Ned Snell

SAMS
Teach Yourself

to **Create**
Web Pages

in **24** Hours

SECOND EDITION

A Division of Macmillan Computer Publishing
201 West 103rd St., Indianapolis, Indiana, 46290 USA

Sams Teach Yourself to Create Web Pages in 24 Hours, Second Edition

Copyright © 1999 by Sams Publishing

International Standard Book Number: 0-672-31716-8

Library of Congress Catalog Card Number: 99-63542

Printed in the United States of America

First Printing: September 1999

01   00   4

Trademarks

All terms mentioned in this book that are known to be trademarks or service marks have been appropriately capitalized. Sams Publishing cannot attest to the accuracy of this information. Use of a term in this book should not be regarded as affecting the validity of any trademark or service mark.

Warning and Disclaimer

Every effort has been made to make this book as complete and as accurate as possible, but no warranty or fitness is implied. The information provided is on an "as is" basis. The author and the publisher shall have neither liability or responsibility to any person or entity with respect to any loss nor damages arising from the information contained in this book or from the use of the CD-ROM or programs accompanying it.

ACQUISITIONS EDITOR:
Mark Taber

DEVELOPMENT EDITOR
Damon Jordan

MANAGING EDITOR
Charlotte Clapp

PROJECT EDITOR
Carol Bowers

COPY EDITOR
Patricia Kinyon

TECHNICAL EDITOR
Gina Carrillo

PROOFREADERS
Betsy Smith
Wendy Ott
Maryann Steinhart

INDEXER
Heather Goens

SOFTWARE DEVELOPMENT SPECIALIST
Aaron Price

INTERIOR DESIGN
Gary Adair

COVER DESIGN
Aren Howell

PRODUCTION
Stacey DeRome
Ayanna Lacey
Heather Miller

Contents at a Glance

Contents

About the Author

NED SNELL has been making technology make sense since 1986, when he began writing beginner's documentation for one of the world's largest software companies. After writing manuals and training materials for several major companies, he switched sides and became a computer journalist, serving as writer and eventually as an editor for two national magazines, *Edge* and *Art & Design News*.

A freelance writer since 1991, Snell has written 12 computer books and hundreds of articles and served as Reviews Editor for *Inside Technology Training* magazine. Between books, Snell works as a professional actor in regional theater, commercials, and industrial films. He lives with his wife and sons in Florida.

Dedication

For my family.

Acknowledgments

Thanks to the folks at Sams Publishing—especially Mark Taber and Damon Jordan.

Tell Us What You Think!

As the reader of this book, *you* are our most important critic and commentator. We value your opinion and want to know what we're doing right, what we could do better, what areas you'd like to see us publish in, and any other words of wisdom you're willing to pass our way.

You can fax, email, or write me directly to let me know what you did or didn't like about this book—as well as what we can do to make our books stronger.

Please note that I cannot help you with technical problems related to the topic of this book, and that, due to the high volume of mail I receive, I might not be able to reply to every message.

When you write, please be sure to include this book's title and author as well as your name and phone or fax number. I will carefully review your comments and share them with the author and editors who worked on the book.

Fax: 317-581-4770
Email: webdev_sams@mcp.com
Mail: Mark Taber
        Associate Publisher
        Sams Publishing
        201 West 103rd Street
        Indianapolis, IN 46290 USA

Introduction

Books that aim to teach beginners how to create a Web page almost always start out the same way: They tell you what a Web page is and why you might want one of your own.

I figure that if you picked up this book, you've already been online (at least a little), you've seen a Web page, and you know why you want one. So I won't waste even one of our 24 hours together on that stuff. Instead, I'll get you creating your own Web pages as quickly and simply as possible.

In fact, before your first three hours are up, you'll already know your way around the easy-but-powerful Web page creation program (Microsoft FrontPage Express) included on the CD-ROM that comes with this book, and you will already have created your first Web page. How's that for cutting to the chase?

> Before proceeding with the lessons in this book, it's a good idea to go to Appendix A, "Setting Up the Programs on the CD-ROM," learn about the programs on the CD-ROM, and set them up on your PC. You'll begin using them in Hour 2, "Getting Started with a Web Authoring Program," so, when you get to Hour 2, I'll remind you to set up the programs in case you have not already done so.

Who I Wrote This Thing For

To understand this book without even breaking a mental sweat, you do not need to be any kind of Internet expert or computer guru.

If you can operate basic programs (such as a word processor) in Windows 95, 98, or NT, and if you can surf from page to page on the Internet, you already know everything you need to know to get started with this book.

By the end of this book, you'll know not only how to create cool-looking Web pages for yourself or your business, but also how to publish them on the Web for all to see.

Why Do I Need the Programs on the CD-ROM?

Well, you don't need them, exactly. Technically, you can create a Web page using a simple text-editing program or word processing program—and here you'll learn a thing or two about how to do it that way.

But for nearly everybody, Web page creation is quickest and easiest when you use a top-notch Web page editor. That's why this book includes a complete copy of FrontPage Express, plus a set of other valuable tools for bringing your Web pages to life.

The Web-authoring program included with this book, FrontPage Express, is a scaled-down version of Microsoft's FrontPage program. The Express version is a fully-capable authoring program in its own right, but does not include every bell and whistle featured in FrontPage.

Given that FrontPage is the most popular commercial Web authoring program in the world, learning Web authoring on FrontPage Express has a distinct benefit: It is the best possible preparation for moving up to FrontPage, if you choose to take your Web authoring skills into the Big Leagues.

In fact, the CD-ROM at the back of this book contains Microsoft's Internet Explorer 5 suite (see Figure I.1), which includes not only FrontPage Express but also the Internet Explorer 5 Web browser, the email program Outlook Express, and more—everything you need to create Web pages *and* enjoy the Internet. (Although the Internet surfing stuff in Internet Explorer 5 is terrific, you don't have to use it. You can do your Web page authoring in FrontPage Express and still use another Web browser, such as Netscape Navigator, if you prefer.)

Because I know you have FrontPage Express, I demonstrate many Web page creation techniques in that program to help you get started. By the end of this book, you'll know how to do just about anything in FrontPage Express.

But this book is not limited to FrontPage Express, and neither are you. Along the way, you'll explore important Web authoring concepts that will enable you to quickly learn and use just about any other Web authoring program. You'll also discover a number of powerful techniques that don't involve FrontPage Express at all. And in the final hour of this tutorial, I'll introduce you to a variety of other popular Web page creation tools, so you can decide where to go when you outgrow FrontPage Express.

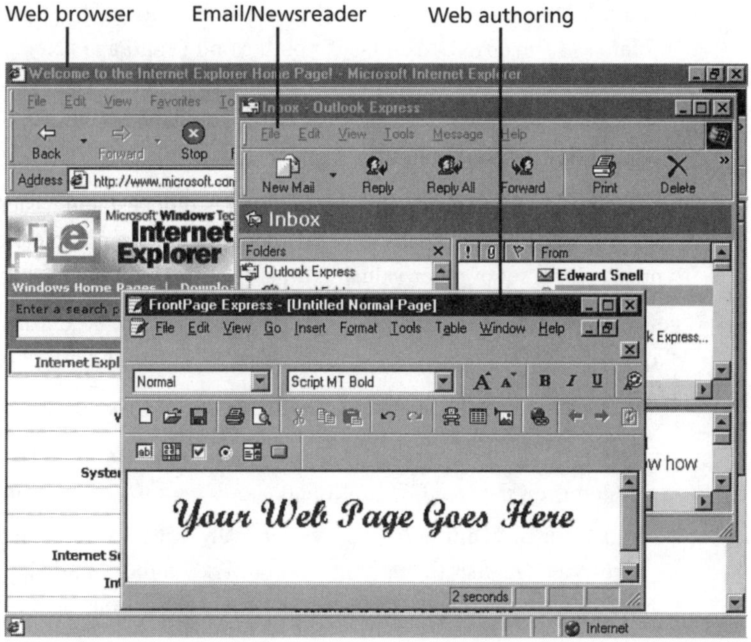

Web browser   Email/Newsreader   Web authoring

FIGURE I.1

*Included with this
book, Internet
Explorer 5 has the
FrontPage Express
Web page editor, a
Web browser, and
other Internet tools.*

How to Use This Book

This book is divided into six parts, each four hours long:

Part I, "First Steps, First Web Pages," kicks off with an easy primer on the technology behind a Web page and a Web page's basic anatomy. After that, you'll learn your way around in FrontPage Express, and even create your very first Web pages.

Part II, " Titles, Text, and Tables," moves ahead to the nitty-gritty of Web authoring, getting your text into the page and making it look exactly the way you want it to look. You'll also pick up handy techniques like creating tables and saving typing time by copying text from other documents.

Part III, " Linking to Stuff," lays out for you the wonderful world of links. You'll find out not only how to add links to your Web pages, but also how to link to stuff other than Web pages, such as newsgroup messages or email addresses.

Part IV, "Adding Pizzazz with Multimedia," shows how to add audiovisual content to your page, including pictures, backgrounds, sound, video, and animation.

Part V, "Fine-tuning Your Page," shows how to create those nifty "fill-in-the-blanks" forms, AND then takes you beyond FrontPage Express, showing how to use other tools on the CD-ROM to create frames, put multiple links in one picture, and add other advanced (but not too tough) Web page features.

Part VI, "Getting It Online," takes you step-by-step through publishing your pages on the Internet and shows you how to test, update, and publicize your pages. It also shows you how to expand your skills to new tools and techniques.

As you can see, the parts move logically from easy stuff to not-so-easy stuff—so it's generally best to read the hours in order. But here and there, I'll tip you to stuff you can skip if you're not immediately interested in a particular activity or technique.

After Hour 24, you'll discover two valuable appendixes:

Appendix A, "Setting Up the Programs on the Bonus CD-ROM," describes the programs on the free CD-ROM and shows how to set them up on your computer.

Appendix B, "Online Resources for Web Authors," contains a directory of Web pages you can visit to learn more about Web authoring, pick up great new Web authoring programs, or gather picture files, animations, and other fun stuff to spice up your own creations.

Finally, there's a Glossary, although I must point out that I use very, very little technical terminology, and I explain it to you whenever I do. So you'll probably never need the Glossary. But just in case you want a glossary, you've got one. I aim to please.

Things You'd Probably Figure Out by Yourself

As you go along, you'll run into a variety of different tip boxes and other special elements. When you do, you'll immediately recognize what each element offers—they really require no explanation. But just for the record, you'll see the following:

"To Dos," New Terms, and Special Element Boxes

Here and there, I use step-by-step instructions, called "To Dos," to show you exactly how to do something. I generally explain how to do that thing in the text that precedes the steps, so feel free to skip 'em when you want to. However, any time you feel like you don't completely understand something, do the steps, and you'll probably get the picture before you're done. Sometimes we learn only by doing.

NEW TERM I call attention to important new terms by tagging them with a New Term icon. It won't happen often, but when it does, it'll help you remember the terms that will help you learn to create Web pages.

You'll also see three kinds of special element boxes:

 A Tip box points out a faster, easier way to do something, or another way to save time and effort. These boxes are completely optional.

A Note box pops out an important consideration or interesting tidbit related to the topic at hand. They're optional, too, but always worth reading (otherwise, I wouldn't interrupt).

 A Caution box alerts you to actions and situations where something bad could happen, like accidentally deleting an important file. Because there's very little you can do in Web authoring that's in any way dangerous, you'll see very few Cautions. But when you do see one, take it seriously.

Q&A Session

At the end of every hour, you'll find a few quick questions and answers explaining interesting stuff that wasn't included in the hour because it didn't directly contribute to teaching yourself how to create Web pages (even though it's interesting).

One More Thing

Actually, no more things. If you have not already done so, skip to Appendix A and follow the steps to set up the programs on the CD-ROM. Then start the clock and hit Hour 1. Twenty-four working hours from now, you'll know Web page authoring inside out.

Thanks for spending a day with me.

PART I

First Steps, First Web Pages

Hour

HOUR 1

Understanding Web Authoring

I can hear your motor running, so I know you're ready to dive in and start creating Web pages. But before building that first page, you need to acquire that rudimentary understanding of how Web pages are born and do some planning about what you want your page to be like.

In this hour, you'll get a quick tour of what Web pages and Web sites are made of. At the end of the hour, you will be able to answer the following questions:

- What are Web pages made of, and how do they work?
- What's HTML, and why should I care?
- How does multimedia—pictures, sound, video, and animation— become part of a page?
- What are *extensions* and why do they matter?
- How should I approach organizing multiple pages into a complete Web site?

Anatomy of a Web Page

There are other optional parts, but most Web pages contain many of the elements described in this section. It's important to know what these parts are because the principal task in Web authoring is deciding what content to use for each standard part, and a principal challenge is dealing with the different ways each browser treats the different parts. (More on that later.)

Parts You See

The following are the elements of a Web page typically visible to visitors through a browser (see Figure 1.1):

FIGURE 1.1

Some of the common parts of a Web page.

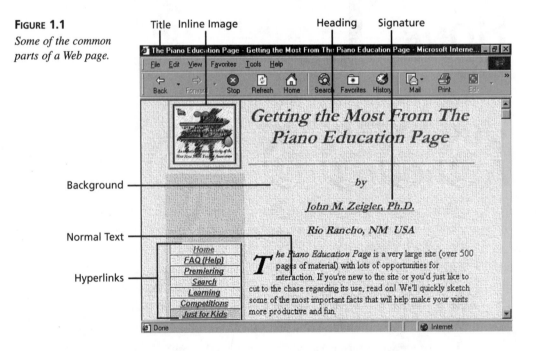

- A *title*, which graphical browsers (most Windows, Macintosh, and X Windows browsers) typically display in the title bar of the window in which the page appears.

The real title of a Web page does not appear within the page itself, but as the title of the browser window in which the page is displayed.

However, most pages have another *title* of sorts, or rather, text or a graphic on the screen doing the job you typically associate with a title in books or magazine—sitting boldly and proudly near the top of the page to give it a name.

1

- *Headings*, which browsers typically display in large, bold, or otherwise empha- sized type. A Web page can have many headings, and headings can be *nested* up to six levels deep; that is, there can be subheadings, and sub-subheadings, and so on.

- *Normal text*, which makes up the basic, general-purpose text of the page. Traditionally, Web authors refer to lines or blocks of normal text as *paragraphs*. But in the parlance of the Netscape Editor, *any* discrete block of words on the page is called a paragraph—whether it's a heading, normal text, or something else that is determined by *properties* assigned to that paragraph.

- A *signature*, which is typically displayed at the bottom of the page. A signature usually identifies the page's author and often includes the author's (or Webmaster's) email address so visitors can send comments or questions about the page. The email address is sometimes formatted as a mailto link, so visitors can click it to open their email program with a message pre-addressed to the author.

- *Horizontal lines*, which dress up the page and separate it into logical sections.

- *Inline images*, which are pictures that are incorporated into the layout of the page to jazz it up or make it more informative.

- *Background color or pattern*, which is a solid color or an inline image that, unlike regular images, covers the entire background of the page so that text and other images can be seen on top of it.

- *Animations*,which can be text or pictures that appear within the layout of the Web page but move in some way. Pictures can flash on and off or cycle through simple animations, and text can flash or scroll across the screen.

- *Hyperlinks* (or simply *links*) to many different things: other Web pages, multimedia files (external images, animation, sound, video), document files, email addresses, and files or programs on other types of servers (such as Telnet, FTP, and Gopher). Links can also lead to specific spots within the current page.

- *Image maps*, which are inline images in which different areas of the image have different links beneath them.

- *Lists*, which can be bulleted (like this one), numbered, and otherwise.
- *Forms*, which are areas in which visitors can fill in the blanks to respond to an online questionnaire, order goods and services, and more.

Parts You *Don't* See

In addition to the stuff you see in a Web page, the page—or rather, the set of files making up the page—has a number of other elements that can be included. These elements aren't usually visible to the visitor, but here are their effects:

- *Identification*—Web page files can include a variety of identification information, including the name (and/or email address) of the author and special coding that helps search engines determine the topic and content of the page.
- *Comments*—Comments are text the author wants to be seen when the HTML code of the page is read directly, not when the page is displayed in a browser. Comments generally include notes about the structure or organization of the HTML file.

NEW TERM   *HTML,* short for *Hyper Text Markup Language*, is the computer file format in which Web pages are stored. An HTML file is really just a text file with special codes in it that tells a browser how to display the file—the size to use for each block of text, where to put the pictures, and so on.

- *JavaScript code*—Within an HTML file, lines of JavaScript program code can add special dynamic capabilities, like a time-sensitive message, to the page.
- *Java applets*—In separate files, Java program modules can enhance interaction between the visitor, the browser, and the server. Java is very popular for writing interactive games that can be played on the Web, for example.
- *Imagemap and forms processing code*—Program code used to process imagemaps and interactive forms.

To Do: Identify the parts of a Web page

▼ To Do

1. Open your Web browser, connect to the Internet and go to any Web page you like. (You can use the copy of Internet Explorer included with this book, or use any other browser you may have.)
2. Look at the title bar of the window in which the browser appears (the bar along the very top, where you usually see the name of a program you're using). You'll probably see the title of the Web page you're viewing there and name of the browser program you're using.

▼

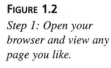

FIGURE 1.2

Step 1: Open your browser and view any page you like.

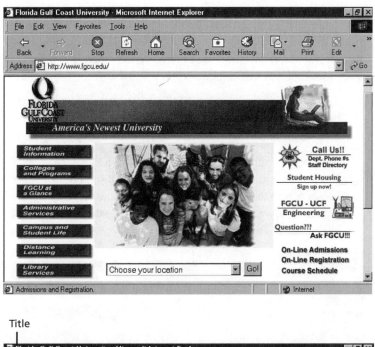

FIGURE 1.3

Step 2: Find the Web page's title in the browser's title bar.

Title

3. Explore the page (and others), and see if you can identify any other parts described earlier in this hour. (Refer back to Figure 1.1 if you need to.)

In most browsers, a status bar appears at the very bottom of the window. Whenever you point to a link (without clicking), you may see in the status bar the address to which that link leads.

Besides exploring where links lead, you can learn about the picture files you see in a Web page. Point to a picture, right-click, and then choose Properties from the menu that appears. A dialog box appears to tell you the filename, file size, and file type of the picture to which you pointed.

Using these techniques, you can develop your Web authoring skills by learning more about the design of the Web pages you visit.

How a Web Page Works

When you author a Web page, no matter how you go about it, what you really end up with is an HTML file that can be published on a Web server.

NEW TERM An HTML file (see Figure 1.4) contains all of the text that appears on the page, plus HTML tags.

These *tags* are codes in an HTML file that tell a browser what to do. For example, if the tag <b> appears before a word, and the tag </b> appears after the word, those tags tell browsers to show that word in bold type when displaying the page.

Besides controlling the formatting of the page, the tags in an HTML file label each chunk of text as a particular element of the page. For example, HTML tags identify one line of text as the page's title, blocks of text as paragraphs, certain lines or words as links, and so on. Other HTML tags designate the filenames of inline images to be incorporated into the page by the browser when the page is displayed.

FIGURE 1.4

The HTML source file of the page shown in Figure 1.1.

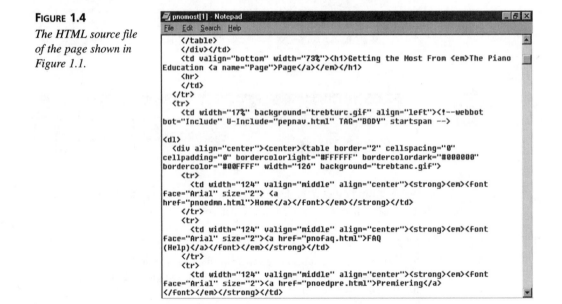

A Web browser is a program that knows how to do at least two things:

- Retrieve HTML documents from remote Web servers (by using a communications protocol called HTTP, about which you need know nothing right now)
- Interpret the HTML tags in the document to display a heading as a heading, treat a link like a link, and so on

What's important to remember is that the HTML tags do not offer you the kind of control over the precise formatting of a page that you would have in a word processor. HTML mostly just identifies what's what. Each browser decides differently how to format those elements onscreen.

NEW TERM *Extensions* are special additions to the standard HTML language, usually created by a browser maker to enable that browser to do stuff that's not included in HTML. See "Extensions: Love 'Em!, Hate 'Em!," later in this hour.

At this writing, the two most popular browsers—various versions of Netscape Navigator and Internet Explorer—comprise the overwhelming majority of the browser market. While there are subtle differences in the HTML tags each supports, the perpetual competition between these two has resulted in two browsers that display most Web pages identically. This means that, to most potential visitors on the Web, your Web page will look roughly the same as it does to you in Communicator.

To folks using browsers other than the two bigshots, your page will always show the same text content and general organization, but its graphical content and other aesthetics might vary dramatically browser to browser. In fact, in some cases, pictures and any other graphical niceties might not show up at all.

> You can download the browsers shown in Figures 1.5 and 1.6 and display your pages in them to see how your work appears in various browsers. Web addresses for getting these browsers appear in Hour 23, "Testing and Updating Your Page."

To illustrate this browser-to-browser variation, Figures 1.5 and 1.6 show the exact same Web page shown earlier in Figure 1.1. Figure 1.1, however, displays the page through Netscape Navigator, while Figures 1.5 and 1.6 show it through two other browsers: Cello and DosLynx, respectively. Compare these two figures and observe how the presentation differs in each.

DosLynx, the browser shown in Figure 1.6, is a *text-only* browser for DOS. (You still remember DOS, don't you?) Disappearing rapidly from the Web (but still out there), these browsers cannot display inline graphics and display all text in the same size typeface, though important elements, such as headings, can be made to stand out with bold type or underlining. Some people use text-only browsers out of choice, although most do so because they lack the proper type of Internet account or the proper hardware for a graphical browser.

FIGURE 1.5

The same page as Figure 1.1 shown in Cello.

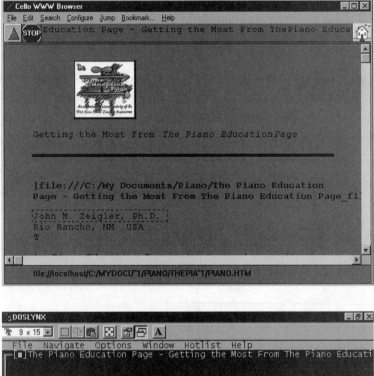

FIGURE 1.6

The same page as Figure 1.1 and 1.5 shown in DosLynx.

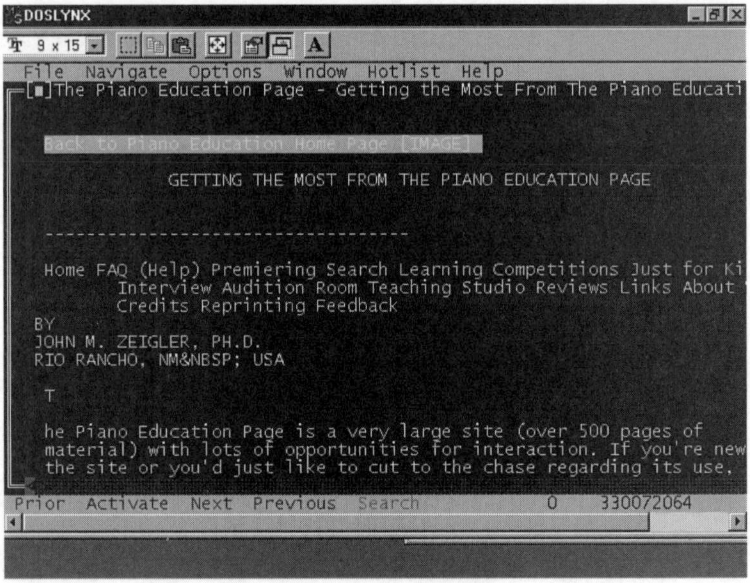

 In addition to those using text-only browsers, others online can't see graphics because they have used the customization features in their browsers to switch off the display of graphics (which speeds up the display of pages).

Although text-only browsers have all but disappeared, as a new Web author it's important to keep in mind the possibility that some folks can't see the pictures in your pages. For them, you need to make sure the text in the page gets the job done, whether the pictures appear or not.

To Do: Examine the HTML source code of a Web page

1. View any Web page through your Web browser.
2. Change the view of your browser so that it shows the raw HTML source code of the page:

   In Internet Explorer 5 (included with this book), choose View, Source.

   In Netscape Navigator, choose View, Page Source.

   In another browser, look for a menu option that mentions "Source" or "HTML."

FIGURE 1.7

Step 1: View any page.

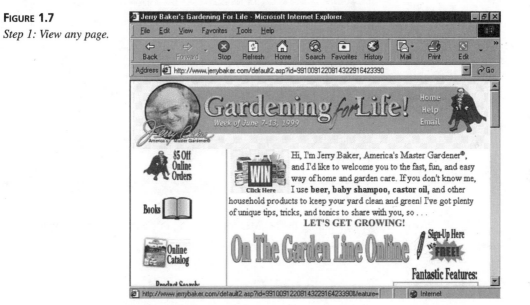

FIGURE 1.8

Step 2: Choose a menu item that displays the HTML source code of the page you're viewing.

▼   3. Explore the HTML code. Don't worry if a lot of it looks like gibberish—you don't
       really need to be able to "decode" an HTML file on sight. But if you look closely,
       you'll see the following within the various codes:

       The actual text that appears on the page

       Filenames of pictures in the page

       Web addresses to which the links point

FIGURE 1.9

*Step 3: Explore the
code, just to get a feel
for what a Web page is
really made of.*

▲   4. When finished examining the HTML source code, close the window in which the
       code appears to return to normal browser view.

Pictures, Sound, and Other Media

Because an HTML file contains only text, the graphics that you see in Web pages, and
the multimedia you can access from them, are not exactly a part of the HTML source
file, itself. Rather, they're linked to the page in either of two ways:

* *Inline images* are graphics files whose filenames and locations are noted in the
  HTML file itself and identified as images by tags. Inline images are images incorporated into the layout of the page—all of the images you see through a browser
  when you access the page.

- *External media* are image, sound, or video files whose names and locations appear as links in the HTML file. These files do not appear or play automatically as part of the page. Instead, the page shows links that, when activated, download the file to play or display it.

Whether inline or external, the media files you use in your Web pages challenge the browsers that will be used to view your page. The browser must be capable of displaying graphics to display inline graphics. External media files can be played by the browser itself, or, more commonly, played by helper applications (or plug-ins) opened by the browser.

When choosing to incorporate media into your page, you'll have to consider carefully the file types you use. The text-only rule of HTML files is what allows users of many different types of computers to access Web pages. Graphics files are less likely to be readable by a wide range of systems, and sound and video files even less so. Even within the confines of PCs and Macintoshes, you'll need to consider whether your media will be supported by a broad spectrum of browsers and/or helper applications. You'll learn more about this in Hour 13, "Getting Pictures for Your Page."

Extensions: Love 'Em!, Hate 'Em!

HTML is standardized so that any Web browser can read any Web documents—sort of.

Here's the deal: All modern browsers support HTML 2, a very well-established set of tags set by the committees that oversee Internet standards. Standardization is good, because it provides Web authors with a way to ensure that most browsers will be able to read what they publish. Because any browser can understand and interpret all of the HTML 2 tags, authors need only stick within the confines of those tags to ensure that their pages are accessible to the biggest possible online audience.

The problem with standards, though, is that they evolve slowly. On the Web, only downloads are permitted to be slow; *evolution* is required to be *fast*. Think about it: The first graphic browser emerged four years ago, and now we're talking real-time video. The entire birth and maturation of the Web as a graphic, interactive environment has taken place within a single presidential administration. Yikes!

HTML 2 includes support for all of the basics—headings, normal text, horizontal lines, lists, links, inline pictures, and so on. But now there's HTML 3 and even HTML 4, which include all of the HTML 2 tags but also add tags for stuff like the following:

- Centered and right-aligned text
- Tables

- Frames
- Math functions
- Ways to position text alongside inline images (instead of just above or below images)

> When creating pages for a company intranet, where all users may have the same browser, you may not need to consider the extensions issue—you can apply all tags supported by the browser.

Leading browsers, including both Navigator and Internet Explorer, support all of HTML 3, and even most of HTML 4. Still, the pace of Web page enhancement is so great that both Netscape and Microsoft continue to incorporate in their browsers new tags and other capabilities that are not part of any approved HTML standard. These new tags are called *extensions*.

NEW TERM   An *extension* is an HTML tag that makes some new capability possible in a Web page but is not yet part of the formal HTML standard.

When used in a Web document, the effects of these extensions can usually be seen only through a browser that specifically supports them. Of course, Navigator supports all of Netscape's extensions, and Internet Explorer supports all of Microsoft's. However, not all browsers support all extensions. That's why you need to be careful with 'em.

In general, when an incompatible browser accesses a page that uses these tags, nothing dire happens. The fancy extension-based formatting doesn't show up, but the meat of the page—its text and graphics—remain readable.

> Authors who want to take advantage of extensions are concerned that some visitors are not seeing the page in its full glory. That's why, more and more, you see messages like Best when viewed through Netscape Navigator, or Enhanced for Internet Explorer on Web pages. That's the author telling you that he or she has used extensions—and if you want to enjoy all the features of the page, you'd best pick up a compatible browser.

Ways to Organize a Web Site

Finally, before you dive into creating Web pages, you must give some thought to the following issues:

- How can my message be broken down into an organized series of topics?
- How long a Web page, or how many Web pages (linked together into a Web site), will be required to say what I have to say?

> After you've developed and refined the topic breakdown and outline of your message, you might find that you've already composed the headings for your Web pages.

Jot down a list of the topics or subtopics your document will cover. How many do you have, and how much material will be required for each topic? After this simple exercise, you'll begin to get a good sense of the size and scope of your document.

Now look at the topics. Do they proceed in a logical order from beginning to end, with each new part depending on knowledge of the parts that came before? Or, does the material seem to branch naturally to subtopics (and sub-subtopics)? How might you reorder the topics to make the flow more logical, or group related topics together?

As you work on your breakdown (not *that* kind of breakdown—your topic breakdown), a simple outline begins to emerge. The more you refine the outline before you begin composing your document, the more focused and efficient your authoring will be. More importantly, the resulting Web document will present your message in a way that's clear and easy to follow.

> To plan a document with three or more pages, *storyboard* it by roughing out each page on a piece of paper to decide which information belongs on each page. Tape the papers to a wall and draw lines or tape strings to plan links among the pages.

While you're building your outline, consider the logical organization of your presentation and how its material might fit into any of the common organizational structures seen on the Web:

Billboard—A single, simple page, usually describing a person, small business, or simple product. Most personal home pages are this type. They'll often contain links to related (or favorite) resources on the Web, but not to any further pages of the same document. (The Netscape Page Wizard builds this type of page.)

One-page linear—One Web page, short or long, designed to be read more or less from top to bottom. Rules are often used to divide up such a page into virtual "pages." Readers can scroll through the entire page, but a table of contents and targets can be used to help readers jump down quickly to any section. This type is best used for fairly short documents (less than 10 screenfuls) wherein all the information flows naturally from a beginning to an end.

Multipage linear—Same general idea as one-page linear, but broken up into multiple pages that flow logically, one after the other, from beginning to end, like the pages of a story. You can lead the reader through the series by placing a link at the bottom of each page, leading to the next page.

Hierarchical—The classic Web structure. A top page (sometimes confusingly called a *home page*) contains links to other pages, each covering a major subject area. Each of those pages can have multiple links to still more pages, breaking the subject down further and getting into even more specific information. The result is a tree structure, like the one shown in Figure 1.10.

FIGURE 1.10
A hierarchical structure.

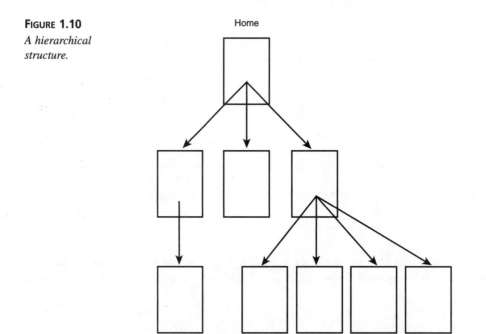

Web—A Web structure (see Figure 1.11) is a hierarchical structure without the hierarchy. It's a multipage document in which any page can have a link leading to any other page. There may be a "top" page, but from there, readers can wander around the Web in no particular path. Web structures are loose and free-flowing and are, therefore, best suited to fun, recreational subjects or to subjects that defy any kind of sequential or hierarchical breakdown. (Hint: Before you resort to a Web structure, make sure your message really calls for one—you might just be having trouble focusing.)

FIGURE 1.11

A Web structure.

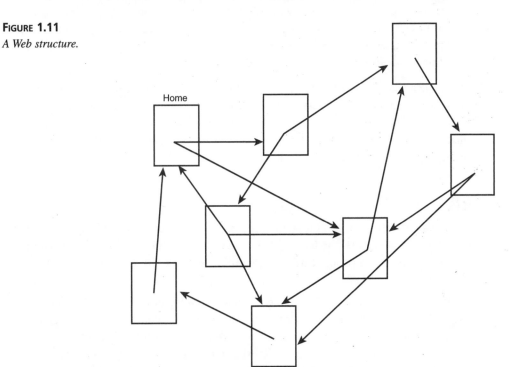

There are other ways to organize information; variations on each of the structures presented here. But one of these structures should resemble the general shape of your message, and thus your document. To put it another way, if you can't yet decide which of these structures is best for the Web page you want to create, you need to play with your message some more and break it down in different ways until a structure reveals itself to you.

Summary

You can, if you so choose, create your Web page by getting some good coffee, sitting down, and fiddling for awhile with a Wizard (see Hour 3, "Wizarding Up a Personal Home Page") or any Web page editor. In the end, you'll have an HTML file suitable for publishing (if not for reading).

But will it be a file that achieves your goals for wanting a Web page in the first place? If you're looking for cyber-friends, will your page appeal to them? If you're looking for clients or customers, will your page make you look better than your competitors do? If you're offering useful information, are you doing so in a way that visitors to your page will find intuitive and easy to navigate?

To create a page that hits its mark, you must first ground yourself in the basics of how a Web document works, and what it can and cannot do. That's what you've picked up in this hour. I didn't attempt to dictate how your document should look, feel, or operate—that has to be your inspiration. But I've tried to feed your thoughts so that you can make informed choices during whatever tasks you choose to take on next.

Q&A

Q **So basically, you're telling me I can do all these cool things to my page, but I should stick with the boring stuff since the cool stuff is based on extensions and also some people can't see graphics. Isn't that, well, ever so slightly a bummer?**

A Bummer—not. In practice, it's really not such a big deal. First of all, remember that the overwhelming majority of the folks browsing the Web can view graphics, and most use a browser that can cope with most extensions. So even if you go completely nuts with pictures and extension-based formatting, your page will look great to most people. By using techniques I'll show you in later hours, you can accommodate the graphics-impaired or extension-impaired so that your page is as useful to them as to everyone else.

But still, it's important to remember that just because you're writing a page *in* a Microsoft Web page editor doesn't mean you're writing it solely *for* users of Microsoft's Internet Explorer. A smart author makes his or her document informative and cool to look at *as well as* accessible to all.

Hour **2**

Getting Started with a Web Authoring Program

When you work in a WYSIWYG Web page editor (like FrontPage Express, included with this book), your page looks (with minor exceptions) just the way it will look to most visitors on the Web.

That's a powerful convenience; without it, Web authors have had to guess about the appearance of their page while fiddling with all the HTML code. To check their work, they had to open the file in a browser, and then go back to the HTML code to make adjustments. With a WYSIWYG editor, you can see and do it all in one window, live and in color.

This hour examines the general operation of FrontPage Express so you'll know your way around when you approach the specific authoring tasks coming up in later hours. At the end of the hour, you will be able to answer the following questions:

- How do I open FrontPage Express?
- How do I start, save, and reopen Web pages in FrontPage Express?

- How do I test the way my page will look online?
- Can I print my work?

 This hour assumes you have already installed the programs from the CD-ROM included with this book, as described in Appendix A, "Setting Up the Programs on the CD-ROM."

Opening FrontPage Express

When you install FrontPage Express (as shown in Appendix A), a shortcut for opening the program is automatically added to your Windows Start menu.

- To open FrontPage Express, click the Start button, and then choose Programs, Accessories, Internet Tools, FrontPage Express (see Figure 2.1).

- To close FrontPage Express, choose File, Exit, or click the X button in the upper-right corner of the FrontPage Express window (see Figure 2.2).

FIGURE 2.1

Opening FrontPage Express.

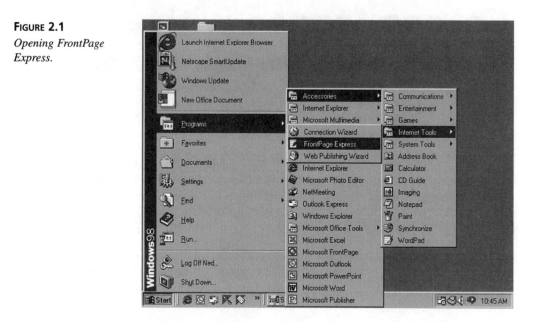

FIGURE 2.2

Closing FrontPage
Express.

X button

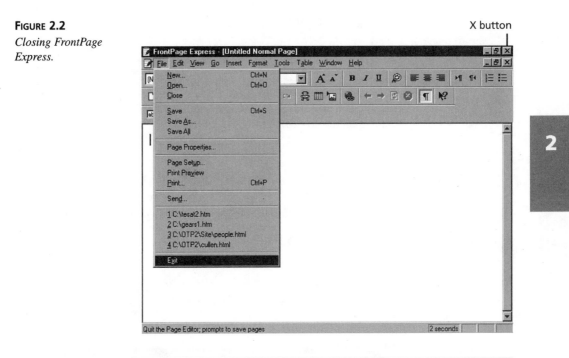

2

When FrontPage Express opens, it automatically opens a new, blank Web page file. You can start typing right away to begin creating your first Web page.

Exploring FrontPage Express's Toolbars

You perform many activities in FrontPage Express by clicking buttons on its three toolbars: Standard, Format, and Forms (see Figure 2.3). You learn much more about these toolbars over the next 22 hours; for now, it's enough just to know where they are.

Most buttons are pretty easy to identify by their icons. But note that every button (or list box) on the toolbars has a "tooltip," a name that appears to identify the button.

To learn the name of any button or list box, point to it (don't click) and pause a moment. The name of the button will appear.

To quickly see the names of all the buttons in one toolbar (to help you locate a particular button), point to the button or list box that's farthest left, until its tooltip appears (don't click). Then slowly move the point to the right, along the row. As you pass each button, its name appears.

FIGURE 2.3

*You do most things in
FrontPage Express by
clicking buttons and
picking from list boxes
on the three toolbars.*

Standard

Forms   Format

The toolbars appear as three rows of buttons near the top of the FrontPage Express window, and each can be displayed (for ready use) or hidden (to free up more screen area for examining your creations). The following To Do shows how to hide and display toolbars.

To Do: Hide and display toolbars

1. Open FrontPage Express, and look at the three rows of buttons beneath the menu bar.

2. Click View. In the menu, a check mark appears next to the name of each toolbar that's currently displayed.

FIGURE 2.4

*Step 1: Open
FrontPage Express
and check out the
toolbars.*

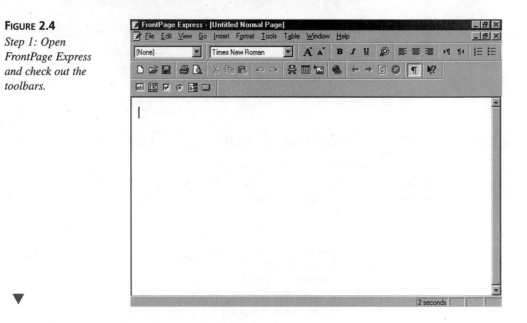

▼

FIGURE 2.5
Step 2: Open the View menu.

3. To hide a toolbar, click its name.

▲ 4. To redisplay a toolbar you've hidden, repeat steps 2 and 3.

Starting a New Web Page

In Hour 3, "Wizarding Up a Personal Home Page," you'll learn how to use FrontPage Express's Personal Home Page Wizard to get a head start on creating a great Web page. But rather than use the Wizard, you can start a completely blank Web page and fill it in any way you wish, as shown in the following To Do.

It really doesn't matter which way you start—what matters is that you know about both methods, so you can choose the one you need on any given day.

To Do: Start a new page file

1. Choose File, New.

2. Choose Normal Page, and then click OK.

FIGURE 2.6
Step 1: Choose File, New.

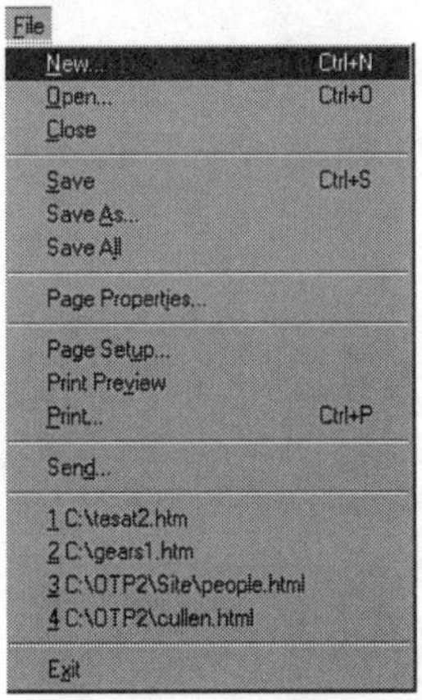

File	
New...	Ctrl+N
Open...	Ctrl+O
Close	
Save	Ctrl+S
Save As...	
Save All	
Page Properties...	
Page Setup...	
Print Preview	
Print...	Ctrl+P
Send...	
1 C:\tesat2.htm	
2 C:\gears1.htm	
3 C:\OTP2\Site\people.html	
4 C:\OTP2\cullen.html	
Exit	

▼

▼

FIGURE 2.7

Step 2: Choose Normal Page, OK.

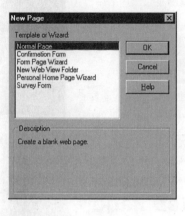

The other choices on the New dialog box—Confirmation Form, Form Page Wizard, and Survey Form—all help you add interactive forms to your Web site that your visitors can use to answer questions or provide feedback (see Hour 19, "Designing Fill-in-the-Blanks Forms").

3. Start typing and formatting the contents of the page (which you will learn to do in upcoming hours of this book).

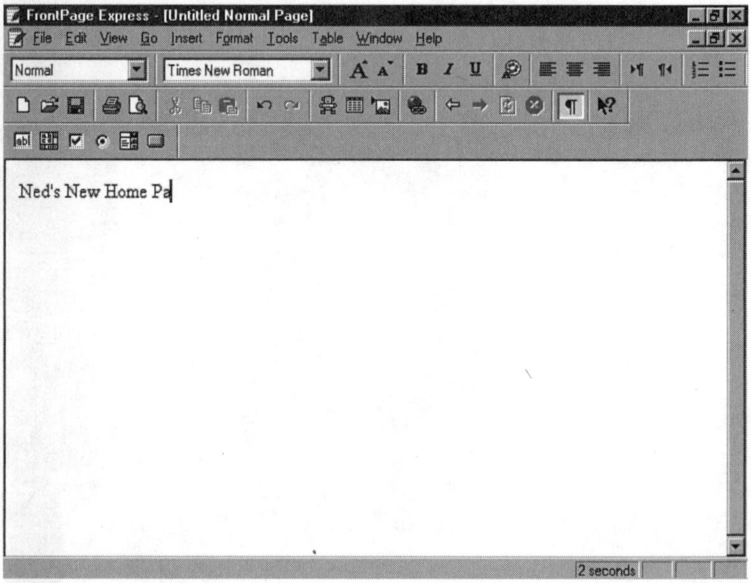

FIGURE 2.8

Step 3: Type away!

▲

Saving and Naming Files

Whether you create it with the Wizard (see Hour 3) or from scratch, you need to save your new Web page file early and often.

About Web Page Filenames

When you save a file in FrontPage Express, you give it a name—presumably the name by which it will be stored on a Web server when published. And when it comes time to publish a Web page, names can be tricky.

For example, Windows 95, 98, NT, and even the Macintosh all allow you to use spaces and punctuation in filenames, but you should not do so when naming Web page files. FrontPage Express will permit you to do it, but when you attempt to publish the files, you'll find that browsers cannot open them.

In general, as long as you use an extension of .htm or .html and eliminate spaces and punctuation, you can give your page files any name you like. However, you can avoid certain kinds of compatibility problems by making sure your filenames conform to the "8.3" filename rule: The filename must be no more than eight characters with an extension of no more than three (.htm, not .html); for example

`nedsnell.htm`

Also, when a page will be the "top" page of a multipage Web presentation, standard practice is to name it `index.html`. Most Web servers are configured to open the file `index.html` automatically when a visitor specifies a Web site address or directory but not a specific file. However, this only works if you have your own directory on the server. Usually, you will. But if you share a directory with others, odds are you won't be the first to post a file called `index.html`, so the server won't accept your document. For this reason, it's sometimes best to choose your server (see Hour 21, "Publishing Your Page") and find out about its naming guidelines before settling on final names for your HTML files.

When creating a multipage Web site, it's important to save all of the page files in the same folder on your PC. Doing so will not only make publishing easier, but it will also simplify other tasks, such as creating links between pages.

The best approach is to create a new, empty folder on your PC and store in it all of the files that make the site—including not only the HTML files, but other files that come into play, such as picture files.

To Do: Saving a file

1. Click the Save button on the Standard toolbar, or choose File, Save.

2. Click As File.

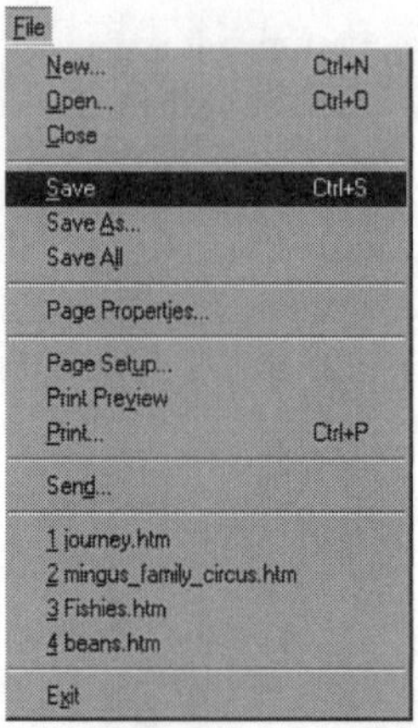

FIGURE 2.9

Step 1: Choose File, Save.

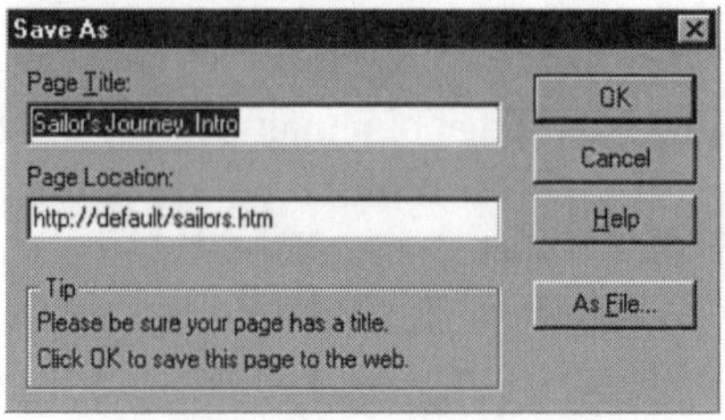

File	
New...	Ctrl+N
Open...	Ctrl+O
Close	
Save	Ctrl+S
Save As...	
Save All	
Page Properties...	
Page Setup...	
Print Preview	
Print...	Ctrl+P
Send...	
1 journey.htm	
2 mingus_family_circus.htm	
3 Fishies.htm	
4 beans.htm	
Exit	

FIGURE 2.10

Step 2: Click the As File button.

Save As

Page Title:
Sailor's Journey, Intro

Page Location:
http://default/sailors.htm

Tip
Please be sure your page has a title.
Click OK to save this page to the web.

OK
Cancel
Help
As File...

In the dialog box shown in Figure 2.10, notice that there's a space for you to give your page a title. FrontPage Express has automatically filled in text from the top of the page to serve as its title. (If the page is blank, the automatic title will be "Untitled Normal Page.")

You can easily change a page's title at any time, and there's a lot to consider in choosing a page's title. So for now, just accept whatever title FrontPage automatically gives your page. In Hour 5, "Choosing a Title, Text Colors, and Other Page Basics," you will learn how to change that title—and to pick a title that really works for your page.

3. Choose a folder in which to save the page file. (To create a new folder to save in, click the Create New Folder button.)

Figure 2.11

Step 3: Pick a folder.

2

4. Click the Save button on the Save As File dialog box.

After the first time you save a file, you'll no longer need to perform steps 2-4 when you save again. Simply performing step 1 saves the file.

Editing Pages You've Saved

As you work on Web pages, you'll probably create them over a series of editing sessions. You'll need to open existing files and close them when you're done. The following To Do shows how to close files and how to reopen them each time you want to work on them.

To Do: Closing and reopening pages

1. To close a page file (without closing FrontPage Express), choose File, Close.

2. To open one of the page files you've used recently, choose File, and then choose the page's filename from the bottom of the File menu.

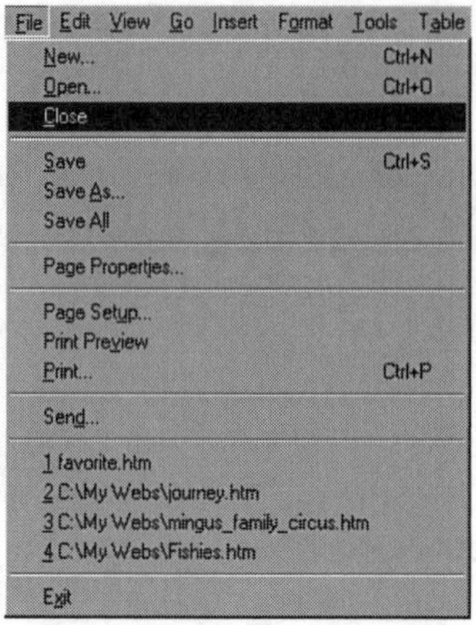

FIGURE 2.12
Step 1: Choose File, Close to close a file.

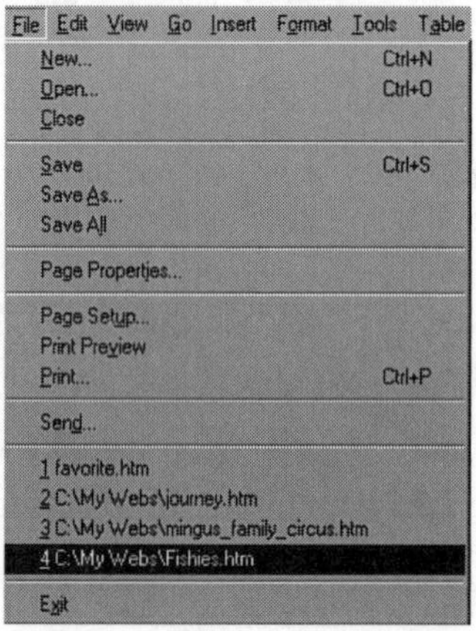

File	Edit	View	Go	Insert	Format	Tools	Table

New...   Ctrl+N
Open...   Ctrl+O
Close

Save   Ctrl+S
Save As...
Save All

Page Properties...

Page Setup...
Print Preview
Print...   Ctrl+P

Send...

1 favorite.htm
2 C:\My Webs\journey.htm
3 C:\My Webs\mingus_family_circus.htm
4 C:\My Webs\Fishies.htm

Exit

FIGURE 2.13
Step 2: To open a file, click its name at the bottom of the File menu.

File	Edit	View	Go	Insert	Format	Tools	Table

New...   Ctrl+N
Open...   Ctrl+O
Close

Save   Ctrl+S
Save As...
Save All

Page Properties...

Page Setup...
Print Preview
Print...   Ctrl+P

Send...

1 favorite.htm
2 C:\My Webs\journey.htm
3 C:\My Webs\mingus_family_circus.htm
4 C:\My Webs\Fishies.htm

Exit

Opening a Page File You Haven't Used Lately

If a file you want to edit is not among the files you've edited most recently, its name won't appear on the File menu as shown in step 2 of the preceding To Do. Here's how to open any Web page file on your PC.

To Do: Opening any page file on your PC

1. Choose File, Open.

FIGURE 2.14
Step 1: Choose File, Open.

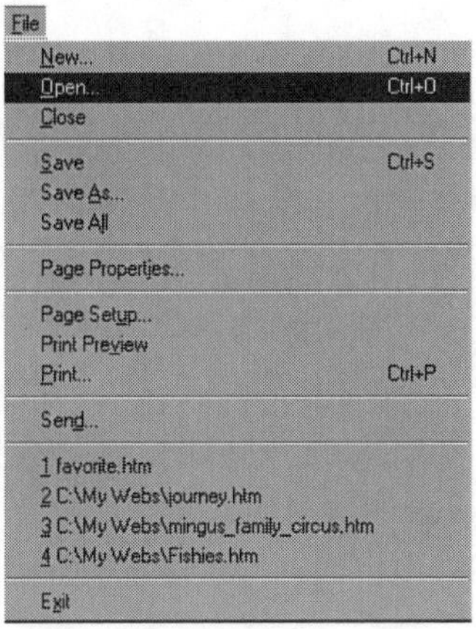

File	
New...	Ctrl+N
Open...	Ctrl+O
Close	
Save	Ctrl+S
Save As...	
Save All	
Page Properties...	
Page Setup...	
Print Preview	
Print...	Ctrl+P
Send...	
1 favorite.htm	
2 C:\My Webs\journey.htm	
3 C:\My Webs\mingus_family_circus.htm	
4 C:\My Webs\Fishies.htm	
Exit	

2. Click Browse.

FIGURE 2.15
Step 2: Click the Browse button.

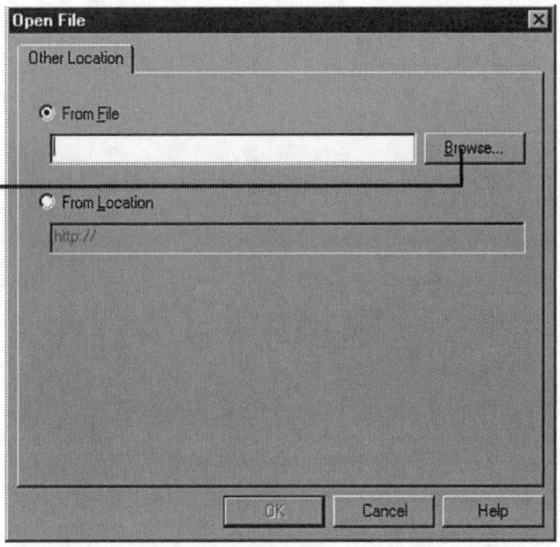

Browse button ————

Open File

Other Location

⊙ From File

Browse...

○ From Location

http://

OK   Cancel   Help

3. Use the Look In list to navigate to the folder where you've stored the page file.

4. Choose the file's name from the Open File dialog box, and click Open.

2

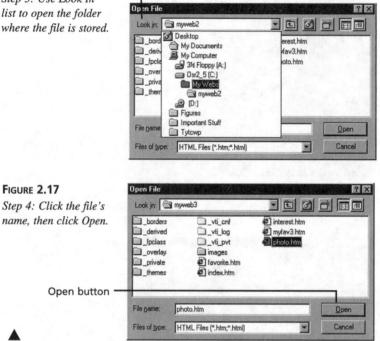

Figure 2.16
Step 3: Use Look In list to open the folder where the file is stored.

Look in list

Figure 2.17
Step 4: Click the file's name, then click Open.

Open button

Checking Out Your New Page in a Web Browser

In FrontPage Express, your Web pages will appear pretty much the same as they will when viewed through a browser and the Internet. Still, it's a good idea to preview your page through your Web browser from time to time to evaluate its true appearance.

It's also a good idea to check out the page in a few different browsers, to make sure it looks OK to everyone online, no matter what browser they use. You learn more about testing your page's appearance in Part VI, "Getting It Online."

To Do: Opening your page in your Web browser

1. Close FrontPage Express.
2. In Windows, locate the file icon for your Web page file.

FIGURE 2.18
*Step 1: Close
FrontPage Express.*

FIGURE 2.19
*Step 2: In Windows,
locate the file's icon.*

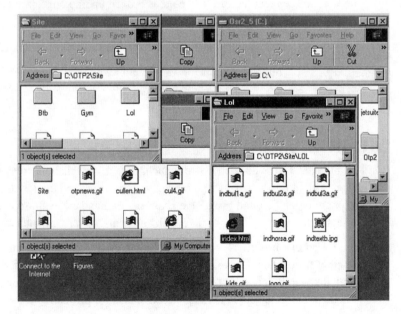

3. Open the file by double-clicking its icon.

> On your PC, you may have several different Web browsers installed. But there is always one browser that's configured as your "default" browser. The default browser is the one that will always open automatically to show you a Web page file when you double-click that file's icon.

Printing Pages

When developing your pages, you may find it useful to print them from time to time. Reviewing printouts of your pages may help you see typos or other errors you might miss when reading a page online (a trick of the eyes).

To print a page you're editing, click the Print button on the toolbar or choose File, Print. The page is printed exactly as it would be from a Web browser—text formatting and pictures are included on the printout, but any background patterns you may have added are omitted to keep text legible. The page is broken up into appropriately sized chunks to fit on paper pages.

> Although you might want to print your pages for reference, do not rely on printouts as accurate representations of your page's appearance online.

Summary

FrontPage Express does a lot—too much, in fact, for this hour to even scratch the surface. Still, in this hour you've wrapped your arms around the job and learned how to get into, out of, and around FrontPage Express. As mundane as those tasks are, they're the essential foundation to productive Web authoring. You're on your way.

But for all that it is, there's one thing FrontPage Express is not: smart. It can't tell you whether the content you've created is well organized, well presented, or well written. And although it applies HTML tags to your document dutifully, it cannot tell you whether you've selected the most effective tags for presenting the content at hand.

Thus, FrontPage Express is a replacement only for time and labor, not for judgment. To author an effective Web document, you must acquire a sense of Web aesthetics. You'll pick up much of this sense as you work through this book. But you must also study other pages you see online and mentally catalog the design aspects and content approaches that sing to you—and those that annoy, bore, or baffle you, as well.

Q&A

Q Opening FrontPage Express from the Start menu can be kind of a drag, having to go all the way to Programs, Accessories, Internet Tools. Isn't there a shortcut?

A Well, there's no shortcut—but you can make one yourself:

1. Click the Start button, and then choose Programs, Accessories, Internet Tools.

2. Right-click the item for FrontPage Express, and in the menu that appears, click Copy.

3. Click anywhere on the Windows desktop, to close the menu.

4. Right-click the Windows desktop, and in the menu that appears, click Paste.

A shortcut to FrontPage Express appears on your Windows desktop. To open FrontPage Express anytime, just double-click the shortcut.

HOUR 3

Wizarding Up a Personal Home Page

I write books (but you knew that). And because I write books, budding writers are always asking me how I can write so much so quickly. The trick, I tell them, is not to worry about the quality of your writing as you write. Just spill it all out as quickly as you can, then go back later to rewrite and polish. Start by digging up the raw clay, and then mold and shape it into what you want. If you fuss over each sentence as you go along, writer's paralysis sets in.

The same philosophy works for Web pages. There's nothing more frightening than facing a blank page you know you have to fill in. But, if you can conveniently create a basic page that's maybe 80 percent finished, you have the raw material you need to get you over the hump. Just edit and add to that page until you have what you want.

That's the idea behind FrontPage Express's Personal Home Page Wizard, a facility that helps you crank out a raw home page in minutes. At the end of the hour, you will be able to answer the following questions:

- What's the Personal Home Page Wizard, and how do I make it work?
- What do I do with the page when I'm done?
- At this stage in the game, what do I need to know about Web page publishing?

What (and Where) Is the Page Wizard?

You're familiar with wizards. They're the friendly, automated routines that lead you step-by-step through otherwise complicated tasks, such as installing programs. You start the Personal Home Page Wizard from a simple menu item in FrontPage Express.

Like any wizard, the Personal Home Page Wizard tells you everything you have to do. You just start it up (as described shortly, in the first To Do in this hour), read each screen, and do what you're told. In a few minutes, you'll have a basic page like the one shown in Figure 3.1.

FIGURE 3.1

A sample home page produced by FrontPage Express's Personal Home Page Wizard.

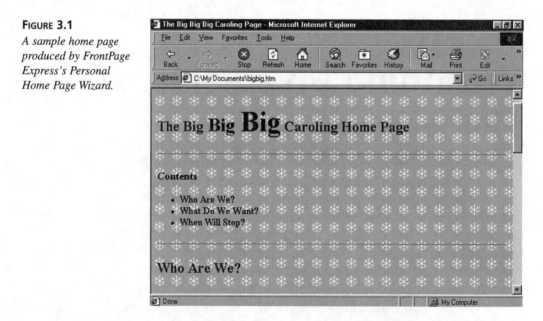

The basic page created in the Personal Home Page Wizard is ready for editing in FrontPage Express. You can finish up by editing just a little (changing any of the sample text that doesn't apply to you) or a lot (adding text, pictures, a background, and so on). In the remaining hours of this book, you'll learn all the steps you need to edit the basic page—or any page—into your masterpiece.

Should I Use the Page Wizard?

When you make choices in the Personal Home Page Wizard, your entries are automatically plugged into the appropriate spots in a Web page template. The template used is a very simple, straightforward home page—no more, no less.

NEW TERM A *template* is a finished Web page file that you can edit and customize to create a new page of your own much more quickly than starting from scratch. See Hour 4, "Starting Pages in Other Programs."

The template used by the Page Wizard is designed for a personal home page and is effective in that regard, even if it is a little short and overly simple. By making a few creative choices when filling in the blanks and then tweaking the page a bit in FrontPage Express, you can also use the Wizard to create a simple business page.

Whether you should use the Wizard depends on whether the overall organization of the resulting page is reasonably close to what you want to achieve. If you want a dramatically different look for your page, or if you plan to build an elaborate Web document made up of multiple linked pages and files, you may be better off with another startup strategy, such as the following:

- Transforming other documents you already have created in other programs into Web pages (see Hour 4)
- Using a "page generator" other than the Personal Home Page Wizard, to get a different style of page (see the Q&A at the end of this hour)
- Brave the void and start from scratch (see Hour 5, "Choosing a Title, Text Colors, and Other Page Basics")

> Since running the Personal Home Page Wizard takes only a few minutes, I recommend trying it out, even if you may choose in the end to go another way.
>
> Doing so is good practice, and also provides you with a practice page of sorts that you can use to conveniently try out techniques as you go along through the remaining 21 hours of this book.

Running the Wizard

Before diving into the Wizard (as you will in the following series of To Dos), it's a good idea to learn how to use each of four buttons you will see on most dialog boxes you'll see while running the Wizard (see Figure 3.2):

FIGURE 3.2

Most dialog boxes displayed by the Wizard have four buttons you use to work your way through: Next, Back, Cancel and Finish.

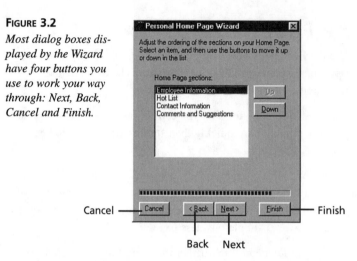

Cancel — Back — Next — Finish

- *Next*—Clicking Next takes you to the next dialog box in the Wizard. As you finish with each dialog box, you click Next to go on to the next one.

- *Back*—Clicking Back takes you backward to the previous dialog box (just as clicking Back in a Web browser takes you back to the previous Web page). Use Back if you change your mind and want to go back and change selections you made on a previous dialog box.

- *Cancel*—Quits the Wizard and creates no page. No fair, no foul. You can start over, any time you want.

- *Finish*—Creates the page, based on the choices you've made so far. Ordinarily, you won't click Finish until you've reached the very last dialog box the Wizard offers. But after you gain some experience, you may know—partway through the Wizard—that the defaults are what you want in all remaining dialog boxes. You may then click the Finish button, if it's available, without moving through the remaining dialog boxes.

As you work through the Page Wizard, you'll notice that certain buttons are faded—"grayed out"—and won't function. A button is grayed out when that button's function is not permitted (or possible) on the current dialog box.

For example, on the Wizard's first dialog box, the Back button is grayed out, because there's no place to go back to—you're at the beginning.

To Do: Run the Personal Home Page Wizard

1. Open FrontPage Express.
2. Choose File, New.

> You must choose File, New (as described in step 2) to display the dialog box shown in Figure 3.3 and start the wizard. Clicking the New button on the Standard toolbar does not display this dialog box; it just opens a new, blank page.

3. Click Personal Home Page Wizard, and then click OK.

3

FIGURE **3.3**

Step 3: Choose Personal Home Page Wizard.

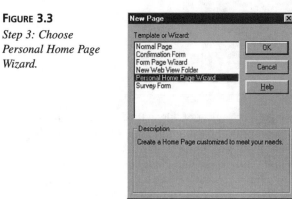

> In Figure 3.3, you may notice another wizard mentioned: The Form Page Wizard. This Wizard helps you quickly build an interactive, fill-in-the-blanks form. You learn to use the Form Page Wizard in Hour 17, "Editing HTML."

4. Change the check boxes so that check marks appear only next to the kinds of information you will want to include on your Web page. (For practice, leave check marks only next to Employee Information, Current Projects, Hot List, and Contact Information.) When done, click Next.

Remember: When you're done with the Wizard, you can edit, expand or enhance your page any way you like. So don't worry about making perfect choices at this point. Just take your best shot.

FIGURE 3.4

Step 4: Check the check boxes of the types of information to feature on your page.

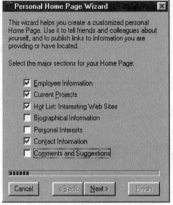

For illustration purposes, the remainder of this To Do assumes that you have left check marks only next to Employee Information, Current Projects, Hot List, and Contact Information.

Feel free to make different choices, but note that the Wizard may then present you with a slightly different series of dialog boxes than those described in this To Do. No biggy: Just read each dialog box, do what the Wizard tells you to, and you'll do fine.

5. Type a simple filename for your Web page file. (Remember to end the name with `.htm`.)

6. Click in the box beneath Page Title, type a descriptive title for your page, and then click Next.

In Hour 5, you'll learn more about coming up with a good title. For now, just type whatever you like in step 6.

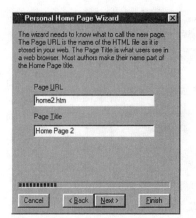

FIGURE 3.5

Step 6: Give your page a title.

7. Review the list of items, and change the check boxes so that check marks appear only next to items you want to include. (For practice, leave check marks next to Job Title and Key Responsibilities only.) When done, click Next.

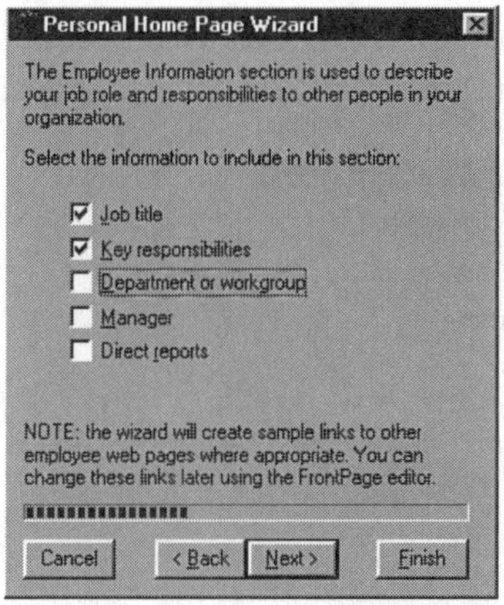

FIGURE 3.6

Step 7: Check the check boxes of items you want included in your page.

8. Type a few words describing a current project, hobby, or other activity, and then press Enter to start a new line.

9. Describe another project or hobby, and press Enter again. Continue adding to the list, being sure to press Enter after each item.

10. Click the name of the style in which you want your list to be formatted. When done, click Next.

▼

FIGURE 3.7

Step 8: Type up a description of your project or hobby.

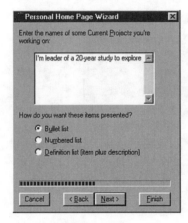

Bullet List style puts an attractive "bullet" character before each item, Numbered List style numbers the list items from one up, and Definition List style provides extra space following each item for a description of the list item, which you can type later.

See Hour 7, "Formatting Text," to learn more about list formatting.

FIGURE 3.8

Step 10: Choose a style for your list.

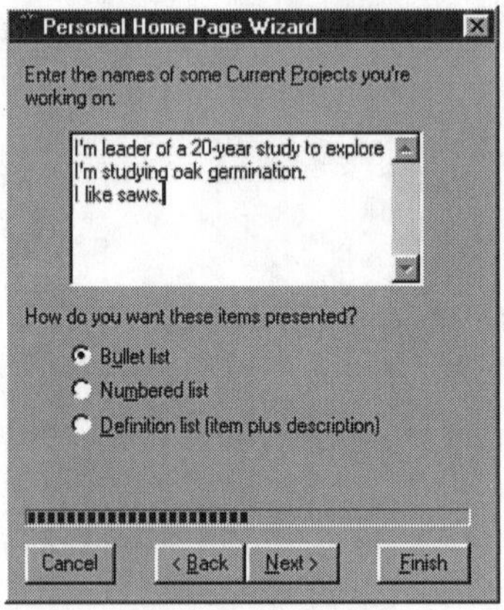

The Wizard whips up a snazzy list of links—a "Hot List"—so your visitors can jump straight from your page to other pages you'd like to share with them.

But these links are "dummy" links—ones that don't go anywhere—until you tell them where to go, as you learn to do in Hour 10, "Making Links." The Wizard just helps you get started, like always.

▼

▼ 11. Click the name of the style in which you will want the links in the Hot List formatted, and then click Next.

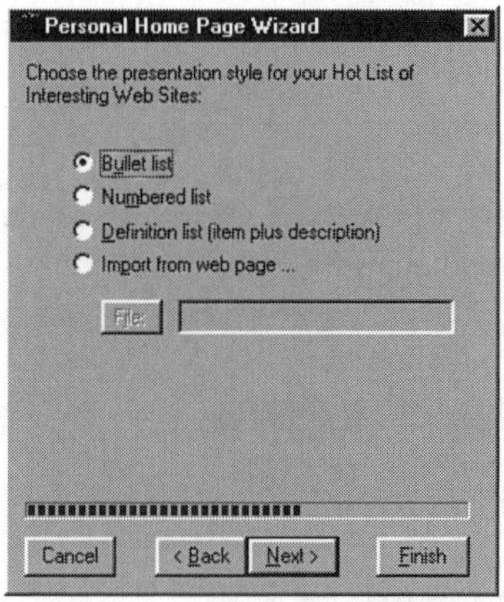

FIGURE 3.9

Step 11: Choose a style for the Hot List.

> When you have more experience creating Web pages, you may choose the fourth item, Import from Web Page. This item copies a list of links from another page.
>
> See Hour 10, "Making Links," to learn more about copying links from other pages.

12. Change the check boxes so that check marks appear only next to items you choose want to include. (For practice, leave a check mark only next to E-mail Address, to add a signature to the bottom of the page.) Click Next.

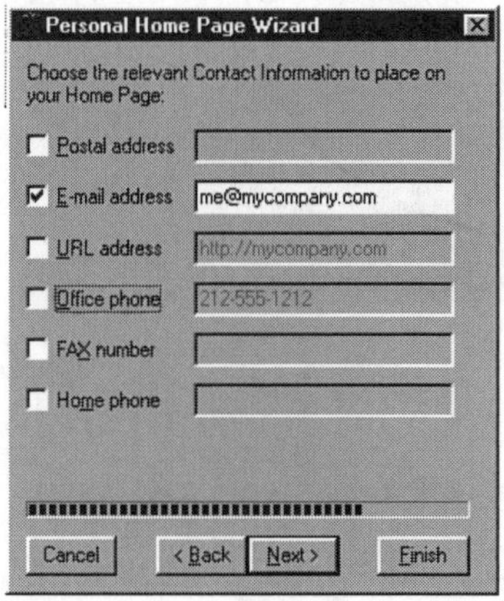

FIGURE 3.10

Step 12: Check the check boxes of items you want to include.

▼

▼

On a business Web page, it's often appropriate to include a postal address
and a telephone number. But for privacy's sake, never put your home phone
number or mailing address on a Web page. Anyone who wants to contact
you may do so by email.

13. In step 4, you decided which of the many available sections to include on your per-
    sonal page. Now you get to choose the order in which those sections are presented.
    Click the name of a part of the page whose position you wish to change.

FIGURE 3.11

*Step 13: Click the
name of a section
whose position in the
page you wish to
change.*

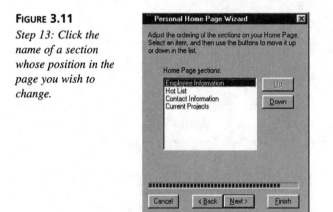

14. To move the item higher on the page, click Up. To move the item lower on the
    page, click Down.

15. Repeat steps 13 and 14 to change the position of any other part of the page you
    want, and, when the order appears the way you want it, click Next.

FIGURE 3.12

*Step 15: Repeat steps
13 and 14 until the
order of page sections
appears the way you
want.*

▼

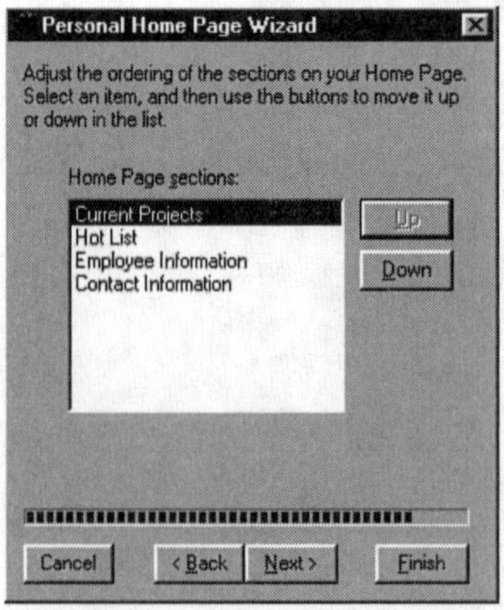

▼   16. Click Back several times, reviewing the choices you made in earlier tasks. Make any changes you want, and then click Next until you return to the final dialog box.

17. Click Finish to create the page.

18. Save the finished page.

FIGURE 3.13
Step 18: Save the finished page.

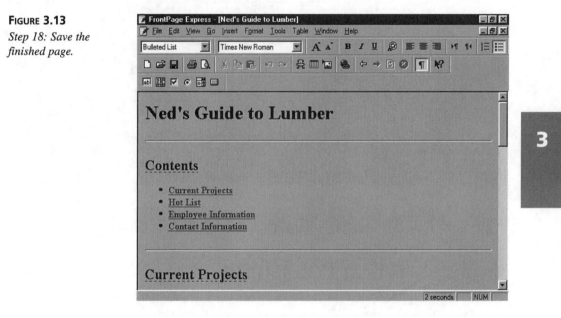

19. Use the techniques described in the remaining hours of this book to change the
▼   page any way you want!

FIGURE 3.14

Step 19: Fiddle around with it, and make it your own!

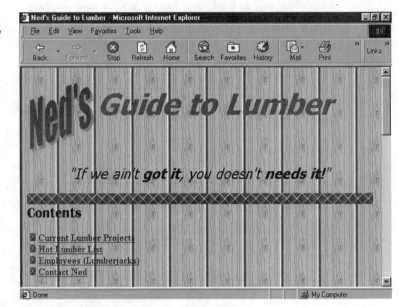

Understanding Publishing

You won't learn all the ins and outs of publishing your page online until Part VI of this book, "Getting It Online." But right now is a good time to begin learning what publishing is all about.

In a nutshell, publishing a Web page is a simple matter of uploading all of the files that make up the page into a designated directory on a Web server (or intranet server, if you intend your document to be used just by folks within a local intranet).

NEW TERM To *upload* is to send files from your computer to a server computer, such as a Web server. (It's the opposite of downloading—receiving files from a server). When you publish a Web page, you upload its files to a Web server.

Most servers—whether Web or intranet—are guarded by security systems that prevent unauthorized users from storing files there. To publish, you must contact the administrator of the server on which you want to publish and obtain the following:

- Permission to upload files to the server
- The name and path of the directory in which the administrator wants you to store your files

- The specific steps required for uploading files to the server (the exact procedure varies somewhat)
- A username and password that you will use while uploading to identify yourself properly to the server's security system (so it will permit you to copy the files)

> If you obtain your Web server space from your Internet provider or online service, the username and password you use to upload Web pages to the server may be the same as the username and password you use to connect to the Internet.
>
> To learn more about getting server space for your Web page, see Hour 21, "Publishing Your Page."

3

When you are ready to upload files, you will do so through a *communications protocol* supported by the server. The required protocol is almost always either of the same two protocols most often used for downloading files on the Internet: FTP (used for downloading files from an FTP server) or HTTP (used for downloading Web pages and other files from Web and intranet servers to browsers).

FrontPage Express includes a built-in publishing facility, the Microsoft Web Publishing Wizard, that lets you publish your pages straight from FrontPage Express, using either the FTP or HTTP protocols. You learn how to run the Wizard—and to publish in other ways—in Hour 21.

Summary

The Personal Home Page Wizard offers a quick, easy way to build a complete, properly designed Web page. It's ideal for building a first personal home page and for creating a basic page you'll later enhance and expand with FrontPage Express.

Q&A

Q Are there other wizards available to create other kinds of basic pages?

A My yes! In fact, there are dozens of such tools. Some are wizards, and work very much like the Personal Home Page wizard. Others are not strictly wizards, but you use them the same way: You fill in the blanks, make a few choices, and out pops a finished HTML file, ready for editing.

All of these tools—wizard and non—are sometimes collectively called *page generators*. Each builds a different kind of page, in a different style. (That's why it's smart to play around with several different ones, to discover the page generator whose output comes closest to the type and style of page you want.)

Some page generators create pages that are far more sophisticated than those created by the Personal Home Page Wizard, featuring pictures, backgrounds, forms, and more. But all page generators have one thing in common: After you use any of them, you can open the files they create in FrontPage Express and edit them to you heart's content.

Some page generators are built into other programs; in Hour 4, you'll learn about page generators built into Microsoft Word, Publisher, and other programs. Other page generators are programs unto themselves, usually available as shareware you can download from the Web and run on your PC. Still other page generators run entirely online; only the resulting HTML file is saved on your PC, when you're done.

You'll find Web addresses for a variety of page generators listed in Appendix B, "Online Resources for Web Authors," under the heading "Page Generators."

Hour 4

Starting Pages in Other Programs

Time is tight for you—it's an issue. How do I know this about you? Well, of all the beginner's Web-authoring books out there, you picked up the one that promised to deliver within a specific time frame. Given what I know about you, I'm placing special emphasis on anything that can get you a great Web page quicker.

Aside from the Personal Home Page Wizard you discovered in the previous hour, nothing saves time better than using a template, or using content you've already created in another program, such as a word processor. In this hour, you'll explore both of these head-starts to Web pages. At the end of the hour, you will be able to answer the following questions:

- How can I turn stuff I already have on hand—such as a résumé or brochure I typed in my word processor—into a Web page without having to start over?

- Can I use a word processor or desktop publishing program to create a Web page?

- What's a *template*, where do I find templates, and how can I use 'em to save time and effort starting a page?

Starting in Your Word Processing, Desktop Publishing, or Other Program

A Web page, when you think about it, is just a document. It's a document that happens to be saved in the HTML file format, but other than that, it's not different from documents created in other document-producing programs, such as word processors (Microsoft Word, WordPerfect), desktop publishing programs (Microsoft Publisher, Adobe PageMaker), and presentation programs (Microsoft PowerPoint).

If those programs could save the documents you create as HTML files, they would be fully functional Web-authoring tools, right? Well, in most cases (unless you're still using versions from a few years ago), these programs can optionally save the files you create as HTML files.

So if you have these programs, you may be able to

- Open documents you've already created—your résumé, recipes, stories, ads, brochures, petitions, whatever—and in a few clicks transform them into HTML files, ready to be edited and enhanced in FrontPage Express (with no retyping!).

- Start new Web pages in these programs, to take advantage of features in those programs before moving the job over to FrontPage Express. For example, Word has spell-checking and grammar-checking, and FrontPage Express does not. In a long page with lots of text, mistakes are easy to miss. You may prefer to create such pages in Word and spell-check 'em there before saving the file in HTML format and switching to FrontPage Express.

- Create and publish the file entirely in another program, and never move over to FrontPage Express. If the Web authoring capabilities in the other program accomplish what you want, you always have that option.

The next few pages describe ways you can use a few popular programs to start Web pages. Recent versions of many other popular document-creation programs for Windows 95/98/NT offer similar capabilities.

If you create a document in another program, save it as an HTML file, and then open it in FrontPage Express for further development, you may see a variety of little question-mark icons sprinkled about the page.

Though distracting, these icons usually do not indicate any real problem. To learn more, see "Importing Various Types of Files into FrontPage Express," later in this hour.

When you want to turn the entire contents of an existing document into a Web page, the techniques in this hour are a great way to begin.

But if all you want to do is to copy a portion of a document—a few paragraphs, say, or a table—into a Web page, you need not bother with these techniques. Instead, you can easily copy text, tables, pictures, and links from any Windows program and paste that content into any Web page you're editing in FrontPage Express. See Hour 5, "Choosing a Title, Text Colors, and Other Page Basics," to learn how to use copy & paste.

Starting Web Pages in Word

With each new version, Microsoft turns Word into something more of a hybrid Web-authoring/word processing program. There are good Web-authoring capabilities built into Word 97, and even better ones in Word 2000.

In either program, you can save any file as an HTML file so it can be published as a Web page or opened and edited in FrontPage 2000. And in either, you can create new Web pages from scratch, based on wizards and templates in Word. The following To Do's show how to use these features in Word 2000.

Depending on the installation options you select when installing Word (or Microsoft Office, with Word included), the Web authoring capabilities in Word may or may not be included in the installation.

If you find that you cannot perform the following To Dos, it probably means that Word's Web authoring tools were left out of your installation. To add them, insert your Word or Office CD-ROM, start the installation program, choose Add/Remove Components, and be sure to select the Web authoring components when updating your installation.

4

To Do ▲

To Do: Save a Word file as a Web page

1. Open the file in Word.

2. Choose File, Save as Web Page.

FIGURE **4.1**

Step 2: In Word, choose File, Save as Web Page.

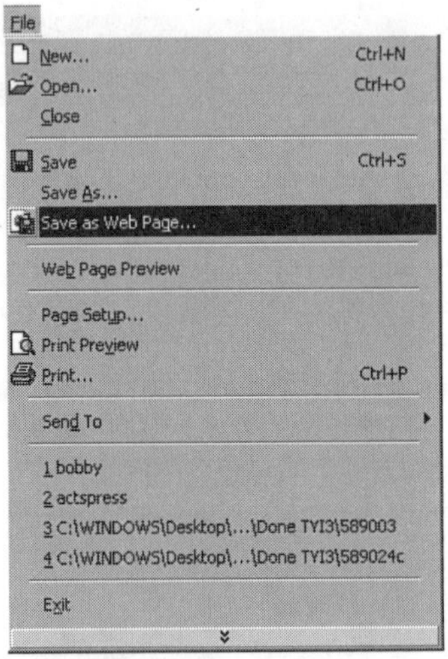

3. Choose a folder and click Save.

FIGURE **4.2**

Step 3: Choose a folder and click Save.

▲

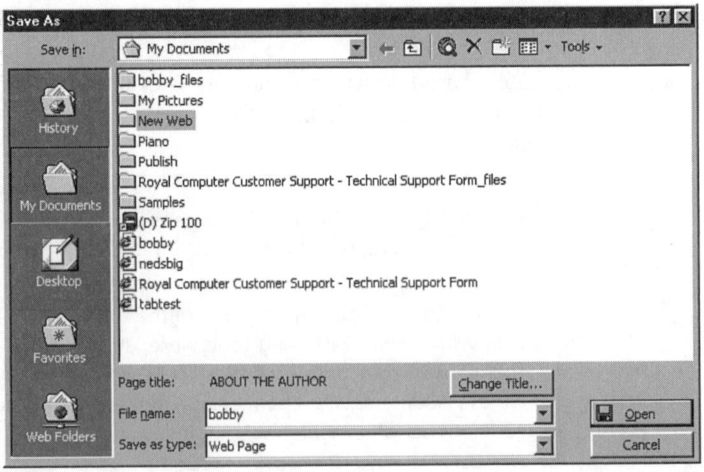

To Do: Start a new Web page in Word 2000

▼ To Do

1. Open Word.
2. Choose File, New.
3. Click the Web Pages tab.

FIGURE 4.3

Step 3: Click the Web Pages tab.

Web pages tab ———

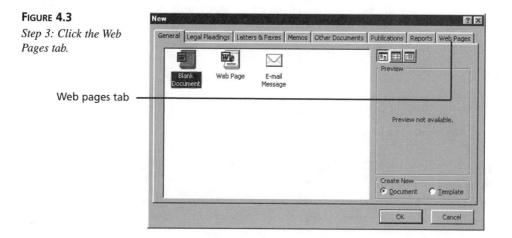

4. Choose the template icon whose name best matches the type of page you want to create, and double-click it.

FIGURE 4.4

Step 4: Choose a template.

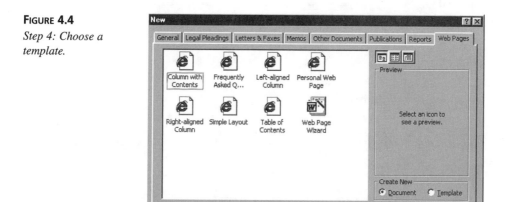

▼

In step 4, observe that in addition to the various kinds of Web page templates, there's an icon for Web Page Wizard. Double-click that icon to open a Wizard that will lead you step-by-step through creating a new Web page.

The results are a lot slicker than what you get with FrontPage Express's Personal Home Page Wizard (see Hour 3, "Wizarding Up a Personal Home Page"), but also a lot more complex and difficult to edit effectively.

If you have Word, I recommend giving Word's Web Page Wizard a spin, just for practice. But I also advise not attempting to create anything critical with it until you gain some more experience.

5. Edit the file in Word as much as you like, and save it. The file is already an HTML file, so at any time you can switch from Word and work on the page in FrontPage Express, or publish it.

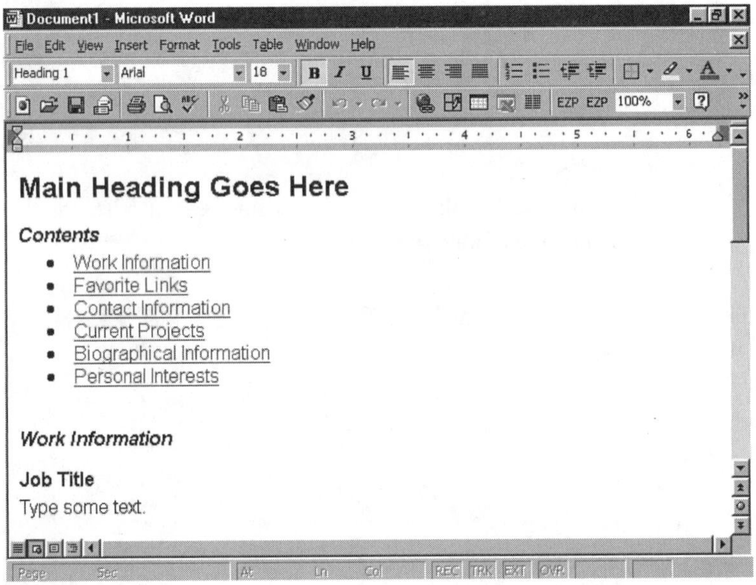

FIGURE 4.5

Step 5: Edit the file, and save it.

After your new Web page opens in Word, you may notice that Word looks a little different from what you're used to. There are toolbar buttons you don't recognize, and new menu items, too.

These are the tools of Word's Web Layout view, a special view in which Word's tools are changed to those you need for working on a Web page. Word always switches to Web Layout view automatically when the file you're working on is an HTML file.

Making Web Pages in Publisher 2000

Like Word, the desktop publishing program Microsoft Publisher enables you to create new Web pages and convert existing publications to HTML files.

Given that Publisher is a program designed for creating print publications that have far more sophisticated layout and formatting than is possible in a Web page, don't be surprised if publications take on a very different appearance when you convert them.

Publisher faithfully carries over all of your text and pictures and the general organization of the publication, and it does the best it can to preserve the overall design, but ultimately, the Web version is never an exact match for the print version. (Nor should it be—design principles from the print world do not always apply online.)

- To convert an existing Publisher 2000 publication to a Web page, open the publication and then choose File, Create Web Site from Current Publication. (Note that if the publication includes more than one print page, Publisher will make each page into a separate HTML file and provide links on each page for jumping to the others.)
- To start a new Web site in Publisher 2000, see the following To Do.

To Do: Start a new Web page in Publisher 2000

1. Open Publisher 2000.
2. In the Catalog, in the list of Wizards, choose Web Sites.

FIGURE 4.6

Step 2: Click Web Sites in the list of wizards.

Web Sites Wizard —

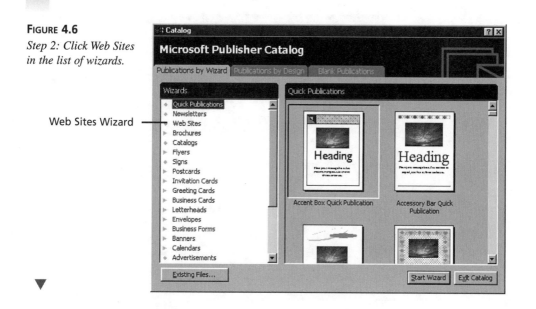

3. Click the Web site design that catches your fancy, and then click Start Wizard.

FIGURE 4.7

Step 3: Choose a Web site design, and then click Start Wizard.

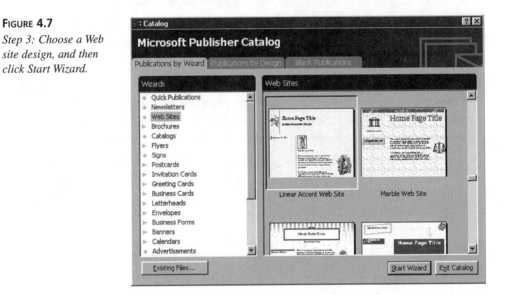

4. Use the Wizard options, or Publisher's regular editing tools, to edit the page as you want.

FIGURE 4.8

Step 4: Edit your new Web site.

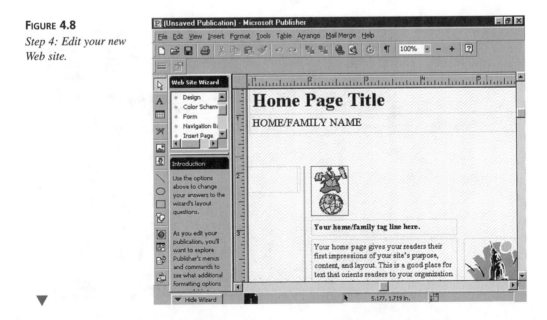

▲ 5. When it's time to save, choose File, Save As Web Page.

Importing Various Types of Files into FrontPage Express

Simply by choosing File, Open, you can open any HTML file in FrontPage Express, whether it was created there or in another program (see Hour 2, "Getting Started with a Web Authoring Program").

But suppose you have a document in another file format, and either don't have the right program to edit it, or have found that that program cannot convert the file to HTML?

You may be happy to discover that you can *import* many different kinds of files into FrontPage Express—convert them to HTML files you can then edit in FrontPage Express and publish on the Web. The next To Do shows how.

Before you get there, though, note that imported files (and Web pages started in other programs, like Word and Publisher) usually wind up showing some funky little question mark icons in FrontPage Express, like those shown in Figure 4.9.

FIGURE 4.9

Question mark icons indicate formatting instructions FrontPage Express does not understand.

Question mark icons

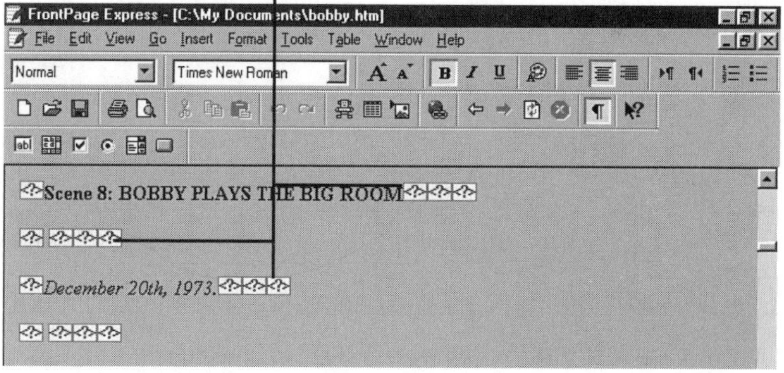

4

The question marks indicate spots in the file that contain formatting instructions (carried over from the other program) that FrontPage Express does not know what to do with. Although they're a drag to look at, they may not indicate any real problem; there are certain kinds of formatting that FrontPage Express doesn't understand which are nonetheless perfectly acceptable in a Web page.

You can cut these icons (and any formatting they might apply) just as if they were typos: Click 'em and press your Delete key. But before doing that, view the file through your browser (as described in Hour 2). You may find that you like the formatting and may choose to leave some of the little buggers alone.

Depending upon the file type you start with, the results of importing a file may come into FrontPage nicely formatted, or in something of a mess.

But even when the formatting doesn't import cleanly, you'll almost always successfully import any text in the original file, which saves you the trouble of retyping it. Reformatting usually goes a lot faster than retyping.

To Do: Import a file from another program into FrontPage Express

1. In FrontPage Express, choose File, Open.

2. Use the Look In list to navigate to the folder containing the file you want to open.

FIGURE 4.10

Step 2: Use Look In to navigate to the folder containing the file to import.

Look in list

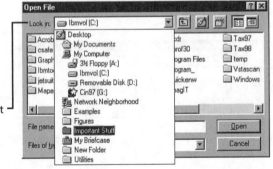

When you get to the folder containing the file, don't worry if its icon and name don't show up in the list of files in the Open dialog box. The file will appear there after you perform step 3.

▼ 3. Open the Files of Type list, and choose the file type of the file you are importing.

FIGURE 4.11

Step 3: Choose the file's type from the Files of Type list.

Files of Type list ──

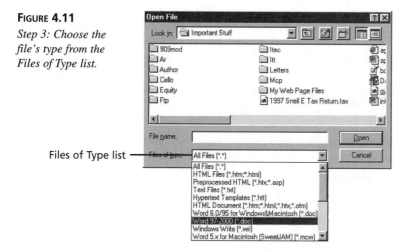

4. Click the file's icon in the list of files, and click Open.

FIGURE 4.12

Step 4: Choose the file, and click Open.

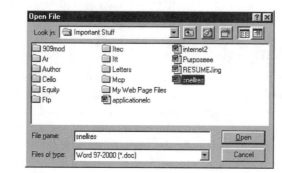

5. When you save the file, it will be saved as an HTML file.

Suppose you get to step 3 of the preceding To Do, and the file type you need does not appear in the Files of type list?

If there's any program on your computer that *can* open the file you want to import, you have two options. Begin by opening the file in that program, and then do the following:

1. Choose File, Save As, and then open the Save As dialog box's Save as Type list. If you see any file type listed that is among the file types FrontPage Express can import, save the file in that format and then import it.

4

or

2. Use copy & paste (see Hour 5) to copy anything you want from the original document to a Web page in FrontPage Express.

Working with Templates

If Web pages were waffles, templates would be Bisquick.

NEW TERM A *template* is a ready-made Web page you can simply edit—replacing the template's text with your own—to quickly create a new, custom Web page that retains some design elements of the template.

As a head start to Web pages, templates offer a quicker and easier way to build Web pages than starting from scratch, and they also allow you greater flexibility in the design of your document than is possible with a wizard like FrontPage Express's Personal Home Page Wizard or Word's Web Page Wizard.

Templates are especially valuable when you need to create a rather complicated page—perhaps one that you feel exceeds your own authoring skills—and aren't quite sure how to approach it.

What's a Template?

A template is simply an HTML file filled mostly with meaningless, boilerplate content instead of the real thing. The prefabricated file has already been organized and formatted with paragraph properties, horizontal lines, and other bells and whistles you learn to create later in this book. A template also can include many of the basic content elements of a Web page: title, headings, body, signature, appropriate links, and so on. (If you don't recognize these parts of a page, review Hour 1, "Understanding Web Authoring.")

By replacing the boilerplate content with your own content and leaving the decorative stuff alone, you can quickly create an attractive, effective Web page without having to fuss much over its organization or formatting. Of course, if you decide you want to change the formatting or organization of a page created from a template, you can, just as you can edit any HTML file in FrontPage Express.

Figure 4.13 shows a template for a human resources department page. Figure 4.14 shows a page I created by replacing the template's text with my own. Compare the figures and observe that the only difference between the two is text content. Notice how I was able to take advantage of the template's organization, fancy horizontal lines, and character formatting while still making it my own.

FIGURE 4.13

An unedited template viewed in the browser window.

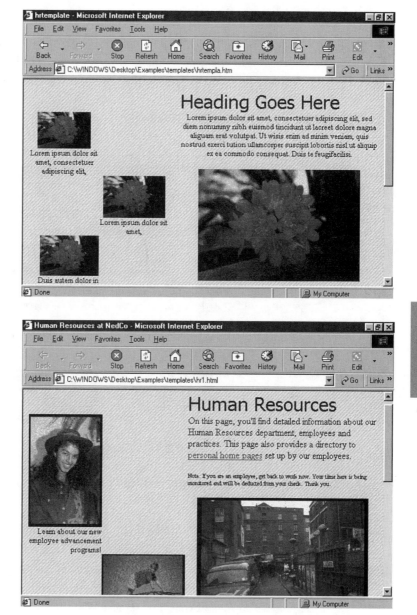

FIGURE 4.14

The template edited into a real page with the addition of real content.

Where to Find Templates

You can find templates in lots of places. Web authoring programs, like the full version of Microsoft FrontPage 2000, usually contain a bunch.

At this point, your best bet is to look online. You can find plenty of good, copyright-free templates in Web authoring sites. The following URLs offer a few good starting points:

- Web Diner's Templates Page (see Figure 4.15) at `www.webdiner.com/templates/`
- BAM Technologies's Web Templates Page at `bamtech.hypermart.net/templates.htm`
- Templates from the Spider's Group at Stanford at `www-pcd.stanford.edu/mogens/intro/templates.html`

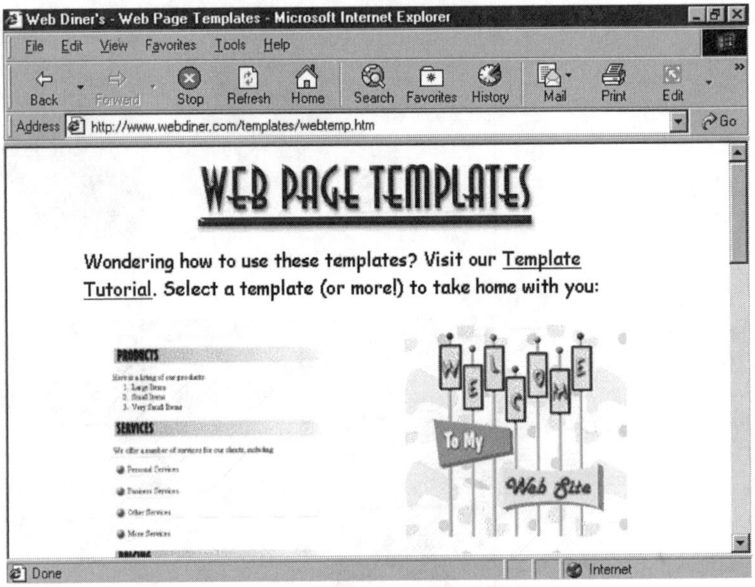

FIGURE 4.15

Web Diner is one good resource for free Web page templates.

Note that a copy of any template you find online must be saved to your hard drive before you can edit it.

Depending on how the template is presented online, there are two ways you can get a template onto your hard drive:

- If the template is offered as a file (or, more likely, as a set of files in a ZIP archive), just download it to your PC like any other file (and unzip it, if necessary).
- If the template appears in your browser as a Web page, you need to save that page to your hard drive. While viewing the page in Internet Explorer, choose File, Save As.

Editing a Template into Your Own Page

After a template has been saved on your hard drive, you can edit, expand, reformat, or delete any part of it. In a few cases, you might find that you don't need to change much of anything—anywhere the template already says what you want to say, leave it alone.

Most of the text you'll see, however, must be replaced or deleted. You'll learn in detail how to edit Web pages in upcoming hours, but just to get you started (templates, after all, are for those who want to work quickly), the following are a few quick editing techniques:

- To replace an entire paragraph, highlight the paragraph from beginning to end by moving the mouse pointer to the left of the paragraph and double-clicking. Then type your new content. The paragraph is instantly deleted and replaced with whatever you type. Your new paragraph takes on the same paragraph properties as the one you've replaced.

- To replace only a portion of a paragraph, highlight the portion you want to replace (click and hold at the start of the selection, drag to the end, and release), and then type your content. The highlighted section is deleted and replaced with what you type.

- To delete an image, click it once (to select it) and press the Delete key.

The only trick to editing a template is to change the content without screwing up the existing formatting. To that end, it's helpful to imagine that, in between each set of paragraphs, there are hidden formatting instructions that must not be lost or corrupted during editing.

To make sure that you don't accidentally alter the formatting, avoid doing anything that would delete the space between paragraphs. For example,

- When the edit cursor (the tall vertical bar that appears whenever you type or edit text) appears at the very beginning of a block of text, do not press the Backspace key.

- When the edit cursor appears at the very end of a block of text, do not press the Delete key.

- If you do change the properties inadvertently, click the Undo button on FrontPage Express's Standard toolbar before you do anything else.

4

Summary

Talk about putting the cart before the horse! It's only four hours into the tutorial, and you have yet to learn the basics of putting text, pictures, and links into a Web page. But you already know three ways—the Personal Home Page Wizard, starting in other programs, and templates—to crank out a pretty respectable page.

Since you've already experienced the rush of instant gratification, the next four hours provide an opportunity to settle down and work closely with the most important part of any Web page: the *words*.

Q&A

Q Can I make my own templates?

A Sure. In fact, doing so can save you a lot of time if you create many similar pages.

To make your own templates, just build a page containing the elements that you tend to reuse from project to project. Create new pages by opening and editing that template file, making sure to save the creations with new filenames (using File, Save As) so that the template itself remains unaltered and ready to serve up the next new page.

Q Can I copy cool pages I visit online to use them as templates?

A Yes and no. (Don't you just *hate* answers like that?)

Technically, sure, you *can* grab any page you see online, save it on your PC, open it in FrontPage Express and edit it. One way to do this is to visit the page in Internet Explorer 5, and then click the Edit button on IE5's toolbar. That button opens the page in whatever program on your PC is set up as your "default" Web page editor. (That's probably FrontPage Express, but if you happen to have another authoring program installed, the file may open in that program.) You can then edit and save the file on your PC.

Another way to get the same result is to visit the page, and then choose File, Save As from IE5's menu bar. A dialog box for saving the Web page files (pictures and all) on your PC opens. After you save the files, you can disconnect from the Internet and open the files in FrontPage Express for editing.

But even though you *can* do this, you probably shouldn't. For one thing, the page and its contents (including pictures) may be copyrighted, which means using any part of it is a big fat no-no. And even if it is not copyrighted, it's someone else's work, so you'll bring bad karma on yourself if you steal it. You may be tempted to think that if you change all the words and pictures, and just borrow the layout, it's OK. Well, in most cases the underlying HTML code may be copyrighted, too, so you're still busted.

And for another thing, you don't *need* to copy anybody else's work. You have the tools to do anything you want, on your own, and within the next 20 hours, you'll have the skills. All you'll need after that is a little practice.

4

PART II
Titles, Text, And Tables

Hour

HOUR 5

Choosing a Title, Text Colors, and Other Page Basics

There's the forest, and then there are the trees.

In Web authoring, the trees are the content—the words, the pictures, the links. But before you start planting pines, it's smart to deal with a few quick, easy elements that affect your page at a higher level: the title, custom colors, and other stuff that defines the shape and function of the forest.

At the end of the hour, you will be able to answer the following questions:

- What are "page properties," and how do I choose them?
- How can I change a page's title, and how do I know if I've come up with a title that works?
- How do I apply custom colors to the text and background in my page?
- How can I add identification information to my page that will help it get listed properly in search pages online?

About Page Properties

Everything you learn in this hour has to do with stuff that's generally described as *page properties*, settings that affect the overall look and function of your page.

Unlike all other parts of your page, such as the page's text and pictures, you do not create the page properties within the work area in FrontPage Express. Instead, you use a special Page Properties dialog box (see Figure 5.1), which you open by choosing File, Page Properties.

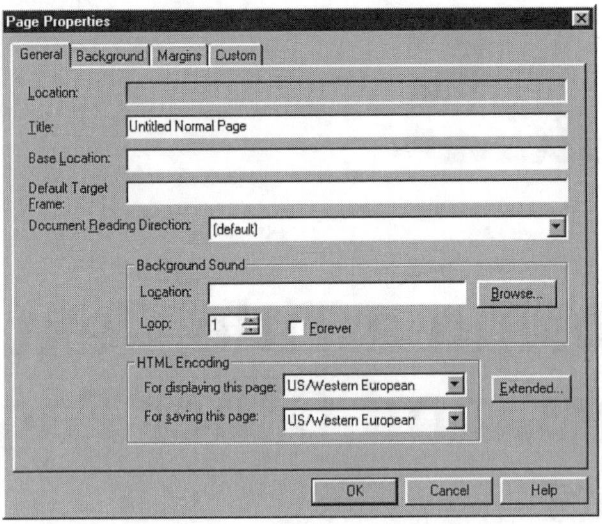

FIGURE 5.1

The General tab of the Page Properties dialog box.

You use the Page Properties dialog box to change your page's title, choose a scheme of complimentary text and background colors, and embed special identification information that does not actually appear on the page, but helps search tools (such as Yahoo! or Alta Vista) properly catalog your pages.

Choosing an Effective Page Title

While every Web page must have a title, entering one in FrontPage Express is not required. As you know from Hour 2, "Getting Started with a Web Authoring Program," if you neglect to create one, FrontPage Express invents one when you first save the page, using whatever text it happens to find at the top of the page.

However, it's very important that you enter a carefully worded title, because the title describes your page to the Web in myriad ways.

For example, when a visitor to your page creates a bookmark or favorite for your page in his or her browser, the title typically becomes the name of the bookmark or favorite, as shown in Figure 5.2.

Also, Web directories (such as Yahoo!) and spiders (programs that build Web directories by searching the Web and cataloging its contents) use the title as a primary reference for what the page is about. Give your page a poorly worded title, and it may not come up in the hit list when folks search on the very topic your page covers.

> When people use Yahoo!, Excite, and other Web-searching tools, you want them to find your page when your page really matches what they want, and *not* to find your page when it's not a good match. Entering a good, descriptive title is one step in ensuring that.
>
> After the title, the next most important property for helping people find your page is the *keywords* you can add in the Page Properties dialog box. See "Helping Search Pages Catalog Your Page," later in this hour.

FIGURE 5.2

Page titles become bookmark or favorite names in browsers.

Favorites
  Add to Favorites...
  Organize Favorites...
  📁 IBM sites   ▶
  📁 Links   ▶
  📁 Media   ▶
  📁 Other useful sites ▶
  📁 Software Updates   ▶
  Easy Choice
  Kelley Blue Book
  MSN
  Ned's Guide to Lumber
  Orlando Theatre Project
  Product Information Page
  Radio Station Guide
  Web Events

5

Don't confuse the page title with any big, bold heading that may top a Web page and serve as its apparent title. Remember, by the time a visitor sees that top-level heading, he or she has already arrived at your page and is presumably already interested in its subject. So that top heading can be more creative than the real page title—even subtle. But the true title must be descriptive, not clever.

Remember: The title entered in Page Properties does not appear on the page itself, but in the title bar of the browser window in which the page is displayed.

An effective title should accurately describe the contents or purpose of your page. It should also be fairly short—no more than six to eight words—and its most descriptive words should appear first.

In a bookmark list or Web directory, there's often room for only the first few words of a title, so your title needs to be short, and those first few words must be meaningful.

The following are some good titles:

Sammy's Racquetball Directory

The Video Store Online

All About Trout Fishing

Marvin C. Able's Awesome Home Page

Weehauken, NJ Events for July

In these good examples, notice that the most specific, important descriptor appears within the first three words: Racquetball, Video, Trout, Marvin C. Able, and Weehauken, NJ Events.

Notice also that the fewest possible words are used to nail down the page. In the first example, you learn in three words that this page is a directory of racquetball-related information and that it's Sammy's directory (to distinguish it from any other racquetball directories). What more do you need to know?

The following, for comparison, are some lousy titles:

My Home Page

Things to Do

Schedule of Events

A Catalog of Links and Documents Provided as a Public Service for Persons Researching Population Trends

In the first three crummy examples, the titles are nondescript; they contain nothing about the specific contents of the page. The last example, although containing some useful information at the end, would be trimmed down to its first four or five words in a bookmark list, and those first few words say nothing useful.

Now that you know a little more about effective titles, you may want to change the titles of pages you've already started developing. The following To Do shows how.

To Do: Change a page's title

1. In FrontPage Express, open (or create) the page file whose title you want to change.
2. Choose File, Page Properties.

FIGURE 5.3

Step 2: Choose File, Page Properties.

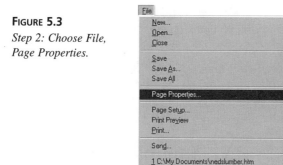

3. On the General tab, find the page's current title in the box marked Title.
4. Click in the box to locate the edit cursor there.

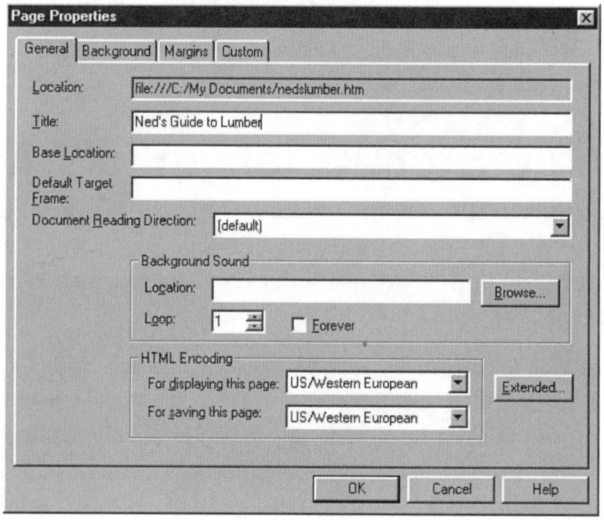

FIGURE 5.4

Step 4: Click in the Title box, so you can edit the title there.

5

▼

5. Use your Delete and Backspace keys to delete any unwanted parts of the current title (or all of it).

6. Type your new title, and then click OK.

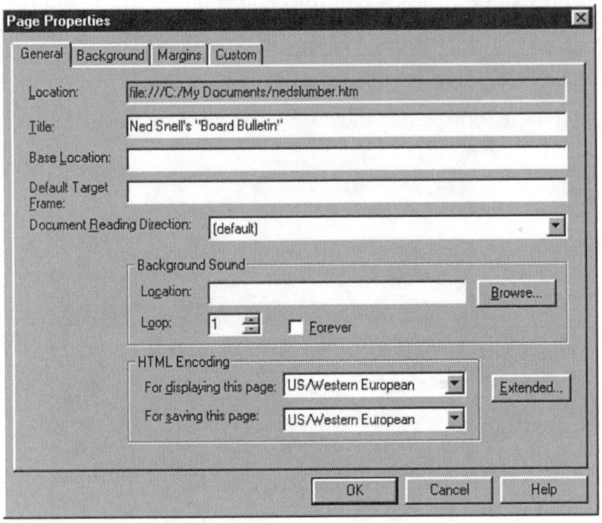

FIGURE **5.5**

Step 6: Type your new title.

When typing your new title, be careful to capitalize and spell it exactly as you want it to appear in a title bar or bookmark list.

Don't bother trying to use character formatting, such as bold or italic, in the title. No character formatting is possible within the text-entry areas in the Page Properties dialog box, and even if it were, it wouldn't show up anywhere titles typically appear.

▲

Choosing Custom Colors for a Whole Page

In general, the visitor's browser—including Netscape Navigator and Internet Explorer—chooses the colors for the text and background of a page. This frees folks to choose color schemes they find pleasing to their own eyes, and to have all Web pages show those colors, unless...

Unless the Web author (that's you) has applied *custom colors*. Custom colors are selected colors for the background and text that override the browser's color settings, so that the Web author—not the browser—controls the color of text and the background.

Note that custom colors affect only text and background colors. They have no effect on the colors in pictures or in picture backgrounds (see Hour 14, "Adding Pictures (and Picture Backgrounds)"). Pictures are always displayed with whatever colors they were created with, regardless of any settings in the page properties or the browser.

You can assign custom colors separately for each of the following page elements:

- *Background*—The entire background area of the page can be a solid custom color. The background color always sits behind text or images in the page, never covering them, obscuring them, or affecting their color.

Choosing Format, Background from FrontPage Express's menu bar opens the Background tab of the Page Properties dialog box. From there, you can change the background exactly as described in steps 4 and 5 of the upcoming To Do.

The menu item is just a faster way to get to the background tab than choosing File, Page Properties, and then clicking the Background tab.

- *Normal text*—All text in the page that is not a link.
- *Hyperlink text*—All links in the page except those that are active or visited (described next).
- *Visited Link text*—Links that the visitor has previously used through his or her browser. In your own travels online, you may have noticed that when you return to pages you've visited before, links you've used before appear in a different color from those you've never clicked.
- *Active Link text*—Immediately after a link has been clicked by the visitor, it may remain visible for a few moments while the browser retrieves the file to which the link points. While the link remains visible, it changes color to indicate that it has been activated.

5

The text colors you select in Page Properties automatically affect the page elements they're supposed to, freeing you to forget about text color when composing your page.

But note that, as you work on your page, you can selectively choose the color of any block of text to give it special emphasis. The color you choose need not be one of the colors you selected in Page Properties; it can be any color you want. To learn how to choose the color of a selected block of text, see Hour 7, "Formatting Text."

To Do: Choose custom colors

1. Open the page whose colors you want to choose.
2. Choose File, Page Properties.

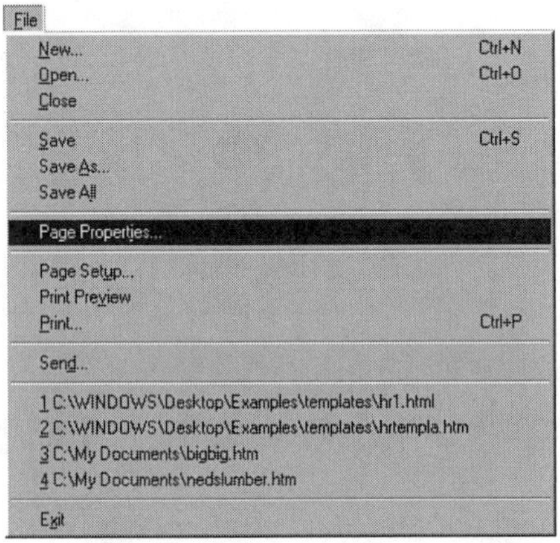

FIGURE **5.6**

Step 2: Choose File, Page Properties.

File	
New...	Ctrl+N
Open...	Ctrl+O
Close	
Save	Ctrl+S
Save As...	
Save All	
Page Properties...	
Page Setup...	
Print Preview	
Print...	Ctrl+P
Send...	
1 C:\WINDOWS\Desktop\Examples\templates\hr1.html	
2 C:\WINDOWS\Desktop\Examples\templates\hrtempla.htm	
3 C:\My Documents\bigbig.htm	
4 C:\My Documents\nedslumber.htm	
Exit	

3. Click the Background tab (see Figure 5.7).
4. Click the arrow on the Background list box to open the list (shown in Figure 5.8).
5. Click the color you want to use for the background.

Be careful that the text and link colors you choose stand out against the background color. For example, if you select a dark background color, all of the text colors must be light so that the text will be legible atop the background.

▼   6. Repeat steps 4 and 5 for the other color lists (see Figure 5.9): Text (for normal
               text), Hyperlink, Visited Link, and Active Link.

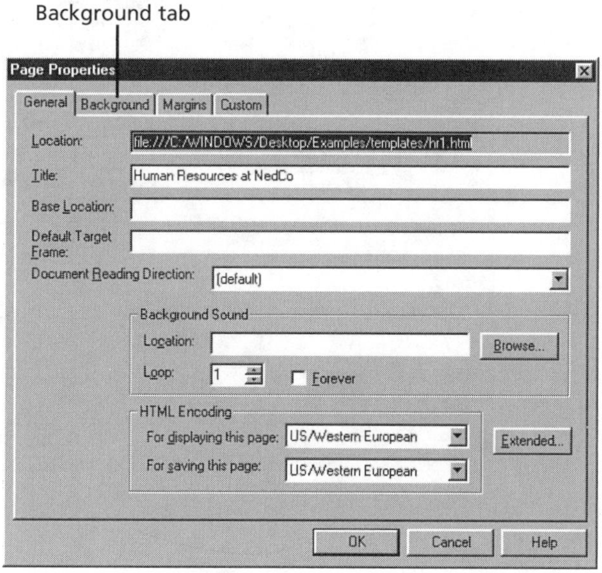

FIGURE 5.7

Step 3: Click the
Background tab.

Background tab

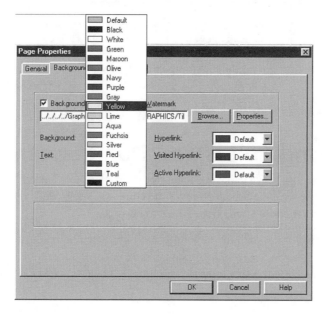

FIGURE 5.8

Step 4: Open the list to
choose a color.

5

▼

Step 6: Choose the text
and link colors.

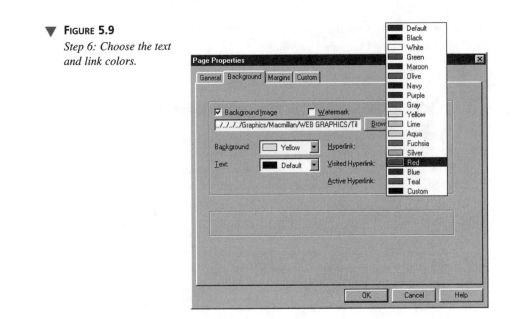

7. Click OK.

Choosing the top item in any color list, Default, assigns no particular color. Instead, it allows the color for that object to be determined by the color settings in the visitor's browser.

Because the color the browser chooses might not show up properly with other colors you've selected, never choose Default unless you choose Default for *all* colors in the page.

Choosing Colors You Don't See in the Lists

Suppose that, when choosing colors for the background and text (as described in the preceding To Do), the lists don't show the color you want. Well, you can optionally display a wider variety of colors from which to choose.

At the bottom of each list of colors, you'll find the choice Custom (look back at Figure 5.8). Click Custom to open a dialog box (see Figure 5.10) on which you can create and select colors different from those shown in the list.

FIGURE **5.10**

Choose Custom from
any color list to open
this palette with many
more choices.

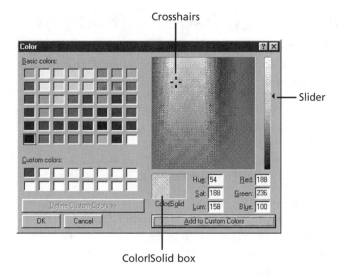

Crosshairs

Slider

ColorlSolid box

- To create a new color, drag the crosshairs on the big square palette, and the slider on the vertical color scale to the right of the palette, until you see the color you want displayed in the ColorlSolid box. Then click the Add to Custom Colors button. The color appears in one of the squares under Custom Colors, in the lower-left part of the dialog box.

- To apply a custom color to the background or text, click its square, and then click OK.

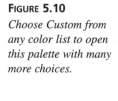

Do what you want, but bear in mind that it's sort of a waste of time to get too esoteric when choosing colors. Visitors will be running monitors with varying color capabilities and browsers with varying levels of support for colors, so it's unlikely that the colors will appear to others in the precise hue you choose.

In other words, it's meaningful to fuss over whether to make text red or blue. But to click Custom so you can choose that *exact* shade of Mediterranean sea blue (the one the bridesmaids wore at your wedding) because it's a half-shade brighter than the blue that's in the color list...well, that's probably splitting hairs.

If a very specific color is essential to your design, it's better to use that color in a picture (or picture background) you create. See Hour 13, "Getting Pictures for Your Page."

5

Helping Search Pages Catalog Your Page

Most folks who publish a Web page want it found by everybody online who may have a remote interest in the page's topic. (If you intend to keep the Web page you're creating a big fat secret, you can skip this part.)

Obviously, the key to exposing yourself is to ensure that the page shows up in the major (and minor) search pages, such as Yahoo! (www.yahoo.com), Excite (excite.com), and Alta Vista (altavista.com). If your page is about Duck Diseases, you want to be sure that whenever anyone enters the search term "sick duck," "duck illness," or "shaggy beak," a link to your page will appear high in the list of results.

In some cases, you must manually register your page with a search tool, or use a Web promotion service to do it for you (you learn to do both in Hour 22, "Announcing Your Web Presence"). But many search pages catalog the contents of the Web automatically. These search pages use programs, sometimes called crawlers or spiders, that roam around the Web, give Web pages a quick glance, and then attempt (with varying success) to automatically assign each page to one or more related categories. The more accurately your pages are categorized by these programs, the more likely they are to be found by exactly the folks you want to attract.

The most important step in ensuring that the spiders categorize a page correctly is giving it a good, descriptive title, as described earlier in this hour (all spiders look at page titles). But you can increase the accuracy with which you'll be categorized by adding keywords to your Page Properties. Many spiders (but not all) read keywords in a page's properties and regard them as clues to the page's proper category. If your page is about bicycles, adding the keywords "bicycle," "bike," "cycling," "cycle," "cyclist," "Huffy," and so on may increase the chances that those interested in cycling find your page through searches.

The following To Do shows how to add keywords in FrontPage Express.

To Do: Add keywords to your Page Properties

1. Open the page for which you want to add keywords.

2. Choose File, Page Properties.

3. Click the Custom tab (shown in Figure 5.11).

4. To the right of the box labeled User Variables (the lower box), click the Add button (see Figure 5.12).

▼ FIGURE 5.11
Step 3: Click the Custom tab.

Custom tab

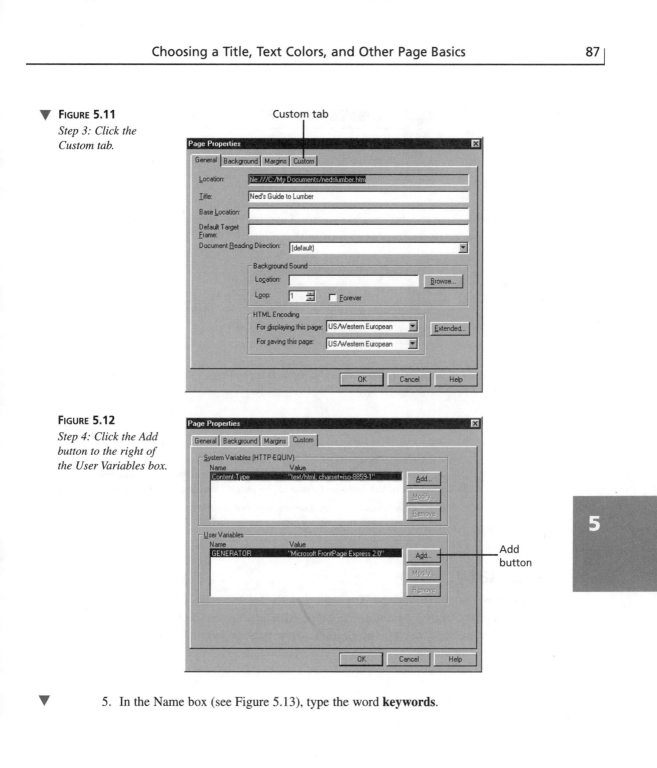

FIGURE 5.12
Step 4: Click the Add button to the right of the User Variables box.

Add button

5

5. In the Name box (see Figure 5.13), type the word **keywords**.

FIGURE **5.13**

Step 5: In the Name box, type the word **keywords**.

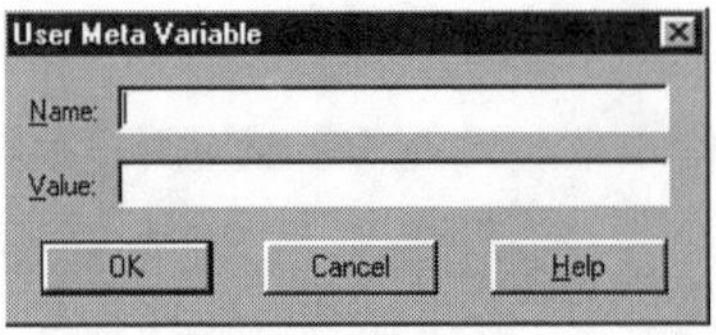

> **User Meta Variable** ☒
>
> N̲ame: [_____]
>
> V̲alue: [_____]
>
> [OK]   [Cancel]   [H̲elp]

6. In the Value box, type your keywords. Put a comma (but no spaces) between keywords, as shown.

FIGURE **5.14**

Step 6: Type your key-words, separated by commas.

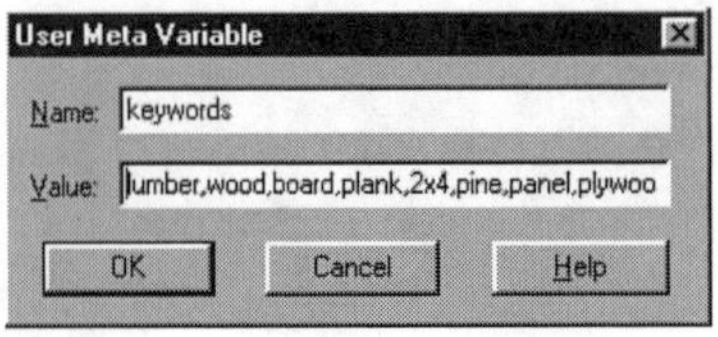

> **User Meta Variable** ☒
>
> N̲ame: [keywords_____]
>
> V̲alue: [lumber,wood,board,plank,2x4,pine,panel,plywoo]
>
> [OK]   [Cancel]   [H̲elp]

7. Click OK to close the User Meta Variable box, and then click OK again on the
   Page Properties dialog box.

> When typing your keywords, favor the singular form of a word (bike not
> bikes). However, when the changes that make a word plural are more exten-
> sive than just the addition of the final "s" (goose and geese, for example),
> include both the singular form and the plural form as separate keywords.
>
> To use a two-word term as a single keyword, connect the two words with a
> dash (bike-racing).

Summary

Choosing your page properties is a snap, and it's also important. Doing it not only starts
defining your page's appearance and purpose, but also forces you to begin thinking more
clearly about those aspects. There's nothing like thinking up a title to help you focus
your plans for your page.

Q&A

Q I've seen these cool backgrounds online, some that look like marble or other textures, and others that are pictures. How do I do those?

A Easy. Instead of using a background color, you can use a picture file to create a graphical background for a page, as you learn to do in Hour 14.

Note that if you do use an image for the background, the background color setting is irrelevant—an image background overrides a background color.

Q Hey! There's lots of stuff on the Page Properties dialog box you didn't cover! What about Base Location! What about Default Target Frame! How do I know I don't need to choose margins?

A Well, I could spend a few pages explaining all of this stuff. But we have only 24 hours together, and the bottom line is that all the options on the Page Properties dialog box I didn't explain are best left alone, especially if you're a beginner.

For example, using the Base Location box will foul up the way links behave when you test your page on your PC before publishing it. It's there to satisfy a minor need of some experienced Web authors, but it can only cause you aggravation.

Similarly, the Margins put blank margin space above and/or below your Web page. But margins created this way are not supported in many Web browsers, and you're really better off not confusing your page layout options with margins.

When you venture to Page Properties, fiddle with your title, change colors, and add keywords. Ignore the rest. Remember: What you don't change can't hurt you.

5

HOUR 6

Adding and Editing Text

Somebody once said to me, "Writing isn't so tough: All you have to do is find a quiet spot and open a vein."

That's true, actually, but to the extent that writing a Web page can be made less immediately life-threatening, a WYSIWYG editor does just that. The principal job in creating the text of a Web page involves two main tasks: getting the text into the file (by typing it, copying it, or importing it) and assigning paragraph properties to each block of text. The properties tell browsers how to present that text.

In this hour, you'll learn how to get text into your Web page files, format it by assigning properties, and edit it. Dealing with the text first is usually the best way to build a Web page; it forces you to think about and resolve issues related to the organization and flow of content. At the end of the hour, you will be able to answer the following questions:

- What are the basics of creating the text elements of a Web page?
- How do I control the text's general appearance and position on the page?

- How do I type special characters that don't appear on my keyboard, such as copyright symbols?
- How can I save time and typing with cut and paste, copy, and other text-entry tips?
- How do I edit the text?

Understanding Paragraphs and Their Properties

What makes a particular paragraph a heading or something else are the properties you assign to the paragraph. Assigning properties to a paragraph is no different from assigning a style in a word processor, and usually it's just as easy. In a nutshell, you type a line or block of text, and then assign properties to that paragraph to identify it as a heading, text paragraph, or whatever. *Voilà.*

NEW TERM   FrontPage Express calls each discrete chunk of text—all the text between paragraph marks (the character you type when you press Enter)—a *paragraph*, whether it's a heading, one line in a list, a multiline paragraph, or just a bunch of words.

Note that paragraph properties apply only to entire paragraphs. For example, you cannot format two words in the middle of a paragraph as an address and the rest of the paragraph as a heading. Either the whole paragraph is one thing, or the whole paragraph is something else.

What Each Paragraph Property Does

The most important paragraph properties are described in the following sections and are shown in Internet Explorer (and most other browsers) as they appear in Figures 6.1 and 6.2.

Normal

Use *Normal* for general-purpose text—like what you're reading right now. Most browsers display Normal paragraphs in a plain font with no special emphasis (such as bold or special color). Normal is the meat and potatoes of your Web page.

Headings

Use headings the way you see them used in this book: to divide and label the logical sections of the page or Web page. There are six levels of headings, ranging in relative importance from 1 (most important or prominent) to 6 (least important or prominent).

Because the level 1 heading is the most prominent, it is often reserved for the apparent title of your page—the one that appears within the page itself (not to be confused with the Web page title entered in Page Properties).

In most browsers, a level 1 heading is displayed as the biggest, boldest text on the page. Level 2 headings are smaller and not bold, or they are de-emphasized in some other way. Level 3 gets less emphasis than 2 but more than 4, and so on. (Six levels require a lot of variation, and the difference between headings only one level apart is barely distinguishable in some browsers, as you can see in Figure 6.1.)

Text-based browsers, which can't display varying font sizes, use bold, underline, or even numbers to show the varying heading levels.

FIGURE 6.1

Paragraphs and their properties: headings, normal text, and address.

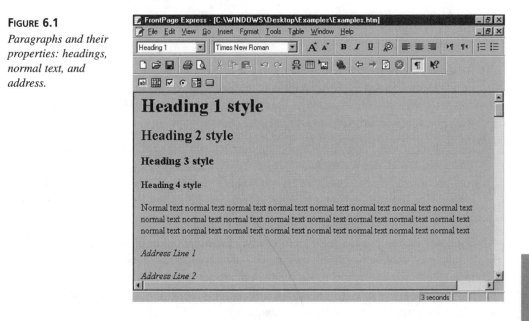

You can use whatever heading levels you want, but in general, obey the numbers. Subheadings within a section should have a higher level number than the heading for the section. For example, a section that begins with a level 2 heading might have level 3 subheadings under it. The subsections under the level 3 heads might have sub-subsections with level 4 heads, and so on.

Address

Use *Address* for creating an *address block*, a line or many lines identifying someone, which usually lists an email address, a snail mail address, or other contact information.

The Address property is used most often for the signature at the bottom of the page, but it can be used to give any address information on your page a unique style that sets it apart from other text. Most browsers display address blocks in italic type.

> Assigning the Address property to an email address on your page does not, by itself, make the address a mail-to link that a visitor can click to send email. However, an email address with the Address property can be a mail-to link—you just have to make it one.
>
> To learn how to create a mail-to link, see Hour 10, "Making Links."

Formatted

Formatted might seem like a misnomer because text assigned the *Formatted* property is in fact less formatted by the browser than any other kind. What *formatted* means in this context is *preformatted*—you have already lined up and spaced the text in a particular way, and you want browsers to leave that formatting alone.

Typically, browsers capable of displaying *proportionally spaced* fonts (such as TrueType's Arial, or even the snappy font you're reading now) use those fonts for most text because they look better than typewriter-style *monospaced* fonts (such as Courier New). Also, browsers ignore tabs, extra spaces, and blank lines (extra paragraph marks) in HTML files.

Suppose that you want to show a text chart or table on your page, or words arranged in a certain way. Tabs are *verboten*, so you need to use spaces and a monospaced font to make the words line up right. But if browsers are permitted to do their regular thing with that text, they will strip out the extra spaces, display the text in a proportional font, and generally screw up your lovely alignment job.

> You can use the Formatted property to create the effect of tables in your Web page, but you can also create real tables that look much better (see Hour 8, "Organizing Text with Tables and Rules").

For example, observe the careful alignment of columns and the use of a monospaced font in the simple table shown in Figure 6.2. This table uses the Formatted property. Notice how the browser's display font and regularity of spacing differs in the formatted table from the other text in the figure.

FIGURE 6.2

Paragraphs and their properties: formatted text.

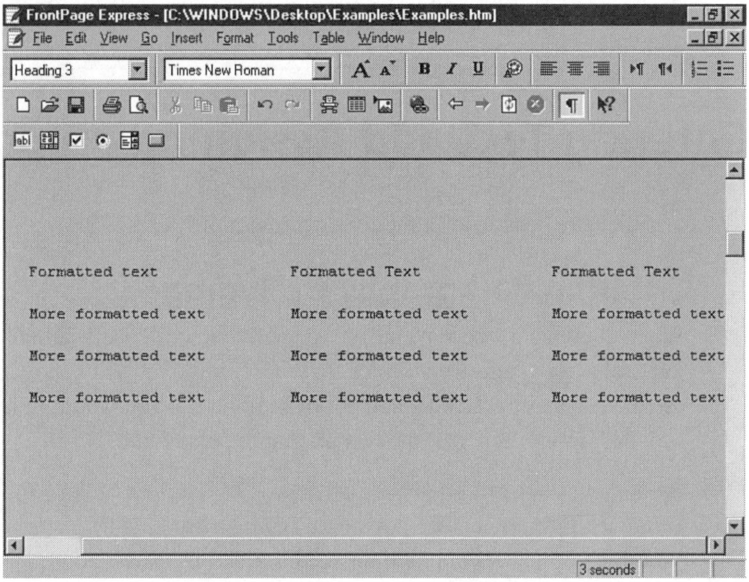

Formatted text	Formatted Text	Formatted Text
More formatted text	More formatted text	More formatted text
More formatted text	More formatted text	More formatted text
More formatted text	More formatted text	More formatted text

Numbered Lists and Bulleted Lists

The Numbered List and Bulleted List properties format lists on your page. Each item in a list is a separate paragraph.

For more about lists, see Hour 7, "Formatting Text."

You can apply paragraph properties in whatever way suits you. (There are no HTML police—at least not yet....) But it's good practice to think of these properties as a way to determine the role a paragraph plays in your page, not its appearance.

For example, there's no technical reason that you can't write a lengthy paragraph and make it a heading, rather than normal text, to make it stand out on the page. But different browsers use different methods to make a heading look like a heading; some make headings big and bold, others underline, and some even number headings according to their levels. Some Web search engines catalog pages according to heading contents because

6

headings generally contain subject information. Putting ordinary paragraph information into a heading might generate some screwy hits on your page from Web searches.

Use properties conservatively, according to their designated roles. Save your artistry for character formatting, images, backgrounds, and other ways you can spice up a page.

Entering Text and Assigning Properties

You can add text to a page and assign properties to that text in several different ways, all of which are described in the following sections.

Entering Paragraphs by Typing

When you create a new Web page, the edit cursor appears automatically at the very top of the Web page. Type away. To correct mistakes and make changes as you go, use the Backspace, Delete, and Insert keys just as you would in any Web page. To end a paragraph and start a new paragraph, press Enter.

By default, your paragraphs are all set as Normal text (unless you select a different paragraph property before you begin typing a paragraph). You can change them to other paragraph properties at any time, as described in the section titled "Assigning Paragraph Properties to Existing Text," later in this hour.

Typing Symbols and Special Characters

Sometimes, you'll need characters that don't appear on your keyboard, such as the copyright symbol or the accented characters used in languages other than English. For such occasions, FrontPage Express offers its Symbol menu.

1. Point to the spot in the text where you want to insert the character, and click to position the edit cursor there.
2. Click Insert, and then choose Symbol.
3. Click the symbol you want to insert. After you click it, it appears next to the Insert button.
4. Click Insert to insert the character.
5. Click Close.

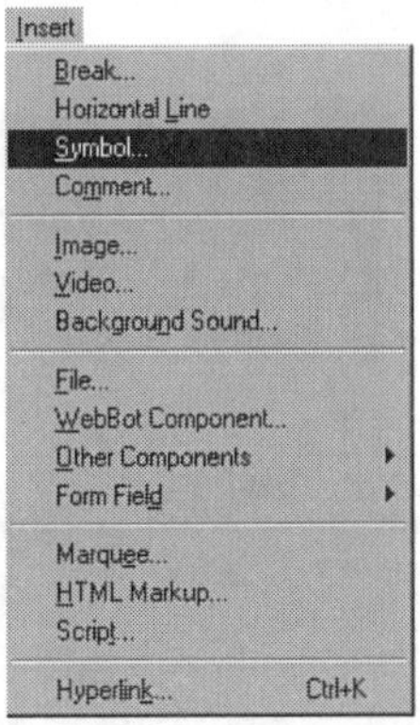

FIGURE 6.3

Step 2: Choose Insert, Symbol.

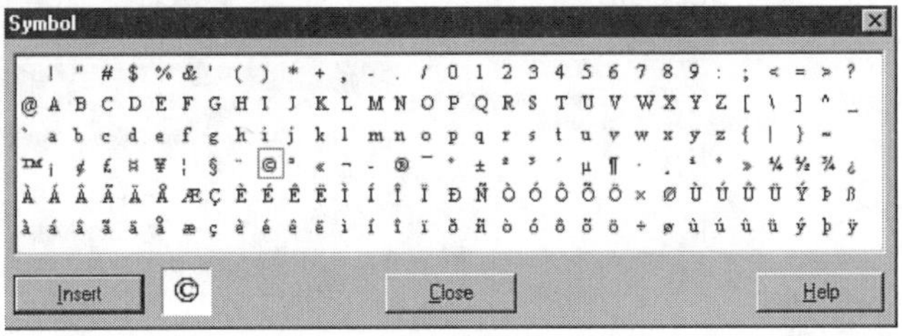

FIGURE 6.4

Step 3: Click the symbol you want.

Copying Text from Another Document

The following To Do describes how to copy text from another document in Windows—such as a word processing file or spreadsheet file—and place it in FrontPage Express so that it can be incorporated in your Web page. This is a convenient way to use preexisting text, such as portions of your resumé or a description of your business, in your Web page without retyping it.

> If you want to use most or all of another document's contents in a new Web page, you may find it more convenient to simply convert that document into a new Web page rather than using Copy and Paste as described here.
>
> To learn how to convert an existing word processing file or other document into a new Web page, see Hour 4, "Starting Pages in Other Programs."

6

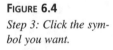

To Do: Enter text with copy and paste

1. Open the application normally used to edit or display the document from which you want to copy, and open the file.

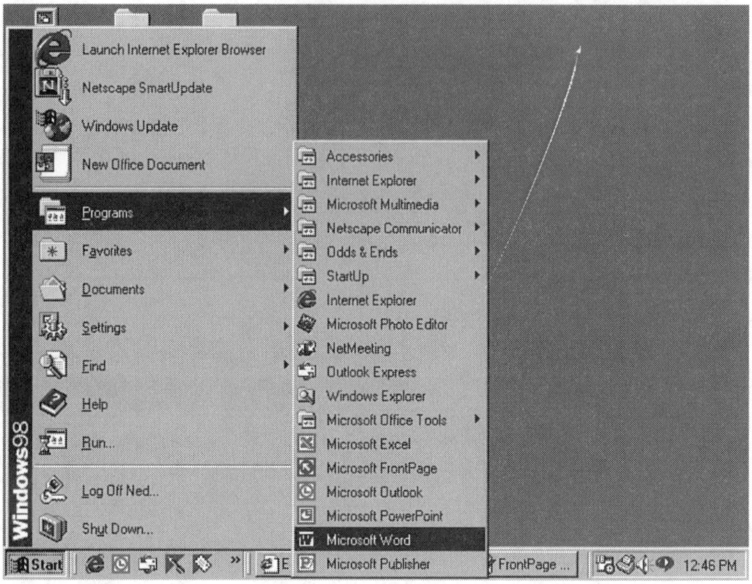

▼

FIGURE 6.5
Step 1: Open the application for the document from which you want to copy text.

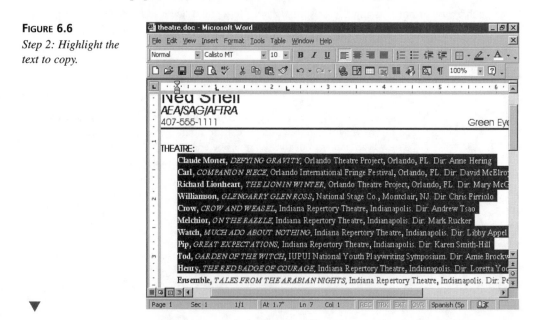

2. Use your mouse to highlight the desired text. (To copy an entire document into your Web page, choose Edit, Select All in the application used to open the Web page.)

FIGURE 6.6
Step 2: Highlight the text to copy.

▼

3. Press Ctrl+C to copy the selection to the Windows Clipboard. (Alternatively, you can click the Copy button on the toolbar or choose Edit, Copy.)

4. Open FrontPage Express and open (or create) the Web page into which you want to copy the text.

5. In the page, click the general spot where you want to copy the text. (If you've just created the Web page, the text must be copied to the top of the Web page where the edit cursor is already located. In a page that already has text, you can click at the start or end of any paragraph to add the selection to that paragraph, or press Enter between paragraphs to start a new paragraph for the selection.)

6. Press Ctrl+V to copy the selection into the page. (Alternatively, you can click the Paste button on FrontPage Express's toolbar or choose Edit, Paste.)

Observe the question mark icons in Figure 6.8. These appear when text you copy carries with it any formatting instructions that FrontPage Express does not know how to interpret and display.

You can easily delete the marks, just as if they were characters. Before deleting them, however, view the page in a browser (as described in Hour 2, "Getting Started with a Web Authoring Program"). The formatting may look just great in a browser, even if FrontPage Express can't quite manage it.

FIGURE 6.7
Step 6: Insert the text.

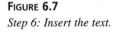

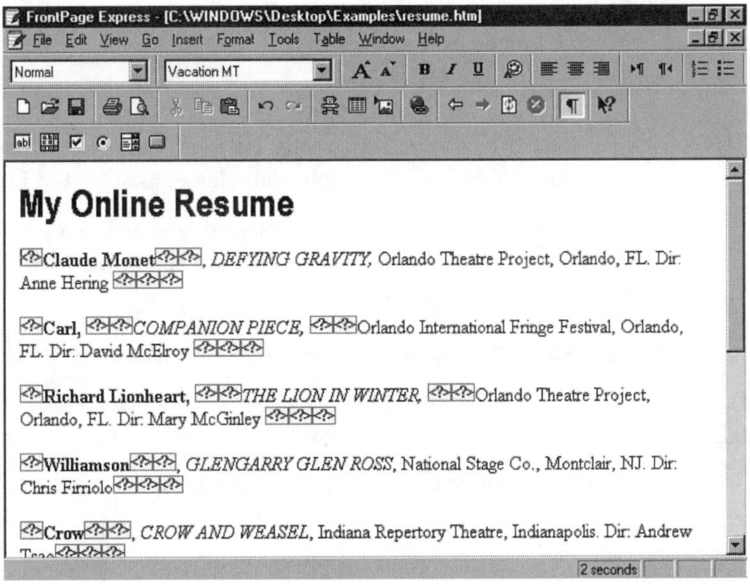

6

▼

When pasted into a blank Web page, the text is automatically assigned the Normal paragraph property. You can then change it to any other paragraph property.

When pasted into a Web page with other paragraphs in it, the text is automatically assigned the same property as the paragraph it is inserted into or adjacent to.

▲

Assigning Paragraph Properties to Existing Text

There are two steps to assigning properties. First, you select the paragraph or paragraphs, and then you choose the properties.

- To select one paragraph, position the edit cursor anywhere within it (either by clicking within the paragraph or by pressing the arrow keys until the cursor arrives within the paragraph). Note that positioning the cursor within the paragraph is sufficient; you don't need to highlight the whole paragraph.

If working *sans mouse*, you can select multiple paragraphs by positioning the edit cursor anywhere in the first paragraph and holding down the Shift key while using the arrow keys to move to anywhere in the last paragraph in the selection.

- To select two or more paragraphs, click anywhere in the first paragraph, drag to anywhere in the last paragraph, and release, as shown in Figure 6.8.

After the paragraph or paragraphs are selected, you assign a paragraph property by clicking the Change Style drop-down list (at the left end of the Format toolbar) and selecting a paragraph style (see Figure 6.9).

To Do: Assign properties and attributes as you type

Although there's a certain logic in entering your paragraphs and then assigning properties, you can do the opposite. To assign properties as you type a paragraph:

1. Click the spot you want the paragraph to go.

▼

*Selecting multiple
paragraphs to assign
them all the same
paragraph property.*

FrontPage Express - [C:\WINDOWS\Desktop\Examples\Examples.htm]

File   Edit   View   Go   Insert   Format   Tools   Table   Window   Help

[None]   Times New Roman

Run to your houses,

fall upon your knees

Pray to the Gods to intermit the plague

That needs must light on this ingratitude

O roar a roar for Nora, Nora Alice in the night
For she has seen Aurora Borealis burning bright!
A furor for our Nora, and applaud Aurora seen
O where throughout the summer has our Borealis been?

3 seconds

FIGURE 6.9

*Use the Change Style
list on the Format tool-
bar to apply a para-
graph style to the
selected paragraphs.*

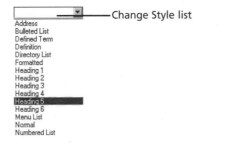————Change Style list

2. Click the Change Style drop-down list on the Format toolbar and select a paragraph style.
3. Type your paragraph. It will appear on the page as you type it, formatted in the
   style you selected. If you press Enter (to end the paragraph and start a new one),
   the new paragraph will take on your selected properties as well.

▼

6

▼

FIGURE 6.10

Step 1: Click where you'll type the new text.

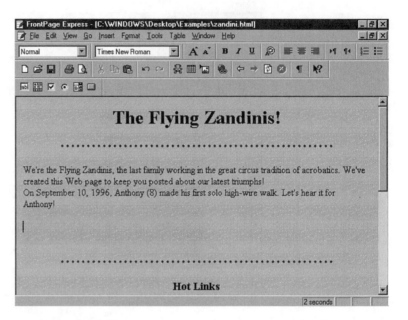

FIGURE 6.11

Step 2: Choose a style.

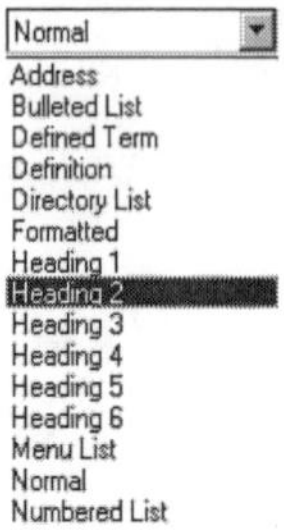

To learn the details of creating and formatting lists, see Hour 7.

▼

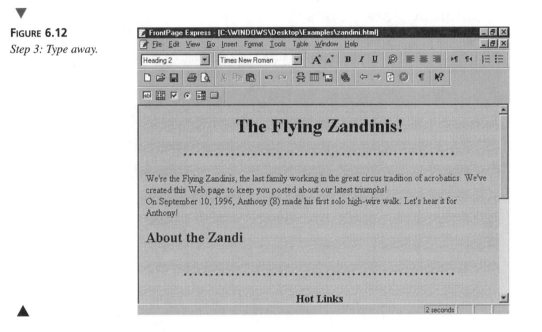

FIGURE 6.12
Step 3: Type away.

Aligning and Indenting Text

On the Format toolbar, you'll find five buttons that control the position of a paragraph on the page (see Figure 6.13).

FIGURE 6.13
The alignment buttons and indent buttons control the position of text within the width of the page.

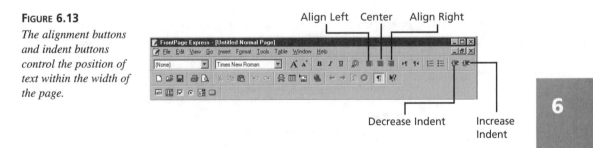

You can use these buttons (as described on the next few pages) on any paragraph, in any style. For example, you can use the Center button to center a paragraph whether the style of that paragraph is Normal, List, Heading 2, or anything else.

6

Aligning Paragraphs

You can align any paragraph any of three different ways (see Figure 6.14): tight up against the left side of the page (left alignment), centered on the page (center alignment), or hard up to the right side (right alignment). The following To Do shows how.

FIGURE 6.14

Left-aligned (the default), center-aligned, and right-aligned text.

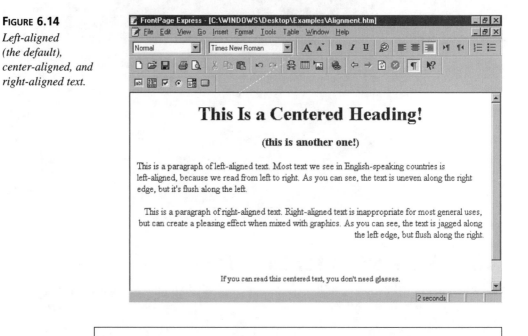

Most of the time, left alignment is best, especially for Normal-style para-graphs. Center can be nice for large headings (such as Heading 1 or Heading 2 style), especially if not used too much. Save right alignment for special needs.

Our eyes are accustomed to left-aligned text, especially for body copy or normal text. A big centered heading looks good on some pages, and right alignment can create a nice effect when text is put to the right of a graphic (see Hour 14, "Adding Pictures (and Picture Backgrounds)"). However, cen-tered normal text paragraphs can appear a bit odd, and centered lists look downright strange.

To Do: Align paragraphs

1. Select the paragraph or paragraphs you want to align.

2. Click one of the three alignment buttons on the Formatting toolbar: Align Left, Center, or Align Right.

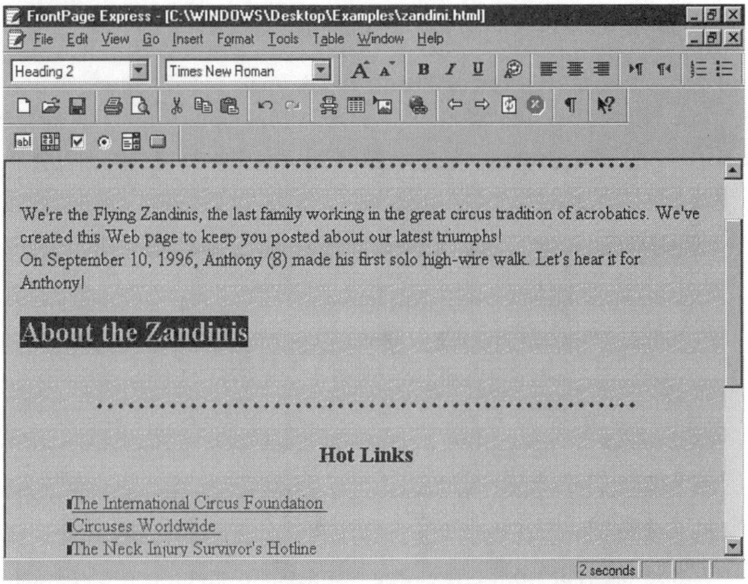

FIGURE **6.15**
Step 1: Select the
paragraph to align.

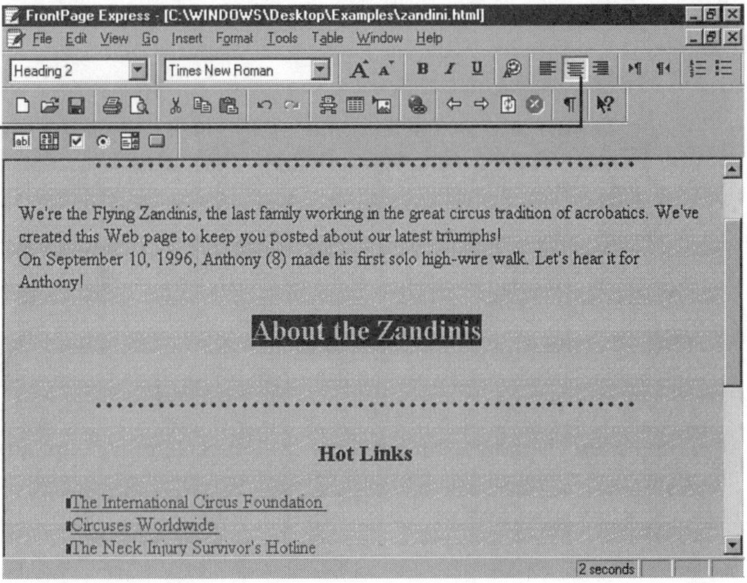

FIGURE **6.16**
Step 2: Click an
alignment button.

Center

Indenting Paragraphs

Besides choosing the alignment of paragraphs, you can *indent* them, pushing them away from the left margin just as you would in a word processor.

FrontPage Express supports multiple indent levels; you can increase the indent several times to push the paragraph farther away from the left margin. Decreasing the indent pulls the text back toward the margin.

- To indent a paragraph, select it, then click the Increase Indent button on the Format toolbar. To indent even farther to the right, click the Increase Indent button again.
- To decrease the indent (move the left edge of the paragraph back toward the left margin), click the Decrease Indent button.

Adding Blank Line Spaces in a Page

Except within the Formatted paragraph style, HTML does not recognize paragraph marks in the HTML file as blank lines or extra blank spaces as extra blank spaces. Thus, browsers generally ignore these characters when displaying a page. To create extra whitespace between paragraphs or extra spaces in a line, Web authors must use the HTML tags for line breaks and non-breaking spaces, respectively.

FrontPage Express, however, figures that when you press Enter multiple times, you want to add whitespace—so it automatically inserts the appropriate tags.

So trust your word-processing instincts: To start a new paragraph, press Enter. And to add a blank line, just press Enter again.

Editing Your Text

Editing a Web page is straightforward, very much like editing any word processing document. To do almost anything, highlight the text you want to change, and then make the change. You can also search for a text string using FrontPage Express's Find in Page tool.

Highlighting Text

To highlight text with your mouse, position the cursor at the start of the area you want to highlight, and then click and hold the left mouse button. Drag to the end of the selection and release the mouse button. Note that you can select as much text as you want in this way: a few characters, a word, a whole paragraph, or a group of paragraphs.

When you drag through an area that includes both text and images, only the text is selected. Images must be selected separately (see Hour 14).

You can also highlight a selection for editing in other ways:

- Double-click a word to select it.
- Double-click at the very beginning of a line to select the first word.
- Double-click at the very end of a line to select the last word.
- Position the pointer to the left of a paragraph and double-click to select the entire paragraph, or single-click to select just the line the cursor is next to.

Replacing Selected Text

When text is selected, begin typing. The selection is deleted immediately and replaced with whatever you type. Any surrounding text that was not highlighted remains unaffected.

You can also replace a highlighted selection with the contents of the Clipboard by clicking the Paste button on the toolbar or by choosing Edit, Paste. (Of course, you must previously have cut or copied something to the Clipboard; see the section titled "Copying or Moving Selected Text," later in this hour.)

Deleting Selected Text

Press the Delete key to delete the selection.

You can right-click selected text to display a context menu with choices for changing properties, for creating links, and for cutting, copying, and pasting. (Refer to Figure 6.5, shown earlier.)

6

To delete the selection from its current location but copy it to the Windows Clipboard so that it can be pasted elsewhere in the page (or into another page or another Windows document), click the Cut button on the toolbar or choose Edit, Cut.

Copying or Moving Selected Text

To copy a highlighted selection, click the Copy button on the toolbar or choose Edit, Copy. Then click in the location where you want the copy to go and click the Paste button or choose Edit, Paste.

To move a highlighted selection, click the Cut button on the toolbar or choose Edit, Cut. Then click in the location where you want the selection moved and click the Paste button or choose Edit, Paste.

Undoing Edits ("Goofs")

If you goof on any edit and wish you hadn't done it, you can undo it.

To undo the last edit you made, click the Undo button on the Standard toolbar (see Figure 6.17).

FIGURE 6.17

To Undo a mistake, click Undo.

Undo

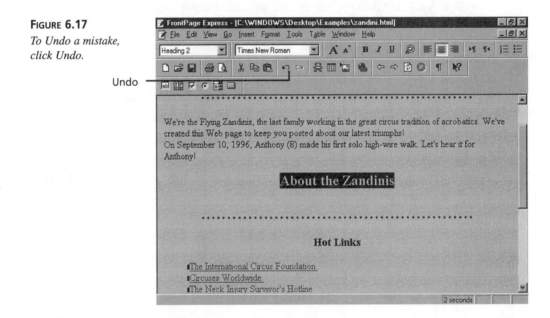

Tips for Good Text Design

It's your page, and far be it from me to tell you what it should look like. However, if you are interested in some of the accumulated wisdom of the Web masters, here are a few things to keep in mind when working with text on your page:

- Write clearly and be brief. Web surfers are an immediate-gratification, fast-food–type lot. To hold them, you must dole out your message in quick, efficient bites.

- Break up your message into pages of reasonable length, and break up pages into at least two or three sections (three is best) delineated by headings, pictures, or horizontal lines (see Hour 7). This makes your page more attractive and inviting and also allows visitors to scan your page easily for items of interest.

- Don't overdo emphasis. Look through your page and watch for overuse of bold, italic, and custom font sizes and colors. Watch also for the use of headings or other properties used to pump up a paragraph that really belongs in Normal text. Let your page's organization (and pictures) create visual interest, and let your choice of words emphasize important ideas. Use bold to light up a word or two and use italic for things that belong in italic, such as book titles or foreign phrases.

- Proofread carefully on your own before publishing. In addition, have someone else check your spelling and critique your writing and layout. (See Hour 4 to learn how to use your word processor to spell check a Web page.)

- Always use a signature (see Hour 10).

Summary

FrontPage Express provides simple toolbar buttons, dialog boxes, and menus for applying properties to paragraphs—the most important activity in building a Web page.

Q&A

Q In second grade I was taught to type two blank spaces after a period, before starting the next sentence. When I try to do that in FrontPage Express (by pressing my keyboard's space bar twice), it won't let me—I get just one space.

A Browsers generally ignore extra spaces, so it's a mistake to use extra spaces to change the appearance of type in a Web page—if you could type two spaces, most browsers would omit the second space when displaying your page anyway. To help you avoid that error, FrontPage Express simply refuses to let you type more than one space character.

If you want that extra space because you're trying to line up rows or columns of text in a particular way, the spacebar isn't the way to do it. Instead, put the text in a table, as described in Hour 8, "Organizing Text with Tables and Rules."

If you absolutely must have multiple character spaces within a paragraph, you have two options: If you use the Change Style list to apply the Formatted style to the paragraph, you can type all the spaces you want—FrontPage Express makes an exception for paragraphs in the Formatted style, and browsers know to display all space characters in such paragraphs. The other method is to actually insert the HTML tag for a blank space.

6

Hour 7

Formatting Text

It's easy—too easy, in fact—to begin thinking that a Web page is made up of three basic parts: text, images, and links. Although that's generally true, it tends to imply that text is for content, images are for show, and links are for action.

The facts are a little muddier than that. Text is first and foremost a vehicle for information, but when text is dressed up in a fancy font or cool color, it contributes both content and design—feeding two brain hemispheres for the price of one. Similarly, organizing text into a bulleted or numbered list affects both content and style.

In this hour, you step beyond paragraph properties and into fancy text formatting. At the end of the hour, you will be able to answer the following questions:

- How do I make attractive lists?
- How do I choose the font and size for text, as I would in a word processor?
- Can I choose the color of text?

Working with Lists

In Hour 6, "Adding and Editing Text," you discovered that you can use buttons on the Format toolbar to create two kinds of lists (see Figure 7.1) in FrontPage Express:

Bulleted list—An ordinary, indented bulleted list.

Numbered list—A list whose items are numbered from top to bottom.

Which kind of list should you create for a given purpose, bulleted or numbered? I dunno. It's your Web site. Do what you feel like.

If you want a principle to guide you, try this: When the order of the items in the list is important, as in step-by-step instructions, use a numbered list. When the order doesn't matter, use a bulleted list.

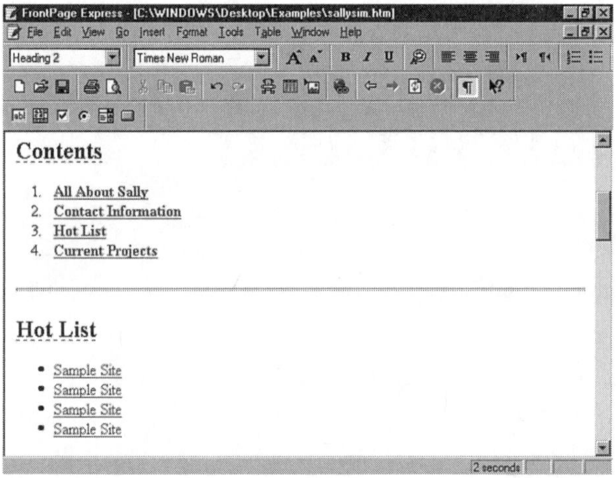

FIGURE 7.1

List styles you can create in FrontPage Express.

But the choices don't stop there! You can take your plain vanilla bulleted or numbered list and change the bullet style or numbering type (see Figure 7.2).

In some pages you see online, you see cool list bullets that are geometrical, multicolored, and even animated.

These are not real bullets assigned by a bullet style attribute, but images inserted right before each line of text. See Hour 14, "Adding Pictures (and Picture Backgrounds)."

FIGURE 7.2

Optional bullet and numbering styles.

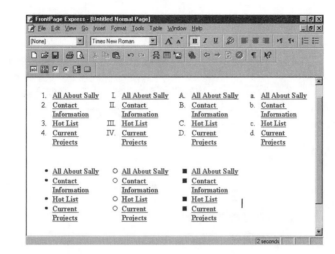

Creating Basic Lists

As with all other text formatting, you create a list by first typing the text of one or more list items; each item is a separate paragraph (press Enter after typing each item), and each item can be as long or as short as you choose. You then apply list formatting as described in the following To Do.

To Do: Create a list

1. Type the list items, pressing Enter after each so that each list item is on a separate line.

FIGURE 7.3

Step 1: Type the list items.

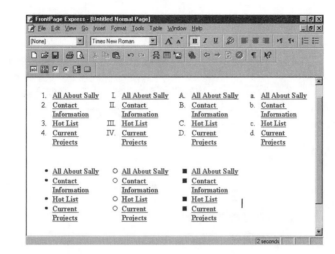

7

▼   2. Select the entire list.

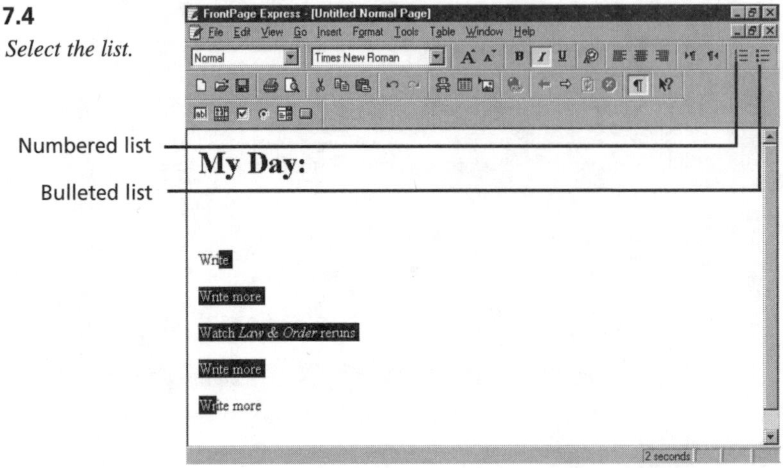

FIGURE 7.4
Step 2: Select the list.

Numbered list ——
Bulleted list ——

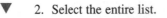

> List formatting is paragraph formatting, so you can select a list by starting the selection anywhere in the first item, and then dragging down to anywhere in the last item.

3. Click one of the two list buttons on the Formatting toolbar: Numbered List or Bulleted List.

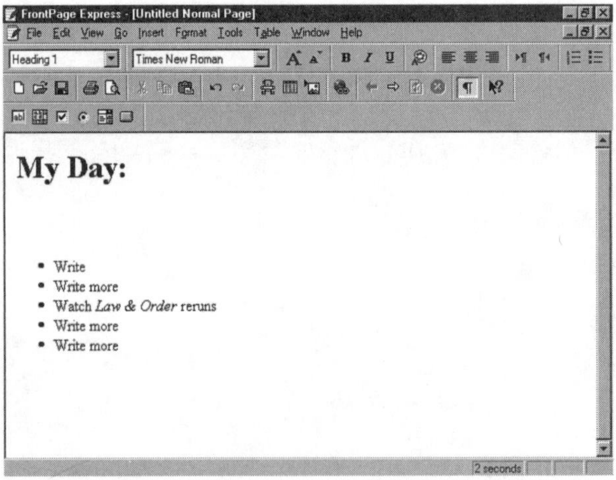

FIGURE 7.5
After Step 3, the list is formatted with the list style of your choice.

▼

The items in a list can be formatted in any style. You can make a list of headings, for example.

However, note that the bullets and numbers at the start of the list usually do not change size, regardless of the size of the text. For that reason, it's best to keep list text in Normal style or as a high-level heading (such as Heading 3 or 4).

If you want really big, bold text for list items, forget about regular list formatting and add graphical bullets (as described in Hour 14) that are big and bold enough to suit the power of the text instead.

Changing the Look of a List

You can make a pretty good-looking list just by clicking a button, as you did in the previous To Do. But you don't have to settle for what you get. You can easily modify the appearance of a list, choosing the numbering style (A B C, I II III, and so on) or bullet symbol.

  1. Select the list.

FIGURE 7.6

Step 1: Select the list.

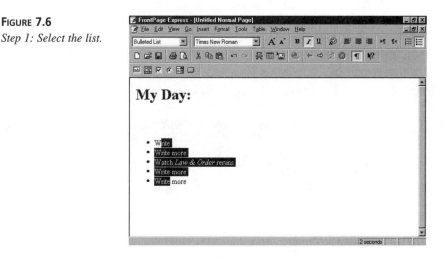

  2. Choose Format, Bullets and Numbering.

  3. Choose the tab for the type of list you want.

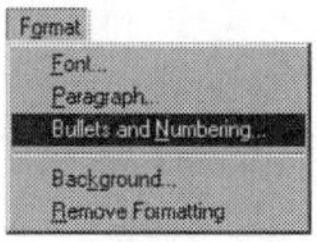

FIGURE 7.7

Step 2: Choose Format, Bullets and Numbering.

7

FIGURE 7.8
Step 3: Choose a tab.

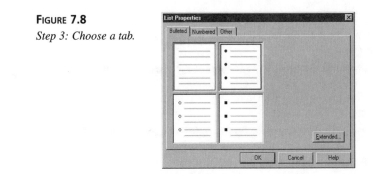

4. Choose the box showing the bullet or numbering style you want to apply.

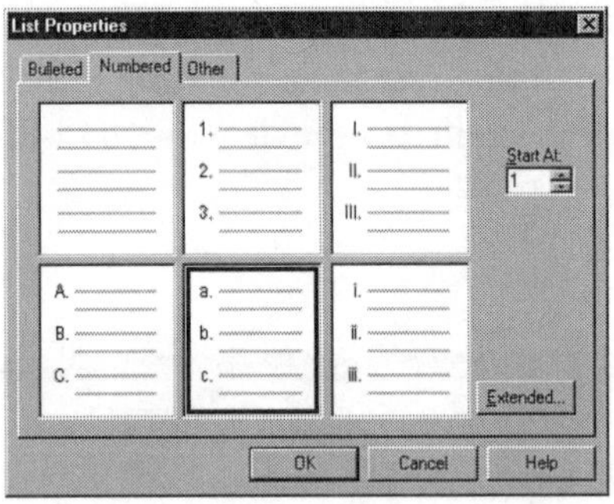

FIGURE 7.9
Step 4: Choose a style.

5. Click OK. The look of the list is changed, as shown in Figure 7.10.

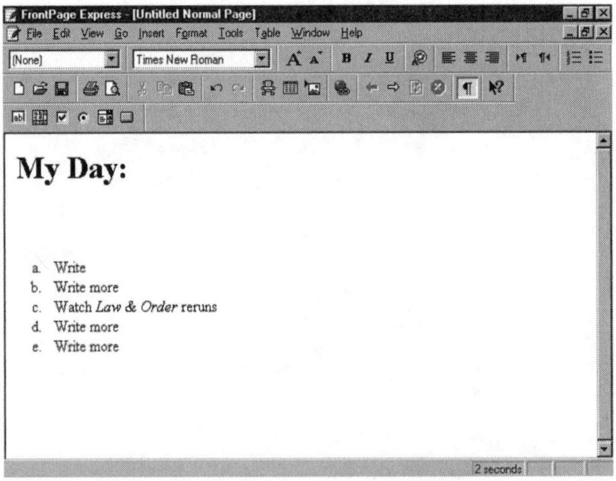

FIGURE 7.10
Old list, new look.

Dressing Up Text with Character Properties

Paragraph properties always apply to a whole paragraph; for example, you cannot make part of a paragraph a heading and another part normal text.

However, you can apply *character properties* to a single character in a paragraph, a few words, a whole paragraph, or a whole document.

 NEW TERM *Character properties* are optional settings you apply to text to change its appearance, such as a particular font (typeface) or bold.

Paragraph properties (such as alignment and indenting) and character properties (such as font or bold) generally work together to define the look of a paragraph and the text within it.

Keep in mind, however, that browsers apply some character formatting to text based on paragraph style alone. For example, they'll automatically show headings in large, bold type. When you apply character formatting, you override any default formatting the browser applies.

The most common use of character properties is to emphasize words by making them bold, italic, or underlined, just as you would when formatting a document in a word processor. But you can also change the color of characters, make them blink, change the font (typeface) or size, and so on.

Besides Font and Size, you can apply other character properties, such as bold, italic, underline, or blinking. You can even choose a color for text.

Some character properties are based on extensions to HTML. As you might expect, anything you can do to text in FrontPage Express is fully supported by our popular friends, Internet Explorer and Netscape Navigator. Among other browsers, however, you'll find a slippery slope of support levels.

Nearly all graphical browsers support relative font sizes. Most support character styles such as bold, italic, and underline; however, some browsers interpret these styles as merely "emphasis" and decide on their own how to show that emphasis. For example, text you make italic might show up underlined (and not italic) in a browser that makes its own rules for emphasizing text. Unusual styles such as superscript and blinking text are not often supported outside the Netscape and Microsoft camps. Text color is an offshoot of custom colors and is supported in any browser that supports custom colors (as long as the visitor has not disabled that support).

7

Font faces and Netscape point sizes are the least widely supported character properties. Many graphical browsers can deal with your assignment of fixed width or variable width as a font face, but specific font choices (such as Arial or Courier) and specific point sizes (as opposed to relative font sizes) are supported almost exclusively by the two leading browsers.

Choosing Fonts

FrontPage Express's Font choices are the fonts installed on your PC. Choosing one of these instructs the browser to use the selected font (or, in a few cases, a font from the same family). The trick is that the font you choose must be installed on the visitor's computer (PC or Macintosh), or the visitor's browser must have a special built-in font viewer.

For example, if you set text in Century Gothic, your visitors will see that font only if they happen to have Century Gothic installed on their computers. Otherwise, the text reverts to a font selected by the browser.

▼ To Do: Choose a font for text

1. Select the exact characters to which you want to apply a new font.

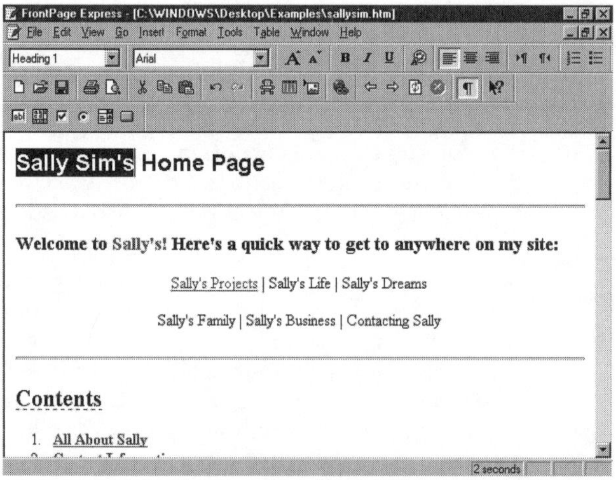

Figure 7.11

Step 1: Select the characters.

> Fonts are a form of character formatting, not paragraph formatting, so they affect only the exact characters you select. To apply a font to a whole paragraph, you must select the whole paragraph.

2. Locate the Change Font list box in the Formatting toolbar. Notice that the box tells the name of the font that's now used for the selected text.

3. Click the arrow on the right side of the list box to open the list.

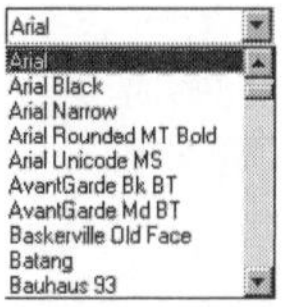

FIGURE 7.12

Step 3: Open the Change Font list.

4. Click the name of the font you want to apply. The change is made, as shown in Figure 7.14.

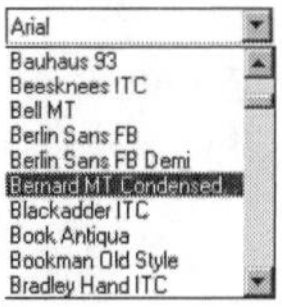

FIGURE 7.13

Step 4: Choose a font.

> Among the font choices you can make in FrontPage Express, three choices are special: Arial, Times New Roman, and Courier. These three choices do not require that the visitor have these fonts; instead, they instruct the browser to use any available font of the same general family.
>
> - Arial is a proportionally spaced *sans serif* font. (Sans serif means it lacks the decorative lips or bars that appear at the points of characters in serif fonts.) A browser on a computer lacking Arial can substitute another sans serif proportional font such as Helvetica.
>
> - Times New Roman is a serif proportional font for which a similar font, such as Century Schoolbook, can be substituted.
>
> - Courier is a monospaced font (like that used to display text in the fixed-width character property or Formatted paragraph property). Another monospaced font, such as Letter Gothic, can be substituted.

7

FIGURE **7.14**
Font applied!

Choosing a Size for Text

The paragraph style determines size. For example, if text set in Heading 3 style looks too small to you, the best solution is to change it to a bigger style, such as Heading 2 or Heading 1. Still, you can fine-tune the size of selected text easily, when the size chosen by the style isn't exactly what you want.

> If you click Increase Text Size and the selected text does not get any bigger, the text is already set at the largest size allowed. Similarly, if Decrease Text Size does nothing, the text is already set at the minimum size allowed.

To Do: Choose the size of text

1. Select the exact characters you want to make bigger or smaller.
2. Locate the two buttons to the right of the Change Font list on the Formatting toolbar.
3. To make the selected text larger, click the Increase Text Size button. To make the selected text smaller, click the Decrease Text Size button. The change is made, as shown in Figure 7.17.

FIGURE **7.15**
Step 1: Select the characters.

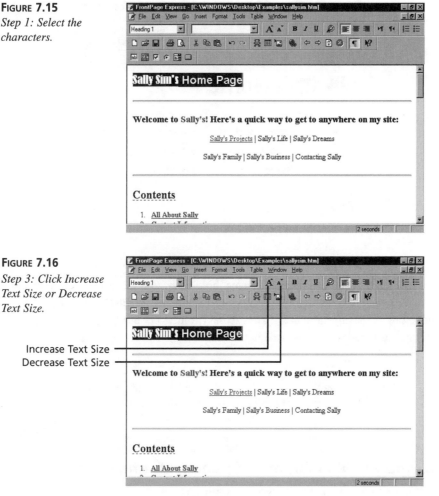

FIGURE **7.16**
Step 3: Click Increase Text Size or Decrease Text Size.

Increase Text Size
Decrease Text Size

You can click the Increase Text Size or Decrease Text Size buttons multiple times to make text a lot bigger or smaller. For example, to make text two levels bigger, click the Increase Text Size button twice.

7

▼

FIGURE **7.17**
Text resized.

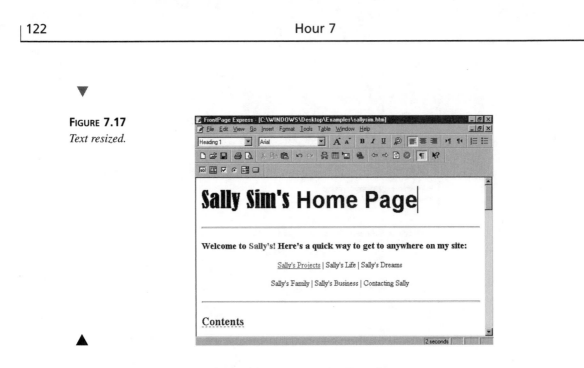

▲

Making Text Bold, Italic, or Underlined

Just as in any letter or report you might create, bold, italic and underlining are valuable
tools in a Web page for making text stand out or for making it match editorial standards
(such as setting book titles in italics). They're easy to use, but use them sparingly; too
much of this stuff makes text busy and hard to read.

> You can combine these kinds of formatting; for example, you can make the
> selected text both bold and italic by clicking the Bold button, and then the
> Italic button.

To Do: Apply bold, italic, or underline text formatting

1. Select the exact characters you want to format.

2. Click a button to format the selected characters: the Bold button, Italic button, or
   Underline button. The change is made, as shown in Figure 7.20.

FIGURE 7.18
Step 1: Select the characters.

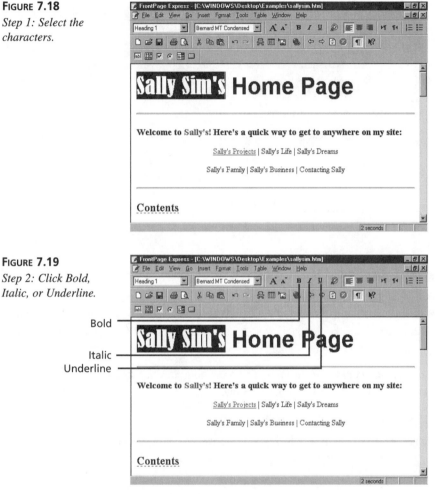

FIGURE 7.19
Step 2: Click Bold, Italic, or Underline.

Bold

Italic

Underline

To remove bold, italic or underlining, select the text and click the button again. For example, to de-bold some bold text, select it and click the Bold button.

7

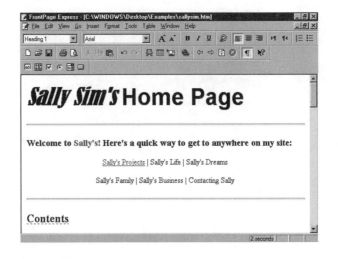

FIGURE 7.20
Italic applied.

Choosing the Color of Text

In Hour 5, "Choosing a Title, Text Colors, and Other Page Basics," you learned how to choose a coordinated color scheme for your Web page—a scheme for making sure that all the colors used for text, the background, and other objects all work together. If you do that, you probably won't be choosing colors selectively for blocks of text.

Still, you may find yourself wanting to give a heading or other selected text its own, unique color. The following To Do shows how.

To Do: Apply a color to text

1. Select the exact characters for which you want to choose a color.
2. Click the Text Color button on the formatting toolbar.
3. Click the colored square containing the color you want to apply, and then click OK. The change is made, as shown in Figure 7.24.

FIGURE 7.21
Step 1: Select the characters.

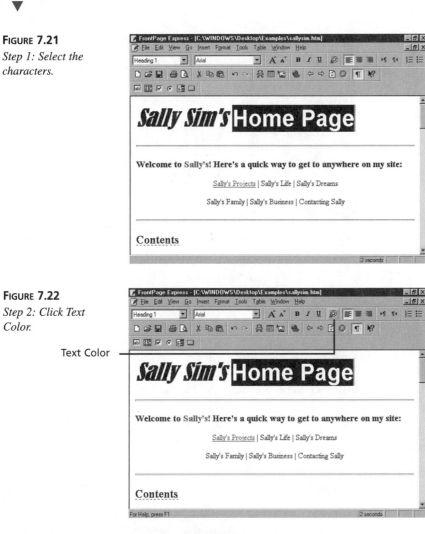

FIGURE 7.22
Step 2: Click Text Color.

Text Color

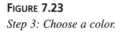

FIGURE 7.23
Step 3: Choose a color.

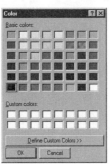

7

> If none of the colors that appear in the color dialog box appeal to you, click the dialog's Define Custom Colors button and a palette appears, which shows all colors possible on your PC as it is currently configured. Click the palette to create a "Custom Color," and then apply that color by clicking the square in which it appears.

FIGURE 7.24
Color applied.

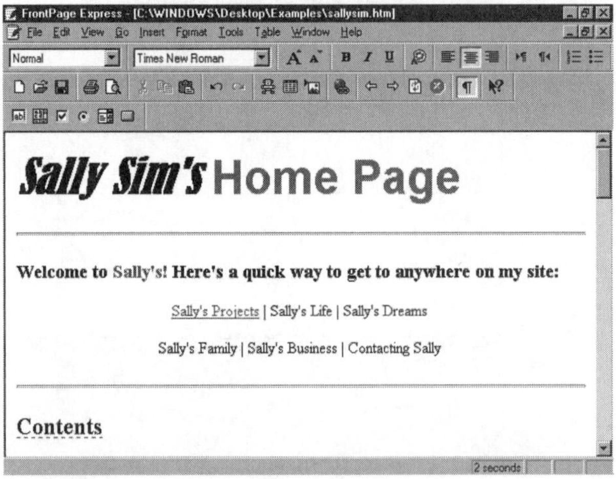

Using the Font Dialog Box to Apply Character Properties

The quickest and easiest way to format text is to use the lists and buttons on the Format toolbar, as you have up 'til now. But there's another way, one that offers you a few other, more esoteric options not found on the Format toolbar: the Font dialog box.

To use the Font dialog box, begin (as always) by selecting the exact characters you want to format. Then choose Format, Font to open the Font dialog box (see Figure 7.25).

Using the lists and check boxes on the Font tab of the Font dialog box, you can apply all of the types of formatting you already know about: font, size, color, and bold, italic, and underlining. You can also choose two additional attributes:

- *Strikethrough*—Strikes a dash through every selected character
- *Typewriter*—Specifies that the browser displaying this page should display this particular text in a monospaced, typewriter-style font

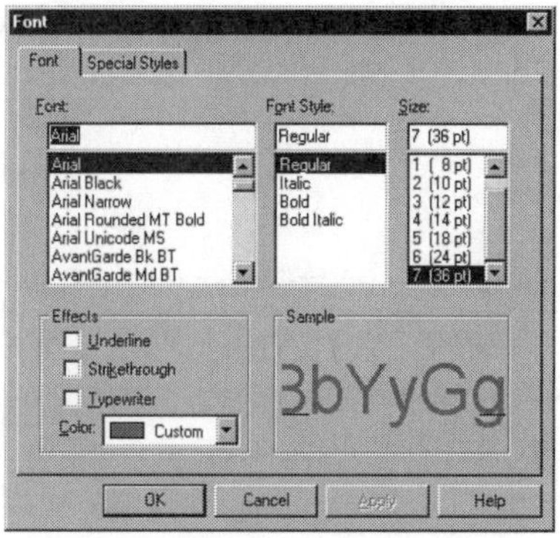

FIGURE **7.25**

*The Font dialog box
gives you one-stop
access to all sorts of
text formatting options.*

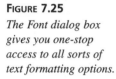

On the Font dialog box's Special Styles tab (see Figure 7.26), you can apply even more
esoteric formatting. Most of these are advanced options that hold little value for most
Web authors and are little used. One option is fun, though: choose Blink to make the text
blink—flash on and off repeatedly—when displayed.

Most options on the Font dialog box's Special Styles tab are enabled by an
extension to HTML. The formatting they apply will show up fine when
viewed through Internet Explorer 4 or 5, but may or may not show up when
viewed through other browsers. Apply this formatting sparingly, if at all.

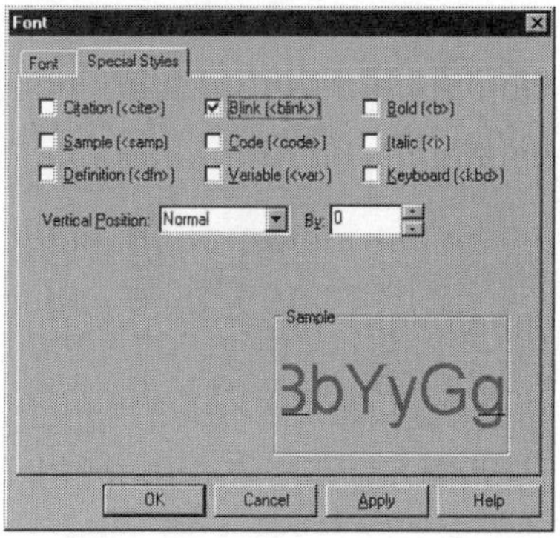

FIGURE **7.26**

*The Font dialog's
Special Styles tab lets
you apply unique
styles, such as Blink.*

Summary

Still think images are the meat of a page's looks? You haven't entered a single image,
and yet you've discovered an easy arsenal of techniques for dressing up a page,
including list formatting, custom colors, and fonts.

7

Sure, you'll still want to use images, but as your pages evolve, always remember that you have these simple but effective design tools available to you.

Q&A

Q Because I can't know what fonts my visitors might have on their computers, shouldn't I steer clear of fancy fonts—especially considering that some browsers don't even support them?

A Actually, fonts are a pretty safe bet. First, keep in mind that when you use fonts, nothing terrible will happen in browsers that can't support them—those browsers simply display the text in their default display fonts.

Second, Windows 3.1, 95, 98, and NT all come with a default set of TrueType fonts, and Macintoshes are equipped with a similar list. If you use fonts from these default lists, you've got a pretty good shot at getting your desired font displayed to most Netscape and Internet Explorer users on PCs and Macintoshes—and that's a majority of the Web surfers out there. You can better your odds by sticking with the three super fonts—Arial, Times New Roman, and Courier—so that computers lacking those fonts can substitute a similar font.

HOUR 8

Organizing Text with Tables and Rules

Between text and pictures, there's a gray area. There are objects that affect the composition and organization of a Web page, but these objects aren't exactly text or pictures; they are tables and horizontal lines (sometimes a.k.a. horizontal rules).

Tables are a great way to organize text in a meaningful, attractive way. And horizontal lines divide pages up visually into meaningful sections, making the page both more appealing and easier to read. In this hour—before moving ahead to pictures in Part IV—you'll learn how to apply these "gray area" techniques to make the most of text.

At the end of the hour, you will be able to answer the following questions:

- How do I insert horizontal lines in my page and control their appearance?
- How do I make a table?

- Can I customize table borders, headings, captions, and other things that affect the table's appearance?
- How can I create really cool Web page layouts by making a table as big as a page?

About Horizontal Lines

The simple, straight lines running horizontally across many Web pages (see Figure 8.1) have always been known in Web parlance as *horizontal rules* because they're created by the HTML tag <HR>—HR for *H*orizontal *R*ule.

Microsoft apparently thinks the term *rule* is confusing, so in FrontPage Express, it's a horizontal *line*.

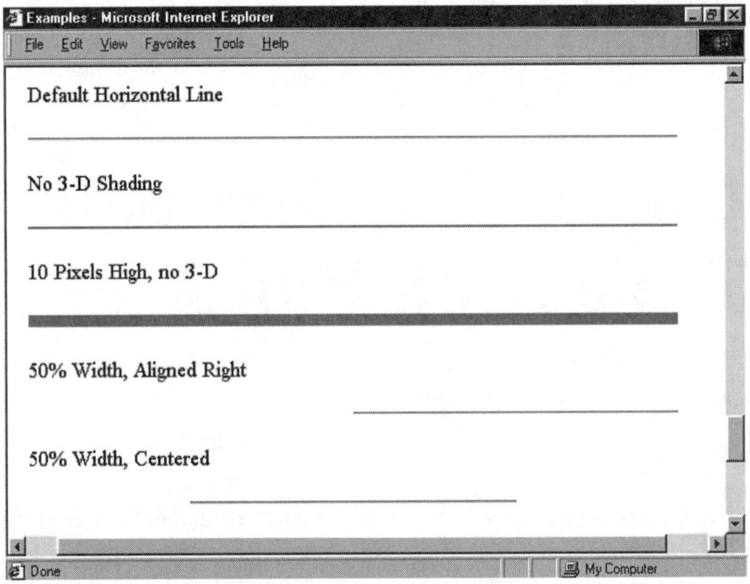

FIGURE 8.1

Horizontal lines are easy to create in various widths and thicknesses, and offer an easy, attractive way to organize a page.

Examples - Microsoft Internet Explorer
File Edit View Favorites Tools Help
Default Horizontal Line
No 3-D Shading
10 Pixels High, no 3-D
50% Width, Aligned Right
50% Width, Centered
Done · My Computer

In some pages you see cool, graphical horizontal lines that zigzag, flash, or scroll. These are not real HTML "horizontal lines," but pictures inserted to achieve the same effect as a line (only cooler).

You learn how to add these picture lines in Hour 14, "Adding Pictures (and Picture Backgrounds)." A nifty selection of pictures to use as cool lines is included on the CD-ROM with this book.

Virtually any browser (even a text-only browser) can show a horizontal line, because any computer system can draw one across the screen (even if it's only with underscores or dashes). Lines are a universal way to add some visual interest to your page and break up logical sections of a page or document to communicate more effectively.

To Do: Add horizontal lines

1. Click in your page at the spot where you want to insert the line.

FIGURE 8.2

Step 1: Click where you want the line.

2. Choose Insert, Horizontal Line.

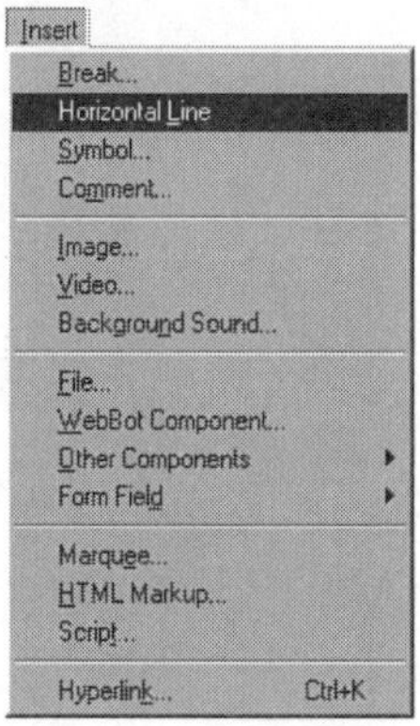

FIGURE 8.3

Step 2: Choose Insert, Horizontal Line.

To Do: Change the look of a horizontal line

1. Double-click a line you've inserted to open the Horizontal Line Properties dialog box.

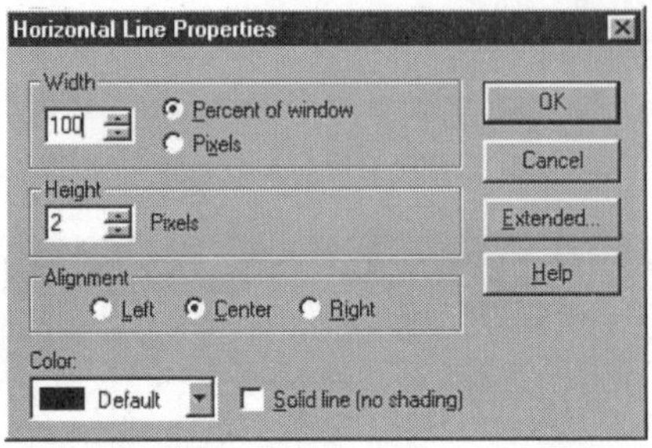

FIGURE 8.4

*Step 1: Double-click
any horizontal line to
open its properties.*

Horizontal Line Properties

Width
[100] ⊙ Percent of window
        ○ Pixels

Height
[2] Pixels

Alignment
○ Left ⊙ Center ○ Right

Color:
[■ Default ▼] ☐ Solid line (no shading)

OK

Cancel

Extended...

Help

> In the Horizontal Line Properties dialog box, always leave the Percent of Window option selected, so that the number you type in Width expresses the width as a percentage of the page's width. Choosing the other option may produce unpredictable results on visitors' screens.

2. To make the line shorter than the full width of the page, type a Width less than 100.

3. Type a number in Height to change the thickness of the line; a higher number makes a thicker line.

4. Choose an Alignment (Left, Right, or Center) and Color for the line, and then click OK. After you click OK, the line will change to match your new settings, as shown in Figure 8.5.

▼ FIGURE 8.5
A line transformed.

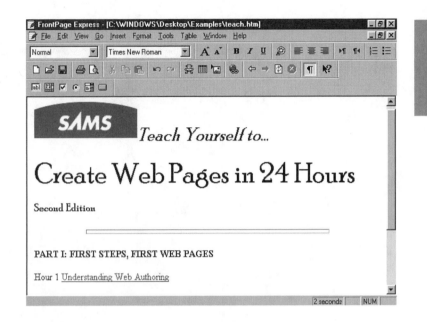

▲

About Tables

A table—regardless of the medium in which it appears—is chunks of information arranged in rows and columns. The grid of rows and columns forms the *cells* in which you can organize text.

 NEW TERM   In a table, the box made by the intersection of a column and a row is called a *cell*; cells contain the table content or *data*.

> You can put text or pictures in a table cell. You learn how to put a picture in a table cell in Hour 14.

Although rows, columns, and data are the minimum requirements for any table, a more elaborate table contains additional elements (see Figure 8.6). It might have column or row headings and a caption above or below it. It might have solid lines, *borders*, appearing on all sides and between cells to form a grid. Note, however, that the borders may be omitted so that cell data is neatly organized in rows and columns, but not boxed up (see Figure 8.7).

FIGURE 8.6
Parts of a table (not all are required)

FIGURE 8.7
A table with no visible borders.

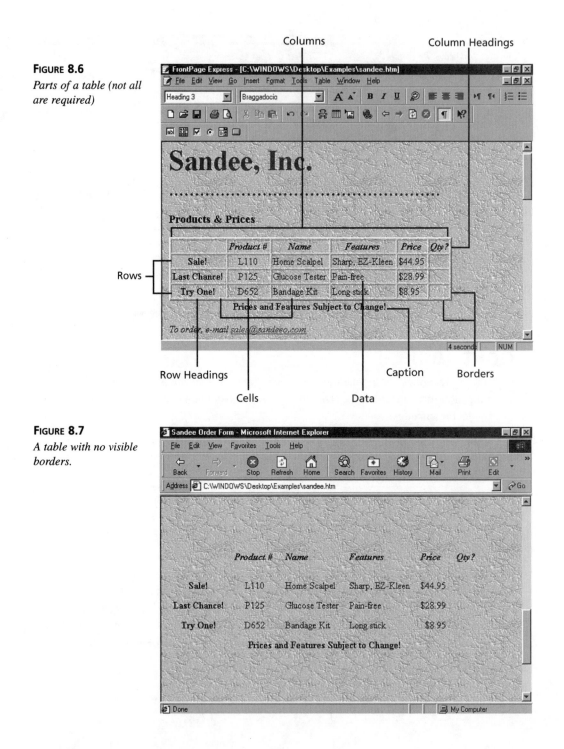

Tables are *transparent*—the page's background color or pattern shows through areas not covered by cell data or borders. However, a table can have its own background (see Figure 8.8), which does not cover the borders or cell data, but does cover the page's background.

There's a lot you can do to format tables to your liking. But keep in mind that the precise formatting of your tables is greatly controlled by the browser displaying it. The height and width of cells is calculated automatically based on the number of columns and the length of the cell content. The width of a column is determined by the width necessary to contain the longest cell data in the column. When the data in a cell is long or when a table has many columns, the cell content may be wrapped automatically to allow the table to fit within the window.

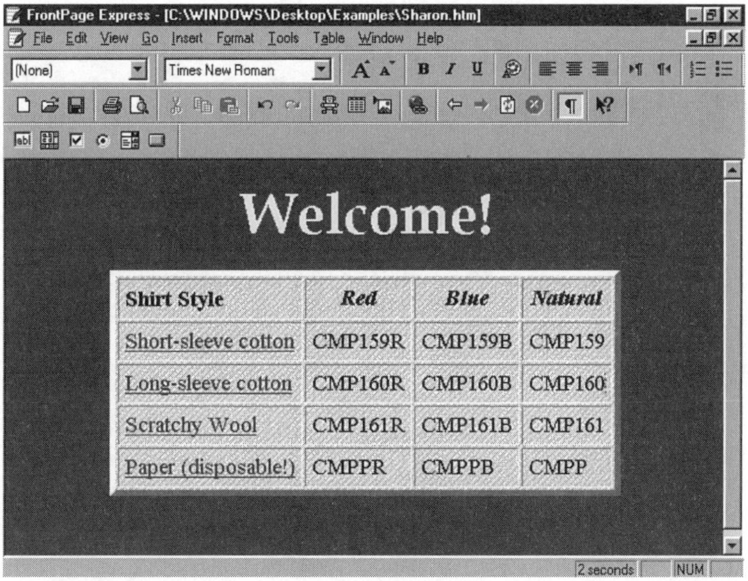

FIGURE 8.8

A table with its own background.

Table Basics

The difficulty of creating tables is directly proportional to how fancy you wanna make 'em. A simple, basic table is a snap, as the following To Dos show. Fancier tables are a little more trouble (as you learn later in this hour), but then, shouldn't they be?

Keep your first tables simple, and get more creative with tables only when you have the basics down pat. You'll do fine.

The best all-purpose way to add a new table is to use Table, Insert Table, as described in the following To Do. It's best because it gives you the opportunity to make a few important decisions about the look of the table at the same time you create it.

However, there's an alternative way to create a quickie table. Just click the Insert Table button on the Standard toolbar. A table grid drops down from the button—four rows high by five rows wide. To create a table, click the cell that would be the lower-right corner of your table; for example, to create a table that's two rows by three columns, click the cell that's in the second row, third column.

After creating a table this way, you can fill in the cells and format the table in any of the ways described in this hour.

To Do: Insert a new table

1. Click at the spot in your page where you want to insert a table.

2. Choose Table, Insert Table.

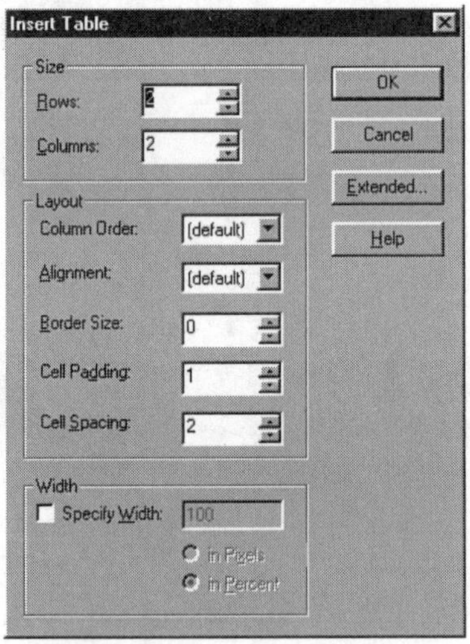

FIGURE **8.9**
Step 2: Choose Table, Insert Table.

3. In Rows and Columns, choose the number of rows and columns for the table.

4. Adjust any of the other options on the dialog box that you want to change. (Note that you can ignore these options for now and adjust them later on the Table Properties dialog box, as described later in this hour.)

5. Click OK.

The dashed lines that show the table borders (see Figure 8.10) and gridlines appear just to show you where your table is—they won't show up when the page is viewed through a browser. That's OK—a table without borders still organizes its contents into rows and columns, and can look pretty cool. But if you really *want* visible borders, you'll learn how to add them later in this hour.

To turn off the display of the dashed lines (so the table appears in FrontPage Express exactly as it would in a browser), choose View, Format Marks. (To show the lines, choose View, Format Marks again.)

FIGURE 8.10

A new table, ready for content or formatting.

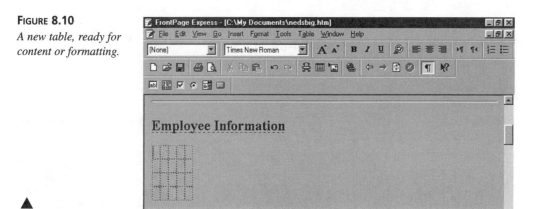

Filling in the Table

There's nothing to filling in the cells of a table—just click in the cell and type away, as the following To Do shows.

When typing in a cell, you can press Enter to start a new paragraph within the cell. You can also apply virtually any type of text formatting you would apply anywhere else in a Web page using the same selection techniques and formatting tools. Specifically, you can apply the following:

- Paragraph styles (normal, headings, and so on)
- Fonts and attributes (bold, italic, color, and so on)
- List formatting (bulleted, numbered)
- Alignment (left, right, center)
- Indenting

The thing to keep in mind about alignment and indenting in table cells is that the formatting is relative to the *cell*, not the whole page or even the table. For example, if you apply Center alignment to text in a cell, the text is positioned in the center of the cell, not the center of the table or page.

> Besides ordinary text, you can also put pictures and links in table cells. To add a link, just type the text in the cell, highlight it, and then create the link as you would any other link (see Hour 10, "Making Links").
>
> To learn how to put pictures in table cells, see Hour 14.

To Do: Add text to table cells

1. Click in the cell in which you want to type.

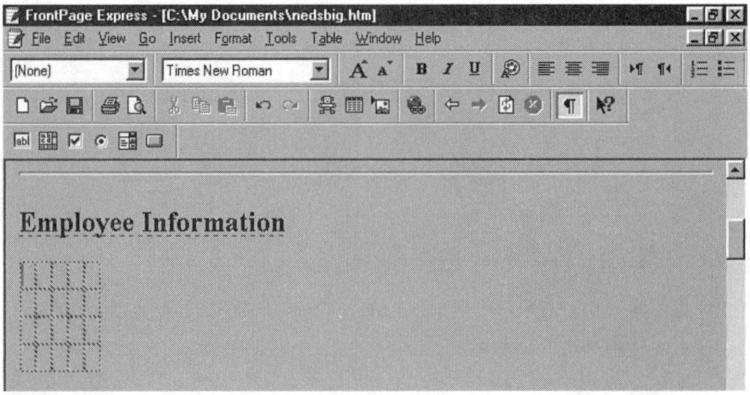

FIGURE 8.11
Step 1: Click in a cell.

FrontPage Express - [C:\My Documents\nedsbig.htm]
File Edit View Go Insert Format Tools Table Window Help

Employee Information

2. Type whatever you want (see Figure 8.12). Observe that the height of the cell expands as necessary to accommodate whatever you type.

3. Press the Tab key to jump to the next cell (or click in the cell you want to fill next).

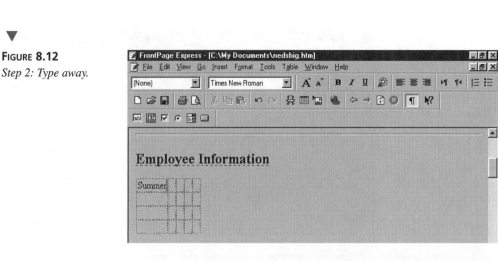

FIGURE 8.12
Step 2: Type away.

FIGURE 8.13
Step 3: Press the Tab key to jump to the next cell and keep typing.

Adding a Caption

NEW TERM A *caption* is a title or other label for a table that appears directly above or below the table (see Figure 8.14). Although the text of the caption does not appear within a table cell, the caption is a part of the table—if you move or delete the table, the caption goes with it.

To add a caption, click anywhere in the table. Choose Table, Insert Caption, and then type the caption text. It appears above the table.

FIGURE 8.14

A caption titles a table.

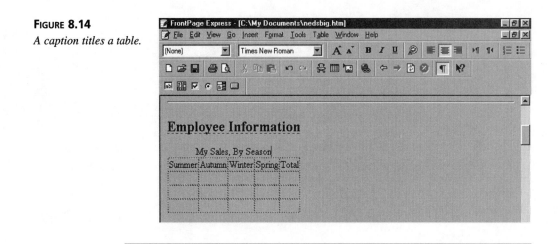

> FrontPage Express automatically puts the caption above the table, but you can move a caption below the table. Click anywhere on the caption, click Table, and then choose Caption Properties. A dialog box appears, giving you two choices for caption placement: Top of Table and Bottom of Table.

Editing and Formatting Tables

So now you've got a table, and you've got formatted text in it. Happy now? If so, congratulations—you're easy to please. If not, note that you can add cool borders to your table, add and delete columns and rows, add a background color...

In short, creating the table is only the beginning. You can do so much more, just by changing settings on the Table Properties dialog box. Read on.

To Do: Dress up tables with borders

1. Click anywhere in the table, and then choose Table, Table Properties.
2. Click the box next to Border Size.
3. Type a number for the width of the borders. For example, type **4** to create a border four pixels wide. The higher the number, the thicker the border.
4. Click OK, and the table border is finished (see Figure 8.17).

8

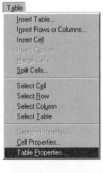

FIGURE 8.15

Step 1: Click in any cell and choose Table, Table Properties.

FIGURE 8.16

Step 2: Click in Border Size.

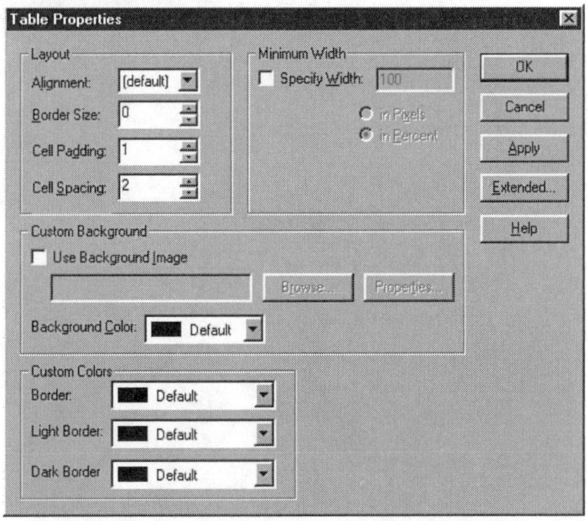

FIGURE 8.17

A nice, fat six-pixel border.

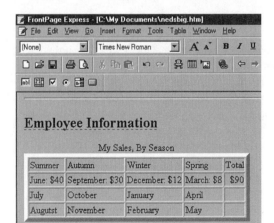

A table border is not one line, it is three lines used together to create a 3D effect: A basic border line, a "light border" (a highlight on the top of horizontal lines and on the left side of vertical lines) and a "dark border" (a shadow on the bottom of horizontal lines and on the right side of vertical lines). You can pick the color for each part of the border, as described in the following To Do.

To Do: Choose custom border colors

1. Click anywhere in the table, and then choose Table, Table Properties.
2. In the Custom Colors section, choose a color from each of the three lists: Border, Light Border, and Dark Border.

FIGURE 8.18

Step 2: Choose each of the three border colors.

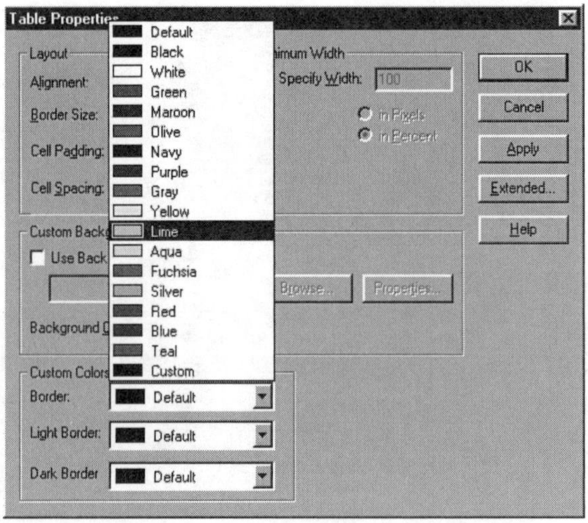

To experiment with borders, border colors, and anything else on the Table Properties dialog box, make any changes on the dialog box, and then click the Apply button instead of OK.

The changes are made in the table, but the Table Properties dialog box remains open, so you can try different settings without having to reopen it.

Keep experimenting, clicking Apply each time, and then click OK when you see what you want to keep, or click Cancel to close the dialog box without making any changes at all to the table.

8

Unless you add a background to a table, the page's background color (or background picture) shows through the table (but does not obscure the table's content or borders). But a table can have its own background, different from that of the page, to make the table—and more important, its contents—really stand out.

The following To Do shows how to give a table its own background color. To learn how to give a table its own background picture, see Hour 14.

To Do: Give a table its own background color

1. Click anywhere in the table, and choose Table, Table Properties.
2. Open the list next to Background Color and choose a color.

FIGURE 8.19

Step 2: Choose a Background color.

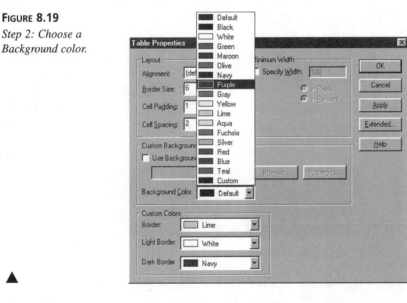

You can use a different background for a selected cell or cells than for the rest of the table; for example, you can give the top row its own, unique background color or image to make column headings stand out.

To begin, click in a cell whose background you want to choose (or any cell in the row or column whose background you want to choose) and choose Table. From the Table menu, choose Select Cell, Select Row, or Select Column. Choose Table, Cell Properties, and then choose a background color from the list.

Creating Column and Row Headings

What's a heading, anyway? Well, it's text that's formatted differently from the rest of the table data (and maybe also enclosed in cells that are formatted differently), so that it is clearly not meant as table data, but as a descriptive label for a row or column (see Figure 8.20).

You can create column or row headings simply by applying unique formatting to the text in the top or bottom rows (column headings) or leftmost or rightmost columns (row headings).

Applying bold or italic, making the font different, increasing the text size, giving the cells containing the headings their own background, choosing a unique text color, or doing all of the above are easy ways to create headings.

FIGURE 8.20

Apply unique text or cell formatting to a row or column to create headings.

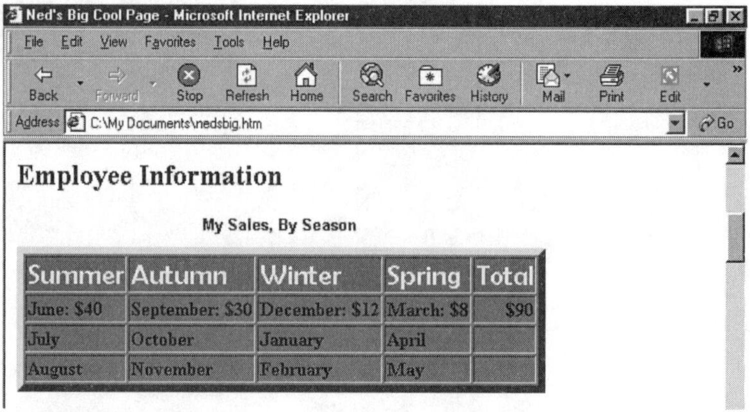

Working with Rows, Columns, and Cells

When you first create a table, as described earlier in this hour, you choose the number of rows and columns, and you get a table that's a nice, regular grid. Often, that'll be just what you want.

But sometimes, after entering some of your data, you'll find you need to add or delete rows or columns. Other times, you might need to create a complex or *irregular* table, one in which a single cell can spread across multiple rows or columns, or where one row has more or fewer cells than others.

In the next few sections, you learn how to manipulate rows, columns, and cells to create precisely the table you want.

Changing the Width or Alignment of a Table

By default, the tables you create fill the full width of the page. You can choose to make your tables narrower than that.

When a table is narrower than the full width of the page, you'll have another decision to make: alignment. Do you want the table to be positioned along the left side of the page (left alignment), on the right (right alignment), or in the center (center alignment)? The following To Do shows how to change table width and alignment.

To Do: Change a table's width and/or alignment

1. Click anywhere in the table, and choose Table, Table Properties.
2. To change width, make sure the Specify Width box is checked, and that the In Percent option is selected. Then enter the percentage of the window you want the table to fill. (For example, enter **50** to make the table half as wide—50%—as the full width of the page.

Specify width here

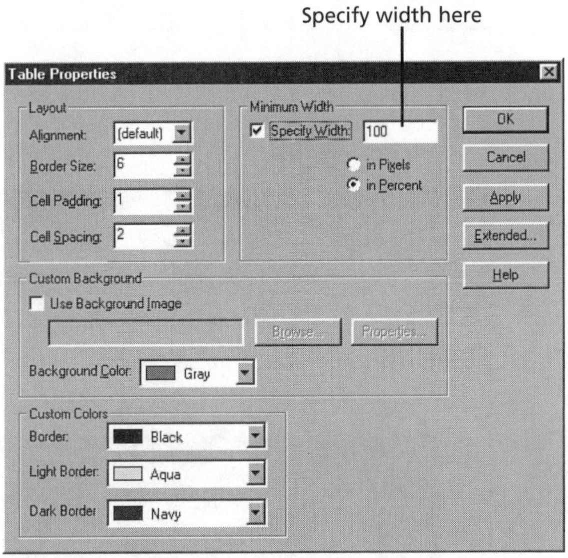

FIGURE **8.21**

Step 2: Change the percentage width.

3. If the width is less than 100%, you may select an alignment for the table. By default, tables are left-aligned. To change that, open the Alignment list and choose Center or Right 9 (see Figure 8.22).

▼

Specify layout
alignment

FIGURE 8.22
Step 3: Choose an
alignment.

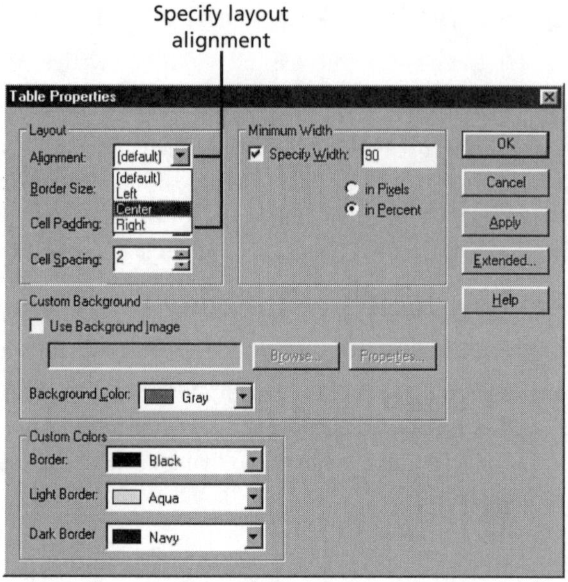

Figure 8.23 shows what you get when you have finished the width and alignment
changes.

FIGURE 8.23
A changed table: 75%
wide, center alignment.

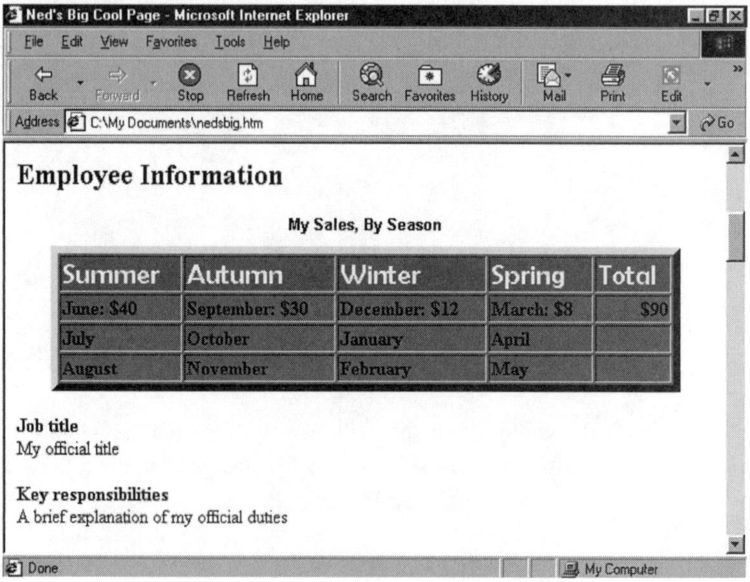

▲

When choosing a width, avoid the In Pixels option. Choosing this option enables you to specify table width as a number of pixels on a screen, rather than as a percent of the window.

But different monitors and computers running at differing resolutions will handle that instruction in unpredictable ways. For example, a table 240 pixels wide appears as about half the width of the screen on a computer configured to use the Windows minimum standard resolution (640×480). But the very same table, on a computer configured for higher resolutions, might fill only 30 percent, 25 percent, or even less of the screen. Stick with percents.

8

Adding and Deleting Rows and Columns

When entering data, you can jump from cell to cell by pressing the Tab key. The Tab key moves among the cells like a reader's eyes, moving left to right across a row, and at the end of a row, it jumps to the leftmost cell in the row below.

But guess what? When you reach the end of the final row and press Tab, a new row appears with the edit cursor positioned in its leftmost cell, ready for a cell entry. This feature enables you to define your table without knowing exactly how many rows it will have. You can simply keep entering data and using Tab to move forward until all of the data has been entered. As you go, FrontPage Express keeps adding rows as they are needed.

Of course, you might sometimes want to add columns, or add new rows between existing rows, rather than at the bottom of the table. The following To Do shows how.

To Do: Add rows or columns

1. Click in a row directly above or below where you want the new row to appear, or in a column directly to the left or right of where you'll want the new column.

2. Choose Table, Insert Rows or Columns.

3. Click Columns or Rows.

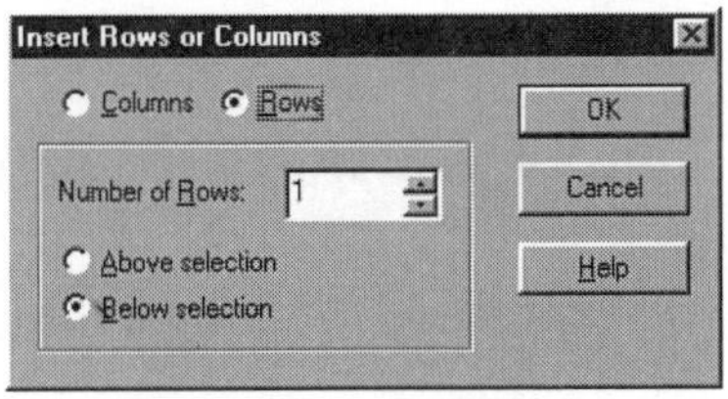

FIGURE 8.24

Step 3: Choose Columns or Rows.

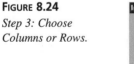

▼ 4. Enter the number of columns or rows to add.

5. Choose where the new rows or columns go:

   - When adding rows, choose Above to insert the new rows above the row you clicked in step 1, or Below to add the new rows below that row.

▲ - When adding columns, choose Left to insert the new columns to the left of the column you clicked in step 1, or Right to insert the new columns to the right of that column.

> To delete a whole table, click anywhere in the table, choose Table, Select Table, and then press your Delete key.

To delete rows or columns, always begin by positioning the edit cursor anywhere in the row or column that you want to delete. Open the Table menu, and use the menu items to select the part of the table you want to delete (Select Row, Select Column, or Select Cell). Delete the selection by pressing the Delete key or by choosing Edit, Cut.

When you delete rows or columns, keep in mind the following:

- Any data in the deleted row or column is deleted too.
- When you delete a row, rows below shift up to fill the gap.
- When you delete a column, rows to the right shift left to fill the gap.

Creating Irregular Table Designs

We think of tables as regular grids, but they don't need to be. A cell can span multiple rows or columns (or a column multiple rows) to achieve certain effects, as shown in Figure 8.25.

To create a cell like those in Figure 8.25, you begin by creating an ordinary table. Then you create the irregularities by *merging* cells (making two or more cells into one, so that one cell stretches across multiple rows or columns, or by *splitting* cells (making one cell into two).

- To merge cells, select the cells you want to merge. (You can select a group of cells by clicking and holding on one and then dragging to select the others). Then choose Table, Merge Cells.
- To split a cell, click in it, and then choose Table, Split Cells.

FIGURE **8.25**

An irregular table design.

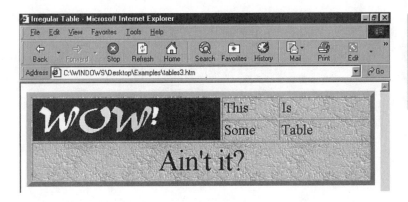

8

> Another technique for creating an irregular table is to nest a table inside a cell in another table, dividing the cell up into mini cells. See the Q&A at the end of this hour for more information about this.

Using a Big Table to Control Page Layout

As you move along through this book, you'll find that it's very difficult to control the exact location of objects in a Web page, the way you would in a desktop publishing program. Generally, you must settle for positioning pictures and paragraphs in rough association with another, and leaving it up to the visitor's browser to arrange the page.

A popular way to get around this limitation is to create a table that fills the entire page, and then put all of the page's contents in table cells (see Figure 8.26). This approach gives you much better control of where objects appear in relation to one another.

> Most new browser versions since about 1996 have supported tables, so you can use tables in your pages—or use a big table to control page layout—with reasonable assurance that nearly all visitors will be able to see your work.
>
> But note that there are just a few folks still online using browsers that do not support tables. If universal access is important to you, you may want to offer an alternative version of your pages that use tables to be sure that absolutely everyone gets your message.

FIGURE 8.26

FIGURE **8.26**

*The dashed lines dis-
played by FrontPage
Express reveal that this
whole page is a table,
which keeps the page
elements neatly orga-
nized.*

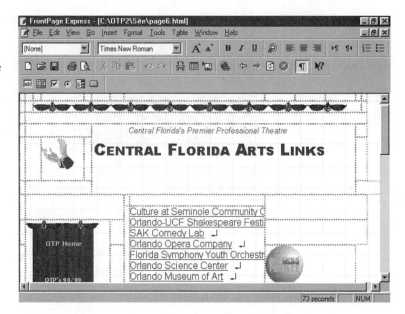

If you use some kinds of templates (see Hour 4), Microsoft Publisher, or Microsoft
FrontPage in your Web authoring toolbox, you'll find that these approaches rely heavily
on tables for page layout. For example, if you create a layout in Publisher and then use
Publisher's tools to convert it into a Web page, you will discover that the resulting page
is a big table. Publisher does this to preserve the organization of the page as faithfully as
possible.

You needn't do anything special to use a big table for page layout. Just start with a completely blank, empty page, and then insert a table. By default, the new table will take up the
full width of the page, and its height will expand as you add the page's contents to the cells.

Advanced Web authoring tools, such as Macromedia DreamWeaver and
Microsoft FrontPage 2000, do enable you to precisely position text and
graphics in a Web page (without using a table), just as you would in a desktop publishing program. In FrontPage 2000, this capability is called *Absolute
Positioning*.

The downside of Absolute Positioning is that it relies on an emerging, non-
standardized set of technologies, collectively called Dynamic HTML (DHTML),
that are now supported in Internet Explorer 5 and in Netscape Navigator 5,
but barely supported anywhere else.

8

If you use Absolute Positioning or other DHTML tools, but still want your Web pages accessible to everybody, you must offer two versions of your pages online: One for those using browsers that support DHTML, another (without Absolute Positioning) for everybody else.

See Hour 24, "Developing Your Authoring Skills," to learn more about advanced Web authoring tools and techniques.

Summary

A simple table is a simple deal. And that's the best way to start—simple. Don't get wrapped up in long, complex tables too soon. Try sticking with simple tables of just a dozen cells or so, not just because it's a good way to learn, but because big hairy tables defeat their own purpose; they confuse visitors instead of informing them. Eventually, you'll move up the table growth curve to tougher, smarter table techniques.

Q&A

Q Can I put a table inside a table?

A Certainly, and you can achieve some interesting effects by using a different border for the table inside (the "nested" table). You can even nest tables within tables within tables.

To nest a table, create the outside, or *parent*, table. Click the cell in which you want to nest a table, and then choose Table, Insert Table to create a new table inside the cell.

Observe that when creating and editing the nested table, some settings will work a little differently. For example, you choose table width not as a percentage of the window, but as a percentage of the *parent cell*, the cell holding the nested table.

Q Sometimes my table looks too crowded, and other times it looks too spaced out. Is there a way to adjust the spacing between cells, or the amount of empty space between a cell's contents and the cell borders?

A On the Table Properties dialog box, two settings control the spacing in a table: Cell Padding and Cell Spacing.

Change the number in Cell Padding to adjust the spacing between the contents of a cell and the walls around that cell. Raising the number in Cell Padding—to, say, 3 or 4—creates more space around the cell contents, making the cell seem less crowded.

Change the number in Cell Spacing to adjust the amount of space between the cells. A higher number moves cells farther apart.

PART III
Linking To Stuff

Hour

HOUR 9

Understanding Links

Links are one of the great mysteries of Web authoring. Everything else is up-front and visible; everything else just has to look right. A link, on the other hand, has to do something—it has to act right. Links are mysterious because what they do when they are activated is not immediately visible to the naked eye.

Fortunately, creating links is surprisingly simple. The only tricky part is correctly phrasing the underlying URL. With an eye toward the real linking pitfalls, this hour shows what links are all about. At the end of the hour, you'll be able to answer the following questions:

- What are the two parts in every link?
- What kinds of stuff can a link lead to?
- How do I properly phrase the URLs for linking to all types of remote Internet resources, including Web pages, email addresses, and so on?
- What's the difference between a *relative* link and an *absolute* link, and why does it matter?

What's in a Link?

Every link has two parts. Creating links is a simple matter of choosing a spot on the page for the link and then supplying both parts:

- The *link source*, the actual text (or graphic) that appears on the page to represent the link. When a visitor activates a link, he or she clicks the link source to activate the unseen URL underneath.

- The URL describing the page, file, or Internet service to be accessed when the link is activated.

You can create menus or directories of links, like those in Figure 9.1, by making each link a separate line in the List Item paragraph property. Links don't have to be on separate lines, as Figure 9.1 shows. You can use any words or phrases in your page as links, including headings (or words in headings), words in normal paragraphs, list items, or even single characters in any paragraph property.

FIGURE 9.1

Links (underlined) in text and by themselves in a menu.

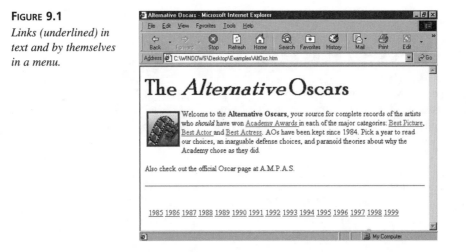

The link source takes on the paragraph properties of the text it is inserted into or closest to, but you can change the paragraph properties of the link source at any time, just as you would for any other text. The underlying link is undisturbed by such changes.

What's Linkable?

A link can point to any resource that can be expressed in a URL or to *local files* (files residing on the same server as the page containing the link). That includes not only remote Web pages and other pages and files residing on the same Web server as your document, but also newsgroups and articles within them, email messages, and Gopher and FTP servers. In your travels on the Web, you've already encountered links pointing to all such resources.

NEW TERM A link can point to a specific location within a Web page—even to a specific location within the same page containing the link. For example, in a long Web page, each entry in a table of contents can be a link pointing to a specific section of the page (see Figure 9.2). This allows visitors to navigate quickly and easily within the page. The spots within pages to which a link can point are called *bookmarks*.

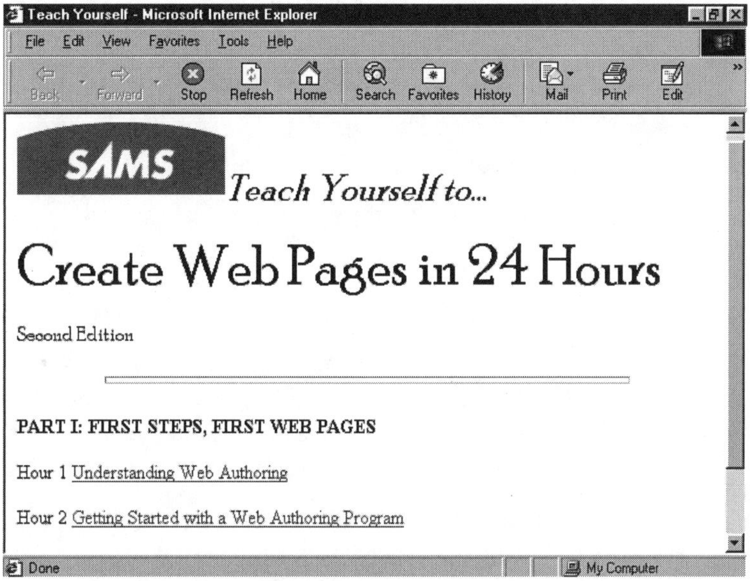

FIGURE 9.2

A menu (table of contents) made up of links to pages within the same document or site.

To create a link, you use the same procedure regardless of the type of resource to which the link points. However, for each type of resource there are issues you must consider when composing the URL for the link. The next several sections describe in detail the special considerations for each type of URL.

Web Pages

Web pages are the most commonly linked resource, and for good reason: You can bet that anybody viewing your Web page can view any other Web page, so links to Web pages are a reliable way to provide information. Linking to Web pages also allows your visitors to apply a consistent set of navigation techniques; Gopher directories, for example, can be a little baffling to newer Web surfers.

> The easiest way to ensure that a URL is properly expressed is to copy it directly from the Web. See the section titled "Copying Links" later in this hour.

URLs pointing to Web pages always begin with the protocol designator `http://`. The protocol is followed by the Web server hostname, the directory path to the page file, and the actual HTML file of the page, as follows:

```
http://hostname/pathname/file.HTM
```

In some cases, you can omit the filename. Some Web servers have default files they display automatically whenever someone accesses the server or a directory without specifying a filename. For example,

```
http://www.mcp.com/
```

accesses the default page for the server `www.mcp.com`, and

```
http://www.mcp.com/publications/
```

accesses the default page for the directory `publications` on the server `www.mcp.com`.

Note that the preceding directory examples end in a slash. You should always use a slash to end an HTTP URL that does not end with a filename; the slash instructs the server to access the default file (usually `INDEX.HTML`). Some servers can still access the default file if you leave off the slash, but some won't. In a link, use the slash for safety's sake.

Finally, always be careful to follow the exact capitalization of the URL as it would appear in Navigator's Location box when you view the page. Many Web servers are case sensitive and won't recognize the directory or filename if it is not properly capitalized.

Bookmarks in Pages (Anchors)

Web pages can contain predefined locations to which links can point. These spots are called *anchors* in HTML (and are created with the <a> tag—*a* for *Anchor*). In FrontPage Express, they're called *bookmarks*. You'd think Communicator, with its salty lighthouse and ship's wheel logos, would have kept the nicely nautical anchor nomenclature, but the bookmark it is. Go with it.

You can add bookmarks to your own Web pages and then link to those bookmarks from elsewhere in the same page or from other pages you create. In addition, you can create links to point to any existing bookmarks in other pages on the Web.

When you create a bookmark, give the bookmark a name. You create links to bookmarks as you do to a Web page, with one difference: You add the name of the bookmark to the URL you enter for the link.

> You can use a *relative pathname* to point to a bookmark in another file stored on the same server (to link from one page of a multipage document to a bookmark in another page in the document, for example). See the following section titled "Local Files."

9

Local Files

Just as you can link to resources on any server, you can also link to resources residing on the same server as your Web document. Obviously, this is what you would do when linking among the pages of a multipage presentation. But you might also choose to link to anything on your local Web server that relates to the topic of your page, such as another Web document or a text file containing related information.

> Technically, the pathnames you enter to create links to local files are not URLs. When you're creating a link, however, you enter these pathnames in the same place you would enter a URL for linking to a remote resource. That's why I refer to them generically as URLs.

When you phrase the URLs to create links to local resources, you have to consider the differences between *relative* pathnames and *absolute* pathnames.

Relative Pathnames

Relative pathnames include only the information necessary to find the linked resource from the document containing the link. In other words, the path given to the file is *relative* to the file containing the link; from outside that file, the information supplied as the URL for the link is insufficient to locate the file.

> If you use FrontPage Express's one-button publishing to publish your document on the server, don't worry much about relative and local pathnames. FrontPage Express takes care of that automatically, as explained in Hour 21, "Publishing Your Page." Still, to assert full control over your Web project and to be able to resolve any problems that might arise, it's important that you understand the principles behind these pathnames.

For example, suppose all of the pages of your multipage document share the same directory on the server, and one of those pages is called `FLORIDA.HTM`. To link from any page in your document to `FLORIDA.HTM`, you need enter only the filename as the URL for the link. For example,

`FLORIDA.HTM`

Suppose all pages but the top page reside in a folder or directory called `STATES`, and that this folder is within the same folder containing the top page. To link from the top page to `FLORIDA.HTM` in the `STATES` directory, you would enter the directory and filename, separated by a slash. For example,

`STATES/FLORIDA.HTM`

This approach works as far into the folder hierarchy as you want. Just be sure to separate each step in the path with a slash. For a file several levels beneath the file containing the link, you might enter

`ENVIRO/US/STATES/FLORIDA.HTM`

Now, suppose you're linking from a page lower in the directory hierarchy to a page that's higher. To do this you must describe a path that moves up in the hierarchy. As in DOS (and in FTP servers), a double period (`..`) is used in a path to move up one level. For example, let's create a link from the `FLORIDA` page back to the top page (call it `TOP.HTM`), which we'll assume is one level above `FLORIDA`. For the URL portions of the link, you would enter

`../TOP.HTM`

If `TOP.HTM` were three levels above `FLORIDA`, you would type

`../../../TOP.HTM`

 Use relative pathnames to link together the pages of a multipage document on your PC. Because the paths are relative, when you publish that document to a server, the inter-page links will still work properly. See Hour 12, "Using Links to Build a Web Site."

Finally, suppose you want to link to a local file that resides in a folder that is not above or below the file containing the link but is elsewhere in the hierarchy. This would require a path that moves up the hierarchy and then down a different branch to the file. In such a case, you use the double periods to move up and then specify the full directory path down to the file.

For example, suppose you want to link from

`ENVIRO/US/STATES/FLORIDA.HTM`

to

`ENVIRO/CANADA/PROVINCE/QUEBEC.HTM`

The phrasing you need is

`../../../CANADA/PROVINCE/QUEBEC.HTM`

The three sets of double periods move up to the ENVIRO directory; then the path down from ENVIRO to QUEBEC.HTM follows.

> On DOS and Windows systems, a relative or absolute path might include the letter of the hard drive, but it must be followed by a vertical bar (¦) rather than the standard colon. For example,
>
> `C¦/STATS/ENVIRO/CANADA/PROVINCE/QUEBEC.HTM`

Absolute Pathnames

Absolute pathnames give the complete path to a file, beginning with the top level of the directory hierarchy of the system. Absolute pathnames are not portable from one system to another. In other words, while composing a multipage document on your PC, you can use absolute pathnames in links among the pages. However, after you publish that document, all of the links become invalid because the server's directory hierarchy is not identical to your PC's.

In general, you'll use absolute pathnames only when linking to specific local resources (other than your own pages), such as FAQs, residing on the server where your page will be published.

Absolute pathnames are phrased just like relative pathnames, except that they always begin with a slash (/), and they always contain the full path from the top of the directory hierarchy to the file. For example,

`/STATS/ENVIRO/CANADA/PROVINCE/QUEBEC.HTM`

Other Internet Services

In addition to Web pages and their bookmarks, links can point to any other browser-accessible servers. But before linking to anything other than a Web page or a bookmark, keep in mind that not all browsers—hence not all visitors—can access all of these other server types.

Nearly all browsers can handle Gopher and FTP. Less common is mail access, and even less common is newsgroup access. Netscape Navigator has native support for both. Other browsers open helper applications for mail. For example, Internet Explorer opens Windows 95's Exchange mail client when a mailto link is activated. Still, many browsers have no news or mail access.

Gopher

Pointing straight to a Gopher server to display the main directory there is pretty simple. You simply build the URL out of the `gopher://` protocol designator and the gopher server hostname, as follows:

```
gopher://gopher.umn.edu
```

Beyond that, pointing to a specific file or subdirectory on a Gopher server gets tricky, often involving port numbers and a complex system of paths, so there's no simple set of rules for specifying the path to a Gopher file in a URL. Therefore, the best way to point to a particular Gopher file is to use any of the following techniques:

- Explain in your Web page the menu choices required to navigate from the main directory to the file and then link only to the server.

- Using Navigator, connect to the Gopher server and click menu items to navigate all the way to the Gopher resource. Then copy the link from the Location box to your document (as described in Hour 10, "Making Links").

- Search for a Web page that carries the same information as the Gopher resource (these are becoming increasingly common), so that you can avoid linking to the Gopher server at all.

FTP

Using a link to an FTP server, you can point to a directory or to a specific file. If the link points to a directory, clicking the link displays the list of files and subdirectories there (see Figure 9.3), and each listing is itself a link the visitor can click to navigate the directories or download a file. If the link points to a file, the file is downloaded to the visitor's PC when he or she activates the link.

> If you create a link to an HTML file residing on an FTP server, clicking the link downloads the file and displays it, just as if it were on a Web server.

FIGURE 9.3
An FTP directory.

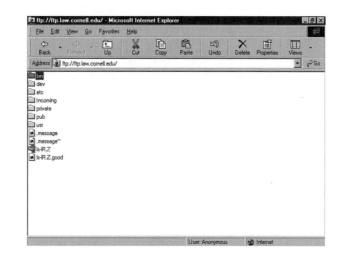

9

To link to an anonymous FTP server, use the protocol designator `ftp://`, followed by the name of the FTP server, the path, and the filename (if you are linking to a file), as the following examples show:

> Observe that you do not end an FTP URL with a slash when linking to a directory. This differs from an HTTP URL, where a slash is always advisable except when accessing a specific HTML file.

`ftp://ftp.mcp.com`   Links to Macmillan's anonymous FTP server and displays the top-level directory

`ftp://ftp.mcp.com/pub`   Links to Macmillan's anonymous FTP server and displays the contents of the PUB directory

`ftp://ftp.mcp.com/pub/review.doc`   Links to Macmillan's anonymous FTP server and downloads the file REVIEW.DOC from the PUB directory

> You can link to non-anonymous, password-protected FTP servers. However, in most cases such servers have been set up precisely to prevent public access. A URL to a non-anonymous FTP server includes a username and password for accessing that server, so anyone who accesses your page can access the FTP server—or read the URL activated by the link to learn the password.
>
> Obviously, you should never create a link to a non-anonymous server unless you have express permission to do so from the server's administrators.

Getting such permission is unlikely.

To link to a non-anonymous FTP server for which you have permission to publish a link, you phrase the URL exactly as you would for anonymous FTP, except that you insert the username and password (separated by a colon), and an @ sign between the protocol and the path, as shown in the following:

`ftp://username:password@ftp.mcp.com/pub/secrets.doc`

This URL downloads the file `secrets.doc` from a password-protected server for which the username and password in the URL are valid.

News

A link can open a newsgroup article list or point to a specific article within that list. Although both newsgroups and the articles they carry come and go, a link to the article list might be valid for years. On the other hand, a link to a specific article might be valid for only a few days—until the article ages past the server's time limit for newsgroup messages, at which point the article is automatically deleted from the server.

Thus, the best use of news links is to point to the article list of a newsgroup whose topic relates to that of the Web document. If a newsgroup contains an article that you want to make a long-term part of the page, copy it into a separate file and link to that file, or simply copy it into a Web page.

Before copying a news article into a page, check for copyright notices in the article. Whether it's copyrighted or not, email the author and request permission to use the article.

To link to a newsgroup to display the current article list, use the protocol designator `news:` followed by the name of the newsgroup. (Note that a `news:` URL omits the double slashes used in HTTP, FTP, and Gopher URLs.) For example, the following are valid news links:

`news:alt.video.dvd`

or

`news:news.announce.newusers`

To link to an article, find the message ID in the article's header (see Figure 9.4); it's often enclosed between carats (< and >) and/or labeled *message ID* by most newsreaders. (Exactly how it appears depends upon which newsreader program you use.)

To phrase the URL, use the protocol designator `news:` followed by the message ID. Note that you do not include the carats, and you do not need to include the newsgroup name in the URL:

9

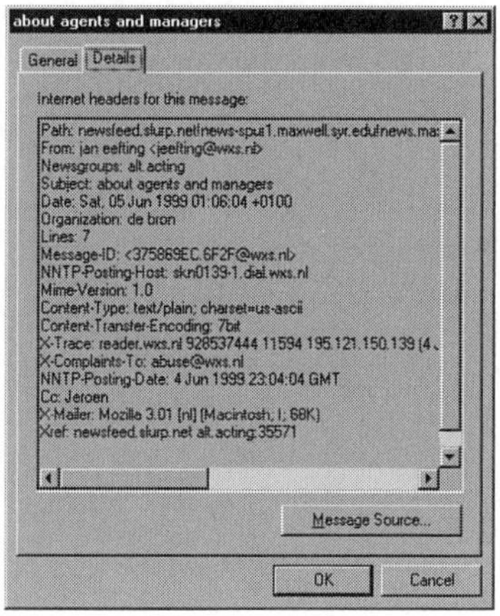

FIGURE 9.4

A news article header in Outlook Express, showing the Message ID (it's labeled "Message-ID," and appears about halfway down the list).

Mail

Mail URLs can be the most difficult to goof up. You enter **mailto:** followed by an email address. That's it. (Note that a mailto: URL omits the double slashes used in HTTP, FTP, and Gopher URLs.) For example,

```
mailto:nsnell@mailserver.com
```

> Before putting an email address other than your own in a link, ask permission from the addressee.

The most common use of mailto: links is in a signature at the bottom of a page. (You learn how to create a signature in Hour 10.) But you can use a mailto: link anywhere it makes sense to offer your readers a way to contact you or someone else.

To Do: Study links

Follow these steps to explore the way the links you see online are phrased.

1. Connect to the Internet and open your Web browser. (Use the Netscape Navigator browser included with this book, or Internet Explorer. These steps may not work with other browsers.)

2. Go to any page you like, and locate a link on it.

3. Point to the link (don't click), and then look in the status bar at the bottom of the browser window. The URL to which the link point appears there, shown exactly as it is phrased in the HTML file.

4. Explore other links this way. In Web pages you visit regularly, try to find links to:

   • Other Web pages

   • Bookmarks

   • Files

   • FTP directories

   • Email addresses

Summary

As you discover in the next three hours, creating links is pretty easy. In fact, making the link is the easiest part, especially if you copy the link from elsewhere. Phrasing the URL just right is the hardest part. Now that you understand the ins and outs of URLs, in the next hours you'll pick up some tips for ensuring you get 'em right when you make links.

Q&A

Q I'm still fuzzy on this whole relative/absolute path business, and I have a headache. Can I just stay stupid on this one and hope everything works out in the morning?

A To some extent, you can. Just trust FrontPage Express. When making links to local documents, use the Browse button in the Link Properties dialog box to choose files, so FrontPage Express can phrase the path for you. Then use FrontPage Express's publishing features (see Hour 21) to publish your document instead of handling the uploading on your own. FrontPage Express automatically adjusts the local file links and uploads all the linked files so that the links still work on the server.

HOUR 10

Making Links

By design, this is an easy hour. The only hard part about making links is understanding how they work, and getting the URL right—and you learned all about that in Hour 9, "Understanding Links." In this hour, you'll put that knowledge to work.

But I haven't given up making things easy yet. You're also about to discover a variety of ways to make picking up the URLs for your links quicker, easier, and more accurate. At the end of the hour, you'll be able to answer the following questions:

- How can I make linking easier and more accurate by copying and pasting URLs?
- How do I create a new link?
- Can I create a signature for my page so visitors can conveniently send me email?
- How do I get rid of a link?

As you know, links can be attached to text or pictures. However, you won't learn how to add pictures to your pages until Hour 14, "Adding Pictures (and Picture Backgrounds)."

Although most of what you learn in this hour applies to both text and pictures, you won't pick up the specifics of making picture links until Hour 14.

Changing Where an Existing Link Leads

If you used FrontPage Express's Personal Home Page Wizard to start a page (as described in Hour 3, "Wizarding Up a Personal Home Page"), your page already contains some links: The "Hot List" (see Figure 10.1).

But right now, those links are phonies—they lead nowhere. The following To Do shows how to make them point wherever you want.

FIGURE **10.1**

If you followed the steps in Hour 3 to create a Personal Home Page, now's the time to add real links to your Hot List.

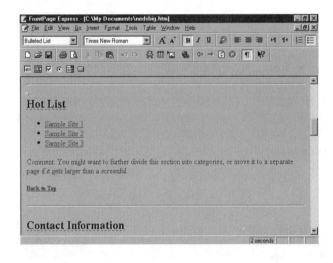

You can, of course, edit the link source to change it from "Sample Site" to anything you like. But when you edit link source text, sometimes you inad-vertently remove the link formatting—you change it from a link source to ordinary text. If that happens to you, just remake the link as described in the "Creating New Links from Scratch" section, later in this hour.

To Do: Change the links in your personal home page

1. Come up with a Web site address you like. (If you need a suggestion, try http://www.mcp.com.)

2. Open your Personal Home Page in FrontPage Express.

FIGURE 10.2

Step 2: Open your page in FrontPage Express.

3. Right-click a Sample Site link, and choose Hyperlink Properties.

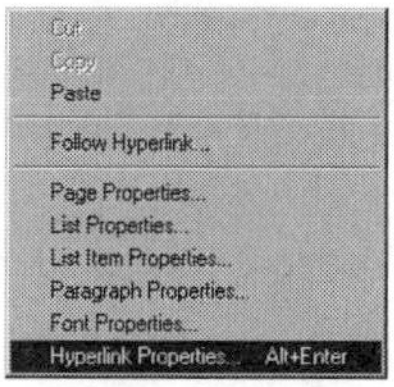

FIGURE 10.3

Step 3: Right-click a link, and then choose Hyperlink Properties.

4. Make sure that the World Wide Web tab is selected.

5. In the box labeled URL, type the complete URL. Be sure to include the **http://** part at the beginning.

6. Click OK. The link source is now a link that points to a URL you chose.

> Before publishing a page that contains links to other Web sites, visit those Web sites and look for the email address of the person responsible for the site: the Webmaster. As a courtesy, email the Webmaster to ask if it's OK to publish a link to the site.

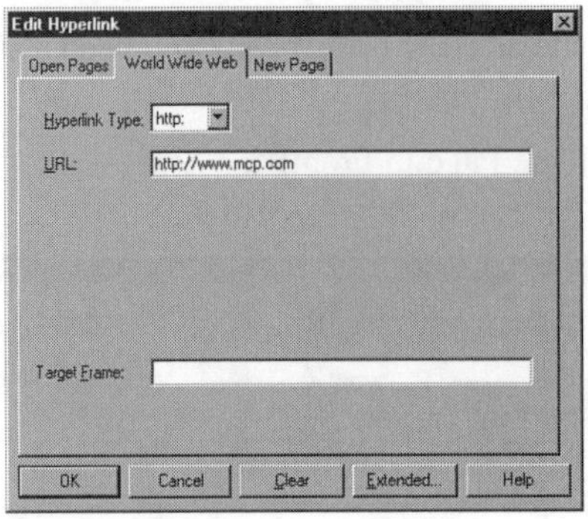

FIGURE 10.4
Step 5: Type the URL.

Creating New Links from Scratch

Creating a new hyperlink is a two-part job:

- First, you create the link source, the text (or picture) that a visitor would click to activate the link.
- Next, you attach the URL to the link source.

The following To Do shows how easy it is to create a new link to a Web page.

> Sometimes you want the link source to match the URL itself. For example, instead of linking the URL www.yahoo.com behind the link source "Click to go to Yahoo!", I could make the link source that appears in the page simply www.yahoo.com.
>
> When that's all you want to do, making links is awfully easy: Just type the URL in your Web page. Anytime you type a URL or email address in a page in FrontPage Express, it becomes a link the instant you type a space following it (or press Enter). Note that there's no need in this case to type the http:// part, although doing so won't hurt.
>
> If FrontPage Express turns a URL into a link, and you don't want it to be a link, remove the link from the text as described later in this Hour under "De-Linking Text."

To Do: Create a new link to a Web page

1. Type and format the text that will serve as the link source.

FIGURE 10.5

Step 1: Type the link source—in this case, a "Kid's Page".

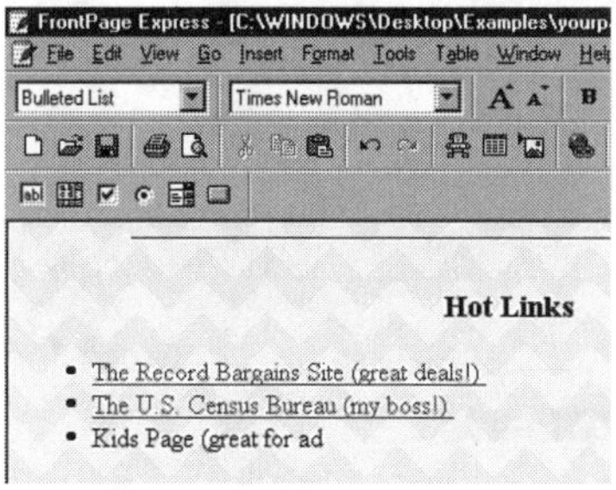

Although you can apply character formatting (such as fonts or italics) to the link source text you create, it's best not to. Just apply the paragraph style you want to use, and leave it at that.

Browsers usually display link source text with unique formatting (usually underlining and a blue color) to help the visitor instantly identify links on a page. You don't want your character formatting to make finding links tricky for your visitors by changing the link source formatting they're accustomed to seeing.

2. Select the text.

FIGURE 10.6

Step 2: Select the link source.

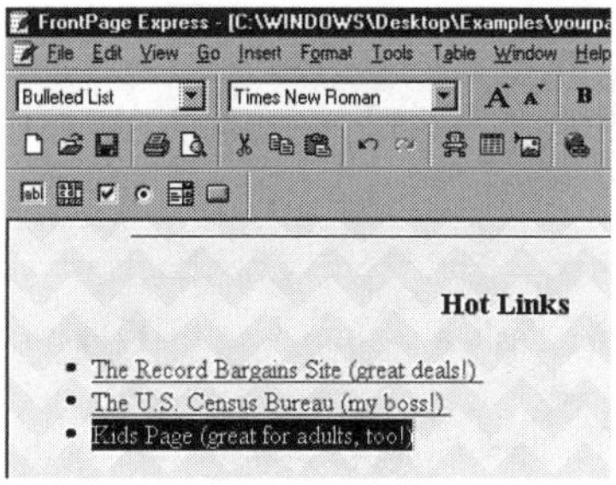

3. Click the Create or Edit Hyperlink button on the Standard toolbar.

4. Make sure that the World Wide Web tab is selected.

5. In the box labeled URL, type the complete URL and click OK. Be sure to include the http:// part at the beginning.

▼

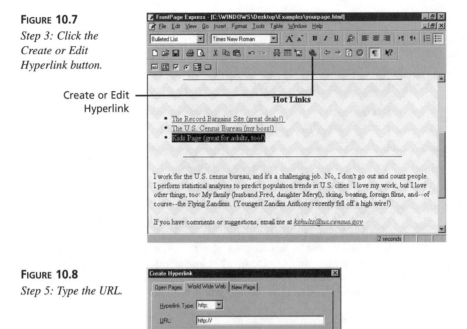

FIGURE 10.7
Step 3: Click the Create or Edit Hyperlink button.

Create or Edit Hyperlink

FIGURE 10.8
Step 5: Type the URL.

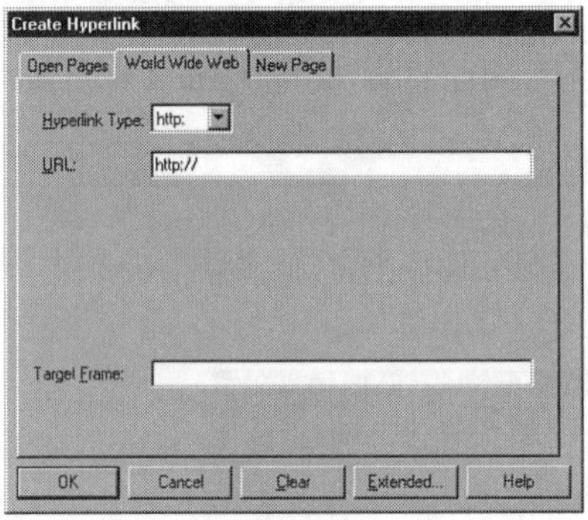

You can use a picture as a link source, so that clicking the picture activates the link (see Hour 14).

You can even put multiple links in one picture, so that clicking each part of the picture leads to a different place. You learn how to do this in Hour 20, "Putting Multiple Links in One Picture."

▲

Creating a Signature (Linking to Email)

A *signature* is really nothing more than some sort of generic sign-off message that has an email address embedded within it. A few stock wording choices—in popular flavors—are

Inviting—Comments? Questions? Email me at `nsnell@mailserver.com`

Formal—If you have any comments or questions regarding this page, contact `nsnell@mailserver.com`

Efficient—Feedback: `nsnell@mailserver.com`

Traditionally, the paragraph containing the signature uses the `Address` property, though that is not required.

What is required is a mailto link—a link that, when clicked, opens the visitor's email program and starts a new message, pre-addressed to an email address specified in the link. Mailto links let you provide your visitors with an easy way to contact you (or anyone else you choose).

10

> The link source of a mailto link need not show the exact email address, because most visitors' email programs will use the right address automatically when they click the link.
>
> However, some visitors use Internet software that doesn't support mailto links; they see the link source OK, but nothing happens when they click it. So always include your exact email address somewhere in the signature (if you really want to be contacted).

To Do: Create a signature

1. Click where you want the signature to be located (usually at or near the very end of the page, and type the signature message, including the email address.

2. Select some text in the message—your name or an email address—to serve as a link source for the mailto link.

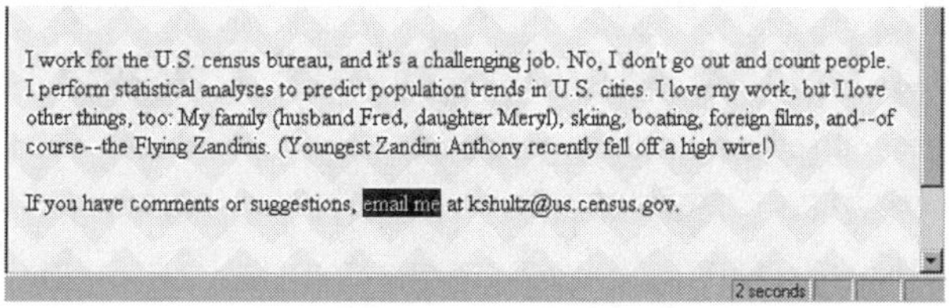

FIGURE 10.9
Step 2: Select the part of the signature that will be an email link.

I work for the U.S. census bureau, and it's a challenging job. No, I don't go out and count people. I perform statistical analyses to predict population trends in U.S. cities. I love my work, but I love other things, too: My family (husband Fred, daughter Meryl), skiing, boating, foreign films, and--of course--the Flying Zandinis. (Youngest Zandini Anthony recently fell off a high wire!)

If you have comments or suggestions, email me at kshultz@us.census.gov.

3. Click the Create or Edit Hyperlink button on the standard toolbar.

4. Make sure that the World Wide Web tab is selected.

5. In the Hyperlink Type box, choose mailto:. The word "mailto" appears at the start of the URL box.

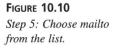

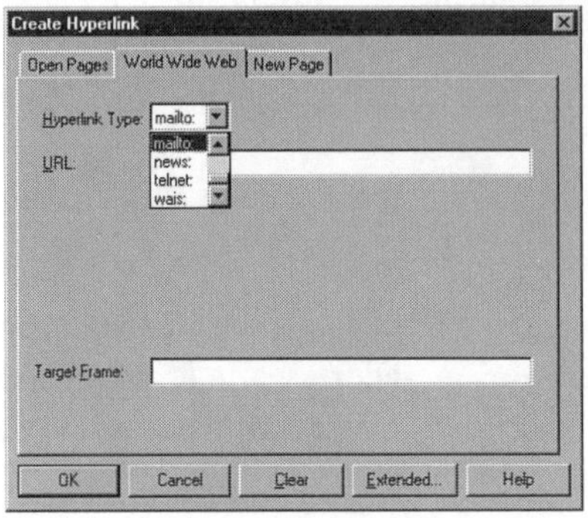

FIGURE 10.10

Step 5: Choose mailto from the list.

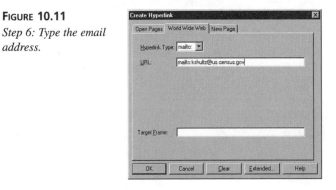

6. Right after the mailto:, in the URL box, type the complete email address.

FIGURE 10.11

Step 6: Type the email address.

7. Click OK.

Copying Links from Other Pages

Anywhere you see a hyperlink, you can easily copy it from your Web browser right into a FrontPage Express page by using copy and paste techniques.

In fact, a page you've just accessed on the Web makes the most reliable source for a link. If you copy the URL of a file while viewing it and paste it as a link into a page you're creating, you can trust that the link will probably work properly (until and unless the page or other resource is moved or removed).

Sources for copying links include

- The Address box in your browser (where the URL of the current page appears)
- The Bookmarks list (in Navigator) or the Favorites list (in Internet Explorer)
- The header of a news article in your Internet newsreader program
- The header of a mail message in your email program
- Any link appearing in a Web page

When copying a link into your page, keep in mind the following:

10

- The link source may or may not be copied, depending on what browser you use; instead, the link source that appears in FrontPage Express may sometimes be the URL itself. To give the link a name to appear instead of its URL, edit the link as described in the "Editing Links" section, later in this hour.
- The link takes on the paragraph properties of the paragraph it is inserted into or closest to. Remember, though, that a link can accept any paragraph properties or character properties—though in most browsers, the character properties cannot override the default way links are displayed. That's a good thing, actually, because you don't want your formatting to disguise the fact that a link is a link.

To Do: Copy and paste a link

Copying and pasting, in case you've forgotten, is a two-part deal. First, you copy something to the Windows Clipboard and then you paste it from the Clipboard into the place you want it to go. You can accomplish each half of the job in several ways. There are several ways to copy and several to paste, and you can combine any copy method with any paste method and get the same results.

From the following lists, pick a copy method you like, pick a paste method you like, and put 'em together.

To copy

- A link to the Web page currently appearing in your browser (Netscape Navigator or Internet Explorer)—Right-click the URL in the Address box, and then choose Copy from the menu that appears (see Figure 10.12).

▼

- A link shown in a Web page—Right-click the link, and choose Copy Link Location (if Navigator is your browser) or Copy Shortcut (if Internet Explorer is your browser)(see Figure 10.13).

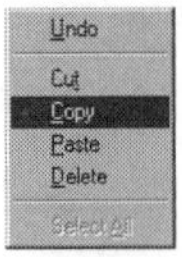

FIGURE 10.12

Copying a link to the current Web page.

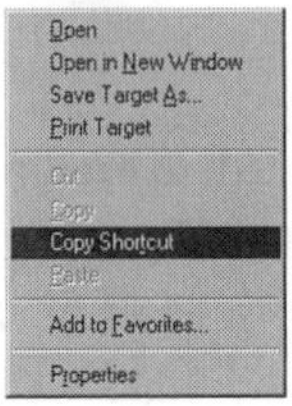

FIGURE 10.13

Copying a link from a link in a Web page.

- A link appearing in Navigator's Bookmarks list or Internet Explorer's Favorites list—Right-click the desired bookmark and choose Copy Location from the menu.
- A link appearing in the header of a news or mail message—Open the message and locate the desired link in the message header. Right-click the link, and choose Copy Link Location.

To paste a link from the Clipboard into your page, do the following:

1. In the open page in FrontPage Express, click the spot where you want to insert the link.

▲ 2. Choose Edit, Paste.

Checking That Links Lead Where They're Supposed To

When you've created links that lead from your page to other pages online, the only way to make absolutely sure that links lead where they're supposed to is to test the links online, *after* you've published your page. Still, you can do a pretty reliable prepublishing link check at any time, right from within FrontPage Express.

1. Connect to the Internet, open FrontPage Express, and open the page file whose links you want to test.

2. Point to a link you want to test, and click so that the edit cursor appears there.

FIGURE **10.14**
Step 2: Click a link.

3. Click Tools, and then choose Follow Hyperlink.

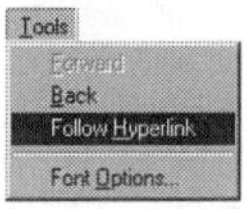

FIGURE **10.15**
Step 3: Choose Tools, Follow Hyperlink.

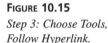

> Even if your links work, be careful to test them again, online, after you have published your page.
>
> You learn more about testing your links in Hour 23, "Testing and Updating Your Page."

Editing Links

You can change anything about a link: the link source, the URL, the type of link, and more. That's handy if you decide to change the wording of the link source, or if you need to update a link when the URL of the page it leads to changes.

*   To change a link source, just edit the text any way you want. Usually, the link behind the source is undisturbed by the editing. If, after editing the source, you see that the link is gone or that it is not connected to the exact words you want anymore, just highlight the text and re-create the link.

*   To change the URL or any other "behind the scenes" aspect of a link, right-click the link and choose Hyperlink Properties from the menu that appears (see Figure 10.16). The Edit Hyperlink dialog box that appears shows the exact same options as the Create Hyperlink dialog box, so change what needs changing, and click OK.

10

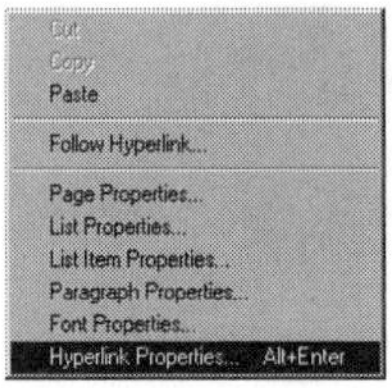

FIGURE 10.16
To edit a link, right-click it and choose Hyperlink Properties.

De-Linking Text

Suppose you want to remove a link from your page but keep its link source text on the page. You could simply delete the link and retype the text. That's a solution for a link or two, but if you want to kill all the links in a large section or entire page, you'd find all the retyping tedious.

The following To Do shows how to revert a link into ordinary text on the page.

To Do: Remove a link (leave the link source)

1. Right-click the link and choose Hyperlink Properties.

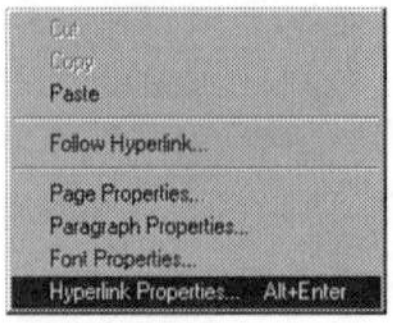

FIGURE 10.17
Step 1: Right-click the link and choose Hyperlink Properties.

2. Click the Clear button.

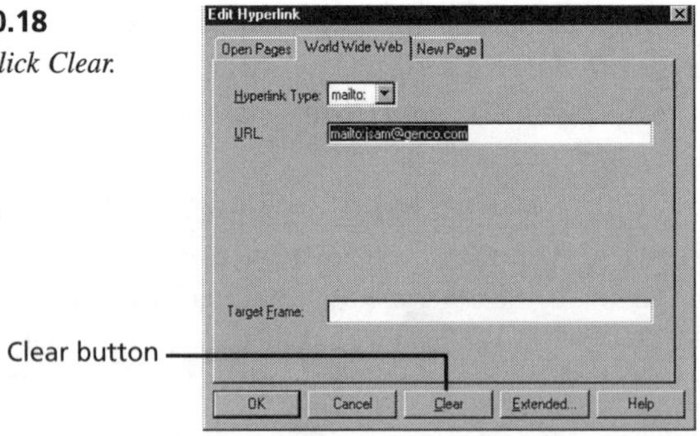

FIGURE 10.18
Step 2: Click Clear.

Clear button

Summary

Just because you can link everywhere doesn't mean you should. Pages with extraneous links are no more useful than linkless ones. Carefully check out each place to which you'll link. Is it really useful to your readers? Does it provide something new, or simply duplicate material your other links already lead to? Does it appear to be on a reliable server, or one that's often inaccessible or slow?

Your goal should not be to provide your readers with as many links as possible, but with a choice selection instead. And it goes without saying that you must check, update, and add to your links often. Do that and your visitors will return often.

Q&A

Q **If I want to offer quick access to other resources related to my page, can I link directly to a category listing in a Web directory, such as Yahoo! or the WWW Virtual Library?**

A Sure, and many people do that. As always, it's proper to email the Webmaster of any directory you link to and request permission.

Also, try not to get too specific; link at the most general point in a directory's hierarchy that pertains to your topic, and let the visitor navigate down to the specifics. Broad categories in directories are fairly stable and remain in place for years. Very specific directory listings low in the hierarchy might disappear or change names, invalidating any links to them.

10

Hour 11

More Ways to Link

If Web pages were books and links were a card catalog, bookmarks would be thumbtabs.

Let me explain. Just like a card catalog entry, a link takes you only to a whole document—a Web page—not to any particular place *within* that document. That makes links great for general-purpose surfing, getting into the general ballpark of what you want.

But sometimes you want to take your visitors not just to a particular page, but to an exact spot within that page. That's the job of *bookmarks.* In this hour, you expand on your linking skills from Hour 10, "Making Links," learning not only how to create and link to bookmarks, but also how to link to any type of file so your visitors can download files you want to offer them.

At the end of the hour, you'll be able to answer the following questions:

- Where and why would I use bookmarks?
- How do I create a bookmark in a page?

- How do I make existing text into a bookmark?
- How do I create a link that takes the visitor to a particular spot within the page he's viewing?
- How do I create a link that takes the visitor from one page to a particular spot in another page?
- How do I create links that, when clicked, download a file?

Understanding Bookmarks

A bookmark is a hidden HTML tag—hidden in that it is not visible to the visitor, but is visible to you in FrontPage Express (see Figure 11.1) so you can see where you put 'em. In FrontPage Express, a bookmark in a file is indicated by

- A flag icon, when the bookmark marks a spot in the page
- A dashed blue underline, when a bookmark is attached to text

FIGURE 11.1

Bookmarks code in an HTML file.

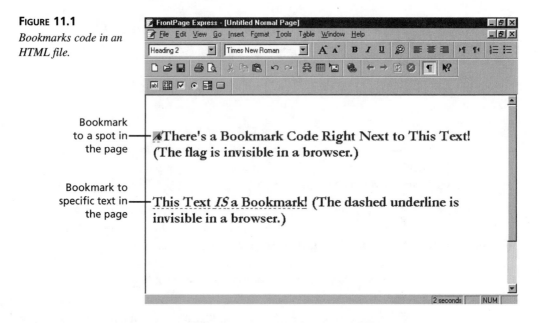

A bookmark provides a location in a page that a link can point to, so that clicking the link takes a visitor to that exact spot, rather than just to the top of the page. A single page can have many bookmarks, each one with a unique name so that a link can point to one and only one particular bookmark. The link that points to a bookmark can be in the same page that the bookmark is in, or in another page.

Why use bookmarks? Well, there are several common scenarios, most involving long Web pages where, without bookmarks, the visitor would have to do a lot of scrolling to locate particular information on a page:

- At the top of a very long Web page (such as a Frequently Asked Questions, or *FAQ*, file), you can include a list of links, each of which points to a different part of the file. The links enable the visitor to jump easily to any part of the file, instead of having to scroll through it to find a particular section.

- You may want to use bookmarks when links on one page refer to particular parts of another page that happens to be a long one. The links can point to bookmarks in the long page, to take the visitor directly there in one click.

- In a frames-based page (see Hour 18, "Dividing a Page into Frames"), links in one frame can bring up particular parts of a file displayed in another frame. Like the other techniques, this reduces the visitor's need to scroll, making a Web site easier to navigate.

I've already said this, but it's important: In HTML code and in some other Web authoring programs (see Hour 24, "Developing Your Authoring Skills"), bookmarks are called *anchors*. In other programs, they may be called *targets*.

You don't need to know that as long as you use FrontPage Express (or FrontPage 2000, which also uses the term bookmarks). But if you move to other Web authoring tools, you'll need to remember that bookmark = anchor or target.

11

Creating Bookmarks in a Page

Before you can begin linking to bookmarks, you must insert those bookmarks in the page. The following To Dos show how to insert bookmarks in a page in FrontPage Express. Note that there are two basic methods: Creating a bookmark that marks a spot, and creating a bookmark that marks certain text.

Which method to use, when? Well, it doesn't really make much difference.

Attaching bookmarks to text makes the most sense when each section where you'll want to put a bookmark begins with a unique heading, as in a FAQ. When that's the case, attaching bookmarks to text saves you the extra step of having to name your bookmarks.

However, the text must be different for each bookmark in the page; no two bookmarks in a file can share the same name.

To Do: Create bookmarks to mark a spot in a page

1. Click at a spot where you'd like a link to lead.
2. Choose Edit, Bookmark.

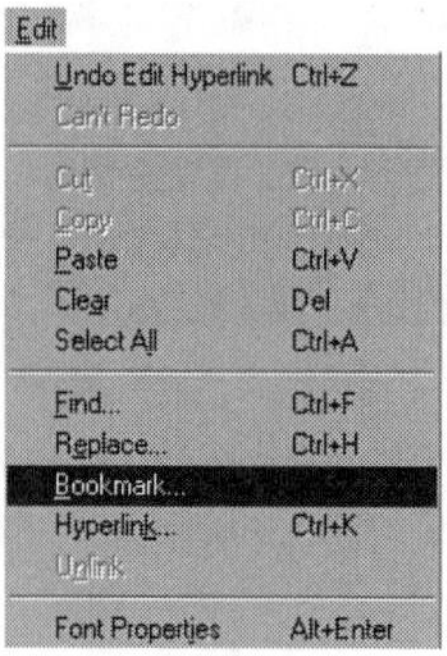

FIGURE 11.2

Step 2: Choose Edit, Bookmark.

Edit	
Undo Edit Hyperlink	Ctrl+Z
Can't Redo	
Cut	Ctrl+X
Copy	Ctrl+C
Paste	Ctrl+V
Clear	Del
Select All	Ctrl+A
Find...	Ctrl+F
Replace...	Ctrl+H
Bookmark...	
Hyperlink...	Ctrl+K
Unlink	
Font Properties	Alt+Enter

3. Type a name for this bookmark, and click OK.

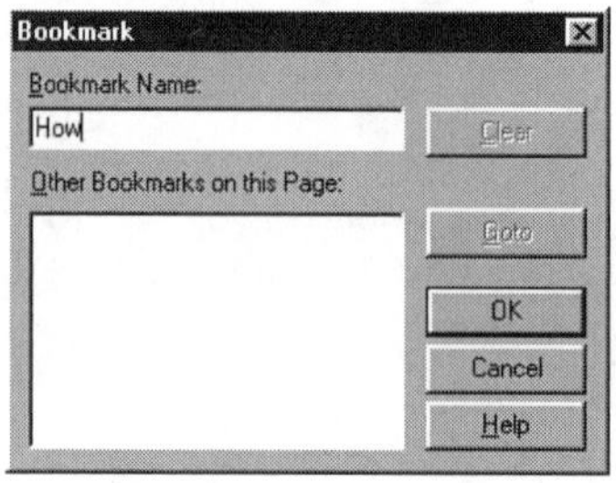

FIGURE 11.3

Step 3: Name the bookmark, and then click OK.

Bookmark

Bookmark Name:
How

Other Bookmarks on this Page:

Clear
Goto
OK
Cancel
Help

▲

To Do: Create bookmarks attached to particular text

1. Select the text to which you want to attach a bookmark.

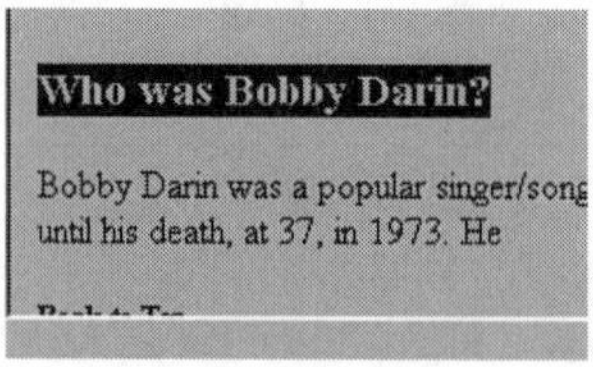

FIGURE 11.4

Step 1: Select the text.

Who was Bobby Darin?

Bobby Darin was a popular singer/song
until his death, at 37, in 1973. He

▼

2. Choose Edit, Bookmark.

3. Observe that the text you selected appears automatically as the bookmark's name. Just click OK.

FIGURE 11.5
Step 3: The bookmark's already named; click OK.

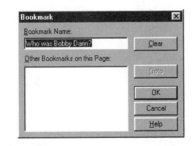

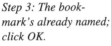

When performing step 1, make sure your selection does not include a paragraph mark. If it does, you'll find that the Bookmarks dialog box won't let you create the bookmark.

To avoid selecting a paragraph character, don't run the selection all the way to the end of a line (make sure the selection ends with a character).

11

Deleting Bookmarks

You can delete bookmarks in several ways:

- If a bookmark flag appears, just click the flag, and then press the Delete key. No flag, no bookmark.

- If the bookmark is attached to text, you can delete the text to delete the bookmark.

- If you want to remove the bookmark but keep the text, click anywhere in the text containing the bookmark, and then choose Edit, Bookmark. On the Bookmark dialog box, click the Clear button (see Figure 11.6).

FIGURE 11.6
Click Clear to remove the bookmark.

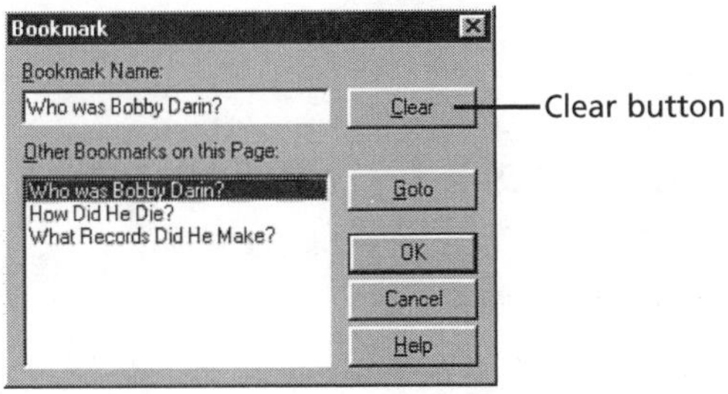

Clear button

Moving Bookmarks

To move a bookmark from one part of a page to another, you can use cut and paste.

Select the flag (or the text to which a bookmark is attached), and click the Cut button on FrontPage Express's Standard toolbar. Then click where you want to move the bookmark, and click the Copy button.

> Note that you can move bookmarks that you've already created links to, and the links will point to the new location without any further modifications.

Linking to Bookmarks

You can create three kinds of links that point to bookmarks:

- A link within the same page as the bookmark to which it points.
- A link in one page that points to a bookmark in another page in a multipage Web site you're creating in FrontPage Express.
- A link in one page that points to a bookmark in another page online that's not one of yours.

In the following pages, you will learn how to link to bookmarks in the same page and to bookmarks in other pages online. See Hour 12, "Using Links to Build a Web Site," to learn how to link from one page of your own to a bookmark in another page of your own.

> In Hour 14, "Adding Pictures (and Picture Backgrounds)," you'll learn not only how to add pictures to your pages, but also how to use a picture as a link source.
>
> It's jumping ahead a little, therefore, to get into pictures here, but I should tell you now that links using any type of link source—text, pictures, or even multilink imagemaps (see Hour 20, "Putting Multiple Links in One Picture")—can point to bookmarks.

Linking to a Bookmark in the Same Page

In FrontPage Express, it's easiest to create links to bookmarks in the same file if you have only the one file open in FrontPage. So that's where you begin, in the following To Do.

As shown earlier, it's customary to put a table of contents at the top of a long page, with each entry in the TOC linking to a bookmark in a section of the page.

If you create a long page of this type, it's also a good idea to put a link on every section that jumps back to the TOC, so visitors can easily jump back and forth from the TOC to desired sections.

Put a bookmark right over the TOC, and insert a link at every section that points to that bookmark.

To Do: Link to a bookmark in the same page

1. To make sure that the page containing the bookmark is the only page currently open in FrontPage Express, open the Window menu and make sure only one file-name appears there.

Window
Cascade
Tile
Arrange Icons
1 C:\My Documents\My Webs\darin.htm

FIGURE 11.7
Step 1: Only one file open in FrontPage Express.

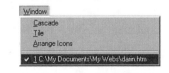

2. Create and select the link source, as you would when creating any kind of link, and then click the Create or Edit Hyperlink button.
3. Click the Open Pages tab.

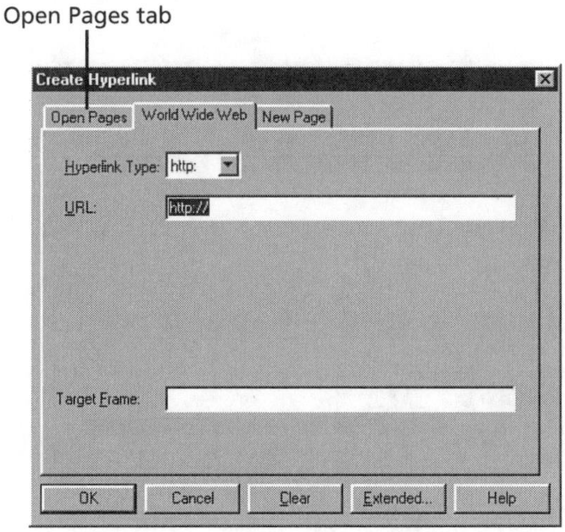

Open Pages tab
Create Hyperlink
Open Pages
World Wide Web
New Page
Hyperlink Type:
http:
URL:
http://
Target Frame:
OK
Cancel
Clear
Extended...
Help

FIGURE 11.8
Step 3: Click Open Pages.

▼   4. Click the arrow on the right end of the Bookmark box to open a list of all book-
        marks in the page.

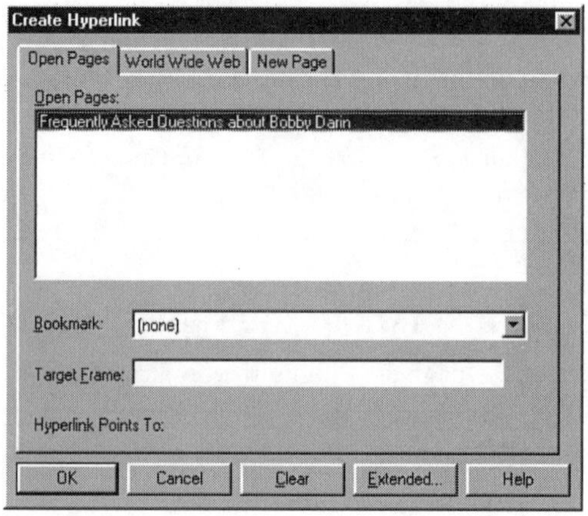

FIGURE 11.9

Step 4: Open the list of bookmarks in the current page.

5. In the list, click the name of the bookmark to which you want this link to lead, and
   then click OK.

Observe that the list of bookmarks is organized alphabetically, by bookmark
name. So find the bookmark you want by name. Don't assume that the
bookmarks are listed in the same order in which they appear in the page—
top to bottom.

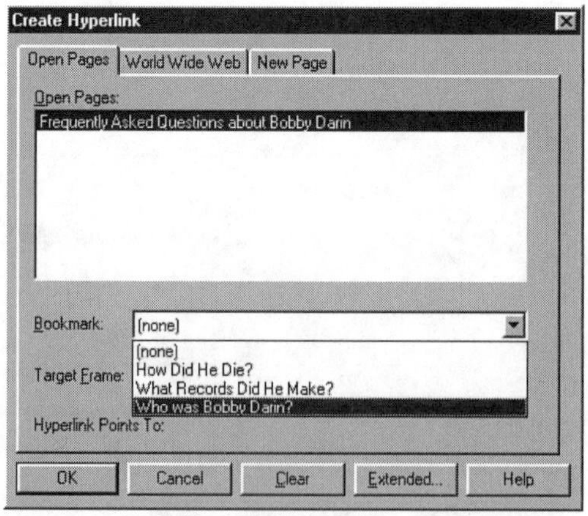

FIGURE 11.10

Step 5: Choose the bookmark.

▲

Test your links to bookmarks like any others while in FrontPage Express. Click the link, and then choose Tools, Follow Hyperlink.

Linking to Bookmarks in Other Pages Online

The easiest way to link to a bookmark in someone else's page online is to find a link on that page that points to the bookmark to which you want to link. For example, if you want to link to a particular part of a FAQ file online, find a link in the FAQ's table of contents that points to that part. Then copy that link from the Web page into your own page using copy and paste, as described in Hour 10.

As always, when linking to pages that are not your own, you should email the Webmaster of the page to which you want to link and ask if it's OK.

Note that some Webmasters may say it's okay to link to the page, but not to bookmarks within the page. This may happen when the page contains advertising or other information the Webmaster wants all visitors to see; linking to bookmarks would allow them to bypass such stuff.

Another method is to learn the bookmark's exact URL, which is made up of the page's URL, a pound mark (#), and the bookmark name. For example, the URL

`http://www.test.com/sample.htm#bookmark1`

points to a bookmark named `bookmark1` in a page file called `sample.htm` on a server called `www.test.com`.

The easiest way to learn the URLs of bookmarks in an online document is to browse to the document in your Web browser and find the links in that document that point to the bookmarks. When you point to a link (don't click), the status bar at the bottom of the window (in Navigator or Internet Explorer) shows the full URL to which that link points—including the bookmark name.

Once you know the complete URL, you can create a link to it like any other link to a Web page, by typing it in the URL box in the Create Hyperlink (or Edit Hyperlink) dialog box (see Figure 11.11).

11

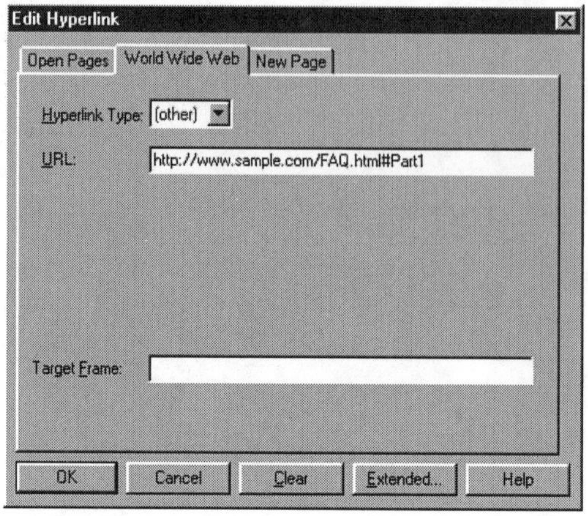

FIGURE 11.11

You can enter a URL that includes a book-mark name right in the Create Hyperlink (or Edit Hyperlink) dialog box.

Creating Links that Download Files

You may have content that you want to offer your visitors, but don't want to turn into a Web page. For example, if you have a long story, report, or other document in a word processing file, it may be better to offer that file for downloading instead of turning it into a Web page (or series of Web pages).

You can offer any kind of computer file for downloading—documents, sound clips, pictures, and so on. The steps for creating links to files are the same—no matter what type of file you want to offer—as the following To Do shows.

One caveat to keep in mind: To use a file you provide, the visitor must have the right program. For example, if you publish a Word file, the visitor must have a program that can display (or convert) Word files to view it. There's not much you can do about this, except to try to offer only popular, widely-used file types, such as Word for documents, `.avi` for video clips, or `.wav` for sound clips (see Hour 15, "Snazzing Up Your Page with Sound, Video, and Special Effects").

To Do: Create links that download files

1. Get the file to which you want to link, and move or copy it to the folder where your Web page files are stored (see Figure 11.12).
2. In the Web page in FrontPage Express, type and format the link source—the text a visitor would click to download the file (see Figure 11.13).

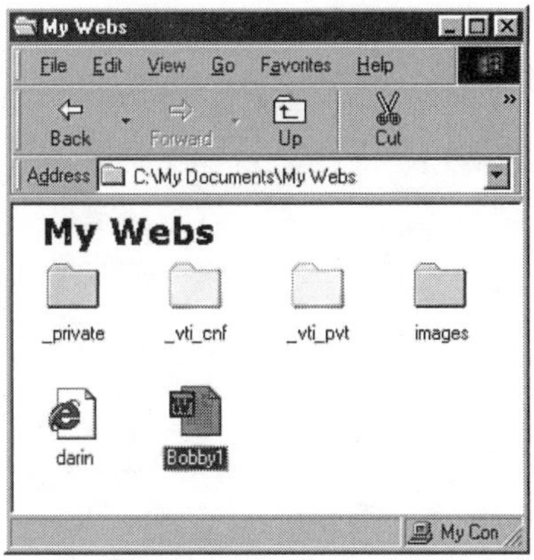

▼ FIGURE 11.12

Step 1: Put the file in the same folder as the Web page file.

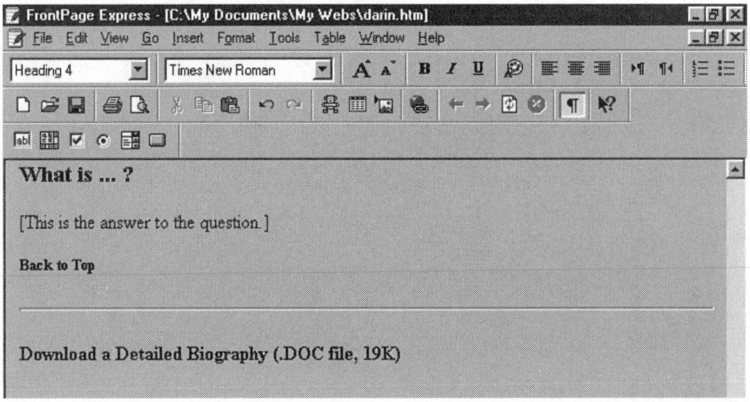

My Webs

File Edit View Go Favorites Help

Back Forward Up Cut

Address C:\My Documents\My Webs

My Webs

_private   _vti_cnf   _vti_pvt   images

darin   Bobby1

My Con

FIGURE 11.13

Step 2: Prepare the link source.

FrontPage Express - [C:\My Documents\My Webs\darin.htm]

File Edit View Go Insert Format Tools Table Window Help

Heading 4   Times New Roman

What is ... ?

[This is the answer to the question.]

Back to Top

Download a Detailed Biography (.DOC file, 19K)

11

In the link source text (or right next to it), it's courteous to tell your visitors the file type (so they can tell whether it's a file they're equipped to view) and size (so they can guesstimate how long it will take to download at the speed of their Internet connection).

3. Select the text of the link source.

4. Click the Create or Edit Hyperlink button on the standard toolbar.

5. Make sure that the World Wide Web tab is selected.

6. In the box labeled URL, type the complete filename of the file (see Figure 11.14). Do not put "http://" at the beginning.

▼

FIGURE 11.14

Step 6: Type the filename, leaving out the "http://" part.

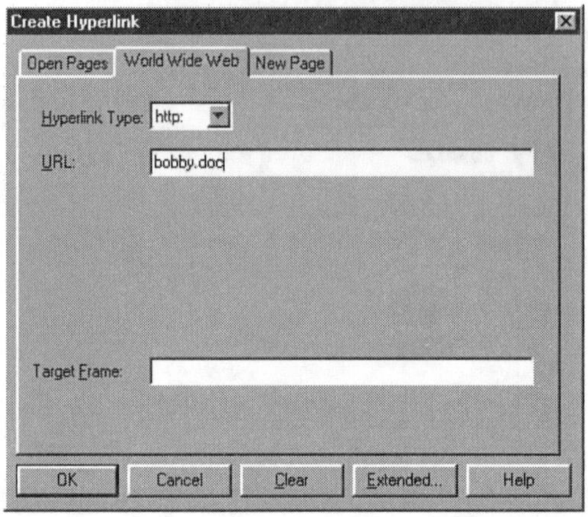

Create Hyperlink	☒

Open Pages | World Wide Web | New Page |

Hyperlink Type: http: ▼

URL: bobby.doc

Target Frame:

| OK | Cancel | Clear | Extended... | Help |

▲   7. Click OK.

When you publish this Web page online, it's essential that you remember to also publish the file to which the link points, and make sure it's stored in the same directory online as the page containing the link; otherwise, the link won't work. See Part VI, "Getting It Online."

Summary

You probably won't use bookmarks often; if you feel you need bookmarks, you should first consider breaking up the page into several, smaller pages. But when it makes sense to publish a lot of information in one file, bookmarks help your visitors wade around in all that information conveniently.

Q&A

Q **Should I finish the rest of my page before adding bookmarks to it? I'm wondering what happens to the bookmarks if I do a lot of editing and formatting to the file after I've added them.**

A In general, it makes sense to complete most other aspects of your page before adding bookmarks. That way, the bookmarks won't get all shuffled around to the wrong spots if you do heavy editing on the page later, such as adding, moving, or replacing large blocks of material.

However, note that most formatting activities don't hurt bookmarks. If a block of text that includes a bookmark has its font or alignment changed, for example, the bookmark will still work (although the icon will appear to take on any alignment changes or indents you apply to the adjacent text).

11

HOUR 12

Using Links to Build a Web Site

There are pages, and then there are *sites*—groups of pages linked together. (The term "Web site" is also used to refer to the server on which those pages are published; see Hour 21, "Publishing Your Page.")

Without carefully created links and bookmarks, a set of Web pages is no site—it's just a bunch of individual, unrelated pages. Link those pages together in just the right way, and they become a cohesive site your visitors can explore to enjoy all that's offered on every page.

In this hour, you'll revisit the various ways a Web site can be structured (first introduced in Hour 1, "Understanding Web Authoring") and learn how and when to deploy each method in your own projects. At the end of the hour, you will be able to answer the following questions:

- How do I link my own pages together, to tie them together into an integrated Web site?

- How do I create the pages of my site at the same time I make the links between pages?

- Can I link from one page to a particular spot in another?

- How do I choose when and whether to build my site as a linear, hierarchical Web or other site structure?

- For each type of structure, what links (and sometimes bookmarks) do I need to insert to link my pages together properly?

- What tips should I apply to make sure that my site is attractive, logical, and easy to use?

> What separates basic Web authoring tools like FrontPage Express from big leaguers like FrontPage 2000? Well, other than a few bells and whistles, the most important difference is that pro tools include *site management* features.
>
> With site management, you can display a diagram of all of the interlinked pages in a Web site. You can add or delete pages, or move pages around, and all of the links among pages are automatically adjusted so that they still lead where they're supposed to. You can apply a *theme* to a Web site, so that all of its pages share a common style.
>
> Starting out, creating single pages and basic Web sites of maybe five pages or so, you don't need site management capabilities. But as you move up to bigger, more complex sites, you should start hinting that, for your next birthday, you want a Web authoring program with site management.

The Basic Act: Linking One Page to Another

FrontPage Express makes it easy to link together pages you've created while they're still on your PC. The trick is to create the pages first, and then build the links as described in the following To Do.

To Do: Link one of your own pages to others

1. Create the Web pages that will make up your Web site, and save them all in the same folder.

2. Type and format the text that will serve as the various link sources.

3. Select the text of one link source.

FIGURE 12.1

Step 1: Create your pages, and store them together in a folder.

FIGURE 12.2

Step 3: Select a link source.

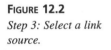

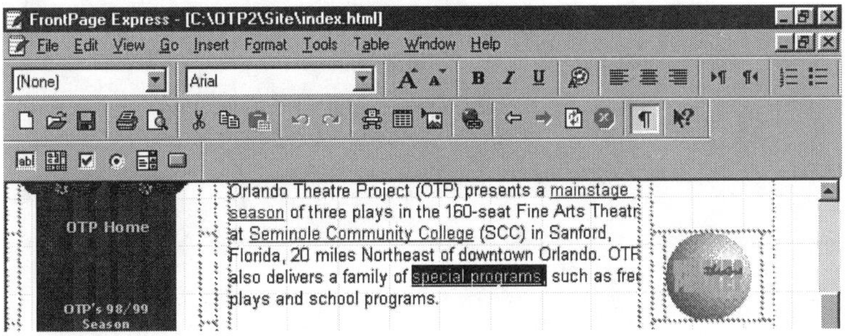

One good way to link pages together is to create a block of links—containing a separate link for each page—and put it at the bottom of every page. That way, your visitors can jump from any page in your Web site to any other with just one click.

Once you've created the block of links, you can use copy and paste to copy it from one page to others (see Hour 6, "Adding and Editing Text"). Or, you can build the block in one page, and then use that page as the template (see Hour 4, "Starting Pages in Other Programs") for all the rest.

Besides (or in addition to) using a block of text links, you can use picture links (see Hour 14, "Adding Pictures (and Picture Backgrounds)") or an imagemap (see Hour 18, "Dividing a Page into Frames") to create a navigation bar, a graphical link block for each page in the site.

12

4. Click the Create or Edit Hyperlink button on the standard toolbar, and make sure that the World Wide Web tab is selected.

▼

5. In the box labeled URL, type the complete filename of the page file to which this link points (including the `.htm` part). Do not put `http://` or anything else at the beginning. The filename alone does it.

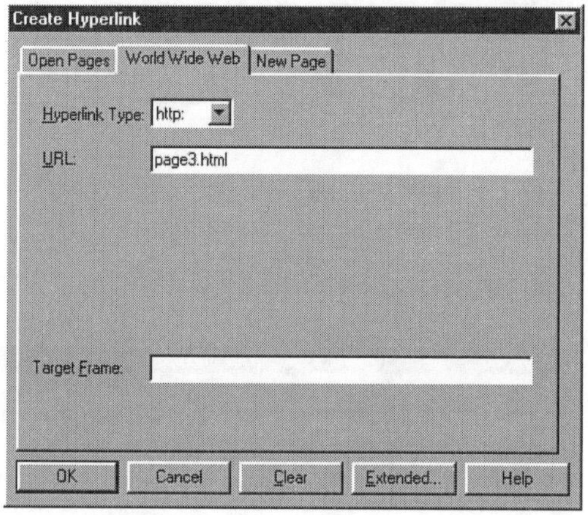

FIGURE 12.3

Step 5: For the link URL, type the filename of the page to which to link.

Create Hyperlink

Open Pages | World Wide Web | New Page |

Hyperlink Type: http:

URL: page3.html

Target Frame:

OK   Cancel   Clear   Extended..   Help

6. Click OK.

When typing your page filename in the URL box, ignore the entry in the Hyperlink Type box. That entry automatically becomes "Other" when you click OK, which is what you want.

▲

Making New Pages When You Make Links to Them

No law says you have to create all your pages first (I just find that a more organized way to work). You can create new page files at the very moment that you create links to them. Then, when you go to fill your pages in, they're already inter-linked. The following To Do shows how.

To Do: Create a new page and the link to that page simultaneously!

1. In a page you've already created, type and format the text that will serve as the link source to the new page.

2. Select the text of one link source.

3. Click the Create or Edit Hyperlink button on the standard toolbar.

4. Click the New Page tab.

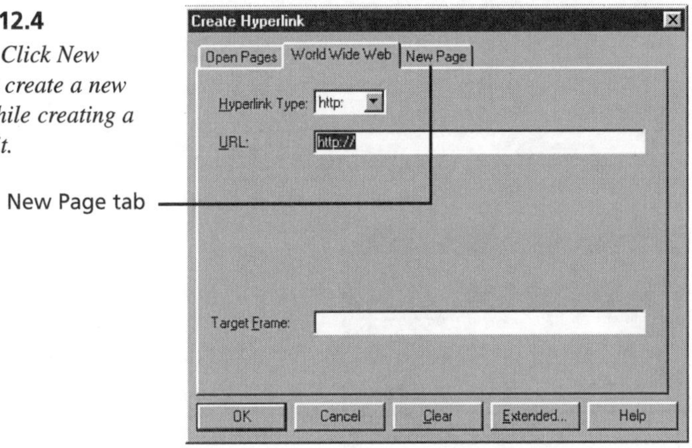

FIGURE 12.4

Step 4: Click New Page to create a new page while creating a link to it.

New Page tab ——

Create Hyperlink

Open Pages | World Wide Web | New Page |

Hyperlink Type: http: ▼

URL: http://

Target Frame:

OK | Cancel | Clear | Extended.. | Help

5. Type a title for the page, and then give it a filename in Page URL.

As Figure 12.5 shows, FrontPage Express fills in the title and filename with ones it makes up out of the text you selected in step 2. You can click OK to accept these, or you can change 'em.

12

6. Click OK. The New Page dialog box opens, just as it does when you choose File, New (see Hour 2, "Getting Started with a Web Authoring Program").

7. Create the new page using any of the options on the New Page dialog box.

▼

FIGURE 12.5
Step 5: Give the new page a title and filename.

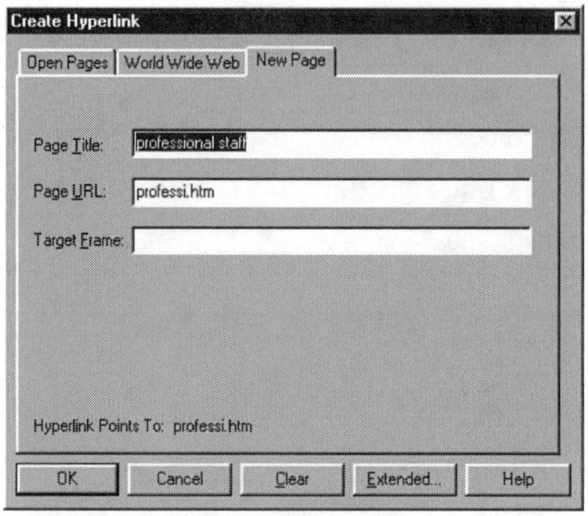

Create Hyperlink
Open Pages | World Wide Web | New Page

Page Title: professional staff
Page URL: professi.htm
Target Frame:

Hyperlink Points To: professi.htm

OK   Cancel   Clear   Extended...   Help

FIGURE 12.6
Step 7: Create the new page.

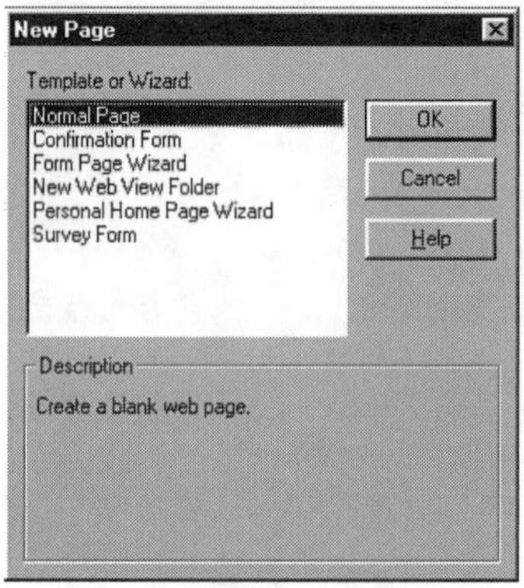

New Page
Template or Wizard:
Normal Page
Confirmation Form
Form Page Wizard
New Web View Folder
Personal Home Page Wizard
Survey Form

OK
Cancel
Help

Description
Create a blank web page.

8. To switch back to the page you started out in (in step 1), choose it from the Window menu.

FIGURE 12.7
Step 8: Use the Window menu to switch among open pages while working.

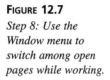

Window
Cascade
Tile
Arrange Icons
1 C:\OTP2\Site\index.html
✓ 2 professional staff

▲

Linking from One Page to a Bookmark in Another

In Hour 11, "More Ways to Link," you learned the fine art of linking to bookmarks, a technique used most often to link from one part of a long page to another. But you can also jump from one of your pages to a particular bookmark point in another of your pages.

To Do: Link to a bookmark in one of your own pages

1. Open the page containing the bookmark, and then open the page that will contain the link, so that both are open.

2. In the page where the link will live, create and select the link source, as you would when creating any kind of link, and then click the Create or Edit Hyperlink button.

3. Click the Open Pages tab.

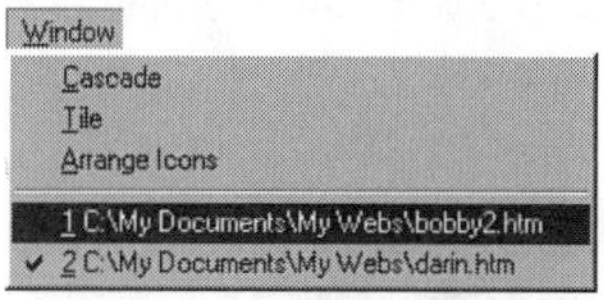

FIGURE 12.8

Step 1: Open both files.

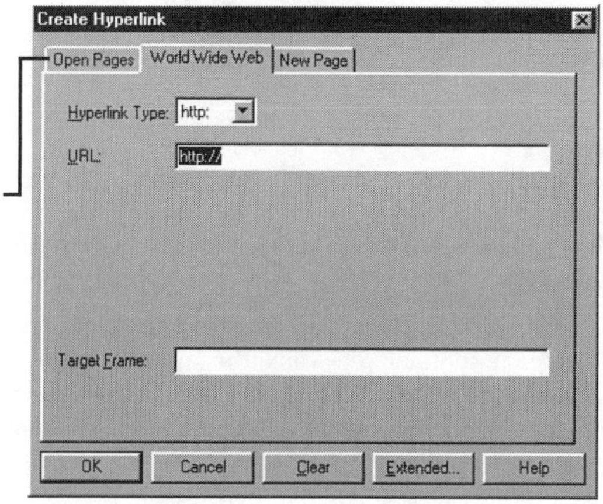

Window
Cascade
Tile
Arrange Icons
1 C:\My Documents\My Webs\bobby2.htm
✓ 2 C:\My Documents\My Webs\darin.htm

FIGURE 12.9

Step 3: Click the Open Pages tab.

Open Pages

Create Hyperlink

Open Pages | World Wide Web | New Page

Hyperlink Type: http:

URL: http://

Target Frame:

| OK | Cancel | Clear | Extended... | Help |

4. Under Open Pages, click the name of the page containing the bookmark.

5. Open the list of bookmarks (which now shows only the bookmarks in the page you selected in step 4), click the name of the bookmark you want this link to lead to, and then click OK.

12

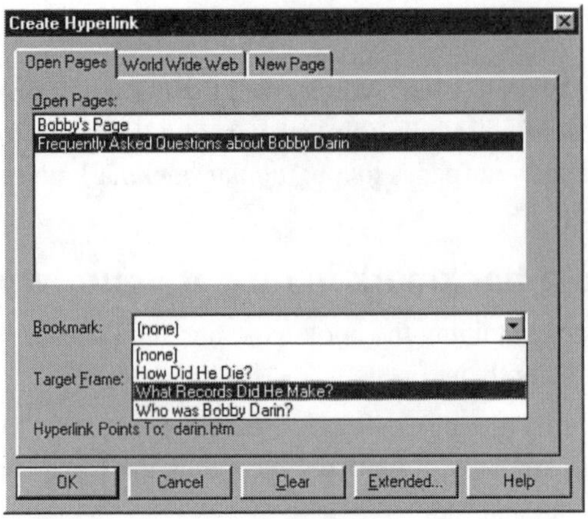

▼

FIGURE **12.10**

Step 5: Choose the file and bookmark.

Create Hyperlink

Open Pages | World Wide Web | New Page |

Open Pages:

Bobby's Page
Frequently Asked Questions about Bobby Darin

Bookmark: [none]

[none]
How Did He Die?
What Records Did He Make?
Who was Bobby Darin?

Target Frame:

Hyperlink Points To: darin.htm

OK   Cancel   Clear   Extended...   Help

6. A warning appears. Click Yes on the warning to create the link anyway (don't worry—see the tip that follows).

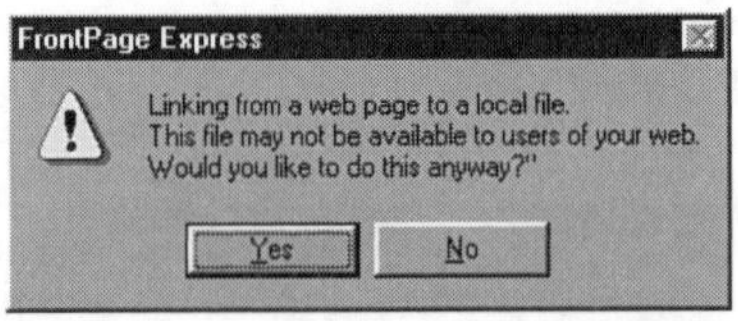

FIGURE **12.11**

Step 6: Ignore the warning and click Yes.

FrontPage Express

Linking from a web page to a local file.
This file may not be available to users of your web.
Would you like to do this anyway?"

Yes   No

▲

Why does that warning appear in the preceding To Do? Well, it has to do with relative and absolute links, which were covered in Hour 9, "Understanding Links." (You skipped Hour 9, didn't you? Admit it. You'll feel better.)

If the page containing the bookmark had been located in a different folder than the page containing the link, the link URL would have pointed not to a filename, but to a file in a particular folder. When you published this page online, the link might not have worked (unless you duplicated the same folder structure online that's on your PC).

But because you started out with both files in the same folder, the link URL contains nothing but the filename and the bookmark name. When you publish (see Hour 21), as long as you publish these files in the same directory online, any links between them will work just fine.

Site-Design Tips

The skills outlined in the preceding To Dos are all you need to stitch multiple pages into a coordinated site. All you need now is a little guidance about ways you can organize information into a Web site. The remainder of this hour offers tips for choosing a site design.

Building a Multipage Linear Site

In a multipage linear site, the pages and links are set up in a way that encourages the reader to read a group of pages in a particular order, start to finish (see Figure 12.12).

This design makes sense when the content your site delivers is made up mostly of medium-sized blocks of text (around one screen) that should be read in a particular sequential order, beginning to end. (Some people call this structure "slide show," because the visitor steps through the pages in order, as in a slide show.)

FIGURE 12.12

The structure of a multipage linear site.

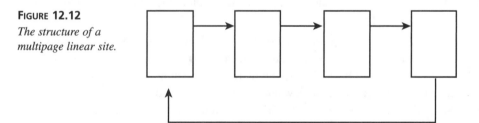

For example, suppose this book were converted into a Web site. Its "hours" serve the reader best when read in order, because each chapter builds on material from the ones before it. So, to encourage the reader to proceed in order, the site would be designed so that the natural flow from page to page (or hour to hour) follows the proper order. Other content that fits this design includes a story that's too long to fit on one page or lengthy step-by-step instructions.

Each page in a multipage linear site features a prominent link, often labeled "Next" or "Continue," that leads only to the next page in order. Other links can be offered as well, but be careful about offering too many links in such pages—they enable the reader to stray from the order, defeating the purpose of the design.

> The Microsoft PowerPoint program (included in most versions of Microsoft Office) is designed to help you quickly build an attractive slide-show presentation.

12

> PowerPoint 97 and PowerPoint 2000 can convert their slide presentations into multipage linear Web sites. They convert each slide into a separate Web page, and then automatically insert the navigation buttons (Back, Next, and so on). It's a fast and easy way to make a Web site from content you may already have on hand.

Tips for Multipage Linear Site Design

When developing a multipage linear Web site, keep in mind the following tips for good design:

- Try to divide the material into pages on which there's just enough content (text and images) to fill the screen. Since the visitor is moving sequentially through the pages, he or she should not have to scroll, too. Putting just the right amount of text on each page enables visitors to conveniently explore the whole site just by clicking the "Next" link that you provide.

- A "Next" link on each page is the only link that's required, and often, the only one you'll want. However, if you can do so without cluttering up the design too much, it's nice to offer a "Back" link (pointing to the preceding page) on each page after the first so the reader can review content, if necessary. Also handy is a "Back to Start" link that points to the very first page, so the reader can conveniently jump from any page to the beginning.

- The very last page in the order should always contain a link back to the very first page, even if you choose not to provide such a link elsewhere.

Working with One-Page Linear Pages

When 1) you have a lot of text to deliver, 2) that text is naturally divided into many small sections, and 3) you want to deliver it in an efficient way, a one-page linear design is a terrific (and often overlooked) approach (see Figure 12.13).

This structure is often applied to lengthy reference material provided as one part of a larger, multipage site, but a well designed one-pager can actually serve as your whole site.

Readers can always scroll through the entire page, but typically, the very top of the page shows a list of links—a table of contents or index of sorts. Each link points to a bookmark (see Hour 11) somewhere down in the page. The links help readers quickly find particular information without having to scroll for it.

FIGURE 12.13

A sample one-page linear design.

TOC Links

Links back to TOC

Bookmarks

Rules

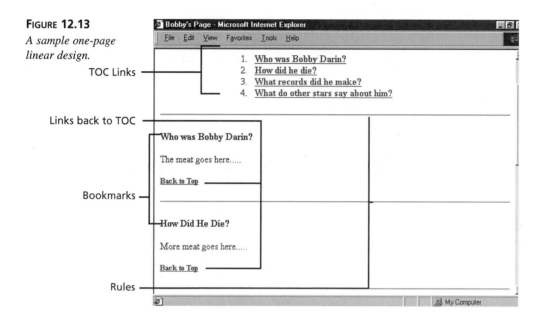

The longer the page and the more separate sections it has, the more important the table of links at the top is.

If a page is only three or four screens long, the visitor can pretty easily explore it by scrolling. Five screens or longer, and you owe your visitors the assistance of some links.

Tips for One-Page Linear Design

When developing a one-page linear design, keep in mind the following tips for good design:

- At the very top of the page, or adjacent to the table of contents, insert a bookmark. Between each logical section of the page, insert a "Back to Top" link that points to the bookmark at the top. This enables the reader to conveniently return to the TOC after reading any section.

- Limit pictures (see Hour 14). The danger of this design is that the long page will contain so much data that it will take a long time to download to the visitor's browser. But text—even a lot of text—moves through the Internet pretty quickly. So if you limit yourself to an image or two, usually at the top of the page, you can lend some visual interest while still enabling the page to download quickly.

12

- Scroll through the page. If the total page exceeds 15 screens, consider breaking it up into a hierarchical or multipage sequential design.

- Use horizontal rules (see Hour 8, "Organizing Text with Tables and Rules") to divide sections of the text visually.

Making a Web-Style Site

In a Web structure, anything goes (see Figure 12.14). Any page can link to any other page, or to all other pages. This structure makes sense when the various pages contain information that is related to information on other pages, but there's no logical order or sequence to that information.

FIGURE 12.14

A Web-style structure.

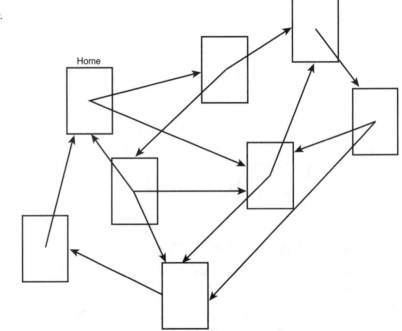

In a Web-style site, there may be a "top" page provided as a starting point (as in a hierarchical site, described later in this hour), but from there, readers can wander around the site in no particular path. Web structures are best suited to fun, recreational subjects, or to subjects that defy any kind of sequential or hierarchical breakdown.

Typically, each page of a Web-style site contains a block of links—often in a column along one side of the page or in a block at the bottom—that lead to every other page in the site (see Figure 12.15).

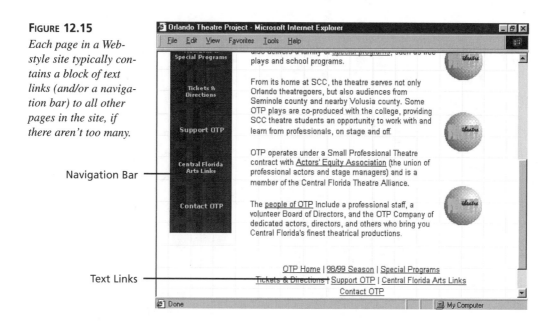

FIGURE 12.15

Each page in a Web-style site typically contains a block of text links (and/or a navigation bar) to all other pages in the site, if there aren't too many.

Navigation Bar

Text Links

Tips for Web-Style Design

When developing a Web-style site, keep in mind the following tips for good design:

- Before you resort to a Web structure, make sure your message really calls for one—you might just be having trouble recognizing the logical organization of your content.

- It's easy for visitors to get lost in a Web-style site. I recommend always including a "top" page that serves as an all-purpose starting point, and then making sure every page in the site contains an easily identifiable link back to the top page. That way, lost visitors can easily get back to a landmark from which to set off down a new path.

Making a Hierarchical Site

The most well-organized design (see Figure 12.16), a hierarchical Web site starts out with a general, "top" page that leads to several second-level pages containing more specific information. Each of these second-level pages leads to third-level pages containing more specific info about the second-level page to which they are linked, and so on, and so on.

12

FIGURE **12.16**
*A hierarchical
structure.*

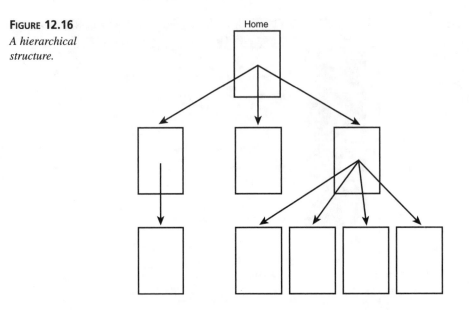

The careful organization of a hierarchical site is not for the mere sake of neatness. The structure of the page actually helps the visitor find what he or she wants, especially when the site carries a lot of detailed information.

For example, suppose the site sells clothes, and I want a dress shirt. The top page might show links to Women's clothes and Men's clothes. I choose Men's and arrive at a second-level page offering links to shirts, pants, and shoes. I choose shirts, and I see a third-level page offering dress and casual. I choose dress, and I'm there. The structure of the page made my search easy, even though the site offers hundreds of items.

Tips for Hierarchical Design

When developing a hierarchical site, keep in mind the following tips for good design:

- As in a Web-style design, be sure that every page in the site contains an easily identifiable link back to the top page, so visitors can easily get back to the top without having to struggle up the hierarchy a level at a time.

- More than with any other design, a hierarchical structure demands that you think and plan the content of each page and the organization of the pages very carefully so the site flows logically. As with my shirt example, visitors should be able to drill intuitively down through the hierarchy to find specific information.

- Keep in mind that you have many levels available to you. Don't try to link the top page to a dozen second-level pages—doing so suggests you have not really figured out the organization. Ideally, each page should lead to no fewer than two pages and no more than seven or eight, in the level below it. Then again, don't follow arbitrary rules. Just be sure the page organization and the natural organization of the content match.

Summary

The organization of pages in a site is not really a Web-authoring challenge: It's a content-management issue. Understand exactly what you're trying to say and how to say it best, and the correct site structure will become immediately apparent to you. All that's left is adding some links (and maybe bookmarks), and you know how to do that already, don't you?

Q&A

Q What if I'm planning to use some content that's naturally sequential, some that's naturally hierarchical, and some that's random? How do I make it all fit one model?

A You don't have to. For more elaborate Web sites, a *hybrid* approach is called for.

A hybrid approach generally starts out hierarchical, with an overview top page to serve as a starting point. But at the second level, that top page might link down to a one-page linear, or to the top page of what will then spread out into a Web structure, or to the first page of a multipage linear slide show, or to the top of a whole new hierarchy.

With a hybrid approach, you can make content at the second and lower levels conform to whatever structure suits it, while still using the top page to hold the whole affair neatly together.

12

PART IV

Adding Pizzazz With Multimedia

Hour

HOUR 13

Getting Pictures for Your Page

In Hour 14, "Adding Pictures (and Picture Backgrounds)", you'll begin adding pictures to your page. But the trickiest part of adding pictures isn't the adding—it's getting the pictures in the first place, and getting them in the proper format. In this hour, you'll learn how, where, and why to get pictures for your page.

At the end of the hour, you will be able to answer the following questions:

- Where can I get pictures for my Web page?
- How can I create pictures of my own?
- What rules—file type, resolution, and other factors—must my picture files follow to appear in a Web page?

About Inline Images

NEW TERM *Inline* images are those that automatically appear within the layout of the page when the page is accessed by a graphical browser.

Computer image files come in many types. Common types include .pcx and .bmp files, which are used most often in Windows, and TIFF (.tif) files, which are often used on Macintoshes and in desktop publishing. However, the most common type of image file used for inline images is GIF (pronounced *jif* and using the file extension .gif). The next most popular type is JPEG (with a .jpg file extension in most systems).

Although images in file types other than GIF or JPEG are inappropriate for use as inline images, most other file types can be used as *external* images (see Hour 15), image files that display outside the browser when the visitor clicks a link.

GIF files (see Figure 13.1) offer certain advantages (see the sections titled "Understanding Interlacing" and "Understanding Transparency" later in this hour), but they are limited to 256 colors (or 256 shades of gray in black-and-white images). For most graphics, especially those originally drawn on a computer, this "8-bit" color is plenty. But for photographs, paintings, and other images taken from life, 256 colors do not permit enough variation in color or shade to present a realistically shaded image; the results can look computerish.

However, GIF's 256-color limitation is not necessarily a big disadvantage. This is true for two reasons:

- Images in 16-bit color (65,000 colors) or 24-bit *true color* (16 million colors) tend to occupy much larger files than 256-color graphics—so much so that they might be inappropriate as inline images because they'll take too long to download to the visitor's browser. (See the "File Size" section, later in this hour.)

- A high proportion of your audience will be running their browsers in 256-color mode anyway, which cannot display the extra color depth and detail possible in 16-bit and 24-bit color graphics. The picture will still show up, but it will look no better than a 256-color image.

However, if you want or need to display more than 256 colors or grays, a JPEG file (see Figure 13.2) can handle it. More important, a JPEG file of a photograph is often a smaller file, which means it appears more quickly on the visitor's display.

FIGURE 13.1

GIF images are usually best suited to highly graphical pictures, such as logos.

(neds.gif 4 k)

FIGURE 13.2

JPEG is a better choice than GIF for photos.

(animals09.jpg 57k)

All graphical Web browsers can display inline GIF images, and a very few can display *only* GIF images. The most popular browsers—Navigator and Internet Explorer—can also display JPEG images.

Another image file format, .png, is supported by some browsers. But GIF and JPEG are much more universally supported, and are thus your best choice for Web graphics.

Creating and Acquiring Image Files

Where can you get images? You can create (or acquire them) in the following ways. The important issue is not where they come from, but their file type, size, and other factors.

Paint/Draw—You can use a paint or draw program to create your inline graphics. Ideally, the program should be able to save your picture as a GIF (or, optionally, JPEG) graphic. If not, you can *convert*…

Convert—If you have existing graphics you want to use in your page that are not in GIF or JPEG format, you can convert them to GIF or JPEG using a paint program or conversion utility, or a conversion utility built into your Web authoring program. (FrontPage Express can convert some file types to GIF automatically.)

13

The software that comes with many scanners, digital cameras, and video capture devices can save images in GIF or JPEG format; when it cannot save in these formats, you can almost always save the file in TIFF format and then use another program, such as Paint Shop Pro (included on the CD-ROM), to convert a TIFF file to GIF or JPEG.

Scan—Using a hand scanner, sheetfed scanner, or flatbed scanner, you can scan photographs or other images and save them (using the scanning software) as GIF or JPEG images. This technique also enables you to draw, sketch, or paint pictures on paper (if you have such skills), and then convert them into computer graphics for use in Web pages.

Shoot—Using a digital camera or computer video camera, you can capture an image from life.

Note, however, that you don't have to create your own images—you can pick up existing images for a wide range of purposes. Collections of *clip art* are available on the Web and in commercial and shareware software packages.

NEW TERM *Clip art* are image files (and sometimes other kinds of media files, such as animations or sound clips) that you did not create but which are made available to you for use in your Web pages or other documents. Clip art libraries can be found on the Web, bundled with some software packages, and on CD-ROM or disk at your local software store.

As a rule, clip art is offered copyright-free, and you can use it any way you want. Some clip art collections are copyright-protected for some uses; be sure to read any copyright notices accompanying any clip art before you publish it in a Web page.

The CD-ROM with this book includes a collection of clip art images for use as list bullets, bars, and backgrounds, which you learn to add in Hour 14.

Also, Appendix B, "Online Resources for Web Authors," shows the addresses of a variety of great clip art libraries online.

Clip art collections on the Web generally offer their wares by displaying the images in a Web page. You can copy these images directly from the Web page into your page using the steps shown in the following To Do.

To Do: Copy clip art from the Web

1. Using Internet Explorer as your browser, visit one of the clip art sites listed in Appendix B.

FIGURE 13.3

Step 1: Visit a clip-art site.

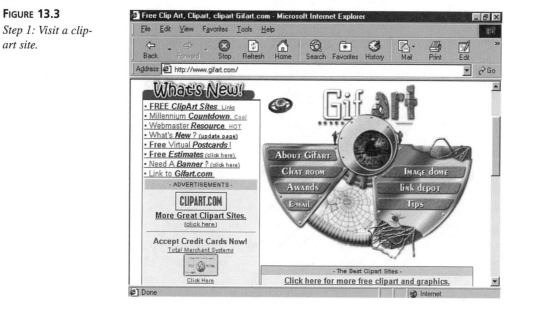

2. Following links and instructions you see on the page, browse around the site until a picture you want to use appears on your screen.

FIGURE 13.4

Step 2: Display the image.

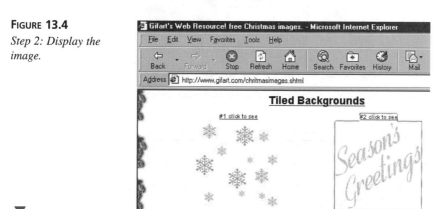

13

▼

▼   3. Right-click the desired image and choose Save Picture As from the pop-up menu.

FIGURE **13.5**

Step 3: Right-click and choose Save Picture As.

Open Link
Open Link in New Window
Save Target As...
Print Target
Show Picture
Save Picture As...
Set as Wallpaper
Set as Desktop Item...
Cut
Copy
Copy Shortcut
Paste
Add to Favorites...
Properties

4. Save the file using the path and filename desired. (The image's filename has been supplied for you, but you can change it. Do not change the extension, which informs browsers of the image's type.)

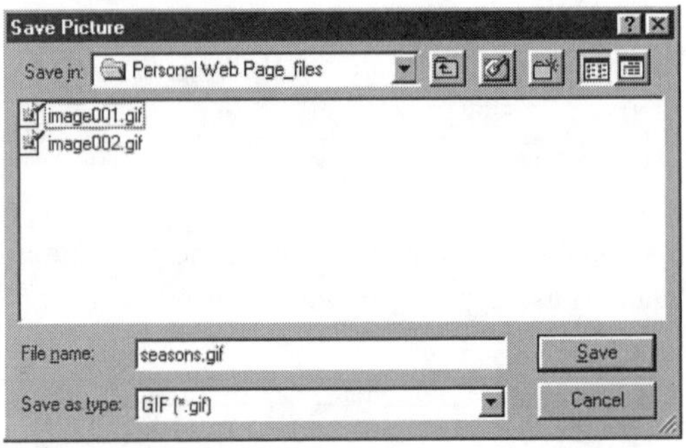

FIGURE **13.6**

Step 4: Save the file on your hard drive.

Save Picture   ? ✕

Save in: 🖳 Personal Web Page_files

📄 image001.gif
📄 image002.gif

File name: seasons.gif   Save
Save as type: GIF (*.gif)   Cancel

5. Switch to FrontPage Express and insert the image into your page as described in
▲   Hour 14.

Using Images from the CD-ROM

The CD-ROM included with this book features a handy collection of JPEG images for a range of uses, including some terrific background textures and cool bullets and rules.

In case you want to use them in your practice pages (or real ones!) as you work through this hour, here's where you'll find them on the CD-ROM. (You can, of course, copy these folders from the CD-ROM to your own hard disk, if you want to.)

In the disk paths shown in the following bulleted list, D: stands for the drive letter of the CD-ROM drive in your PC. For many people, that letter really will be D:. But your CD-ROM drive letter might be E: or another letter, depending on how your PC is configured.

- D:\Gfx\WebGfx contains three folders: Banners (Web banners), Buttons (various styles of navigation buttons you can attach links to), and Textures (background pictures).
- D:\Gfx\Fun contains a collection of fun images.
- D:\Gfx\Photos contains three folders of photographic images: Animals, Everyday, and People.
- D:\Gfx\Backgrounds contains more great images for picture backgrounds.
- D:\Gfx\Business contains business-related photographs.

You can insert a picture directly from the CD-ROM into a page. When you publish, FrontPage Express will publish the image from the CD-ROM right along with the HTML file.

However, I always recommend copying picture files to the same folder where the HTML file is stored (*before* inserting the picture in the page!), to avoid some kinds of complications that can crop up.

To copy a picture file from the CD-ROM to your hard drive, use My Computer to navigate to the CD-ROM folder where the image file is stored, and locate the exact picture you want by using the techniques described in the next section, "Previewing Images in Windows 98." While previewing the image, choose Edit, Copy from the folder's menu bar. Then open the folder containing the Web page file in which you plan to insert the image, and choose Edit, Paste.

13

Previewing Images in Windows 98

Sometimes it can be tricky to find the image file you want just from its filename. There are any number of terrific programs available for "browsing" the images on your hard drive or on a CD-ROM—showing each picture to help you find the one you want.

But if you have Windows 98, you can preview any picture just by single-clicking its file icon in a folder; a preview of the picture appears in the folder window, to the left of the file icons, as shown in Figure 13.7. (If you see no preview, choose View, As Web page, from the folder's menu bar.) Previewing pictures this way makes finding and selecting the right picture easier when you insert images in FrontPage Express.

FIGURE 13.7

You can easily preview most image files in Windows 98.

Important Stuff to Know About Inline Images

Before inserting an image into your page, consider the issues described in the next several sections.

File Type

As a rule, try to use GIF files whenever possible. Doing so ensures that almost any visitor using a graphical browser can see the image.

When you want to publish a more photo-realistic image, or if you have a JPEG file you can't get converted to GIF, you can use a JPEG file as an inline image. If you do, be aware that you're hiding that picture from the folks using browsers that don't support JPEG (who are few).

With either GIF or JPEG, your image editor may give you a choice of color model and resolution. Choose RGB as the color model and 72 dpi as the resolution. These settings offer the best balance between appearance and file size.

File Size

In theory, it takes fewer than 10 seconds for a 20KB image file to travel from a server to a browser over a 28.8Kbps Internet connection. But a host of other factors affect the speed with which an image makes it to a visitor's optic nerve, including the disc access speed of the server, processor speed and available memory in the client PC, performance of the browser software, and multitasking speed.

Still, the one-second-per-2KB rule of thumb is a good way to estimate the speed with which your page will materialize on most visitors' screens. Given that, consider how long you want to make visitors wait to see your whole creation. Popular wisdom says a typical Web surfer won't wait even 20 seconds before moving on—and, of course, popular wisdom is usually wrong. Unless visitors are highly motivated, they might depart early if your page takes as few as 10 to 15 seconds to shape up.

Add up the size of your HTML file and all the inline images you plan to add to it. (If you don't know how to do this, you'll learn in Hour 21, "Publishing Your Page.") The recommended maximum is 30KB—such a page appears, images and all, in about 15 seconds or less. Realistically, though, it's wise to try to keep the whole package to around 20KB.

If you find that your page files are too big and slow, the obvious solution is to use fewer images. Other than that, here are some ways to keep your page compact:

- *Use images that take up less area on the page*—Smaller pictures generally mean smaller files.
- *Use fewer colors*—When drawing or painting an image, use as few colors as you can to achieve the desired effect. When working with clip art or scanned images that contain many colors, use an image editor to reduce the number of colors or the size of the *color palette*. Most editors offer options for making color images black and white, or for posterizing a photograph to give it a graphical look. Either of these options tend to reduce file size dramatically and can result in some nifty effects.
- *Create text-only alternative Web pages*—When your page is heavily graphical, create a second set of all the pages beyond the top page, using the same general content but no graphics. On the top page, provide a link to this text-only version of your page. Visitors with text-only browsers and others who simply don't care to wait for images can use the text version instead.
- *Use thumbnails and external media*—Instead of displaying large GIF or JPEG images inline, use inline thumbnails (see Figure 13.8) or text as link sources to external versions of the images. That way, visitors have the option of viewing or ignoring the images. Visitors wait more patiently for images they choose to view.

13

FIGURE 13.8

Thumbnails, small versions of images.

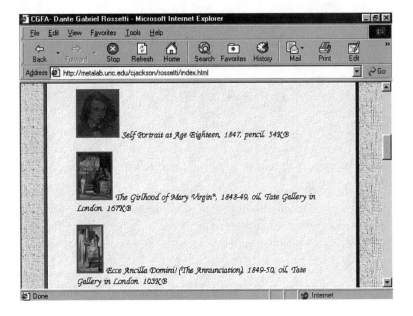

When creating or editing a JPEG picture, you'll have the opportunity to choose a quality setting for the image file.

What's "quality"? Well, JPEG files provide you with the option to sacrifice how good the picture looks in exchange for making the file smaller, so it appears on a visitor's screen more quickly. If you decrease the quality setting (as you learn to do in Hour 14), you may be able to dramatically speed up the performance of the Web page without noticeably degrading the appearance of the picture.

Copyrights

The ease with which images can be scanned, converted, copied, or even captured from the Web itself is a natural invitation to copyright infringement—and, in fact, the Web today is rampant with copyright violations. Smart authors are getting better about inserting copyright notices (see Figure 13.9) prominently on their pages to remind visitors that the work they see is not free for copying.

Regardless of whether it was accompanied by a copyright notice, do not publish any image unless

- You created it yourself by drawing or painting it, or by photographing it with a digital camera. (Note however that publishing a photograph of copyrighted artwork—such as a snapshot of a copyrighted painting in a museum—might violate the copyright.)

- You scanned it from artwork you created or artwork you know to be copyright free.
- You acquired it from a clip art collection whose copyright notice specifically calls the images contained therein "copyright-free" or states clearly that you are authorized to publish the images. (If the copyright notice requires that you label the image with information about its creator, do it.)

If you publish your own artwork on the Web, include on your page a link to a copyright notice in which you reserve the rights to your artwork.

FIGURE 13.9

A copyright notice on a clip art page.

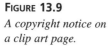

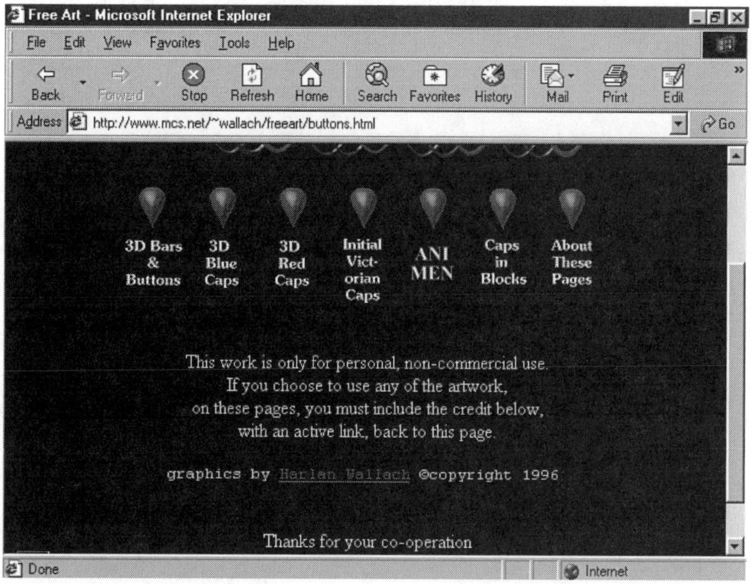

Understanding Interlacing

13

Interlacing your GIF images is one way to speed up the apparent display of images on your page. Interlacing doesn't affect the final look of the image in your page at all and requires no changes to the steps used to insert or format the image in your page. But interlacing does change the way the image materializes on the screen in some browsers.

When it's retrieving a non-interlaced GIF image, a browser typically displays an image placeholder until the entire GIF image has been downloaded, and then it displays the image. If you save your GIF image in interlaced format, browsers that support interlacing can begin to display the image while downloading it. As the image is retrieved, it appears quickly as a blurry rendition of itself and then incrementally sharpens up as more of the image is retrieved.

Interlacing allows visitors to your page to get an idea of what your images look like before they've finished downloading. If the visitor sees what he or she needs to see before the image comes into focus, the visitor can move on without waiting for the finished graphic.

The program you use to create a GIF image might permit you to save the image either as an interlaced GIF or as a non-interlaced GIF. If the program saves only non-interlaced GIF files, you can use a program such as Paint Shop Pro to convert the file to an interlaced GIF.

 In the section titled "Creating Images in Paint Shop Pro" later in this hour, you'll learn how to save a file in interlaced GIF format.

Understanding Low-Res Versions

Another way to give visitors something to look at before the graphics show up is to use your image editor to save an alternate version of the image in a very low resolution (and with a different name than the high-resolution version). You can then define the *low-resolution version* as the image alternative representation when choosing Image Properties for the high-resolution version (as described in Hour 14).

In browsers that support alternative representations, the low-resolution, alternative image displays first, and it appears quickly because decreasing resolution makes the image file smaller. Although the visitor examines the low-res version, the browser loads the full resolution image in the background and prepares it for display. When the full resolution image is ready, it replaces the low resolution version on the page. Like interlacing GIF images, this technique allows visitors to get an idea of what the image represents well before the final image shows up. You can use low-res alternatives for both GIF and JPEG images.

Understanding Transparency

In a GIF image, you have the option to make one color within the image *transparent*. In a Web page, the transparent parts of the image don't show, so whatever is behind the picture—usually a background color or pattern—shows through.

You'll have to deal with transparency more often than you might think. For example, when you paint a picture in most paint programs (including Paint Shop Pro), the file you create contains not only the parts you paint or draw, but also a white or colored background of a particular size. If you insert the picture in a Web page, the background shows up as a colored square or rectangle behind the parts you painted (see Figure 13.10).

However, if you select the image's background color as the transparent color, the background square or rectangle is invisible in a Web page, allowing the page's background to show through.

FrontPage Express offers no built-in control of transparency; you must select the transparent color when you're creating or editing the image. In the next section, you'll learn how to create images in Paint Shop Pro, including how to choose the transparency color. Many other programs also let you select the GIF transparency color. If your favorite paint program does not, you can simply create an image in that program, and then open it in Paint Shop Pro to choose the transparency color.

FIGURE 13.10

In the bottom sample, the image background color is the GIF transparent color, so the page background shows through.

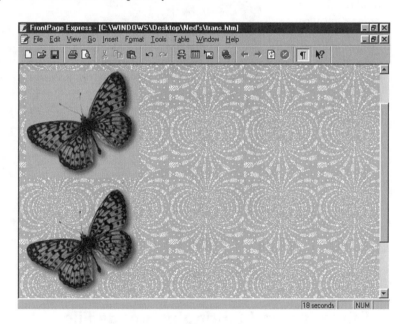

Creating Images in Paint Shop Pro

13

The CD-ROM bundled with this book includes a trial version of Paint Shop Pro, a full-featured paint program you can use to create, edit, and convert images for your Web pages.

In fact, Paint Shop Pro is so sophisticated that I could devote a whole book to it. But you and I have Web pages to write, and truthfully, if I just give you the basics to get you started, you'll discover the rest of Paint Shop Pro pretty easily on your own.

The next several pages explain the basics of using Paint Shop Pro to create, edit, and format images for use in FrontPage Express.

The section that follows assumes you have already installed Paint Shop Pro from the CD-ROM bundled with this book. If you have not, see Appendix A.

Opening Paint Shop Pro

To open Paint Shop Pro in Windows, choose Start, Programs, Paint Shop Pro 5, Paint Shop Pro 5 (see Figure 13.11)

FIGURE **13.11**

Starting Paint Shop Pro 5.

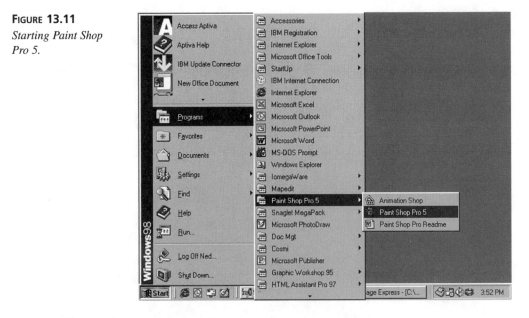

Creating and Editing an Image File

To create a new image, open Paint Shop Pro and start a new image file by clicking the New Image button on the toolbar, or choosing File, New.

The New Image dialog box opens, as shown in Figure 13.12.

In Paint Shop Pro, you don't choose the file type (GIF, JPEG, and so on) when creating the image, you choose the file type when saving it.

In the dialog box, the Width and Height fields define (in pixels) the width and height of the image you will create; you can edit these to your liking or ignore them and adjust the size of the image later. The resolution box lets you raise or lower the resolution of the image; the default choice, 72 dpi, is a good one for creating images that look reasonably good online but don't inhabit very fat files.

> Remember: You want to keep the size of your image files low to make your page appear quickly to visitors online.
>
> The larger the Width and Height, the higher the resolution, and the greater the number of colors, the larger the file. Always use the lowest settings in these categories that give you an image of acceptable quality.

The Image Type drop-down list offers five choices, from an image type that includes only two colors up to 16.7 million colors. Choose 16 colors for simple graphics with few colors, or 256 colors or 256 grays to create more complex, 8-bit images. (GIF files cannot contain more than 256 colors, but JPEG images can.)

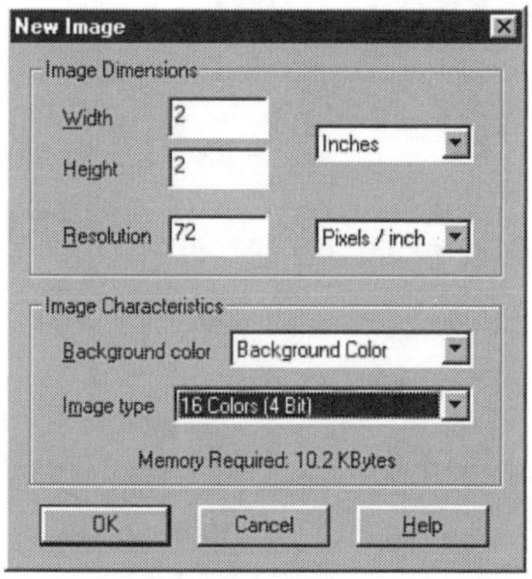

FIGURE 13.12

New Image dialog box.

New Image

Image Dimensions

Width   2
Height   2   Inches ▼

Resolution 72   Pixels / inch ▼

Image Characteristics

Background color Background Color ▼

Image type 16 Colors (4 Bit) ▼

Memory Required: 10.2 KBytes

OK   Cancel   Help

13

Note that after you've made your selections in Width, Height, and Image Type, the dialog box reports the approximate size of the file in bytes ("Memory Required").

After completing the New Image dialog box, click OK to begin painting. An empty window opens (see Figure 13.13), flanked by the toolboxes you will use to paint and edit your new image.

FIGURE **13.13**

New Image window and toolboxes.

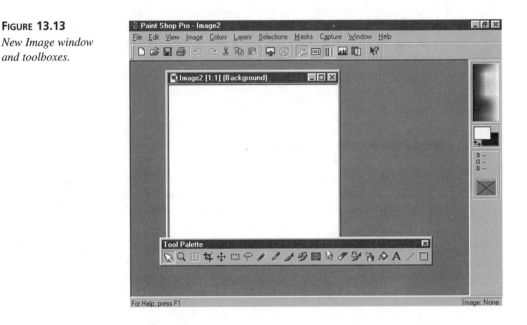

Saving a Picture You've Created in GIF or JPEG Format

Soon after you begin creating your image, you need to save it and choose its file type. The following To Do shows how to save a picture in GIF or JPEG format in Paint Shop Pro.

To Do: Save an image and choose its file type

1. Click the Save button, or choose File, Save (see Figure 13.14). The Save As dialog box appears.

> It's smart to store the image files for a page in the same folder in which you will store and edit the page itself (before publishing it on a server).
>
> At any point between step 1 and step 4, you can use the Save In list at the top of the Save As dialog box to navigate to the folder in which your Web page files are saved. After step 4, the picture file will be saved there.

2. Type a name for the image in the File Name box. Do not type a filename extension (such as .gif); that will be added automatically in step 3.

3. Drop down the Save As Type list (see Figure 13.15) and choose CompuServe Graphics Interchange (GIF) or JPEG from the list. Observe that the appropriate filename extension is added automatically to the filename.

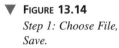

Figure 13.14
Step 1: Choose File, Save.

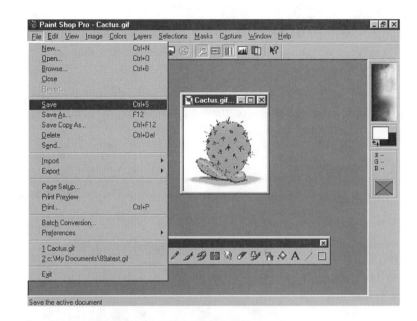

Figure 13.15
Step 3: Choose the file type.

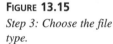

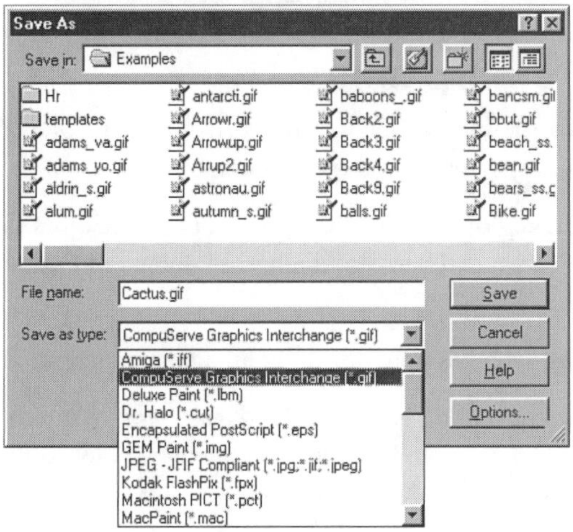

4. Click the Save button on the Save As dialog box.

There are actually two types of GIF file: GIF 87a and GIF 89a. Anytime a graphics program gives you the choice, use GIF89a, which supports interlacing and animation (GIF 87a does not).

13

Choosing GIF Interlacing

When saving a GIF file in Paint Shop Pro, you have the option to save it as an interlaced GIF file.

In Paint Shop Pro's Save As dialog box, after choosing the GIF format in the Save As Type list, click the Options button. On the dialog box that appears, click Version 89a, and then click Interlaced (see Figure 13.16).

 If you have already closed the Save As dialog box and need to reopen it to choose interlacing for a GIF image file, choose File, Save As.

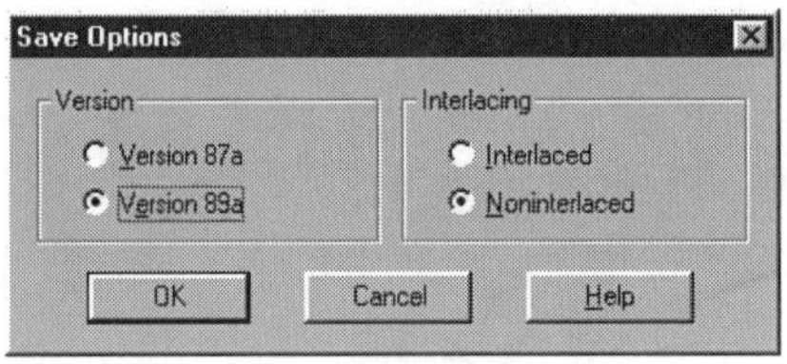

FIGURE **13.16**

Choosing GIF interlacing in Paint Shop Pro.

Save Options		
Version		Interlacing
○ Version 87a		○ Interlaced
● Version 89a		● Noninterlaced
OK	Cancel	Help

Setting GIF Transparency

If you have saved a file in GIF Version 89a format (see the preceding section, "Choosing GIF Interlacing"), you can also add transparency.

To choose transparency options for the GIF file, choose Colors, Set Palette Transparency from Paint Shop Pro's menu bar. The dialog box shown in Figure 13.17 opens. Choose a transparency option:

No transparency—Makes no color in the image transparent; all colors show.

Set the Transparency Value to the Background Color—Automatically determines the current background color and sets the transparency color to match, so that the image background does not show. Use this option to omit backgrounds from images.

 If you make the background color transparent, never use that color in the foreground. Areas of the foreground using the same color as the background will be made transparent as well. (Of course, you can choose to make parts of the foreground transparent to achieve a special effect.)

Set the Transparency Value to the Palette Entry—This option enables you to select a specific color from those in the picture to use as the transparent color.

To test the transparency, click the Proof button on the Set Palette Transparency dialog box. After closing the dialog box, you can also test transparency by choosing Colors, View Palette Transparency from the menu bar.

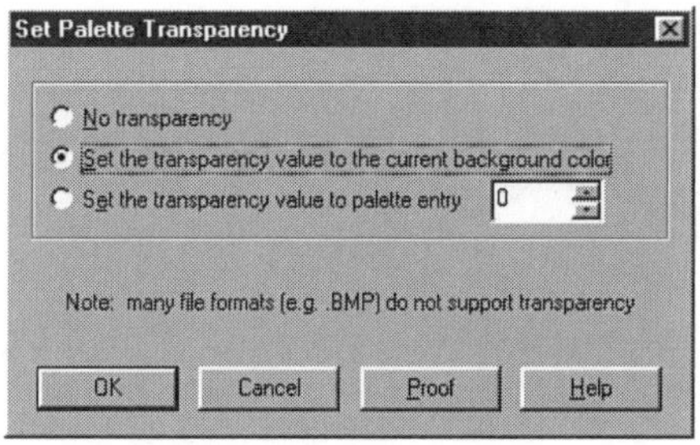

FIGURE 13.17

Choosing GIF transparency options in Paint Shop Pro.

Summary

As you'll see in the next hour, getting your pictures into your pages is pretty simple. Nearly everything that can go wrong with pictures happens because there's something wrong with the file—wrong type, wrong size, and so on. But that won't happen to you now that you know the rules.

Q&A

Q I see that some Web authoring programs, including FrontPage Express, can be used to change the size and other aspects of a picture. Should I do my "raw" image editing in a graphics editor like Paint Shop Pro, and then fine-tune the picture in my Web authoring program?

A Web authoring programs vary in how well they edit pictures, and some work very well. But as a rule, it's best to make a picture exactly the size, shape, and color you want it to be in your graphics editor, and then insert it in a page. Use the Web authoring tool only to adjust the picture's position on the page.

Sometimes, using the Web authoring program to edit other aspects of a picture can deliver unwanted results. For example, if you change the size of a GIF with a transparent background within a Web authoring program, often the transparency information is lost in the process. Such anomalies happen when the Web authoring program does not actually change the image file, but rather applies HTML coding around the picture that modifies the way a browser displays it.

13

HOUR 14

Adding Pictures (and Picture Backgrounds)

Pictures are like salt: Add the right amount in the right way, and your Web page becomes tastier—but add too much, and your visitors will wind up logging off the Internet to go get a soda.

In this hour, you'll learn not only how to add images (and image backgrounds) to your pages and to control the appearance of those images, but also how to use images wisely, for the best effects. At the end of the hour, you will be able to answer the following questions:

- How do I insert images into my Web pages?
- Can I control the alignment, spacing, and even the size of the images?
- How do I create "alternatives" to images, for those whose browsers can't display pictures?
- How do I make an image into a link?
- How do I add a background image?
- Can I create fancy bullets for lists and snazzy horizontal lines?

Inserting a GIF or JPEG Image in FrontPage Express

Before beginning the steps to insert an image in a Web page, first prepare your image file or files as discussed in Hour 13, "Getting Pictures for Your Page." Be sure that the image file is stored in the same folder as the Web page file in which you will insert it. (If it isn't, move or copy it there before beginning the To Do.)

> If the image you want to insert is not in GIF or JPEG format, you can still insert it.
>
> In step 3 of the following To Do, click Browse. In the dialog box that opens, open the Files Of Type list and select the type of file in which the picture is currently stored. (If the file's type is not listed in the Files Of Type list, FrontPage Express cannot use it.) You can then use the dialog box's Look In list to navigate to the folder containing the picture and select it.
>
> When you next save the page, FrontPage Express will offer to convert the file to GIF and save the new GIF file in the same folder as the Web page. (See the section titled "Automatically Getting the Right File Type, Right Folder," later in this hour.)

To Do: Put an image in a page

1. Click in your page at the spot where you want to insert the image.

2. Click the Insert Image button on the Standard toolbar.

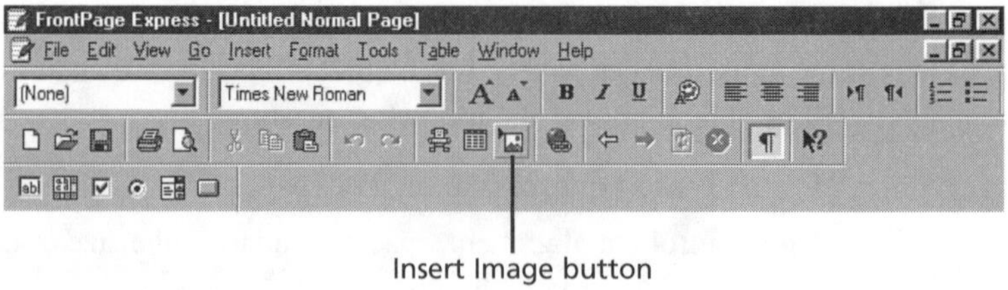

FIGURE 14.1

Step 2: Click Insert Image.

Insert Image button

3. Type the filename of the image.

4. Click OK.

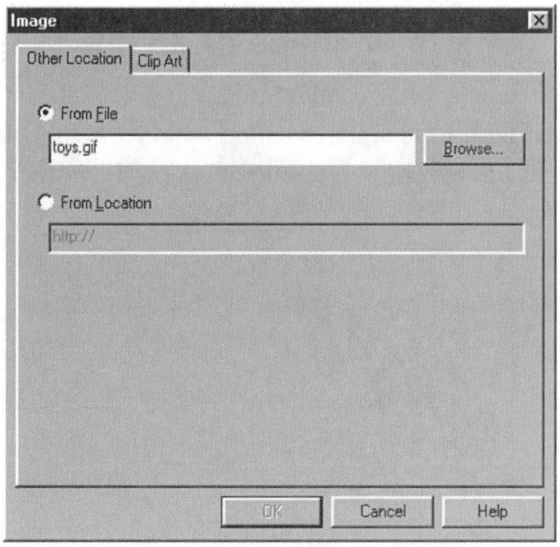

▼

FIGURE 14.2

Step 3: Type the image filename.

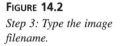

Image	☒

Other Location | Clip Art

(•) From File

toys.gif   Browse...

( ) From Location

http://

OK   Cancel   Help

▲

> To move an image after inserting it, just point to it, click and hold, drag to the new spot, and release.
>
> You can also move an image with cut and paste, just like text. Click the image to select it, click the Cut button, click in the new spot, and click the Paste button.

Changing the Dimensions (Size and Shape) of the Image

From right within FrontPage Express, you can change the size of an image, and you can change its shape, stretching or squeezing (and distorting) it, as you learn to do shortly. But first...

As a rule, you get better results if you choose the size and shape of the image in the application used to create it, or in a good image-editing program (such as Paint Shop Pro), rather than in FrontPage Express or most other Web authoring programs.

Why? Well, FrontPage Express can't really change the dimensions of an image. Instead, it applies tags to the HTML file that browsers use to resize the image when displaying it. A browser is not as sophisticated a graphics scalar as a real image-editing program, and the likelihood of unattractive "artifacts" in the scaled image (such as streaks through the image) or a loss of the transparency of a transparent GIF file is high.

14

With that caveat, the following To Do shows how to change the size and/or shape of an image in FrontPage Express, when doing so seems prudent to you.

To Do: Change the size or shape of an image

1. Click the image to select it. When an image is selected, a temporary border appears around it, dotted with little squares called *handles*. (Observe that some handles are on the corners of the border, while others are on the border lines.)

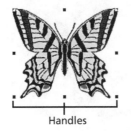

FIGURE 14.3
Step 1: Click the image to select it and display its handles.

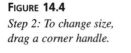
Handles

2. To change the size of an image (without changing or distorting its overall shape), click and hold on any corner handle, and drag to resize the image.

FIGURE 14.4
Step 2: To change size, drag a corner handle.

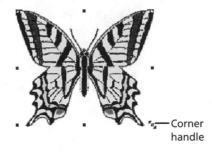
Corner handle

> Dragging a corner handle *toward* the center of the image reduces (shrinks) the image, while dragging a corner handle *away* from the center enlarges the image.

3. To stretch or squash the image vertically (see Figure 14.5), drag a top or bottom handle.

4. To widen or narrow the image horizontally, drag a side handle.

FIGURE **14.5**

Step 3: To change shape, drag a handle that's not on a corner.

5. To deselect the image when finished changing its size or shape, click anywhere in the page except on the image.

> If you decide you don't like the way you changed shape or size immediately after making the change, you can easily restore the image to its previous size and shape by clicking the Undo button.
>
> Later on, after it's too late to use Undo, you can restore an image to its original size and shape at any time. Right-click the image and choose Image Properties from the menu that appears. On the Appearance tab of the Image Properties dialog box, clear the check box next to Specify Size, and then click OK.
>
> To learn more about the options on the Image Properties dialog box, see "Choosing an Image's Layout Options and Other Properties," later in this hour.

Using the Same Image Multiple Times

If you want to use the same image multiple times in a page, you don't need multiple copies of the image with different filenames.

A single copy of an image file on a Web server can appear in the same page—or in several pages—as many times as you like. Just choose the same filename when inserting each copy of the image, or use copy and paste to insert multiple copies of the same image. This technique is especially useful when you use graphical bullets in a list (see "Inserting Fancy Bullets and Rules," later in this hour).

To use copy and paste, insert the image one time, click it to select it, and then click the Copy button on the Standard toolbar. Click in the page where you want the copy to go, and then click the Paste button.

14

You can paste as many copies as you like without having to click Copy again. Until the next time you click Copy, the image stays in the Windows Clipboard, ready to be pasted anywhere you want it.

Deleting an Image

To delete an image, click it once to select it, and then press the Delete key or click the Cut button on the toolbar.

Note that deleting an image merely removes it from the Web page—the file itself is not deleted; it remains on your hard drive to be used another time.

Choosing an Image's Layout Options and Other Properties

After you've inserted an image, you can change its appearance in a variety of ways, all by choosing options on the Image Properties dialog box (see Figure 14.6).

To open the Image Properties dialog box, click the Image to select it, and then choose Edit, Image Properties. (You can also open this dialog box by right-clicking the image and then choosing Image Properties from the menu that appears.)

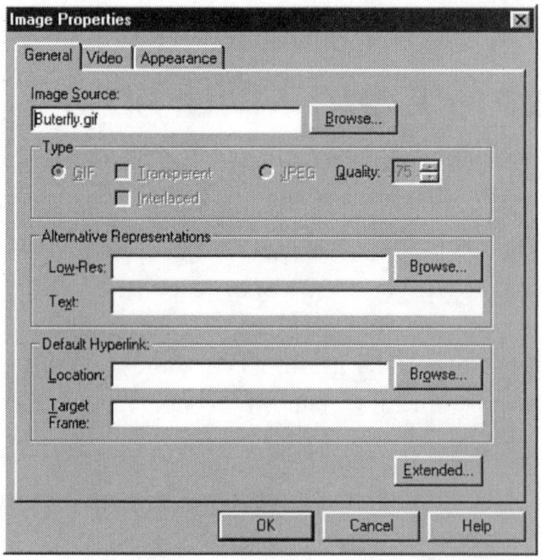

FIGURE 14.6

Use the Image Properties dialog box to change an image's role in the layout of a page.

The next several pages describe ways you can use the Image Properties dialog box to change a picture's appearance.

 The Video tab of the Image Properties dialog box is used only for controlling the display of inline video clips. See Hour 15, "Snazzing Up Your Page with Sound, Video, and Special Effects," to learn more about the Video tab.

Choosing a Picture's Alignment, Spacing, and Borders

On the Image Properties dialog box's Appearance tab (see Figure 14.7), you can choose from among a variety of options that govern the image's position and appearance within the layout of the page.

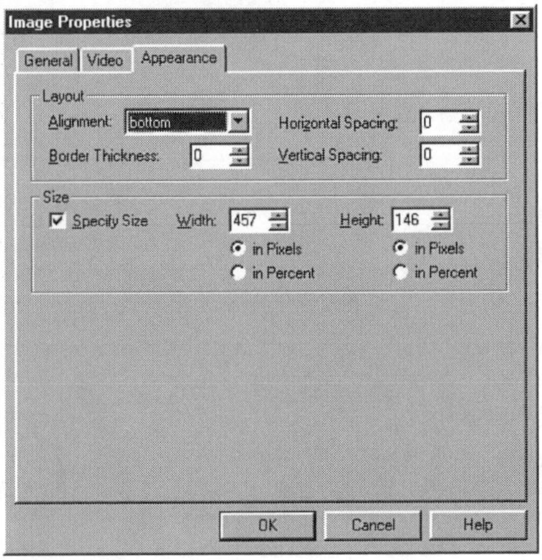

FIGURE **14.7**

On the Appearance tab of the Image Properties dialog box, you control the picture's role in the layout of the page.

Controlling Alignment

A picture's alignment describes its position on the page, and also how it relates to any text adjacent to it.

By default, a picture aligns to the left side of the page (just like left-aligned text). The first line of any text immediately following the picture appears to the right of the picture, near its bottom. If the text runs for more than one line (without an intervening paragraph break, all lines after the first line appear underneath the image. This default alignment is called *bottom* alignment (see Figure 14.8).

14

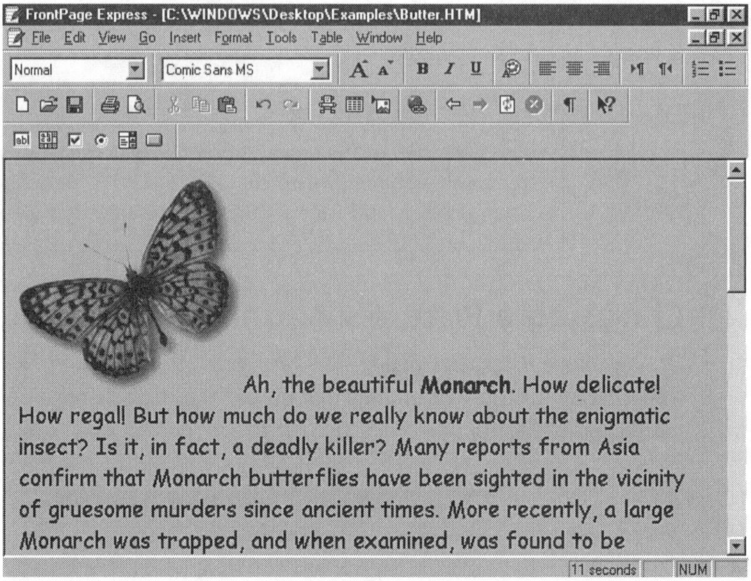

FIGURE **14.8**

The default alignment for images, known as bottom.

FrontPage Express - [C:\WINDOWS\Desktop\Examples\Butter.HTM]

File Edit View Go Insert Format Tools Table Window Help

Normal   Comic Sans MS

Ah, the beautiful **Monarch**. How delicate! How regal! But how much do we really know about the enigmatic insect? Is it, in fact, a deadly killer? Many reports from Asia confirm that Monarch butterflies have been sighted in the vicinity of gruesome murders since ancient times. More recently, a large Monarch was trapped, and when examined, was found to be

11 seconds   NUM

To understand alignment options, you need to understand what the "baseline" of text is. The baseline is the line the letters sit on when you write them. Most letters appear entirely above that line, but a few—such as lowercase j and y—have descenders that drop down below the baseline.

The default, bottom alignment, aligns the baseline with the bottom of the image, so that any descenders actually drop lower than the bottom of the image.

The alignment options beginning with the letters abs (short for *absolute*) ignore the baseline, and align the picture with the exact bottom or middle of the text instead. For example, absbottom aligns the bottom of the image with the real bottom of the text, so that the descenders do not drop below the bottom of the image.

To change a picture's alignment, choose from the options in the Alignment list on the Appearance tab. The other common choices (besides bottom) are:

- middle   The first line of text appears to the right of the image, with the baseline of the text aligned to the vertical center of the image. Any lines after the first line appear underneath the image.

- top   The first line of text appears to the right of the top of the image, with the top of the text aligned to the top of the image. Any lines after the first line appear underneath the image.

- **absbottom** Just like `bottom`, except that the bottom of the image is aligned to the absolute bottom of the text, not the baseline.

- **absmiddle** Just like `middle`, except that the vertical center of the image is aligned to the absolute middle of the height of the text, not the baseline.

- **texttop** The first line of text appears to the right of the top of the image. The top of the tallest letter is aligned with the very top of the image. Any lines after the first line appear underneath the image.

The bottom two alignment options, Left and Right, are special "wrapping" options. Unlike all of the other options, which can put only the first line of text alongside the image, right and left allow multiple lines of text to appear alongside a picture.

- **left** Text wraps alongside the image, with the image to the left of the text (text on the right).

- **right** Text wraps alongside the image, with the image to the right of the text (text on the left). See Figure 14.9.

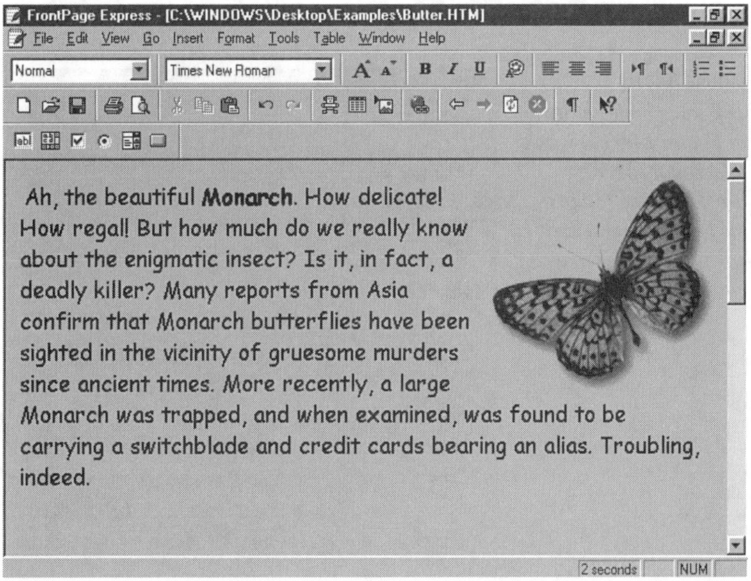

FIGURE 14.9

Left alignment and right alignment (shown here) allow multiple lines of text to wrap alongside an image

FrontPage Express - [C:\WINDOWS\Desktop\Examples\Butter.HTM]

File Edit View Go Insert Format Tools Table Window Help

Ah, the beautiful **Monarch**. How delicate! How regal! But how much do we really know about the enigmatic insect? Is it, in fact, a deadly killer? Many reports from Asia confirm that Monarch butterflies have been sighted in the vicinity of gruesome murders since ancient times. More recently, a large Monarch was trapped, and when examined, was found to be carrying a switchblade and credit cards bearing an alias. Troubling, indeed.

2 seconds | NUM

All of the alignment options are represented reasonably accurately when you view a page in FrontPage Express, but sometimes the representation is not 100 percent accurate. Always evaluate your alignment formatting by viewing the page in a Web browser.

14

Controlling Spacing and Borders

To add a border around a picture, or to change the amount of space between the image and what's around it, use the Border Thickness, Horizontal Spacing, and Vertical Spacing options on the Layout section of the Appearance tab.

- To add a black border all around the image (see Figure 14.10), enter a number of pixels for the thickness of the border in Border Thickness.

> Typing 4 in Border Thickness makes a nice, bold border like the one shown. A lower number makes a finer border; a higher number, a thicker one. A border thicker than about 8 pixels is probably overkill.

- To increase the space between the top and bottom of the image and adjacent text, tables, or other objects, enter a number of pixels in Vertical Spacing.

- To increase the space between the sides of the image and adjacent text, tables, or other objects, enter a number of pixels in Horizontal Spacing.

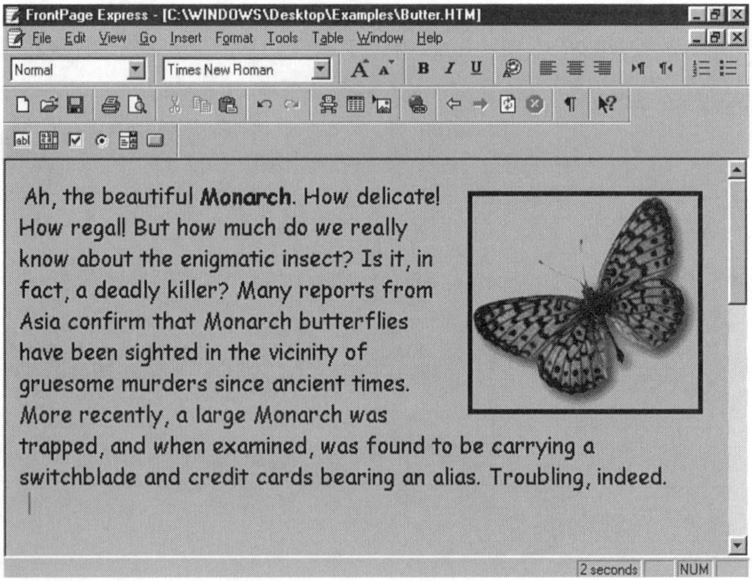

FIGURE 14.10

The same page shown in Figure 14.9 but with additional space around image (30 pixels left and right) and a 4-pixel border indicated.

> FrontPage Express - [C:\WINDOWS\Desktop\Examples\Butter.HTM]
>
> File Edit View Go Insert Format Tools Table Window Help
>
> Normal   Times New Roman
>
> Ah, the beautiful **Monarch**. How delicate! How regal! But how much do we really know about the enigmatic insect? Is it, in fact, a deadly killer? Many reports from Asia confirm that Monarch butterflies have been sighted in the vicinity of gruesome murders since ancient times. More recently, a large Monarch was trapped, and when examined, was found to be carrying a switchblade and credit cards bearing an alias. Troubling, indeed.
>
> 2 seconds   NUM

Alternative Representations

You can help some visitors cope with your images through two special options on the General tab of the Image Properties dialog box (see Figure 14.11):

- *Low-res*—When you plan to use an especially large image file in a page, you may want to supply the filename of another, smaller version of the same image file here. For example, if the page features a very large GIF file—say, 100KB or more—you could use your graphics program to save a version of the same picture that you've reduced to 10KB by decreasing its resolution or other properties. A browser always displays the picture listed in low-res first, and then continues to download the main image. The low-res version gives the visitor something to look at while waiting.

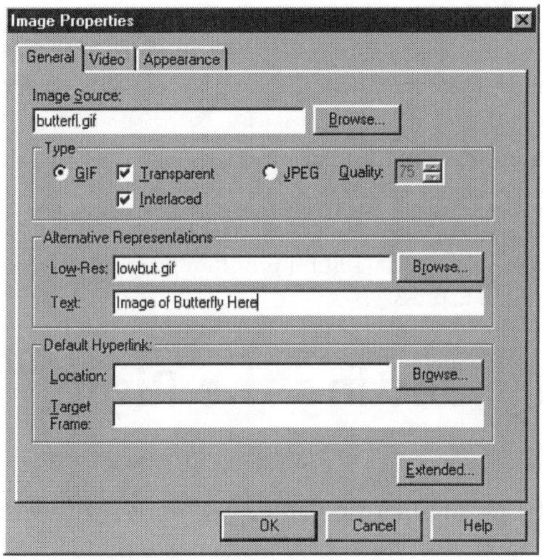

FIGURE 14.11

You can use the Alternative Representations section of the General tab to help some visitors with slow connections or non-graphical browsers.

Low-res versions aren't all that important these days. That's because most folks use pretty fast Internet connections, and because interlaced GIF and progressive JPEG pictures give folks something to look at while the image loads anyway.

If you plan to show an image that's so large that you think a low-res alternative is necessary, I recommend two other solutions instead:

- Try to reduce the size of the picture file. You can do this in your image-editing program by reducing the resolution or number of colors, or by reducing the overall area of the image. If the file is a JPEG file, you can also reduce its size by reducing the Quality setting (see Hour 13, "Getting Pictures for Your Page").

- Supply the big image file, not as part of the layout of the page, but as *external media*. In the page itself, use a thumbnail version of the picture as the source for the link that displays the big picture. See Hour 15.

14

- *Text*—Here you can enter the text you want to appear in place of the graphic in browsers that do not support graphics. Try to supply informative text to replace the idea that was originally communicated by the image. Also, many browsers that support text alternatives will display an image placeholder, something like "<image>", if you don't supply a text alternative representation. The text alternative is not only more informative in such browsers, but also better looking.

Also on the General tab of the Image Properties dialog box, you'll see a Type section containing options for choosing interlacing and transparency (if the image is a GIF 89a file) and JPEG quality setting (if the image is a JPEG file).

These options do not work especially well. I advise leaving these settings alone.

If you want to fuss with GIF interlacing and transparency or JPEG quality, do so in your image-editing program prior to inserting the picture in FrontPage Express.

Automatically Getting the Right File Type, Right Folder

Anytime you insert a picture that's not already GIF or JPEG, FrontPage not only offers to convert the file, but also offers to save the converted file in the same folder as the Web page. I recommend always taking advantage of this feature when it pops into action to keep your pictures together with the Web page file and to make quick work of file conversion.

The first time you save the page after inserting the image, FrontPage Express displays a message like the one in Figure 14.12, offering to "Save this Image to a File." If you click Yes on the dialog box, the converted image file is saved in the same folder as the Web page file. (Its new filename is the same as the original, except that the filename extension is changed to .gif.) Note that all formats are converted to GIF (never JPEG), and JPEG files are not converted at all. (And that's fine.)

FIGURE **14.12**

*When you save a
file containing an
image that's not in
GIF or JPEG format,
FrontPage Express
offers to fix that
situation.*

> If, since your last save, you've inserted multiple images that require conver-
> sion and copying to the Web page's folder, you can click the Yes to All but-
> ton on the dialog box shown in Figure 14.12.
>
> Yes to All instructs FrontPage Express to automatically convert all non-
> GIF/non-JPEG files to GIF and to save all converted image files in the same
> folder as the Web page without prompting you again.

Entering Images in Table Cells

You put an image in a table cell (see Hour 8, "Organizing Text with Tables and Rules")
exactly as you put one in a page. The only difference is that you must first click in the
cell to position the edit cursor there. You can then click the Insert Image button and insert
the picture exactly as you would anywhere else in a Web page.

FIGURE **14.13**

*To insert a picture in a
table cell, click in the
cell right before click-
ing Insert Image.*

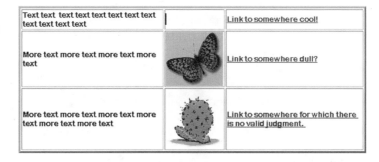

Inserting Fancy Bullets and Rules

No doubt you've seen some highfalutin' pages that feature cool, multicolored graphical
bullets and horizontal lines. These are not actual bullets and lines of the kind you create
with the Bulleted List button and Insert Horizontal Line. Instead, they're just inline
images that *look* like bullets and lines (see Figure 14.14).

14

FIGURE **14.14**
Fancy bullets and rules are just image files used in place of horizontal lines and list bullets.

FrontPage Express - [C:\WINDOWS\Desktop\Ned's\nedslumber.htm]

File Edit View Go Insert Format Tools Table Window Help

Normal   Times New Roman

*"If we ain't **got it**, you doesn't **needs it!**"*

XXXXXXXXXXXXXXXXXXXXXXXXXXXXXXXXXXXXXXXXXXXXXXXXXXXXX

Contents

  Current Lumber Projects
Hot Lumber List
Employees (Lumberjacks)
Contact Ned

Current Projects

6 seconds   NUM

Line-type images, sometimes called *bars,* are simply inserted between paragraphs. The bullets are inserted before individual lines of text, using any paragraph style other than List. (If you use List, you get your cool bullets *plus* the List's bullets or numbers. Icky.)

> To get the best results when inserting a bullet image next to a line of text, align the image using `middle` or `absmiddle` alignment.

> You'll find a great selection of GIF image files for fancy bullets and rules on the CD-ROM at the back of this book.

Using an Image as a Link

As you learned in Hour 9, "Understanding Links," every link has two parts: the *link source* (the thing a visitor sees and clicks) and the URL (or local path and filename) to which the browser goes when the link source is clicked.

Making an image into a link is just a matter of attaching the URL to the image. In fact, it's exactly like creating a text link; the only difference is that you select an image, rather than a block of text, before clicking the Create or Edit Hyperlink button.

To Do: Make an image into a link

1. Click the image you want to make into a link to select it.

2. Click the Create or Edit Hyperlink button on the Standard toolbar.

3. Use the dialog box to create any of the types of links you learned to create in Hour 11, "More Ways to Link"—a link to a Web page, email address, bookmark, and so on.

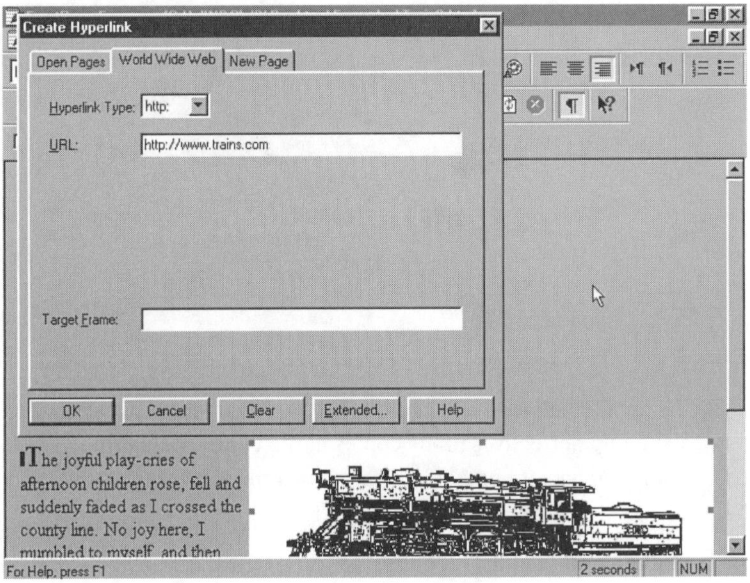

FIGURE 14.15

Step 3: Fill in the Create or Edit Hyperlink dialog box for an image link exactly as you would for a text link.

4. Click OK.

Adding a Picture Background

As an alternative to a background color (which you learned to add in Hour 5, "Choosing a Title, Text Colors, and Other Page Basics"), you can apply as a background a *tiled image*, an image file (GIF or JPEG) repeated across the entire background.

When this image has been designed carefully to match up perfectly with its mates at all four corners, the tiling creates a seamless "texture" effect, as if one enormous image covered the background (see Figure 14.16). Fortunately, the effect is created out of only one small image; accessing an image file large enough to cover a page would choke most Internet connections.

14

You'll find a selection of image files for background textures on the CD-ROM at the back of this book.

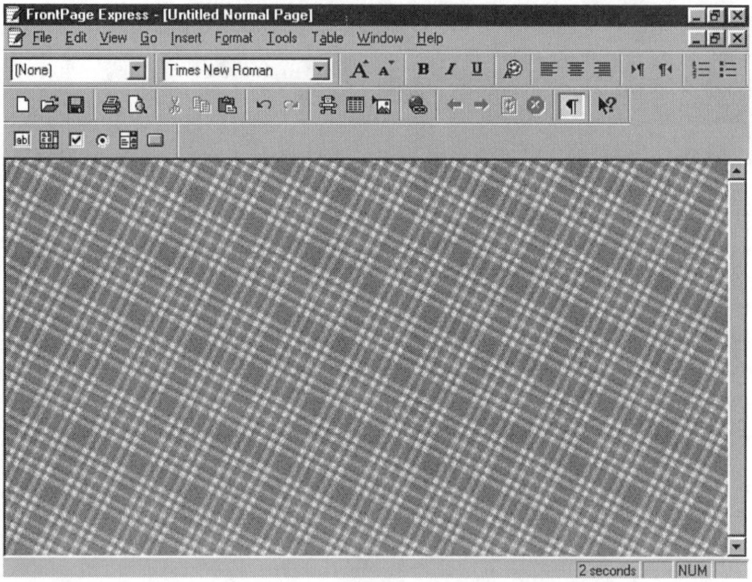

FIGURE **14.16**

A tiled background texture.

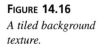

As an alternative to a background texture, you can choose to tile an image that doesn't match up perfectly with its copies at the edges. Using this technique, you can create some fun background effects, as shown in Figure 14.17.

Finally, you can use as a background a single, large image file that covers the entire page background (and thus requires no tiling). Be careful when using this technique to use an image with a low resolution and few colors to keep the image size small and the page's appearance fast.

Most "full page" background images do not actually cover the full background; rather, they often take the form over very tall, narrow bars, like the one shown in Figure 14.18. Because the bar is so tall, the browser does not tile it and left-aligns it on the page. The file itself is reasonably small (the one shown in Figure 14.18 is only about 2KB), yet it lends a graphical flair to the whole page without obscuring text.

FIGURE 14.17

A fun background made of a tiled image.

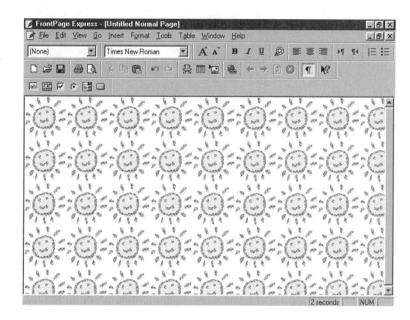

Tiled background images automatically supercede a background color, because they cover the whole background.

But if you use a non-tiled image like the one in Figure 14.18, and the image does not happen to fill the background, you may use a background color along with it. The background color affects only the portion of the background not covered by the image.

Be careful with backgrounds. If you don't choose carefully, you can wind up making your text illegible, or at least hard on the eyes.

Use custom text colors (see Hour 5) to contrast the text with the background. Use light colors to stand out against dark backgrounds, and dark colors to stand out against light backgrounds.

Even with those precautions, a tiled-image background is usually too much when seen behind a page with lots of text on it. A way around this is to use a snazzy tile background behind your logo or brief text on a top page, and then switch to a solid color or no background on text-heavy pages to which the top page links.

14

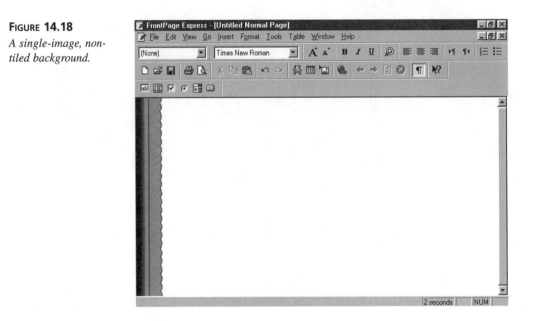

FIGURE **14.18**

A single-image, non-tiled background.

To Do: Add a picture background

1. Store the GIF image you want for a background in the same folder as the page in which you want to use it.

2. In FrontPage Express, open the page to which you want to add a background, and click Format, Background.

FIGURE **14.19**

Step 2: Choose Format, Background.

3. Click the check box next to Background Image to place a check mark there.

4. Click in the box beneath Background Image, and type the filename of the GIF image you want to use. (Or click Browse to navigate to it.)

▼   5. Click OK.

FIGURE **14.20**

Steps 2 and 3: Check background Image, and enter the name of the image file.

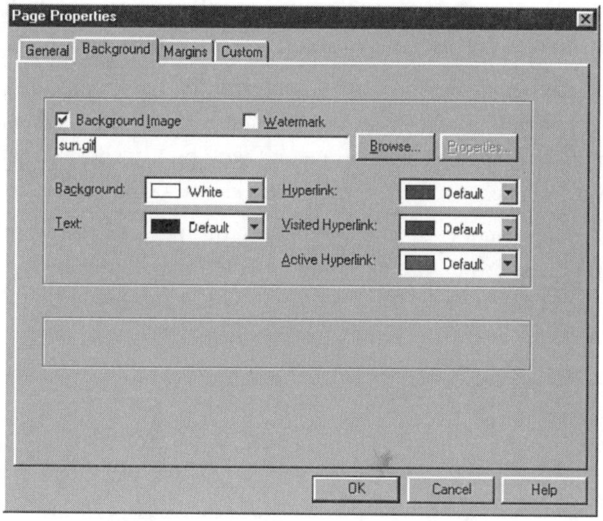

An image background automatically supercedes a background color. If you create an image background, any selection you may have made for background color is irrelevant.

Summary

In the cookie that is a Web page, images are the chocolate chips. And as we all know, the best cookie strikes just the right chip-to-cookie ratio—too many chips is as bad as none at all. (Replace with your favorite ratio-balancing analogy: pizza crust:cheese, peanut butter:jelly, RAM:processor speed, longevity:fun, and so on.)

The issue is not just whether you use graphics, or how many you use, but *why* you use them. Do the images add something useful to your page—like photos of people the page is by or about, or images of products and places described—or are they mere decoration? An image or two added for the sake of style is worthwhile, but only if the image succeeds in actually enhancing style. If it seems like a generic image dropped there merely for the sake of having an image, dump it. Dress your page with careful text formatting, the natural beauty of solid organization, and strong writing.

14

Q&A

Q **You sure are a downer about images. But on the coolest, award-winning pages out there, I see lots of graphics. Aren't you being a little puritanical here?**

A Perhaps—and yes, there are some great, highly graphical sites out there. But for every slickly produced, award-winning site, there are a hundred others that overuse pointless graphics or obliterate text with poorly chosen background textures. The award winners use all their graphics smartly, and for a purpose.

My point is not to discourage the use of images. I just want you to ask yourself the right questions before dumping any old image on your page. You can bet the award winners do.

HOUR **15**

Snazzing Up Your Page with Sound, Video, and Special Effects

At the simplest level, adding a little multimedia zip to your pages is extremely easy, requiring mostly Web authoring skills you already possess. But beyond a few simple tricks, such as background sounds, Web multimedia gets pretty heavy, and quickly escapes the scope of this book.

So, this hour offers two kinds of new wisdom: First, it shows how you can quickly add a little sizzle to your pages through some easy FrontPage Express techniques. Then it introduces you to the big fat hairy world of external media, beginning (but by no means completing) your Web multimedia education without going so far as to blow any of your circuit breakers.

At the end of this hour, you'll be able to answer the following questions:

- How do I add the few types of inline multimedia available (such as inline video and background sounds)?

- How does "external media" work and what can I do with it?
- How do I choose external media types to serve either the widest possible Web audience or a tightly targeted audience?
- How do I insert links to external media in my Web pages?

> There's one important kind of multimedia left out of this hour, one that's well within your capabilities—animated GIF pictures. You learn all about creating and using animated GIFs in Hour 16, "Creating Your Own Animations."

Adding Background Sound

Background sound is a sound clip that plays automatically when the visitor arrives at the page. You can add background sound to a page in FrontPage Express and choose whether that sound should play once, several times, or over and over forever.

> At this writing, background sounds are supported in Internet Explorer, but not in Netscape Navigator. Nothing bad happens when someone uses Navigator to view a page with a background sound—they just don't hear it.
>
> So make sure your background sound doesn't contain anything essential to the page, such as a spoken welcome that's not repeated in regular text.

Finding Sound Clips

Before you can add a sound, you need to have a sound file to use.

A variety of different sound file formats are used on the Web (as you learn later in this hour; see "About External Media"). But for Windows users, the easiest type to deal with is .wav, known as *Wave*.

Wave files (and other popular sound file formats, such as .au and .mid), are available in sound clip libraries online or on CD-ROM. You can download sounds to your PC, and then use them in your Web pages as background sounds or as external media files visitors can choose to play by clicking a link.

You can use Web search tools to search for archives of sound clips in much the same way you search for clip art.

But more often, sound clips are found on pages to which the sound is related. For example, to find sound clips from your favorite TV show, you need to find a site about the TV show.

Using your PC's sound card and a microphone (or the sound card's audio inputs), you can also record your own Wave files. Most sound cards include their own audio recording program; alternatively, you can use Windows 98's own built-in sound recorder by clicking Start, and then choosing Programs, Accessories, Entertainment, Sound Recorder (see Figure 15.1). (In Windows 95, you open Sound Recorder by choosing Programs, Accessories, Multimedia, Sound Recorder.)

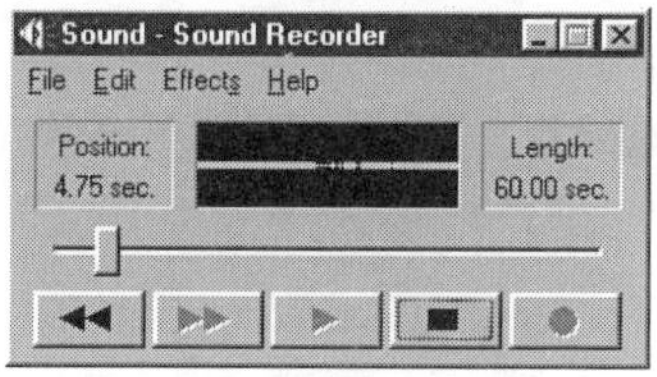

FIGURE 15.1

You can use Windows Sound Recorder and a microphone attached to your sound card to record Wave files for use as background sounds.

After finding or creating your Wave file, you can make it the background sound for your page, as described in the following To Do.

To Do: Add a background sound

1. Store your Wave file in the same folder where the Web page is stored.

2. In FrontPage Express, open the page you want to add the sound to, click File, and choose Page Properties.

3. Make sure the General tab (shown in Figure 15.2) is selected.

4. In the Background Sound section of the dialog box (see in Figure 15.3), click in the box labeled Location, and type the filename of the Wave file.

5. In Loop, type the number of times you want the sound to repeat before stopping, or check the check box next to Forever to make the sound play over and over for as long as the visitor views the page.

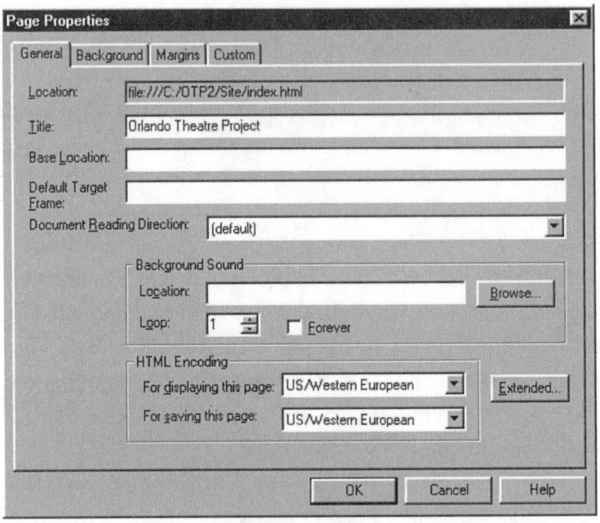

▼ FIGURE **15.2**

Step 3: Select the General tab of the Page Properties dialog box.

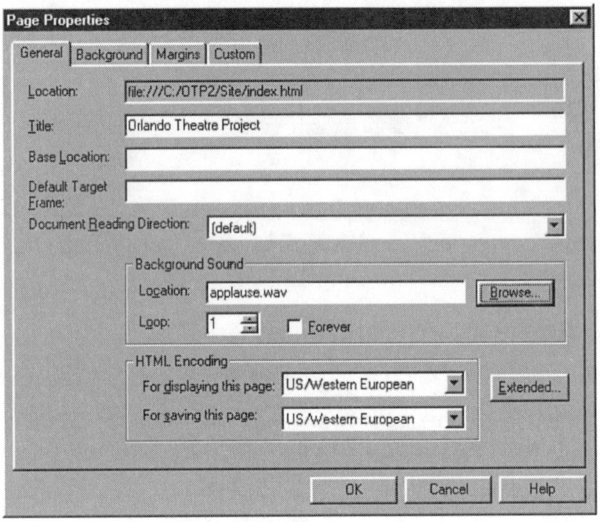

Page Properties

General | Background | Margins | Custom

Location: file:///C:/OTP2/Site/index.html

Title: Orlando Theatre Project

Base Location:

Default Target Frame:

Document Reading Direction: (default)

Background Sound

Location: Browse...

Loop: 1   ☐ Forever

HTML Encoding

For displaying this page: US/Western European   Extended...

For saving this page: US/Western European

OK   Cancel   Help

FIGURE **15.3**

Step 4 and 5: Supply the wave filename, and choose Looping options.

Page Properties

General | Background | Margins | Custom

Location: file:///C:/OTP2/Site/index.html

Title: Orlando Theatre Project

Base Location:

Default Target Frame:

Document Reading Direction: (default)

Background Sound

Location: applause.wav   Browse...

Loop: 1   ☐ Forever

HTML Encoding

For displaying this page: US/Western European   Extended...

For saving this page: US/Western European

OK   Cancel   Help

▲   6. Click OK.

> FrontPage Express can't play background sounds. View the page in Internet Explorer to hear the sound. (Make sure your speakers are switched on!)

Creating a Times Square-Style Animated Marquee

15

 NEW TERM A *marquee* is a short slice of animated text that scrolls through a Web page. The effect is like the scrolling marquee on the *New York Times* building in Manhattan, the one people in movies are always watching for bulletins during a crisis. Marquees are a fast way to add a little action to a page, and are usually used for text you really want the visitor to notice.

> At this writing, scrolling marquees are enabled by a Microsoft extension, and are supported in Internet Explorer but not in Netscape Navigator or in other browsers. Navigator users will see your marquee text as regular, static text on the page.

To Do: Insert a marquee

1. Click the page at the spot where you want to insert your scrolling marquee.

2. Click Insert, and then choose Marquee.

3. Type the text you want to see scrolling along.

FIGURE 15.4

Step 3: Type the text for the marquee.

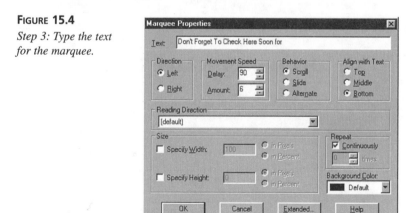

4. You may skip ahead to step 5 to use the default options for Direction, Speed, and so on, or make any changes to these settings you want (see in Figure 15.5).

▼ FIGURE **15.5**

Step 4: Choose options for direction, speed, and so on.

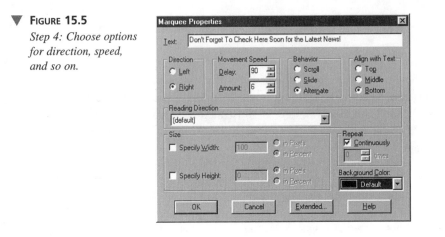

5. Click OK. The marquee text appears in FrontPage Express as a fixed, ordinary heading.

6. View the page in Internet Explorer to see the marquee scroll as it will for visitors who use Internet Explorer.

FIGURE **15.6**

Step 6: View the page in Internet Explorer to see the marquee in action.

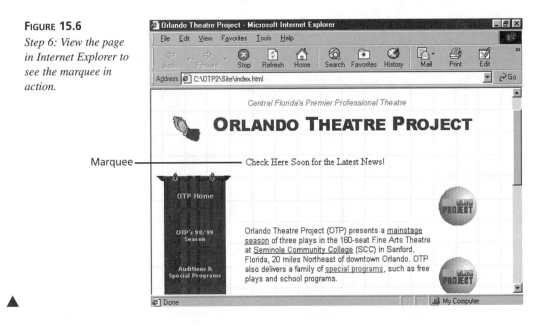

To change the options or text for a scrolling marquee, just double-click the marquee to open the Marquee Properties box, change whatever you like, and then click OK.

15

Inserting an Inline Video Clip

OK, I'll tell you how to add an inline video clip (a video clip that appears within the page layout, like an image), because FrontPage Express provides such a handy way to do it. But that doesn't mean I recommend it...

Here are the problems, in no particular order: 1) The clips work only when the page is viewed through Internet Explorer, not in Navigator or in any other browser; 2) An inline clip may dramatically slow down the performance of your page, annoying visitors; and 3) A nice inline picture or animation (see Hour 16) really makes more sense. Save video for external presentation (see "About External Media," later in this hour).

That said, I know you... There's just no holding you back, is there? The following To Do shows how to add an inline video clip in FrontPage Express.

Before you insert a video clip, you must have one on hand, in AVI format (using the filename extension .avi). You can find such clips online in clip art libraries (see Appendix B, "Online Resources for Web Authors"), or you can create your own AVI files if you have a video capture card in your PC. You can plug a camcorder or VCR into a port on the capture card, play a tape in the VCR or camcorder, and use the card's software to save the incoming video in an AVI file.

Keep in mind that video files are very large. A mere minute can take up several megabytes, which takes up a big chunk of your allotted space on the Web server and also forces long waits for those with slower Internet connections. The video capture software usually offers options for keeping the file size down, at the cost of making the video clip smaller (in the onscreen area) and fuzzier.

If you want a quick way to find an AVI file to use for practice (without downloading one from the Web), use the Windows Find facility and search for *.avi. Odds are the search will turn up a few AVI files you didn't even know you had, deposited on your PC by various programs or Web sites.

To Do: Insert inline video

1. Store the AVI file in the same folder as the Web page (or copy it there).

2. Click the page at the spot where you want to insert your inline clip.

3. Choose Insert, Video.

4. Type the filename of the video clip, and click OK.

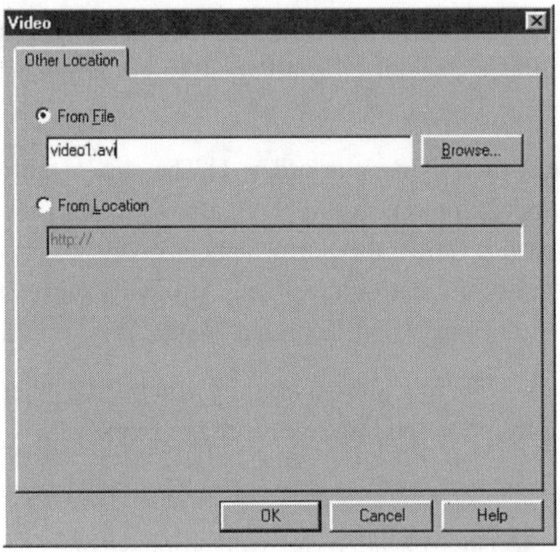

FIGURE 15.7

Step 4: Fill in the clip's filename.

The clip appears as a static image—a freeze-frame, if you will—in FrontPage Express. Using that freeze-frame, you can move the clip, change the size of the window in which it appears, put a border around it, and more, all by using the exact same steps you'd use if it were a GIF or JPEG image.

5. Now choose play options for the clip. Right-click the clip, and choose Image Properties from the menu that appears.

6. In Loop, type the number of times you want the clip to repeat before stopping, or check the check box next to Forever to make the clip play over and over for as long as the visitor views the page (see in Figure 15.8).

7. Under Start, check the optional check boxes to make the clip play On File Open (as soon as the visitor arrives) or On Mouse Over (when the visitor points to the freeze-frame).

8. Click OK, and then open the page in Internet Explorer to test the video clip. (Video does not play in FrontPage Express).

15

▼ FIGURE **15.8**

Step 6: Choose options for how the clip plays.

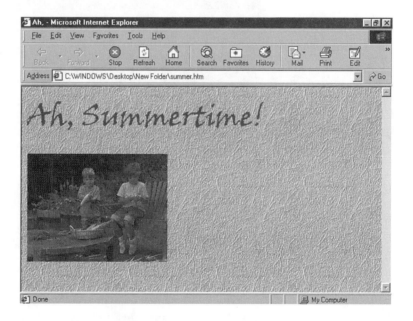

FIGURE **15.9**

Step 8: View the page in Internet Explorer to see the clip in action.

About External Media

Unlike such inline multimedia files as background sounds or inline GIF images, *external* media files do not display or play automatically when a visitor accesses a Web page. Instead, external files are downloaded to the visitor's PC and displayed or played there only when the visitor executes a particular link.

NEW TERM *External media* Refers to media files—images, video clips, sound clips, documents, and so on—to which links in a Web page point.

Often, the browser does not play or display the file itself. Instead, a helper application or plug-in opens to do the job. Some browsers have native support for some types of files, but when the file is set up as external media, the effect is the same as if a helper application were used.

For example, Internet Explorer and Netscape Navigator both have native support for JPEG image files; they can handle JPEGs either as inline or external media. But when a JPEG image is supplied as an external file, it has no home on the page—the browser doesn't know where to put it. So despite its ability to display a JPEG image inline, the browser opens an empty window to show a JPEG image accessed as an external file (see Figure 15.10).

FIGURE 15.10

Viewing an external JPEG image through a browser with native JPEG support.

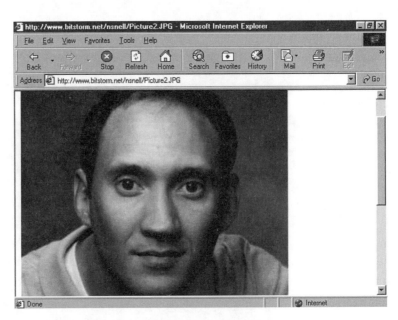

What if the visitor's browser has no native support and no helper application for a particular external media file? When the visitor clicks the link, the browser usually downloads and saves the file on a disk. That way, the visitor can install an appropriate application later to play the file offline. Because unplayable files are downloaded and saved, text-only browser users can still capture media files from the Web and then play them later in an application or a system that supports them.

Understanding Media Types

(Yes, I know, Dan Rather is a "Media Type"… but you won't learn about him here. Stay with me.)

Using techniques for embedding external media, you can build links to any type of file, from video and sound clips to the dynamic link library (.DLL) files used by Microsoft Golf.

Although video and sound clips might be playable by the visitor, the .DLL files from Golf are useless (except to Golf). The important question is not, "What can I supply as external media?" but "What can the browsers and helper applications out there actually play or display?"

Unfortunately, there's a tendency for external media file types to be system-specific, or at least favored by certain systems. Some types of files will play only in Windows, others only in Macintosh, and so on. More commonly, a type of file will work across multiple systems but is favored by one system. For example, Video for Windows (.avi) video clips play natively in Windows but require a special player on a Macintosh.

When you're faced with a choice between formats that don't reach everyone, you have three options:

- Use the most widely supported format, even if it is not universally supported.
- Choose the file type most easily supported by your target audience. For example, professional graphics artists tend to use Macintoshes. If your page and its external media files are aimed at that community, choose file types that favor the Macintosh.
- Offer multiple versions of your media files, each in a different format (see the section titled "Tips for Proper Presentation," later in this hour).

Images

As explained in Hour 13, "Getting Pictures for Your Page," the main image file formats for inline graphics in Web pages are GIF and JPEG. Although GIF and JPEG images can be used inline, there's no reason why you can't offer them as external media instead; in fact, there are some good reasons to do so.

Suppose you had lots of graphics you wanted to show—for example, pictures of products you sell or head shots of your employees or family. Inserting many such images inline will dramatically increase the time required to transmit your full page to a visitor. In such a case, consider using a minimum of inline images in a page that's compellingly organized and written. Then offer your images as external media, from a menu or from *thumbnails* (see the section titled "Tips for Proper Presentation," later in this hour).

Offering images as external media has other advantages as well. When you're using inline images but want to avoid building a page that takes a week to appear on the visitor's screen, you must compromise the appearance of the images by using few colors and by making the images fairly small (covering a small area).

When images are external, you can publish the highest quality images you want to—even full-screen, photorealistic, 24-bit color JPEG images. (True, when the visitor clicks the link to view such images, the wait for such a picture to appear can be long. But by the time a visitor chooses to see external media, he or she has already been pulled into your document and is much more likely to wait patiently.) Professional artists who publish their portfolios on the Web nearly always offer their work as external JPEGs so they can show the best.

Although GIF and JPEG are the only image formats supported inline, any other image format can be used externally. There is, however, one caveat: GIF and JPEG have been favored for a reason. They are broadly supported across the principal graphical systems—Windows, Macintosh, and X Window. Other image file types tend to be supported by applications on one or two systems, but rarely on all three. So although you can offer these alternative image formats, you should convert these and publish them as GIF or JPEG files whenever possible.

- *Publisher's Paintbrush (PCX) and Windows Bitmap (BMP) (the principal graphics formats used in Windows (3.1, 95, NT and 98)*—Graphics created in Windows 98's Paint program or in Paint Shop Pro can be saved in either format. Any Windows-based graphical browser that uses helper applications can display external PCX and BMP files, because Paint can be used as the helper. In the Macintosh world, there is some application support for PCX files, but very little for BMP. As a rule, use PCX or BMP formats only when your intended audience includes only Windows users.

- *Tagged-Image File Format (TIF or TIFF)*—TIFF files are a longtime standard for scanned images, and most scanning software saves TIFF files (along with other formats). TIFF files are great for high-resolution images destined for printing but tend to be rather large as external media in comparison to other formats. TIFF files are used on all types of systems but are not widely supported by applications other than desktop publishing programs.

- *Macintosh Picture (PIC or PICT)*—A Macintosh picture file. The Macintosh has native support for PICT, so any Macintosh visitor to your page can display PICT files. But PICT support is rare beyond the Macintosh world.

15

- *PNG*—A cross-system format that can be displayed on many systems and browsers but is not yet recognized as a standard for inline Web graphics. Still, as a widely-supported format, it's probably your third-best choice (after GIF and JPEG) for a widely-viewable external image file format.
- *XBM*—An X Window bitmap image. X Window systems and most other graphical interfaces to UNIX environments have native support for XBM, so almost any visitor using a UNIX system with a graphical interface can display XBM files. However, XBM support is rare beyond the UNIX world.

Video

Three principal video file formats appear on the Web. Each offers acceptable video quality (by the standards of computer-based viewing), and all three can include audio with the video. MPEG offers the best overall quality, but MPEG files are generally larger than comparable files for similar clips in the other formats.

- *Video for Windows (AVI, or Audio-Video Interleave)*—AVI files, which include both picture and sound, are the standard for video clips in Windows 3.1 and Windows 95/98/NT. AVI is also the required format for inline video (see "Inserting an Inline Video Clip," earlier in this hour). Windows 98's Media Player program has native support for AVI, whereas Windows 3.1 users must install a Video for Windows player to play AVI files. Macintosh users can install players for AVI as well (or use a browser that supplies native AVI support, such as Internet Explorer), but outside of the Windows world, MPEG and MOV files are supported far better.
- *Motion-Picture Experts Group (MPG, or MPEG)*—An independent standard for high-quality audio and video. An MPEG player is required on any system type (recent versions of the Windows Media Player for Win 95/98/NT can play MPEG files, but many users have not upgraded to that player). Still, because MPEG offers such high quality and because there are so many MPEG clips on the Web, most surfers interested in using video have installed an MPEG player.
- *QuickTime (QT or MOV)*—QuickTime is the Macintosh video standard, Apple's counterpart to Video for Windows. All Macintoshes have native support for QuickTime, whereas users of other systems usually must install a player or plug-in (or use a browser that supplies native support). For example, Windows users can install a free QuickTime player from Apple, and the latest version of Windows Media Player can play QuickTime movies.

In addition to these standard file types, there are other types of video/audio file types common on the Web that are *proprietary*—you can only create them if you purchase a particular vendor's program.

For example, you may have watched RealVideo clips or live broadcasts, or listened to RealAudio, in your travels online. You can create such files only with software purchased from the Real Networks company (www.real.com). You may also have visited "shocked" sites loaded with interactivity and multimedia and requiring a ShockWave plug-in in your browser. You can create such sites only with software from Macromedia (www.macromedia.com).

As you grow as an author, you may choose to begin working with such advanced formats. But the cost and complexity of these greatly exceed any real benefit to the beginning Web author. Stick with the non-proprietary audio and video formats for now. You can easily create these with the software included with most sound cards and video-capture cards for PCs.

Audio

Audio is perhaps the most confusing area of Web multimedia. There are many formats now, and a few more emerge each year as developers try to improve the quality or download speed of audio information.

Although some browsers contain native support for some sound formats, the effect is the same as when a helper application is used. A pop-up window opens with controls for the sound, such as Play or Rewind.

- *Basic audio (AU or SND)*—The most common sound format, several browsers and most audio player helpers provide native support for Basic audio. Although Basic audio offers only so-so sound, its combination of wide support and relatively small file size make it the recommended media type except when high audio quality is required.

- *Windows Sound Clip (WAV)*—The sound clip standard for Windows (3.1, 95, 98 and NT). The audio quality is about the same as Basic audio, but the format is not well supported outside of Windows. WAV is best used for distributing sounds to Windows users and is the required format for background sounds (see "Adding a Background Sound," earlier in this hour.)

- *MP3*—Short for MPEG Level 3, MP3 is a relatively new format that can carry CD-ROM–quality digital sound online. It's not as widely supported as the other sound formats yet, but may be within a year or two. MP3 support is included in the latest version of Windows Media Player, and there are dozens of shareware and freeware MP3 players available online. You can also find shareware and freeware programs for recording your own MP3 files.

MP3 is the subject of some controversy right now. Because of its CD-ROM–quality sound, the format has been widely used for distributing perfect copies of popular recordings—some authorized by the copyright holders, some not. The record industry is working feverishly to get some control of the flow of MP3 files online, and changes in the format are imminent.

15

To Do: Link to external media

1. Prepare the external media file, and store it in the same folder as the Web page file.

2. Create the link source in either of two ways:

   • Compose text for the link source.

   • Insert an image for the link source.

FIGURE 15.11

Step 2: Create the link source.

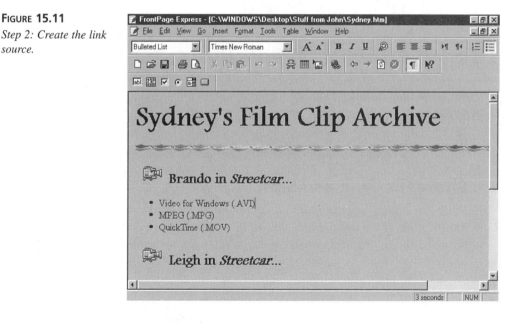

3. Select the link source (by highlighting the text or clicking the image).

4. Click the Create or Edit Hyperlink button on the Standard toolbar.

5. In Hyperlink Type, choose File.

6. In the URL box (see in Figure 15.12), following `file://`, type the filename of the external file.

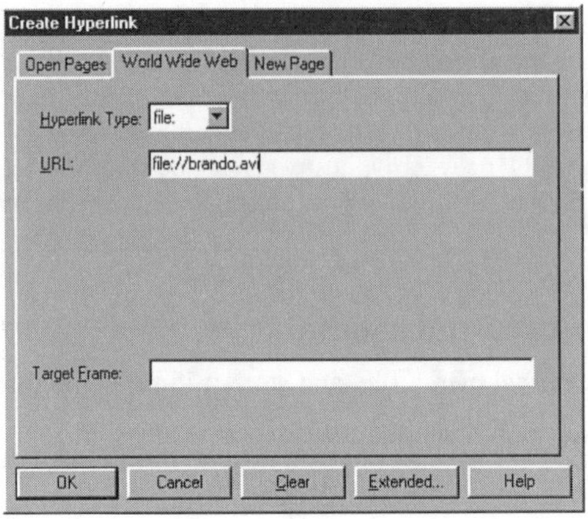

▼ FIGURE **15.12**

Step 6: Fill in the URL.

▲   7. Click OK.

Tips for Proper Presentation

As you can see, making the link to external media is simpler than creating or acquiring the media file in the first place. But the secret to the effective use of external media isn't setting up the link and file. The secret is presenting the link to external media in an attractive, inviting, and useful way.

The next few sections offer tips for properly presenting your external media.

Show File Type and Size

Whenever offering external media, always show the file type and its size (see Figure 15.13) as part of the link (or very close to it) so that visitors can make two decisions before clicking a link in your document:

- Do I have the necessary software to play, display, or run a file of this type?
- Do I have the time or patience to download a file of this size?

Keep in mind that many Web surfers today are still novices, especially when it comes to dealing with external media types. Configuring helper applications baffles many browser users, so they just don't do it. You can make your document newbie-friendly if, in addition to showing the file size and type, you

- Describe what the file type means and what's required to use the file. Don't just say the file is AVI; say the file is a Video for Windows (AVI) file that requires Windows 95/98/NT or a Video for Windows player in Windows 3.1 or Macintosh systems.

- Tell visitors where they can find the helper applications they need to play or display your file. If you know of a good source online, you can even provide a link to that source. That way, a visitor who wants to use your external media file but lacks the right software can jump to the helper application source, get the right helper, and then return to your page. (The visitor can also download and save your external media file, go get the helper, and then play or display the file later, offline.)

- Offer media in multiple formats—both Video for Windows (.AVI) amd QuickTime (.MOV), for example.

FIGURE 15.13
File type and size of an image linked to external media.

Use Descriptive Images as Link Sources

In addition to labeling a link to external media with its file type, it's a good idea to use an image that represents the file type as the link source. For example, a camera icon makes a great link source for any video clip. A sound-related icon, such as an ear or speaker, visually informs visitors that the link leads to a sound file.

Show Inline Thumbnails for Large External Images

As mentioned earlier in this hour, thumbnails are a great way to create meaningful link sources for external images.

A thumbnail is a very small, low-resolution version of a larger image. The thumbnail appears on the page as an inline image and also serves as the link source to the larger, full-resolution image. Thumbnails provide visitors with a general sense of what the full image looks like, so they can decide whether to bother downloading it.

As with any link to external media, you must indicate the file type and size along with the thumbnail. If a group of thumbnails all link to files of the same type and of about the same size, you can describe the files once for the group, as shown in Figure 15.14.

Figure 15.14

Thumbnails linked to larger JPEG images.

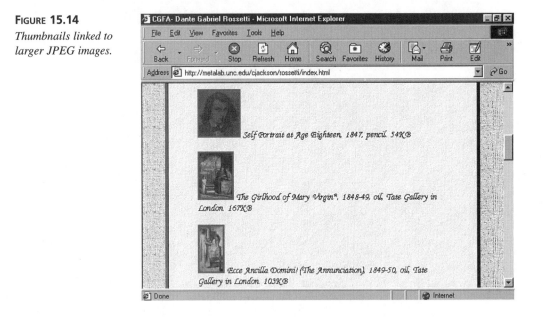

Summary

Embedding external media files in FrontPage Express is a snap: make sure the file is in the right place, build a link, and you're done. The only way you can blow it after that is if you forget to copy the media file to the server when you publish your page—and FrontPage Express can even make sure you get that right (see Hour 21, "Publishing Your Page").

The tricky part is creating or choosing the right type of file to reach either the broadest possible audience or the specific audience you most want to reach. PCs are more common in homes than Macintoshes, so if you're trying to reach homes, it helps to slant your file choices to whatever makes Windows happy. Many, many corporate users, especially those in engineering and technical departments, are on UNIX systems with X Window interfaces. Web authors often overlook the UNIX crowd when choosing media types. If your message is aimed at that crowd, try to aim your media files that way, too.

Q&A

Q If a video clip or other file I like is already available through a link on another Web page, can I simply link to it instead of supplying my own file?

A Sure you can, and doing so is quite common. There are, however, a couple of rules:

First, as always, email the Webmaster of the site to which you will link, and ask permission to link to the site and file.

Second, avoid linking directly to the file. Instead, link to the page on which the link appears. After all, the site providing the file is doing you a favor—the least you can do is give visitors a glimpse of the site's message before retrieving the link. Also, if the site is using the file in violation of a copyright (something that's difficult for you to find out), linking to the page rather than the file better insulates you from sharing the blame for the violation.

When you do create the link, you can use FrontPage Express's support for cut and paste to easily copy the link into your document (see Hour 10, "Making Links").

HOUR 16

Creating Your Own Animations

Ever visit a Web page where you see a spinning logo, steam rising from a picture of a coffee cup, or graphical rules that flash, strobe, and dance? You may not have known it, but you were experiencing *animated GIFs*, a special kind of inline GIF image file that moves when viewed through a Web browser.

You're about to learn how easy it is to create these puppies all by yourself. At the end of this hour, you will be able to answer the following questions:

- What's an animated GIF?
- How do I create the various frames that serve as each step of the animation?
- How do I combine the frames into a single, animated file?
- How do I customize aspects of the way the animation plays, such as how quickly the animation flips through the frames?
- How do I insert an animated GIF into a page?

About Animated GIFs

Animated GIFs are exactly what they sound like: GIF images that move. Unlike other types of multimedia files discussed in this chapter, you can incorporate an animated GIF into the layout of a Web page and control its alignment, borders, and other formatting just like any other inline image (see Hour 14, "Adding Pictures (and Picture Backgrounds)").

But unlike a regular GIF file, an animated GIF can *move*—well, a little. An animated GIF is not a suitable vehicle for a Disney film. Rather, animated GIFs provide very short, simple animations that add a little zip to a page without slowing its download to a crawl. A candle flickers. A cartoon bomb explodes. A horizontal line flashes and undulates. This is the kind of stuff animated GIFs do best.

The hands in Figure 16.1 are an animated GIF; they clap. (I can't prove it on paper, but it's true.) In this Web page, I paired this animated GIF with a *background sound* (see Hour 15, "Snazzing Up Your Page with Sound, Video, and Special Effects") of applause.

FIGURE **16.1**

These hands clap (honest!).

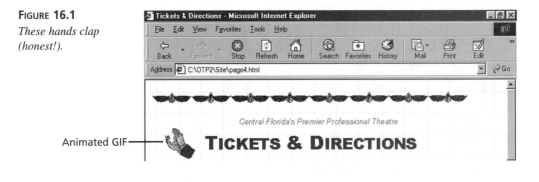

Animated GIF

To learn the addresses of some good clip art sites for animated GIFs, see Appendix B, "Online Resources for Web Authors."

To learn how to copy an image—even an animated GIF—from a Web clip art library to your PC, see Chapter 13, "Getting Pictures for Your Page."

The best way for beginning authors to get animated GIFs is to pick them up as clip art. Dozens of clip sites on the Web feature animated GIFs (see Figure 16.2). You copy these from the Web (copyrights permitting!) by following the exact steps you use for doing so with any GIF file, animated or not (see Hour 13).

FIGURE 16.2

Animated GIFs are easy to find online, and you can copy them to your PC and use them in your pages using the same steps you use for non-animated pictures.

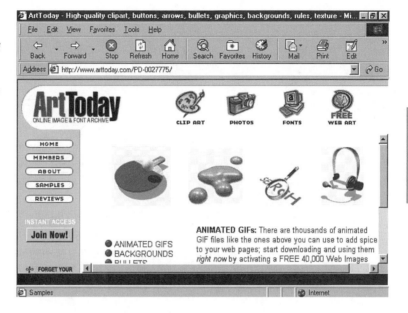

Recent versions of Microsoft Word and Microsoft Publisher can be used to create Web pages (see Hour 4, "Starting Pages in Other Programs"). Note that these programs include a clip art library on CD-ROM that contains a selection of "motion clips," nifty little animations.

The motion clips are not animated GIFs; they're another type of animated graphic. However, when you use Word (97, 98 or 2000) or Publisher (98 or 2000) to create a Web page, any motion clips you've inserted are automatically converted into animated GIFs.

Inserting Animated GIFs into Pages

Once you have an animated GIF file you want to use, insert it in your FrontPage Express document just like any other inline image, by using the Insert Image button or choosing Insert, Image.

FrontPage Express does not include full WYSIWYG support for animated GIFs. When you insert an animated GIF in a page in FrontPage Express, the picture appears to be a static, non-animated one. When you preview the page in a browser, you'll see the animation play.

After inserting an animated GIF, you treat it in FrontPage Express like any other inline GIF image. Using the exact same techniques used for ordinary GIFs, you can

- Position the GIF on the page
- Choose the way text aligns to it
- Drag its handles to change its size or shape (although doing so often produces unattractive results)
- Add extra space or a border around the GIF

You make most of these changes using the Image Properties dialog box, which opens when you double-click the animated GIF image in your page. To learn more, review Hour 14.

> You can use Windows's drag-and-drop to drag an image from a Web page (such as a clip art library) into a page you're creating in FrontPage Express.
>
> I didn't explain that before, in part because I think it's actually easier (and more reliable) to follow the steps I provided than to use drag-and-drop, especially when you consider all the finagling with window sizes you must do to make drag-and-drop practical.
>
> But another reason is that when you drag an animated GIF from one page to another, it loses its animation—it arrives in the page as an ordinary GIF. You can safely drag animated GIFs from one spot in a page to another, but not from page to page.

Creating Your Own Animated GIFs

If you want to create your own animated GIFs, you have two major steps to perform. Although an animated GIF is a single file, it is made up of multiple *frames*, just like a piece of movie film.

Each frame is slightly different from the others (see Figure 16.3); when the frames appear in rapid sequence, the illusion of a single image in motion is created. (Most animated GIFs are made up of a dozen frames or fewer.)

FIGURE 16.3
Like all animation, animated GIFs start out as a series of separate images, or frames.

The two steps in creating an animated GIF are

1. Creating the separate frames
2. Combining the frames into one animation file

Making the Frames

You create each frame as a separate GIF file. For example, using Paint Shop Pro, you could create a single, static GIF image of a closed blossom. After saving that image, you could edit it to show the blossom opening slightly, and then choose File, Save As to save the edited version as a new file. You could continually edit and save new versions of the file to create a series of separate images that, viewed in sequence, show the flower bloom.

If you want a quick way to practice animation, create a series of images as described in the following To Do, and then combine those images into an animation as described later in this hour. The simple animation you're creating will make your name appear to spin around.

To Do: Create a series of images for an animation

1. Open Paint Shop Pro from the Windows Start menu by choosing Programs, Paint Shop Pro 5, Paint Shop Pro 5.
2. Start a new image (File, New).
3. In the New Image dialog box, enter
   - 1 inch for both Width and Height
   - 72 pixels/inch for Resolution
   - Background Color for Background Color
   - 16 Colors for Image Type

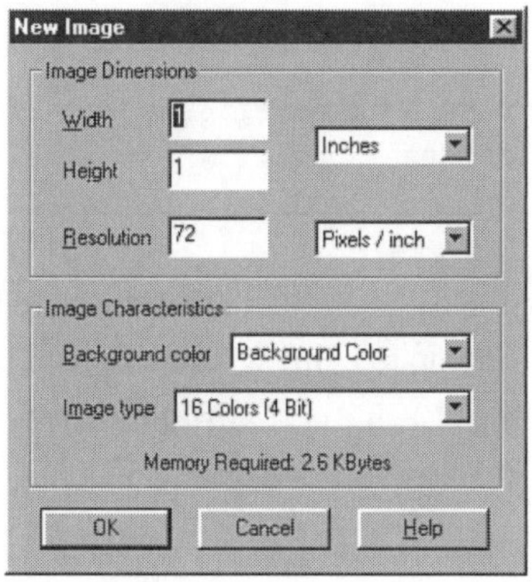

FIGURE **16.4**

Step 3: Configure the first image file.

▼   4. Click OK on the New Image dialog box, and then choose View, Zoom In, 3:1 to make the image appear larger (so it's easier to work with).

   5. On the Tool Palette, click the Text tool.

FIGURE 16.5
Step 5: Click the Text tool.

Text tool

   6. Click anywhere in the image.

   7. Choose any Font and Style you like, and choose a Size of 16 or 18 (if your name is longer than four letters) or 20 if you have a short name. Then type your name and click OK.

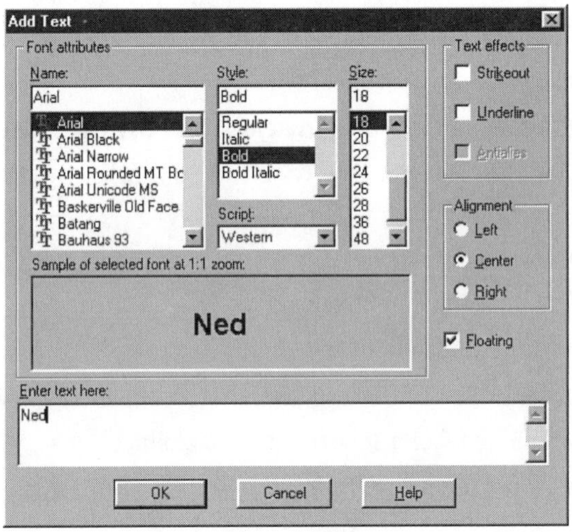

FIGURE 16.6
Step 7: Choose a font and size, and type your name.

> If after step 8 your name is too wide to fit in the window, start over and choose a smaller font size in Step 6.

   8. Drag the outline of your name to where it is nicely centered in the window, and click. Then right-click your name to cement it in its place.

▼   9. Save the file as a GIF 89a interlaced file (see Hour 14). Name it **name1.gif**.

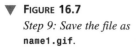

▼ **Figure 16.7**

Step 9: Save the file as `name1.gif`.

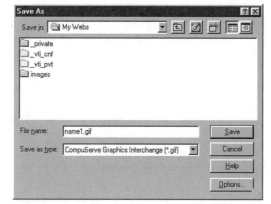

16

10. Choose Image, Rotate.

11. Click the Free option, and type **30** (to rotate the image 30 degrees).

Figure 16.8

Step 11: Rotate 30 degrees.

12. Choose File, Save As, and save the file under a new name: `name2.gif`.

▲

13. Repeat steps 10–12 until you have rotated the name almost completely around. (Your last save should be `name12.gif`.)

Turning Multiple Frames into One Animation

Once you've created the series of frames, you must combine them into a single animated GIF file. Doing so requires a special utility program.

One such program, Animation Shop, is included on the CD-ROM with this book. (It's a part of Paint Shop Pro, so it installs when you install Paint Shop Pro 5.) You can often acquire other such utilities from links on clip art sites that offer animated GIFs.

The following To Do shows how to use Animation Shop's Animation Wizard to combine a series of images into an animation.

> Animation Shop's Animation Wizard offers quite a few options along the way for changing the way the animation is created. To help you learn quickly, and also because most of the time the preselected, default option is the one you'll want to choose anyway, I won't stop to explain every option. Besides, you can change any of these optional settings at any time after finishing the Wizard.
>
> It's best to leave most of these options alone until you gain some basic experience. When you want to know what each option does, consult Animation Shop's Help.

To Do: Combine GIF pictures into an animation

1. Open Animation Shop from the Windows Start menu by choosing Programs, Paint Shop Pro 5, Animation Shop.

2. Choose File, Animation Wizard.

3. Click Next on this dialog box, and also the one after it.

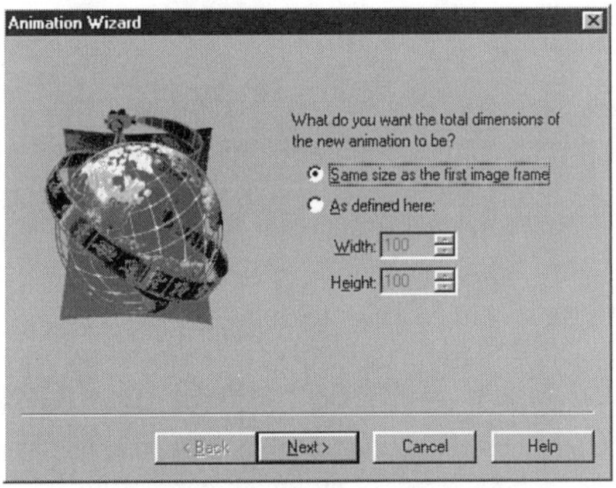

FIGURE **16.9**

Step 3: Click Next on this dialog box and on the next one.

4. Choose Centered in the Frame and With the Canvas Color (see in Figure 16.10), and then click Next.

5. The Wizard asks whether you want the animation to "loop" (play continuously, over and over, as long as the visitor views the page) or play a particular number of times and stop (see Figure 16.11). Choose Yes, Repeat the Animation Indefinitely, and then click Next.

▼ FIGURE **16.10**

*Step 4: Choose
Centered in the Frame
and With the Canvas
Color, and then click
Next.*

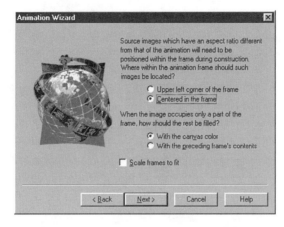

The dialog box shown in Figure 16.11 also lets you choose the "delay" between frames. The higher the number you select, the more slowly the animation will move from frame to frame.

To achieve the smoothest animation, you'll want a high number of frames (10 or so) and a short delay (1 hundredth of a second or so). When you have only a few frames, a short delay may make the animation whiz by too fast to see. The default setting of 10 hundredths of a second is a good choice for this example.

FIGURE **16.11**

*Step 5: Choose Yes,
and then click Next.*

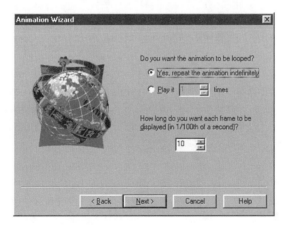

▼

▼   6. The next screen prompts you to select the frame files. Click the Add Image button.

    7. Browse to the folder where the "name" images you created are stored. Hold down the Ctrl key and select all of the frame files. Then click the Open button.

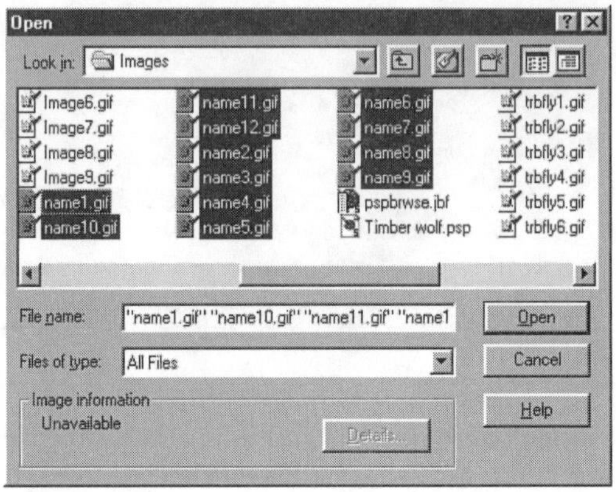

FIGURE **16.12**

Step 7: Select the image files.

    8. Rearrange the image filenames so that they're in numerical order, top to bottom. To move an image's place in the order, click it to select it, and then choose Move Up or Move Down. When done, click Next.

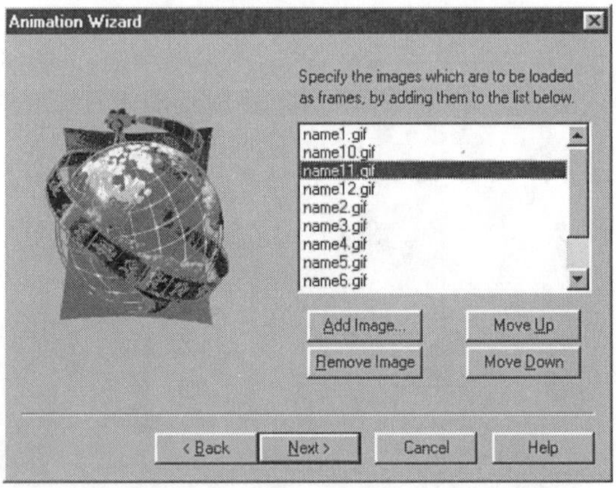

FIGURE **16.13**

Step 8: Put the image files in order.

    9. Click Finish. After a few moments, the frames of your animation appear.

    10. Choose File, Save. Give the animation any name you like, but leave `.gif` as the
▼   filename extension. Click the Save button.

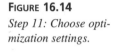 11. Now you get to choose Optimization. Optimization is important, because it keeps the animation file from getting too large and slowing down your page. This small, simple animation won't be a size problem, so you can leave the slider at the top setting, Better Image Quality, and click Next.

FIGURE 16.14
Step 11: Choose optimization settings.

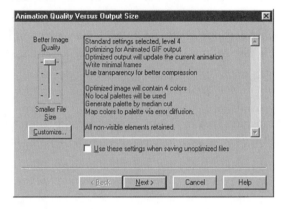

16

 When creating larger, more complex animations, you may prefer to move the slider down a notch or two, sacrificing image quality but creating a smaller file.

To change the optimization settings later, open the animation file in Animation Shop and choose File, Optimization Wizard.

12. Animation Shop creates the final file. Click Next.

FIGURE 16.15
Step 12: Click Next.

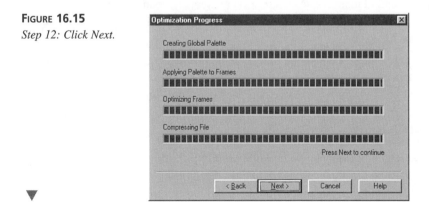

▼   13. Animation Shop reports the final size of the file and other statistics. Click Finish.

14. You may now do any of the following:

- Choose View, Animation to watch your animation in Animation Shop.

- Use Animation Shop's menus to change and fine-tune your animation.

▲   - Open FrontPage Express and insert the animation file you just created in a Web page. (You'll find it under the name you gave it in step 10.) Remember: You'll have to view the page in a browser to see the animation move.

Summary

If you can make pictures, you can make an animated GIF. All it takes is creating a series of images, and then binding them together. It's a fast, easy way to add a little action to a Web page.

Q&A

Q Do animated GIFs affect the download speed of a Web page?

A An animated GIF is an image file, and because it contains multiple frames, it is a larger file than a similar non-animated GIF. As with any image, you must consider whether the effect of an animated GIF is worth the wait it can cause.

The major factors affecting the size (and thus the download time) of an animated GIF file are the number of frames it contains and the screen area it occupies. And of course, if you build an animation out of large, complex files with a great many colors, the animation file will end up large, too, despite optimization. Try to limit screen area and number frames while still creating an effective animation, and choose optimization settings carefully to get the best compromise between image quality and file size.

In addition to the extra download time, note that the animation can increase the memory demand and processor load in your visitor's browser. The impact is generally slight, but a visitor with an overburdened machine—for example, someone running Internet Explorer on a 486 PC with only 8MB of memory—might see a significant degradation when viewing animated GIFs.

PART V

Fine-Tuning Your Page

Hour

HOUR 17

Editing HTML

The easiest and most reliable way to create a Web page is to use a WYSI-WYG editor—that's why I gave you FrontPage Express on the CD-ROM with this book, and that's why you've spent 16 hours with it.

But no matter which editor Web authors use, they often reach a point where they want to do something that's perfectly possible in an HTML Web page, but for which their WYSIWYG authoring program offers no buttons or menu items. If you reach that point, you may want to move beyond FrontPage Express into the realm of the HTML source file itself.

This hour introduces you to HTML source files and how new tags and attributes are applied. At the end of the hour, you'll be able to answer the following questions:

- How can I read and understand an HTML source file?
- How do I insert HTML codes from within FrontPage Express?
- What other tools can I use to edit HTML source code?

How to Read an HTML File

Recall from Hour 1, "Understanding Web Authoring," that an HTML source file consists of four basic elements:

- The text to be displayed on the page
- The filenames of inline images
- The URLs or filenames for links (and the text or image filenames for the link source)
- HTML tags and attributes, which tell browsers which lines are images, links, headings, or normal paragraphs, and so on

The best way to learn about HTML is to study HTML files and compare them with the output in a browser. Figure 17.1 shows a basic Web page displayed in Internet Explorer, and Figure 17.2 shows the HTML source file for the same page.

FIGURE 17.1

A basic Web page, as interpreted by a browser.

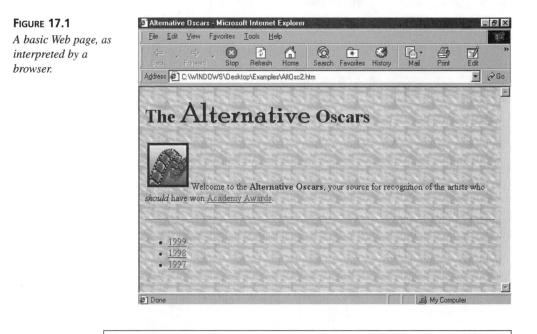

In Figure 17.2, notice that HTML·tags are always enclosed within angle brackets (< >) and that each content element of the page—a paragraph or image filename—is surrounded by a pair of tags. Compare Figures 17.1 and 17.2 carefully, and you'll quickly see how HTML tags tell a browser what to do with the text and files that make up a Web page.

Most Web pages contain more elaborate coding than what you see in the
example illustrated by Figures 17.1 and 17.2. However, this example contains
all the basics and shows how HTML tags are applied. When you understand
this example, you know enough to apply virtually any other HTML tag.

FIGURE 17.2

*The HTML source
code for the Web page
shown in Figure 17.1.*

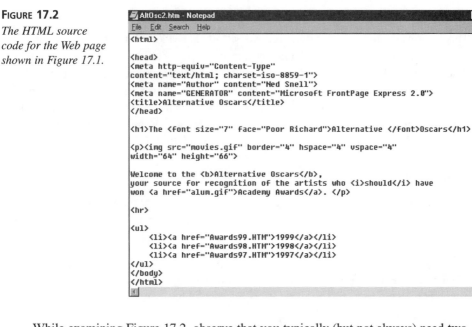

```
AltOsc2.htm - Notepad
File  Edit  Search  Help
<html>

<head>
<meta http-equiv="Content-Type"
content="text/html; charset=iso-8859-1">
<meta name="Author" content="Ned Snell">
<meta name="GENERATOR" content="Microsoft FrontPage Express 2.0">
<title>Alternative Oscars</title>
</head>

<h1>The <font size="7" face="Poor Richard">Alternative </font>Oscars</h1>

<p><img src="movies.gif" border="4" hspace="4" vspace="4"
width="64" height="66">

Welcome to the <b>Alternative Oscars</b>,
your source for recognition of the artists who <i>should</i> have
won <a href="alum.gif">Academy Awards</a>. </p>

<hr>

<ul>
    <li><a href="Awards99.HTM">1999</a></li>
    <li><a href="Awards98.HTM">1998</a></li>
    <li><a href="Awards97.HTM">1997</a></li>
</ul>
</body>
</html>
```

17

While examining Figure 17.2, observe that you typically (but not always) need two
HTML tags to identify a page element: one tag that has no slash (/) inside the first angle
bracket and another that has a slash there. The no-slash version is used to mark the
beginning of a page element, and the slash version (sometimes called the *close* tag)
marks the end. For example, the tag <HTML> at the top of the file marks the very beginning of the entire HTML document, and the close tag </HTML> marks the end.

If you're wondering why you see some tags in uppercase letters and some in
lowercase letters, see the "Q&A" section at the end of this hour.

Now take a look at how the tags, text, and filenames work together to build a page. Every HTML document begins with the following command:

`<HTML>`

This tells the browser that it's reading an HTML document and should interpret it as such. Typically (but not always), the next tag is the following:

`<HEAD>`

This informs the browser that what follows `<HEAD>` is header information. Information entered in the header does not display as part of the page but is important because it describes your document to the browser and to Web search engines and directories. The header portion of an HTML file created in FrontPage Express contains all the information you entered in FrontPage Express's Page Properties dialog box. This includes not only such standard elements as the document title, but also header elements created by FrontPage Express automatically. These are indicated with two types of tags:

```
<META NAME=...>
<HTTP-EQUIV>
```

The next two tags, `<TITLE>` and `</TITLE>`, surround the text of the Web page title. After the title and any other header lines, the tag `</HEAD>` informs the browser that the header is over. Next comes the body of the page, kicked off by the `<BODY>` tag. The body contains everything that displays on the page itself.

The first element of the body in Figure 17.2 is a heading. The heading tags are easy to remember: `<H1>` is a level 1 heading, `<H2>` is a level 2 heading, and so on. The first heading in the example is a level 1 heading:

`<H1>The Alternative Oscars</H1>`

Notice that the end of the heading is marked with `</H1>`.

The inline image (GIF file `movies.gif`) is indicated with the `<IMG SRC...>` tag, like the following:

`<IMG SRC="movies.gif"...>`

Note that the image filename must be enclosed in quotes. In Figure 17.2, optional *attributes* for spacing, image dimensions, and a border around the image appear between the beginning of the `<IMG SRC...>` tag and the close angle bracket (>) that ends it. Attributes are always optional and go inside the tag itself (between the angle brackets).

Observe that the `<IMG SRC...>` tag requires no close tag.

Immediately following the end of the <IMG SRC...> tag comes a normal text paragraph (beginning with Welcome). Note that no tag is required to identify it; any text in an HTML document is assumed to be a normal paragraph unless tags indicate otherwise. However, keep in mind that while entering normal text, you cannot simply type a carriage return to start a new paragraph. To break a paragraph and begin a new one, you must enter the new paragraph tag (<P>). It's proper to end a paragraph with a close paragraph tag (</P>), but doing so is not required.

Embedded within the normal paragraph, you can see a few more tags:

- The set <B> and </B> surrounding Alternative Oscars applies bold character formatting.
- The set <I> and </I> surrounding should applies italic character formatting.
- The tag beginning with <A HREF... creates a link to another page, using the text Academy Awards as the link source. In the link, the <A HREF= portion indicates that, when activated by a reader, the link should open the file or URL named in quotes. The text between the close angle bracket following the filename and the close tag </A> is the text that is displayed in the page as the link source.

Following the normal paragraph is a new paragraph tag that inserts a blank line before the horizontal line (<HR>) that follows. All by itself, the <HR> tag inserts a line; the width=100% is an attribute, one of the optional properties you can apply to a horizontal line's properties' extensions (see Hour 8, "Organizing Text with Tables and Rules").

The <UL> tag starts an unnumbered list. (Look for the </UL> tag that closes the list.) Each list item is surrounded by <LI> and </LI> and contains a link (<A HREF) to another page in the document.

At the bottom of the file, the </BODY> tag closes off the body, and the </HTML> tag indicates the end of the HTML document.

That's it. To learn more about the HTML source code of pages you've created in FrontPage Express or any page you see on the Web, follow the steps in the next section.

Viewing the HTML Source Code of a Document

A great way to learn more about HTML is to study the source code for Web pages. You can study the source code for pages you view on the Web, or look at the underlying source code for pages you create in FrontPage Express. You can even view the source code for a page you're editing, make a small change with FrontPage Express's menus or toolbar buttons, and then view the source code again to see how the HTML code has been changed. Give it a try!

17

To view the HTML source for a page you're looking at

- When in Internet Explorer, choose View, Source.
- When in FrontPage Express, choose View, HTML.

Using FrontPage Express to Insert an HTML Tag

When you've built a document in FrontPage Express but need to add a tag here or there for which FrontPage Express offers no button or menu, FrontPage Express's Insert HTML Markup function allows you to do so conveniently, without having to fuss with the whole HTML source file.

In FrontPage Express, Insert HTML Markup can be used to insert any HTML tag—even those that FrontPage Express inserts automatically when you apply properties to text or an image. However, it's wise to use Insert, HTML Markup only for tags not supported by another menu item or button in FrontPage Express.

The reason isn't just convenience. When you use HTML Markup, the results are displayed as a question mark icon in the document instead of displaying in the FrontPage Express window as they would through a browser; you do not get WYSIWYG results with HTML Markup even when the tag you insert applies formatting that FrontPage Express can usually display.

In the example that follows, you insert the horizontal line tag (<hr>), which is supported by FrontPage Express's menus (see Hour 8). The <hr> tag is used in the example only to provide an easy-to-follow test case without introducing a tag not yet covered in this book.

To Do: Insert an HTML tag

1. Click in the page at the spot where you want the object or formatting applied by the tag to go.
2. Choose Insert, HTML Markup.
3. Type your entry, and then click OK.
4. To see the effects of the tag, save the page, and then view it in Internet Explorer.

▼ **FIGURE 17.3**
Step 2: Choose Insert, HTML Markup.

FIGURE 17.4
Step 3: Type the tag.

17

FIGURE 17.5
Step 4: View the results in your browser.

▲

To edit a tag you've inserted with HTML Markup, double-click the tag's question mark icon. The HTML Markup dialog box opens so you can edit the tag and verify your changes. To delete a tag, click it and press Delete.

Adding Attributes with FrontPage Express's Extended Buttons

When performing many kinds of activities in dialog boxes in FrontPage Express—inserting or formatting an image, for example—you'll see an Extended button somewhere on the dialog box, like the one shown in Figure 17.6. The Extended button enables you to code attributes or other options manually into the HTML tag controlled by the dialog.

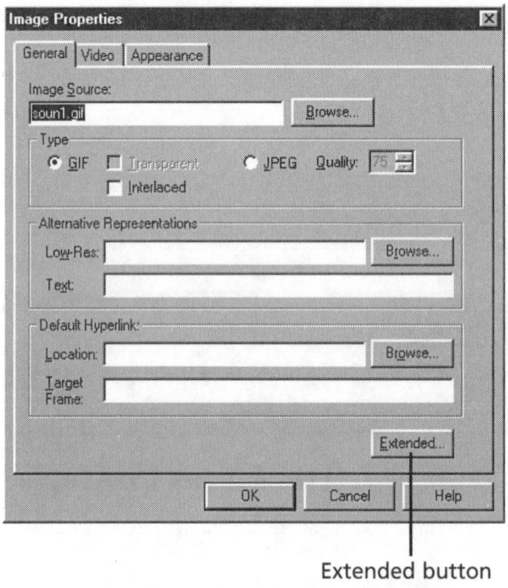

FIGURE 17.6

Where you see an Extended button, you can click it to open a dialog box where you can add optional attributes.

Extended button

However, the Extended button has little immediate value when you're writing HTML. For the most part, all optional attributes you might want to use are already available on the dialog box. Also, the Extended button enables you to insert any attributes or other code between the tag and its closing tag—for example, anywhere between <TABLE> and </TABLE> when you click the Extended button on the Insert Table dialog box. However, this method does not give you control of the position of the added attributes among other attributes within the tags, and position is sometimes important.

I've told you about the Extended button, 'cause it's there and 'cause for all I know, you may find it useful. But if you really want to apply attributes not featured on FrontPage Express's menus and toolbar buttons, I recommend steering clear of Extended and editing the HTML source file, as described in the next section. Doing so, you'll develop greater skill and confidence working with HTML, and you'll avoid niggling little problems that the Extended button can bring about.

Editing an HTML Source File Directly

FrontPage Express's HTML Markup function is terrific for inserting a tag or two in a file, but for more serious HTML work, you'll find it easier to simply edit the HTML source file itself.

In principle, you can use any program capable of saving text files for your HTML editor. (Remember: An HTML file is really just an ordinary text file that's saved with a filename extension of .htm or .html.)

Windows' Notepad program (see Figure 17.7) is ideal, because it edits and saves *only* flat text files. The only thing you must remember is to change the filename extension to .htm or .html when saving the file.

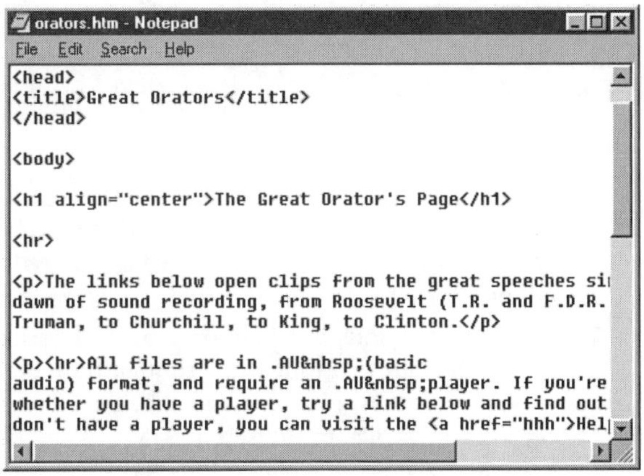

FIGURE 17.7

An HTML file in Notepad.

But although Notepad can do the job, it doesn't offer you much help with the HTML. A better option is FrontPage Express's built-in HTML source editor. To use the editor, open the page whose HTML you want to edit, and choose View, HTML. The View or Edit HTML dialog box opens, as shown in Figure 17.8. There you can make any changes to the HTML you want; when you close the dialog box, you return to editing the page in WYSIWYG mode.

17

When you return to WYSYWYG editing mode, changes you've made to the HTML source file may be indicated by question mark icons, just like the changes you make with the HTML Markup dialog box. To see the full effects of your changes, you may need to view the page in a browser.

FIGURE **17.8**

FrontPage Express features a built-in, color-coded HTML source file editing tool.

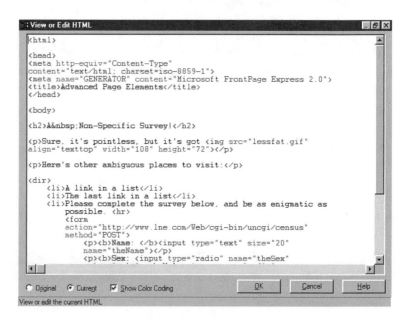

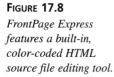

If this book were in full color, you'd see that the HTML code in Figure 17.8 appears in three different colors: Purple for tags, red for attributes, and blue for content (text, image filenames, URLs for links).

The color coding is intended to make the HTML easier to read, to help you distinguish the tags that format the content from the content itself. But the color coding is entirely cosmetic, added by the editor—there's no real color-coding in an HTML file. In a different HTML editor, you may see a different color scheme, or none at all (as in Notepad).

About HTML Assistant Pro

There are WYSIWYG editors that do all the HTML work for you (behind the scenes), and there are flat HTML editors and text editors that let you edit the source code, but give you little or no help with it. Somewhere in between those two extremes lay professional HTML editing tools like HTML Assistant Pro 97, which is included on the CD-ROM at the back of this book. (See Figure 17.9.)

To open HTML Assistant Pro, choose Programs, HTML Assistant Pro 97, Pro 97 from the Windows Start menu. (If the "Congratulations" screen appears, click the Continue with Mission button.)

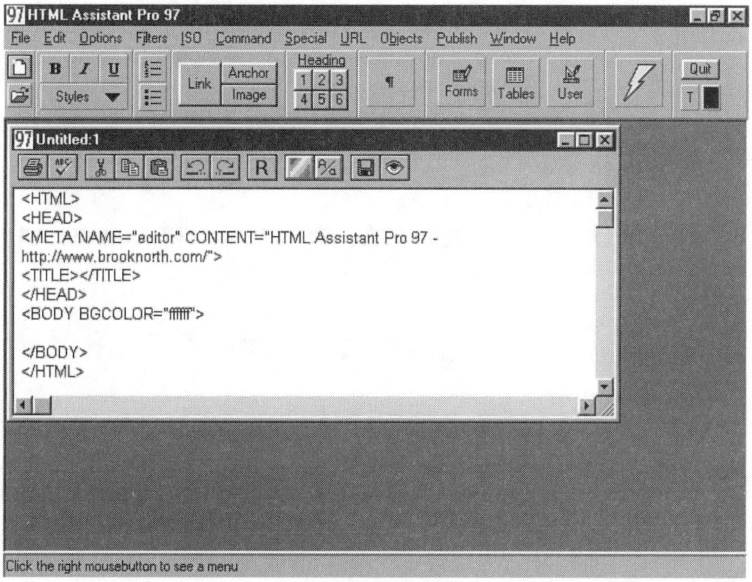

FIGURE 17.9
HTML code being edited in HTML Assistant Pro.

For readers of this book, HTML Assistant Pro provides another important benefit—one that requires no HTML coding.

FrontPage Express includes no facility for creating Web pages with *frames*—pages divided into two or three separate panels that each show a different file. Using a tool built into HTML Assistant Pro, you can easily produce a frames page, with no HTML coding.

In Hour 18, "Dividing a Page into Frames," you'll learn how to create frames in HTML Assistant Pro.

Although an HTML editor produces and edits simple text files, it also offers menus and toolbar buttons to make entering tags more convenient and accurate.

For example, in HTML Assistant Pro, you apply the tags for bold character formatting simply by highlighting text and then clicking the B button on the toolbar (see Figure 17.10). Instead of seeing the text turn bold (as you would in a WYSIWYG editor), you'll see the bold tags (<B>, </B>) appear around the text. These editors don't show you the effects of your coding (you need to view the file in a browser to check its appearance), but they do make working with raw HTML easier, and they help ensure that you enter the codes correctly.

When working in HTML Assistant Pro, you can click the Preview button on the toolbar (the creepy eye; see Figure 17.10) to view the page in the default browser on your PC.

FIGURE 17.10

HTML Assistant Pro's toolbars offer most tools you need for applying tags without typing.

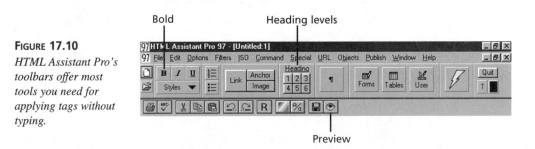

Typically, you compose in HTML Assistant Pro by typing only the text you want to display (or entering filenames for images or URLs for links), highlighting the text with your mouse, and then clicking a toolbar button to apply a set of tags to the selected text. The tags are displayed instantly in the document. For example, you could type a line of text, highlight it, and then click a number (1–6) under Heading in the top toolbar to assign heading tags to the text.

Note too that you needn't manually code such structure tags as <HTML>, <HEAD>, or <BODY>; HTML Assistant Pro adds these automatically when you create the file.

In Hour 24, "Developing Your Authoring Skills," you'll learn about other Web authoring environments, such as Microsoft FrontPage 2000 and Adobe PageMill 3, which you can add to your arsenal as your skills advance.

If you find yourself needing to do a lot of HTML coding to do stuff FrontPage Express doesn't do, you should consider moving up to one of these professional-level Web authoring tools, so you can perform the same tasks more conveniently and in true WYSIWYG fashion.

Summary

Coding HTML is no great challenge. In fact, the beauty of HTML is that coding simple stuff—such as text paragraphs, links, and inline images—is actually simple, and coding more complex elements builds naturally on the skills required for the easy stuff.

As a FrontPage Express author, you won't spend much time coding the simple stuff because FrontPage Express offers buttons and menus for all of it. Instead, you'll lay out most of your document in FrontPage Express, and then use Insert HTML Markup or an HTML editor to code the rest.

Q&A

Q **I noticed in some of the HTML source code examples you showed that the lines of code in the header were indented. What does indenting do?**

A Nothing. The indenting of blocks of HTML code has no effect on the display of the page; it's there for the same reason some editors color-code the HTML when showing it to you. Authors (and most editors) indent portions of code to make the structure of the file easier to understand when a person reads it. Browsers don't care; they pay no attention to indents in HTML source code, so do whatever works best for you.

Q **I've also noticed that tags are sometimes typed in uppercase letters (`<TITLE>`) and other times lowercase (`<title>`). Does it matter which I use?**

A Browsers today don't care whether you use uppercase tags, lowercase tags or both—they pay no attention to the case of the letters used in tags, and the tags have the same effect either way. You may have noticed that FrontPage Express does its tags lowercase (see Figure 17.8), while HTML Assistant does its tags uppercase (see Figure 17.9). Same dif.

For years, the accepted convention among Web authors was to use uppercase tags. Because most of the text content of a page was likely to be lowercase (with uppercase letters only at the beginnings of sentences and on proper nouns), it was thought that using uppercase tags helped the author easily distinguish tags from content. That's the same reason, in this hour, that I mostly used uppercase tags—so they stand out from my description around them.

Given that you'll probably spend most of your HTML coding time editing HTML files originally produced by programs, it pays to stay flexible and cultivate the ability to work either way. In fact, you may want to always do the opposite of what the program does; for example, when editing the all-lowercase HTML code in FrontPage Express's View or Edit HTML dialog box, write your edits in upper-case—that'll make it easier to see what you've changed if you need to resolve a problem later.

Eventually, it's likely that all coding will be required to be lowercase. That's because HTML will one day be supplanted by a new standard, XHTML (see Hour 24), in which tags must be lowercase. But that's still a few years off.

Q I've looked at the source for some pages on the Web, and I've seen lines of text preceded by a <!- tag. The text doesn't seem to be part of the header, but it is displayed nowhere in the browser view of the page. *Que pasa, mi amigo*?

A Any text preceded by <!- is a *comment*, a note inserted in the file to explain some-thing to anyone who might read the HTML source code. Comments are inserted by programmers in all types of program code, including HTML, to help others (or the programmer himself) understand the code when reading it. Comments have no effect on the display or actions of the document, and the text within comments is hidden when the browser displays the document. (In FrontPage Express, you can add comments to the HTML by choosing Insert, Comment.)

HOUR 18

Dividing a Page into Frames

If you've hit a frame-based page in your browsing, you know that they're cool. They make your display look like the control panel of a jet fighter—so many different, independent chunks of information stimulating your brain at once. (If you're not sure what I mean, peek ahead to Figure 18.1.)

It's like picture-in-picture on a new television, for people with eyes so info-hungry that just one program—or one page—at a time provides inadequate sensory input. Of course, frames also greatly expand the author's ability to offer a variety of page navigation scenarios to visitors.

At the end of the hour, you'll be able to answer the following questions:

- What's a frames page really made of, behind the scenes?
- How can I easily create a frames page by using HTML Assistant Pro and FrontPage Express together (with no HTML coding!)?
- How can I create and edit frames in HTML?
- How do I help visitors who don't have frames-capable browsers?

What Does It Take to Make a Frame Page?

In a frame-based page, the content of each frame is contained in a separate HTML page (see Figure 18.1). If the page features three frames, there are at least three separate HTML files, one to appear in each frame.

In addition to those "content" HTML files, there is another HTML file that ties all the others together—the frame definition page.

NEW TERM The *frame definition page* is a special HTML file that creates and controls a frames-based Web page. The file contains the filename of the HTML file that's to be displayed in each frame, plus tags dictating the number and size of the frames.

FIGURE 18.1

A frame-based page.

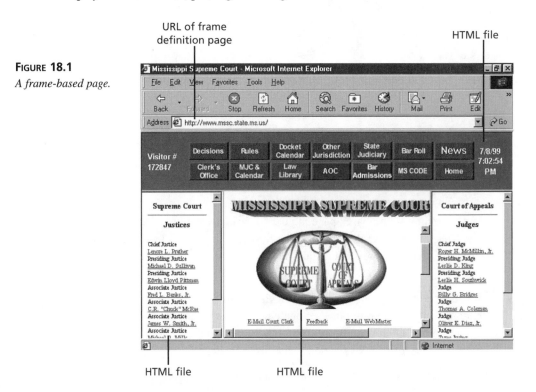

Creating a frame-based page requires three basic steps:

1. Creating the various individual HTML pages that will be displayed within the frames.

2. Creating the frame definition page to define the number, size, and other aspects of the frames.

3. Tying one HTML file to each frame.

> When publishing and publicizing your frame-based page, you will direct visitors to the frame definition page, not to any of the content files displayed within the frames.

The Frame Definition Page

The frame definition page supplies no content to the page; it merely specifies how the page is to be split up and which HTML page is to be displayed in each frame.

In Figure 18.1, the URL shown in the address box is that of the frame definition page; that's the URL a visitor accesses to open the page. The frame definition page then takes care of displaying the pages within the frames.

> In the frame definition page, you can insert a message to be displayed only to visitors who can't see frames. (See the section titled "Accommodating the Frames-Intolerant," later in this hour.)

18

The Frame Content

A separate HTML file, which you compose like any other Web page, supplies the content of each frame. You create and format these pages like any other Web page file; however, when composing files that will be displayed in frames, you must try to account for the size and shape of the frame in which you plan to display it.

Browsers help adjust content for frames: They automatically shorten horizontal lines and wrap text to fit within a frame. Alignment properties are also preserved in a frame; for example, if your text is centered in the page when you compose it, the browser centers it within the frame when displaying it. However, browsers cannot adjust the positions or spacing of images (or images used as rules or bullets); images often make framing difficult.

> Note that each page in a frame can have its own unique background image or color, defined in the content file.

Frames are not created in FrontPage Express, but you can create your content files in FrontPage Express, and then tie them together under a frame definition page you create with HTML or another tool (as you'll do in the next To Do).

Browsers automatically add scrollbars to a frame when the contents exceed the frame size. But a frame page showing a collection of fragmentary files and scrollbars is unappealing, and visitors tire quickly of excessive scrolling—especially horizontal scrolling to read wide text. Whenever practical, make the content fit the frame—or vice versa.

Using HTML Assistant Pro to Create a Frames Page

Because FrontPage Express contains no built-in tools for making frames, you'll need to code the frames directly in HTML or bring in another tool to help. The easier method is to bring in another tool, and lucky you, you have one: HTML Assistant Pro, included on the CD-ROM at the back of this book.

The following To Do assumes you have already installed HTML Assistant Pro from the CD-ROM at the back of this book. If you have not, see Appendix A, "Setting Up the Programs on the Bonus CD-ROM."

To Do: Build a frames page with FrontPage Express and HTML Assistant Pro

1. In FrontPage Express, compose the content pages that will be displayed in the frames. Try to organize and format them, if possible, in a way that will minimize the need for visitors to scroll them in their frames. (But keep in mind that you can always fine-tune them later, after seeing how they look in their frames.)

2. Open HTML Assistant Pro by choosing Programs, HTML Assistant Pro 97, Pro 97 from the Windows Start menu. (If the "Congratulations" screen appears, click the Continue with Mission button.)

3. Choose Special, QuickFrames from the menu bar.

FIGURE **18.2**

Step 3: Choose Special, QuickFrames in HTML Assistant Pro.

▼

Special
QuickFrames... Ctrl+F5

▼   4. Click the picture that matches the style of frames page you want to create.

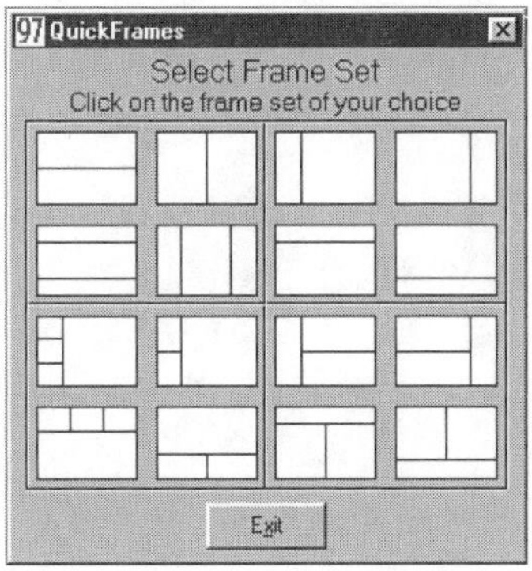

FIGURE 18.3

Step 4: Click the type of frames page you want.

5. In the picture of the frame, click in any frame.

6. Under URL Prefix, click None, and under File Name, click File Name Only.

7. Under Source URL, type the filename of the HTML file you want displayed in the frame you clicked in step 5. (Or click Browse to browse for it.)

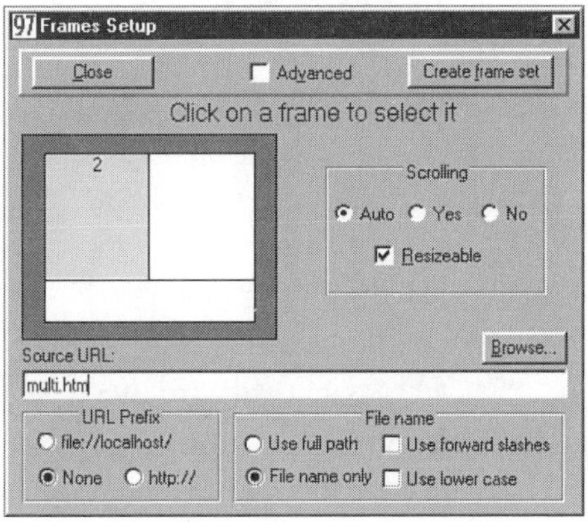

FIGURE 18.4

Steps 5-7: Click a frame in the picture, choose a few options, and enter the filename of the HTML file to appear in that frame.

8. Repeat steps 5 through 7 for all other frames in the picture.

9. When you have supplied a filename for all frames, click the Create Frame Set
▼   button.

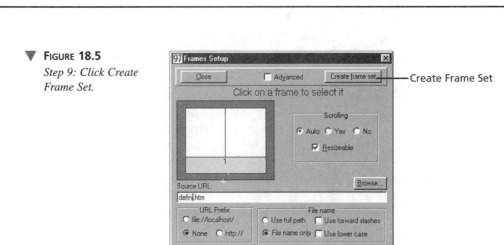

Create Frame Set

10. Choose File, Save, and save the new frame definition page. Be sure to save it in the same folder as its content files (the ones created in step 1).

> If you want to change the number or organization of the frames after creating the frame definition page in HTML Assistant Pro, you must edit the HTML directly; there's no easy dialog box for revising the frames.
>
> An easier technique, however, is to simply create a new frame definition page (choosing new options along the way), and incorporate the same content files as in the previous version. Doing so takes only a minute or two, and is quicker than fussing with the code.

11. Still in HTML Assistant, click the Preview button to see the page displayed in your default browser (see Figure 18.6).

12. Leave your browser open, and open FrontPage Express.

13. Make any changes you want to the content files to improve their appearance in their frames. After changing a file, save it in FrontPage Express, switch to the browser, and click the browser's Refresh (or Reload) button to see the effects of any changes.

▼

▼ FIGURE 18.6
*Step 11: Click the
Preview button to view
the frames page in
your browser.*

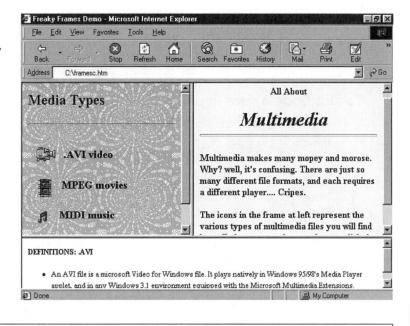

When you publish a frames page to the Web (see Hour 21, "Publishing Your Page"), you must be certain to publish the frame definition page and each of the separate content pages.

Even though you can't view the frames in FrontPage Express, you can open the frame definition page in FrontPage Express and use FrontPage Express's publishing tools to publish the frame definition page. You can finish up by publishing each of the content pages separately.

You can also publish your frames page simply by uploading all of its files via FTP, or by using the publishing tools in HTML Assistant Pro.

After publishing, when publicizing your page (see Hour 22, "Announcing Your Web Presence"), be sure to direct visitors to the address of the frame definition page, not to any of the content pages.

18

Creating Frames in HTML

Most folks' frames' needs will be more than satisfied by HTML Assistant Pro, as shown in the preceding To Do. But if you want greater control over your frames, you'll want to edit the HTML source directly, either in HTML Assistant Pro or in another tool.

> If you don't know how to edit HTML, see Hour 17, "Editing HTML."

To Do: Code a simple page in HTML

1. In FrontPage Express, compose the content pages that will be displayed in the frames. Try to organize and format them, if possible, in a way that will minimize the need for visitors to scroll them in their frames. (But keep in mind that you can always fine-tune them later, after seeing how they look in their frames.)

2. In any HTML editor, create a new HTML file, including the required structure tags and the title for your frames page.

```
<HTML>
<HEAD>
<TITLE>Frames Demo</TITLE>
</HEAD>
   <BODY>
   </BODY>
</HTML>
```

3. Replace the <BODY> tags with <FRAMESET> tags, as shown in the following code. (Note that in a frame definition page, the <FRAMESET> block replaces the <BODY> block, and you cannot include a <BODY> block anywhere in the file.)

```
<HTML>
<HEAD>
<TITLE>Frames Demo</TITLE>
</HEAD>
   <FRAMESET>
   </FRAMESET>
</HTML>
```

   The <FRAMESET> tags enclose the entire definition of the frames. All further coding is inserted between these tags.

4. My frame page will be split into two columns without any rows. Therefore, in the <FRAMESET> tag, I add the COLS attribute. I want the first column to be narrow (30 percent of the window), and the second column to take up the remainder of the window.

```
<FRAMESET COLS="30%,*">
</FRAMESET>
```

> In the <FRAMESET> tag in the example, COLS="*,70%" or COLS="30%,70%" would have the same effect as the entry shown.

▼

5. Having defined the frames, I define their content by adding the `<FRAME SRC>` tag and the filenames of the content files (in quotes). In the columns on the page, the files will be displayed in the same order (left to right) in which they appear in the `<FRAMESET>` block (top to bottom). In the following example, the page file `MULTI.HTM` will be displayed in the first (left) column:

```
<FRAMESET COLS="30%,*">
    <FRAME SRC="MULTI.HTM">
    <FRAME SRC="DESCRIP.HTM">
</FRAMESET>
```

6. Review the completed code of the frame definition page.:

```
<HTML>
<HEAD>
    <TITLE>Frames Demo</TITLE>
</HEAD>
    <FRAMESET COLS="30%,*">
        <FRAME SRC="MULTI.HTM">
        <FRAME SRC="DESCRIP.HTM">
    </FRAMESET>
</HTML>
```

7. Choose File, Save, and save the new frame definition page. Be sure to save it in the same folder as its content files (the ones created in step 1).

8. Test your new page by opening the frame definition page in your browser.

18

FIGURE **18.7**

Step 8: Test the page in a browser.

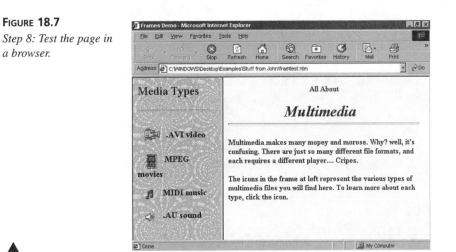

Specifying the Frame in Which a Linked Page Opens

If you code your frame definition pages as shown up to this point in the hour, a link that appears in any of the pages will open its corresponding file in the same frame that holds the link. In other words, if I click a link that's shown in the upper-left frame, the page opened by that link also appears in the upper-left frame, replacing the file that was there.

If you want a link in one frame to open a new page in *another* frame, you must do two things:

- In the <FRAME SRC> lines of the frameset, you must give each frame a name.
- In the links within the content files, you must indicate the name of the frame in which the linked file should open.

Naming the Frames

Using the page created in the preceding To Do as a starting point, we'll name the frames. Add the NAME= attribute to the <FRAME SRC> tag after the filename (and a blank space), as shown in the following code:

```
<FRAMESET ROWS="75%,*">
<FRAMESET COLS"30%,*">
<FRAME SRC="MULTI.HTM" NAME="Icons">
<FRAME SRC="DESCRIP.HTM" NAME="Text">
</FRAMESET>
<FRAME SRC="DEFINI.HTM" NAME="Definitions">
</FRAMESET>
```

It doesn't matter what you call the frames, as long as you give each a unique name. The frame names do not display on the page, just in the source code.

> To name frames while creating them in the Frames Setup dialog box in HTML Assistant Pro, click the Advanced check box. Doing so expands the dialog box to reveal a box in which you can type a name for each frame.

Making Links Point to Frame Names

After naming the frames, you must edit the links within the content files to add the *target*: the name of the frame in which the linked files should open.

That's easy to do when editing the content files in FrontPage Express. When using the Create or Edit Hyperlink dialog box to create or edit a link that you want to open its file in a particular frame, just type that frame's name in the Target Frame box on the World Wide Web tab (see Figure 18.8).

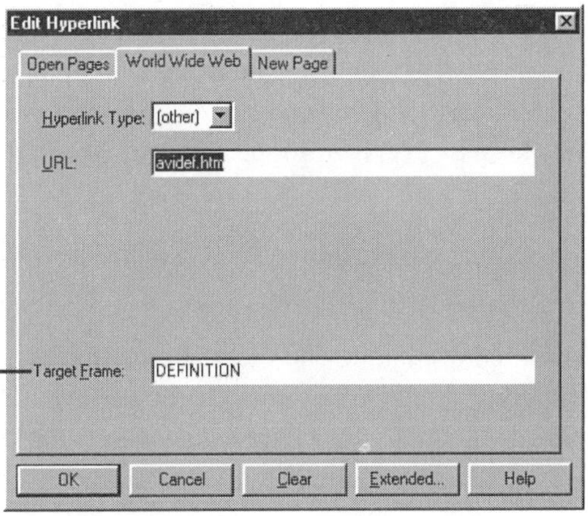

FIGURE 18.8
When adding links to the content files in FrontPage Express, use the Target Frame box to enter the name of the frame in which the page this link points to will appear.

Target Frame

If you'd prefer to code your targets in HTML instead of using FrontPage Express, you must add the TARGET= attribute and the frame name (in quotes) to the link, following the filename, as in the following example:

```
<A HREF="avidef.htm" TARGET="Definitions"></a>
```

When the link shown is executed, the file AVIDEF.HTM opens in the frame named Definitions (the bottom frame), replacing DEFINI.HTM.

Now suppose you wanted every link in the MULTI.HTM file to open its file in the Text frame. When all links are to open in the same frame, you can save time by using the <BASE TARGET> tag in the content file's header. All links in a file containing a <BASE TARGET> tag open their files in the frame named by <BASE TARGET>; you do not need to add any TARGET attributes to the link tags, as in the following example:

```
<HTML>
<HEAD>
<TITLE>
<BASE TARGET="Text">
</HEAD>
<BODY>
page definition goes here
</BODY>
</HTML>
```

All links in the sample content file will open their files in the Text frame.

18

Accommodating the Frames-Intolerant

For all that frames can deliver, they can also make us pay.

Frames generally slow down initial access to a page (because the browser must download multiple files), and when poorly designed, frames force visitors to do a lot of scrolling simply to read the contents of a single page. Frames are supported in all versions of Internet Explorer and Netscape Navigator released since about 1997, and in some other browsers—but not all.

Besides all that, there are many folks online (especially relative newcomers to the Web) who simply don't like navigating frames pages; they find them confusing.

For all of these reasons, many authors who create frames pages also create a non-frames version, with identical content, and give visitors a choice of which version to view (see Figure 18.9). The easiest way to do this is to create a non-frames page that contains links to each of the very same, separate content pages also opened by the frame definition page.

FIGURE 18.9

It's often best to create two separate versions of a site and offer visitors a choice—Frames or No Frames.

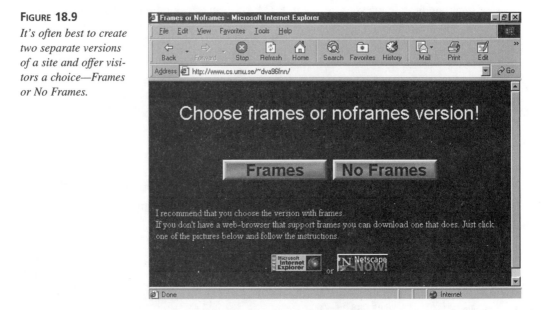

Another useful touch is to add a "noframes" message to the frame definition page. When a visitor using a non-frames–capable browser opens the frame definition page, the message appears in place of the frames. The message can include a link to the non-frames version; for example,

```
Sorry, your browser does not support frames. To view the non-frames version of
the Web site, click here.
```

Two easy ways to create the noframes message are

- Open the frame definition page in HTML Assistant Pro, and look for the <NOFRAMES> tag near the bottom of the file. Replace the sample text there ("This is where to put text that browsers without frames support will display") with your message and URL.

- Open the frame definition page in FrontPage Express. Because FrontPage Express does not support frames, it shows the sample noframes message created by HTML Assistant Pro—it acts, in effect, like a non-frames-capable browser (see Figure 18.10). You can edit the message right there in FrontPage Express, add your URL pointing to the non-frames version, and then save the file.

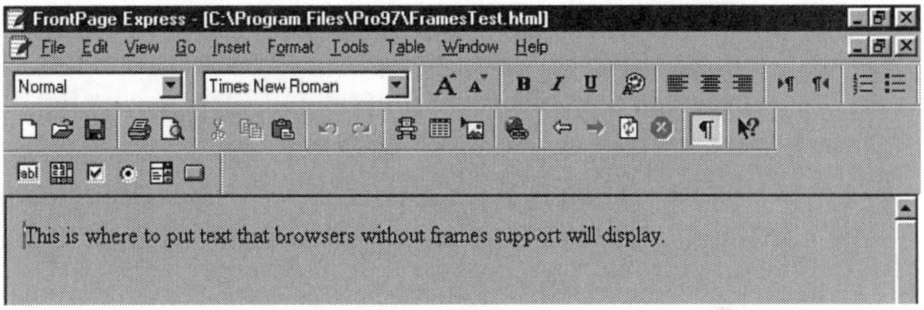

FIGURE 18.10

You can't use FrontPage Express to create the frame definition page, but you can use it to edit the noframes message.

18

Summary

Frames are an exercise in careful choices and organization. Most important among the choices is deciding whether to use frames at all. When you're committed to using frames, always try to supply a useful <NOFRAME> message and an alternative version for the frameless.

Q&A

Q Sometimes, Internet Explorer adds scrollbars to my frames when they're not really necessary. What can I do about that?

A By default, browsers add scrollbars whenever a file's contents seem to exceed the frame. You might be able to eliminate the problem by adjusting the formatting of the content file or the size of the frame in which it is displayed so that the content sits comfortably in the frame.

Keep in mind, however, that just because everything fits in your display does not mean it will always do so in every visitor's browser. Variations in font size, display resolution, and other display factors can cause material that fits in a frame on your computer to exceed the frame on someone else's. Leaving scrollbars enabled helps ensure that all frames-capable visitors will be able to navigate your page.

If you're confident that scrollbars are unnecessary, but they still show up, you can prevent them in two ways: In HTML Assistant Pro, when defining the content page to use for each frame (look back at Figure 18.4), click the No option in the Scrolling box. Or, you can edit the HTML directly, and add the `SCROLLING="NO"` attribute to the `<FRAME SRC>` line for the frame, as shown in the following:

```
<FRAME SRC="sample.htm" SCROLLING="NO">
```

By the way, you can force browsers to display scrollbars on a frame, even when the browser considers them unnecessary, by choosing the Yes option in HTML Assistant Pro, or by adding `SCROLLING="YES"` to the `<FRAME SRC>` line.

Q **I've seen pages online that appear to have frames (parts of the page seem to operate independently of others), but there are no borders or scrollbars between frames. How do I do these?**

A It's easiest to do in HTML Assistant Pro. When defining the frames, click the Advanced check box at the top of the Frames Setup dialog box. The dialog box expands to reveal more options below. For each frame, click the frame in the picture, and then clear the check box labeled Border in the expanded area.

That step removes borders, but scrollbars will still appear if the selection under Scrolling is Auto or Yes. To prevent the scrollbars from appearing, choose No.

HOUR 19

Designing
Fill-in-the-Blanks Forms

You know forms. They're those fill-in-the-blanks' parts of Web pages you use to enter search terms, register with a Web site, make e-purchases and much more. In fact, Web forms are really the only way a Web visitor can send information to a Web site *through* the Web (email doesn't count).

A signature containing your email address (see Hour 10, "Making Links") is sufficient for providing visitors with a way to send you comments and questions. But if your site is visited hundreds or thousands of times a day, or if you want to collect orders or mailing list sign-ups online, you need a more efficient method—a way to collect all of the information sent by visitors, store it in a database, and then work with it in a meaningful way. That's what forms make possible.

At the end of this hour, you will be able to answer the following questions:

- What's involved in creating a form, and why do most beginners need to enlist the aid of a server administrator to get the whole job done?

- How do I create the easy part of a form, the part you actually see in the Web page?
- What do I have to do to get the tricky part of a form (the data processing) done?

Understanding Forms

A *form* is a Web page (or a part of a Web page) that collects information from your visitors by prompting them to select options from lists, check boxes, and use other such *form fields* (see Figure 19.1). When done supplying information, the visitor clicks a Submit button to send the data to the server to be processed.

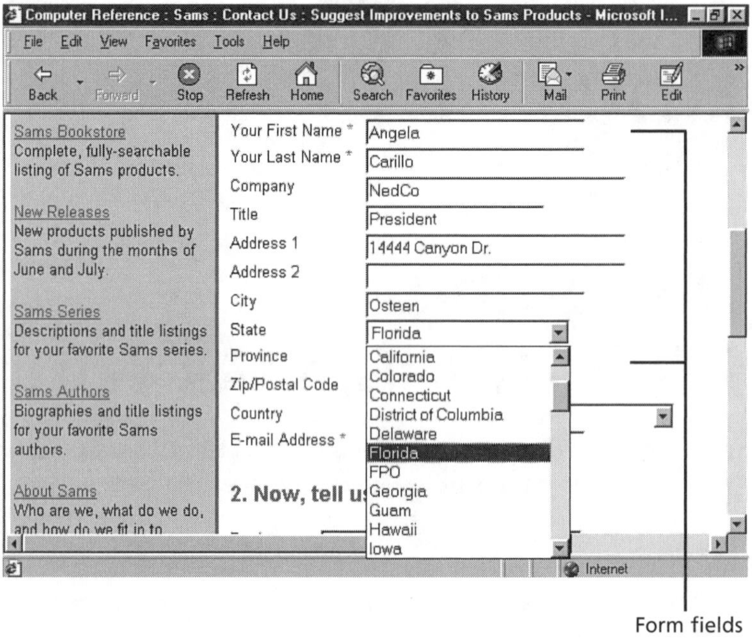

FIGURE **19.1**

Forms use fields to collect information from visitors.

Form fields

Creating the part of a form you *see* is easy—in fact, FrontPage Express can even create one for you, in several different ways. But the part you see is only half of the form; the other half consists of various behind-the-scenes programming for collecting and processing the data visitors enter and storing it in a form that's useful to you.

That processing can happen in several different ways: If the Web server on which you publish the page containing the form is equipped with Microsoft software called *FrontPage Extensions*, you can configure nearly all aspects of processing from within FrontPage Express, and you will need no other programming to process your form.

But if the server does not have the FrontPage Extensions, a short program called a *script* must be custom-written to process your form, and that script must be properly set up on the server. The script can be programmed in any of several different programming languages, including Java, Microsoft Visual Basic, and several other languages, sometimes labeled "CGI" languages. Such programming generally exceeds the capabilities and ambitions of beginning Web authors—although, if you're so inclined, there are plenty of good books to teach you.

For beginners, I think the best approach is this: You worry about what appears on screen, and you let someone else worry about the scripting.

If you will publish on your Internet provider's Web server, you can simply define the form's onscreen appearance (as you learn to do in this hour), and then talk with your Internet provider about how you want the data handled. In all likelihood, the Internet provider will write the script for a modest fee, or arrange to have a reliable programmer do it.

Creating the Visible Form

Again, while the data processing aspects of forms can be tricky, creating the form itself in FrontPage Express is a snap. The next several pages show several different ways you can quickly produce any type of form you desire.

No matter which way you create your form, after you create the form you must deal with how it will be processed.

After using the form-creation method of your choice from this section, be sure to read the final two sections of this hour: "Choosing Options for Fields" and "Controlling the Way Form Data is Processed."

19

Building a Fast, Easy Form with the Form Page Wizard

FrontPage Express includes a Form Page Wizard you can use to create a new page with a lovely form already in it. Based on your selections in a few simple dialog boxes, the Wizard custom builds a form page matched to your needs. After creating the page, you can add text and graphics to it and expand it by adding other page content above and below the form.

The following To Do demonstrates only one of the many different types of forms you can create by making different choices in the Form Page Wizard. Feel free to experiment. If you don't like the results, it's easy to start over.

To Do: Run the Form Page Wizard

1. In FrontPage Express, choose File, New.

2. Click Form Page Wizard, and then click OK.

FIGURE 19.2

Step 2: Click Form Page Wizard, and then click OK.

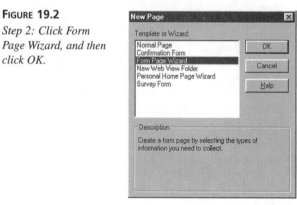

3. Click Next.

4. Type a filename for the page in Page URL and a title in Page Title (just as you ordinarily do in FrontPage Express the first time you save a new page). Then click Next.

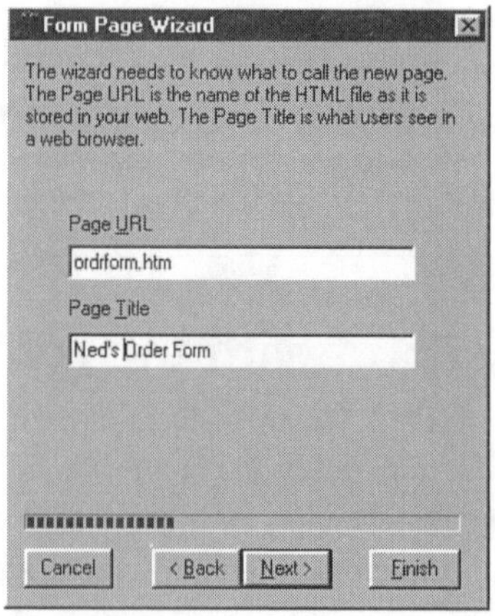

FIGURE 19.3

Step 4: Type a filename and title, and then click Next.

5. Click the Add button.

▼ 6. Choose one type of information to collect in the form, and then click Next.

FIGURE **19.4**

Step 6: Choose a type of information to collect, and click Next.

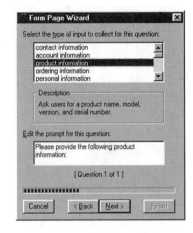

In step 6, after choosing a type of information (but before you click Next), the box at the bottom of the dialog box displays the text that will appear in the page next to the form field created by this step.

You can edit that text right in the box, if you like, before clicking Next. But note that you can also edit the same text in the page after the form is finished.

7. Choose from among any options presented (the options differ, depending on which type of information you selected in step 6). When done, click Next.

19

FIGURE **19.5**

Step 7: Choose options for the information type you selected in step 6.

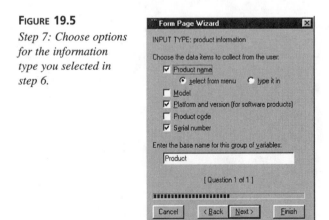

8. Repeat steps 5–7 for each type of information you want this form to collect, and then click Next.

After step 7, you can change the order of the sections in the form by using the Move Up and Move Down buttons to change the order of the list.

9. When the dialog box lists all of the questions you want the form to ask, click Finish.

FIGURE 19.6
Step 9: Click Finish.

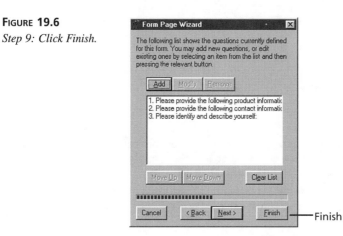

10. Evaluate your form, and edit it any way you want.

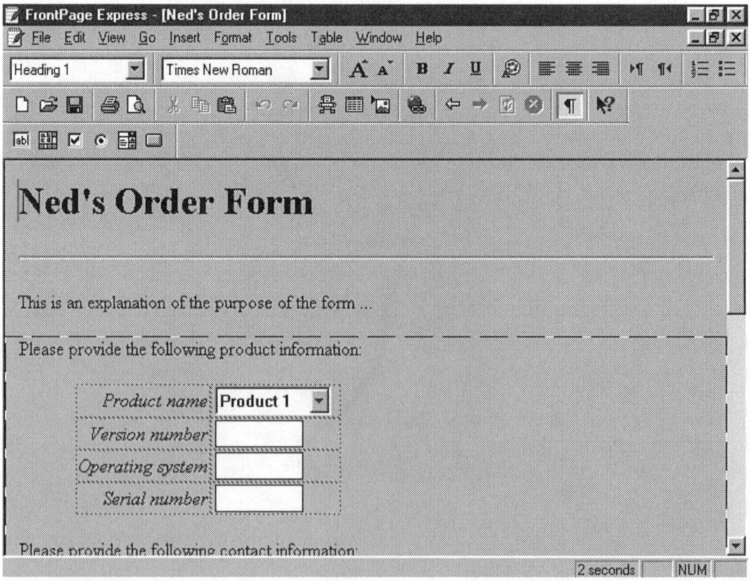

FIGURE 19.7
Step 10: Edit the page in FrontPage Express.

> In Figure 19.7, observe the dashed line above the beginning of the form fields.
>
> When Format Marks are turned on in FrontPage Express, a dashed box appears around the entire form. The box helps you identify where the form begins and ends, and to distinguish between different forms in the same page. (The box does not appear when the page is viewed through a browser.)
>
> To turn Format Marks on (or off), choose View, Format Marks.

Including a Form in Your Personal Home Page

When you use the Personal Home Page Wizard to crank out a quick page (see Hour 3, "Wizarding Up a Personal Home Page"), you have the option to include a simple form in that page.

When checking check boxes to choose the section to include in the page, at the very bottom of the list of sections you'll see a check box for adding a Comments and Suggestions section. If you check that box, a few steps further in the procedure you'll encounter a dialog box like the one shown in Figure 19.8.

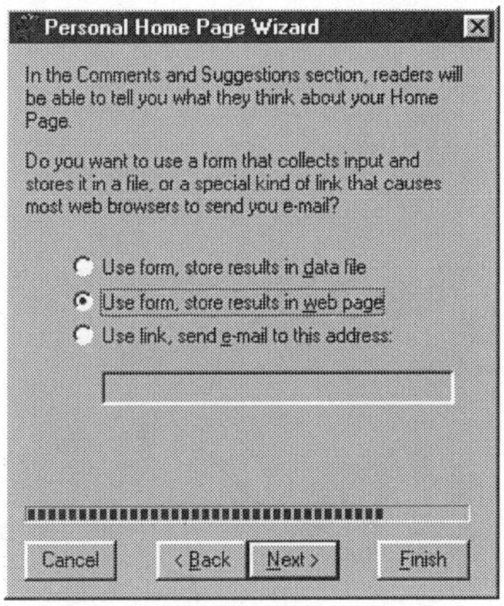

FIGURE **19.8**

If you choose to include a Comments and Suggestions section in your Personal Home Page, the Wizard gives you an opportunity to choose how that form's data will be processed.

19

In the dialog box shown in Figure 19.8, you must choose an option for collecting and processing comments and suggestions from your visitors:

- *Use form, store results in data file*—Inserts a text box in the page in which visitors can type comments. When a visitor clicks the Submit button, the comments are stored in a data file on the server for you to review.

- *Use form, store results in Web page*—Inserts a text box in the page in which visitors can type comments. When a visitor clicks the Submit button, the comments are stored in a Web page file on the server for you to review.

- *Use link, send to this email address*—Omits the form, and instead creates a signature with a mailto: link (see Hour 10) so visitors can send comments to you via email.

> These processing options will work only if the page is published on a server that's equipped with the FrontPage Extensions.

If you select either of the options that create a form, your page will include a form like the one in Figure 19.9 when you finish the Wizard.

FIGURE 19.9

Here's what you get if you include Comments and Suggestions in your personal home page.

FrontPage Express - [Home Page 8]

File   Edit   View   Go   Insert   Format   Tools   Table   Window   Help

Comment: This form will store its results in the HTML file '_private/homeresp.htm'.

Please tell me what you think about this page.

Comments:

From:

[Submit Comments]   [Reset Form]

> In addition to the Personal Home Page Wizard and the Forms Wizard, there's one more choice on FrontPage Express's New Page dialog box (File, New) to create a form: Survey Form.
>
> If you choose Survey Form, there are no further Wizard steps. A sample survey form page appears immediately, ready for you to edit to your liking.

Creating Custom Forms from Scratch

Besides providing wizards for making forms, FrontPage Express also offers the Forms toolbar, from which you can quickly create forms containing precisely the fields you require.

If you do not see the Forms toolbar in FrontPage Express, choose View, Forms Toolbar.

FIGURE 19.10

Use the Forms toolbar to add individual fields to a form.

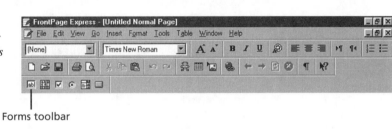

Forms toolbar

When inserting fields, choose fields that match the input you want from the visitor. If you want a short, typed response, use One-Line Text box; Scrolling text boxes are for longer typed responses. Radio buttons and check boxes let visitors choose one or more options shown, while a drop-down menu lets the visitor select a single item from a short list.

19

To add fields (and even insert a whole new form, as you learn in the next To Do), you click buttons on the Forms toolbar:

abl	One-line text box	
🔢	Scrolling text box	
☑	Check box	☑
⦿	Radio button	⦿

Drop-down menu

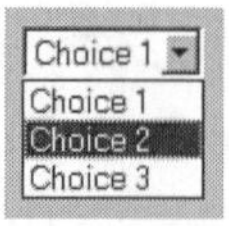

Push button

> When you insert a push Button, it's automatically labeled "Submit" and con-
> figured as the Submit button—the button a visitor must click to send in the
> form data.
>
> To change a button's name, or to make it into a Reset button (a visitor clicks
> the Reset button when he wants to wipe out all previous entries and start
> over), double-click the button to open its Properties dialog box, and change
> it with the options provided.

To Do: Inserting form fields

1. Click in the page where you want the form to go, and then click the Forms toolbar
   button for the type of field you want to add. A new form is inserted (indicated by
   the dashed box), with the field in it.

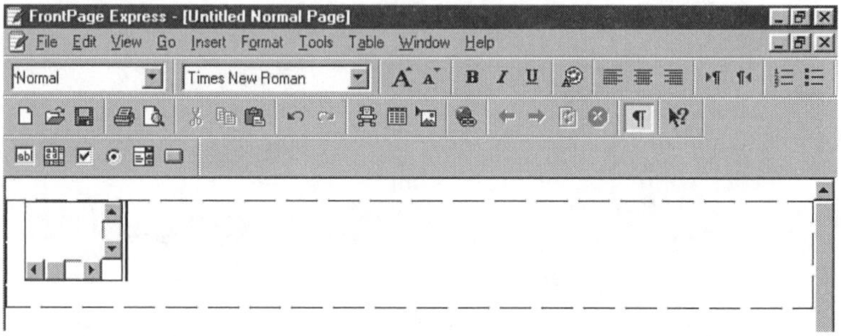

FIGURE 19.11

*Step 1: Insert one field
to automatically start a
new form.*

> To add fields to an existing form, such as one you created with a wizard, just
> click where you want to add the field and then do steps 2–4 of this To Do.
>
> To delete a field, click it (to select it), and press the Delete key.

2. To insert your next field to the right of the first, repeat step 1. To insert your next
   field beneath the first, press Enter to start a new line, and then repeat step 1.

▼ 3. After adding your fields, type a descriptive label or instruction next to each.

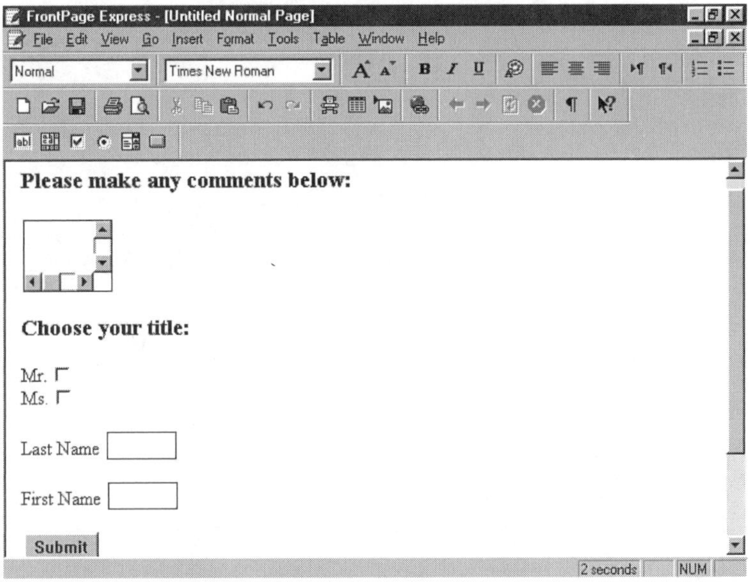

FIGURE 19.12

Step 3: Label your fields.

Observe in Figure 19.7 (earlier in this hour) that the Forms Page Wizard sometimes aligns fields with labels by putting the fields and labels in a table.

You can do the same thing. Begin by inserting a single field in the page to add a new form box. Then delete that field, and the empty form box remains. Click inside the form box, and choose Table, Insert Table to insert a new table inside the form box. Then simply insert your fields and labels inside the table cells as you create them.

19

▲

To Do: Creating the items on a drop-down menu

To create each option a visitor can select with check boxes or radio buttons, you just add another field. But after inserting a drop-down menu, you must add to it all of the items from which the visitor may select.

1. Double-click the drop-down menu field.

2. Click Add.

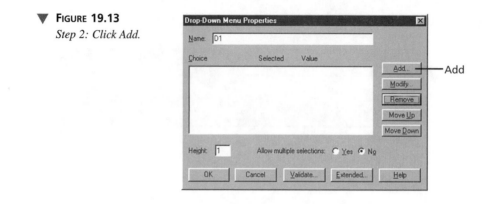

FIGURE 19.13
Step 2: Click Add.

3. In Choice, type the item text, and then click OK.

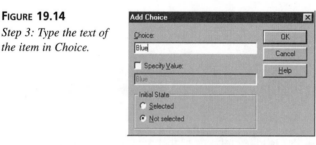

FIGURE 19.14
Step 3: Type the text of the item in Choice.

4. Repeat steps 2 and 3 for the remaining items.

5. Click OK on the Drop-Down Menu Properties dialog box.

> After step 4, you can rearrange the order of items in the list. In the Drop-Down Menu Properties dialog box, click an item whose place in the order you want to change, and then click Move Up or Move Down.

Choosing Options for Fields

Regardless of how the form was created, you can customize the appearance or behavior of any form field. To begin, double-click the field. A properties dialog box opens, like the one shown in Figure 19.15.

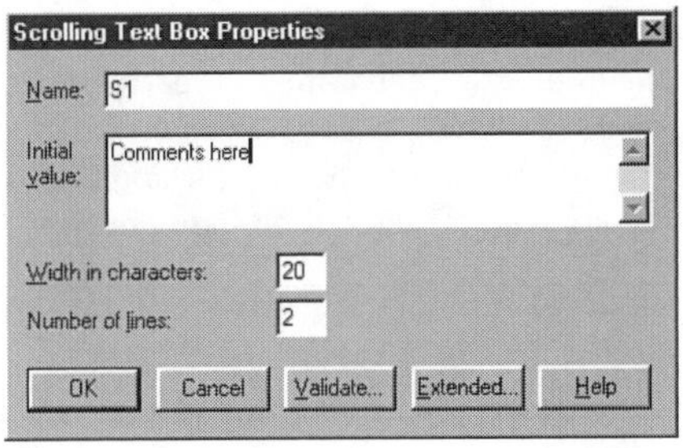

FIGURE 19.15

Double-click any field to change its Properties.

Scrolling Text Box Properties

Name: S1

Initial value: Comments here

Width in characters: 20
Number of lines: 2

OK   Cancel   Validate...   Extended...   Help

The exact options you'll see vary, depending on the type of field you double-clicked. Most options are self-explanatory, such as the Height and Width options that let you set the size of a text box.

> You can change the width of a one-line text box, and the width and/or height of a scrolling text box, using the same techniques you use to size a picture. Just click the field to select it, and then drag its handles.

However, there are three important options you'll see that may not be so self-explanatory:

Name—Every field (and every item in a drop-down list box) has a unique name not used by any other field in the form. These names do not appear in the page; rather, they're used behind the scenes to process the data collected.

Initial Value—In one-line and scrolling text boxes, an optional, default form entry you offer your visitors to save them time. For example, if you predict that most visitors will probably make a particular entry in a text box, you can make that entry appear to be pre-entered on the form. The visitor can always change that entry, but if the initial value is what he would have chosen or typed anyway, he can skip that field. Some Web authors also use the Initial Value to display within the form an instruction for using the form ("Type your address here").

Initial State—In lists, check boxes and radio buttons, you can specify that a particular field or list item is automatically selected, so that visitors who would have made the same selection can skip the field.

19

You choose the initial state separately for each item in a drop-down list. You can do that on the Add Item dialog box when creating the item. You can also change the setting later by double-clicking the list, selecting the item you want to change, and clicking the Modify button.

Controlling the Way Form Data is Processed

Regardless of which method you use to create the visible part of the form, when you're finished, you must also configure the back end—the invisible settings that determine how the data is to be collected and processed.

Again, you must work closely with your Internet Service Provider (ISP) or the administrator of the server where you will publish your pages to set up forms processing. You need to find out whether the server is equipped with the FrontPage Extensions and, if the server is not so equipped, how your form data will be processed on the server (by a Java program, CGI script, and so on).

The following To Do provides a rough overview of the basic steps for defining data handling for a form. But the specific options you select must be determined in consultation with your server administrator.

To Do: Choosing how the form data will be processed

1. Right-click anywhere within the form, and choose Form Properties.

FIGURE 19.16
Step 1: Right-click in the form and choose Form Properties.

Cut	
Copy	
Paste	
Page Properties...	
Form Properties...	
Paragraph Properties...	
Font Properties...	Alt+Enter

2. In Form Name, type a name for this form.

3. From the Form Handler list, choose the way data from this form will be processed:

   • If the server has the FrontPage Extensions, choose WebBot Save Results Component.

   • If the server does *not* have the FrontPage Extensions, choose one of the other options in the list, as directed by your administrator.

▼

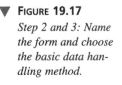

▼ FIGURE **19.17**

Step 2 and 3: Name the form and choose the basic data handling method.

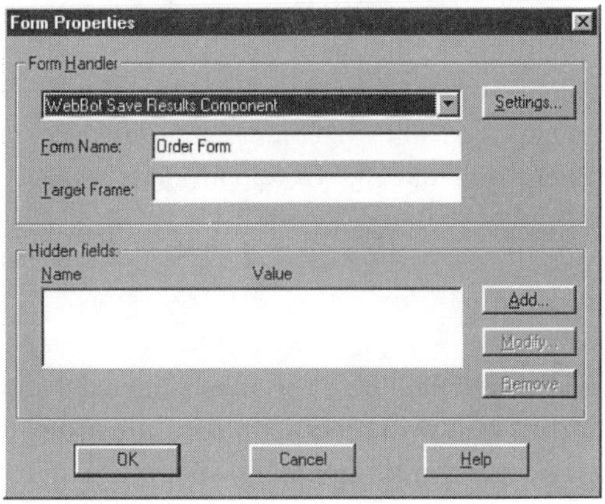

4. Click the Settings button to open a dialog box on which you can select from among various processing options for the type of processing you selected in step 2. When done with that dialog box, click OK to return to the Form Properties dialog box.

FIGURE **19.18**

Step 3: Pick the Settings for the data handler type.

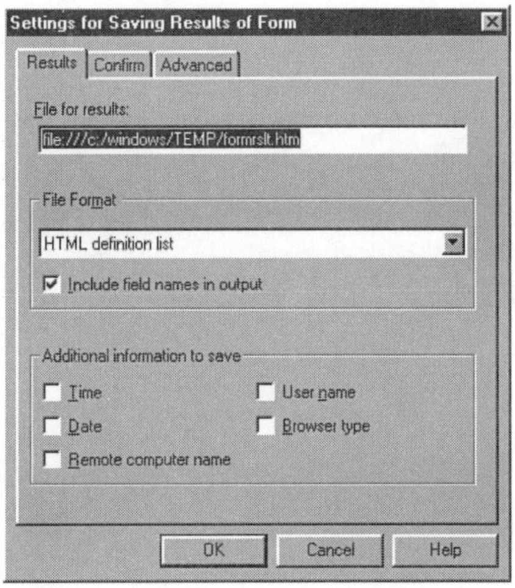

19

▲   5. Click OK.

Summary

As you can see, building a form is easy—even fun. And building the data-handling can be fun, too—but you must be willing to commit yourself to moving a notch higher in your technical expertise. See Hour 24, "Developing Your Authoring Skills," for some suggestions on how to learn scripting.

Q&A

Q So if I write my own script, or if the server has the FrontPage extensions, I don't need to deal with my server administrator when building a form, right? 'Cause I saw him once, and... he scares me.

A No, you'll still need to work closely with the administrator of the Web server to set your form up properly.

Different servers have different rules in force about what kinds of processing users are permitted to do, where on the server the programs must be stored, and so on. These policies are essential to safeguarding the server from computer theft and vandalism.

In fact, security is one reason some server administrators won't install the FrontPage Extensions. Some administrators believe the extensions make it too easy for just anyone to run a program on the server.

But don't be afraid of your server administrator. The next time you see him, just call him Spock, and you'll be fast friends.

HOUR **20**

Putting Multiple Links in One Picture

You've seen 'em—those cool-looking pictures and button bars in Web pages that contain multiple links. Click one button or one part of the picture, and you go one place; click another part, you go somewhere else. It's a pro touch.

But it's not out of your league, now that you have 19 hours of Web authoring training already under your belt. In this hour, you learn how to apply some of the HTML skills from Hour 17, "Editing HTML," and scripting skills from Hour 19, "Designing Fill-in-the-Blanks Forms," to make these multilink pictures happen. At the end of the hour, you'll be able to answer the following questions:

- How do *imagemaps*—those inline images with multiple links—work, anyhow?
- What's the difference between a *server-side* imagemap and *client-side* imagemap?
- How can I add imagemaps to my Web pages, using FrontPage Express in tandem with another program on the CD-ROM, MapEdit?

About Imagemaps

You know that an image file can serve as a link source; clicking the image activates the link. By creating an imagemap, you can make different areas within one image activate different links. Figure 20.1 shows an imagemap.

NEW TERM An *imagemap* is an inline image containing multiple links, each of which is activated when the visitor clicks a different area of the image.

Imagemaps are used for fancy jobs, such as maps—click a country or state, and a link opens a document about it. But they have more mundane uses, as well; for example, most button bars you'll see online are imagemaps. The whole bar is one big GIF file, but the imagemap assigns a separate URL to each button.

FIGURE 20.1

Clicking on different parts of this imagemap activates different links.

The links in an imagemap can point anywhere any other link can point: to another Web page, to an email address, to a bookmark (*target*), to a file for download/display, and so on.

Server-Side Versus Client-Side

An imagemap can be written as a server-based, imagemapping script, or it can be coded into the HTML file itself to be run by the browser, or *client*. When the imagemap code is inserted directly into the HTML file, it's called a *client-side* imagemap. When a script on the server is required, it's a *server-side* imagemap.

To learn more about scripts, see Hour 19.

Which should you create? Well, here's the full poop: Client-side imagemaps are much easier to create than server-side imagemaps. Client-side imagemaps work only when the page is viewed through an imagemap-compatible browser, but fortunately, the overwhelming majority of folks online today use browsers that can handle client-side imagemaps. Client-side imagemaps are supported by

- Every version of Internet Explorer since its debut
- Netscape Navigator versions 2 and later
- Most other browsers derived from Spyglass Mosaic versions 2.1 and higher

These browsers (which together represent over 90 percent of the browsers used on the Web) not only support client-side imagemaps, but server-side imagemaps, as well.

A very small proportion of folks online—those using graphical browsers other than the ones I listed—cannot use client-side imagemaps, but *can* use server-side imagemaps. Of course, those using text-only browsers cannot use any kind of picture links, including any sort of imagemap, whether client or server.

As you know from Hour 19, writing scripts requires more technical expertise than most beginning Web authors care to develop. On top of that, publishing your scripts on a server requires very close collaboration with the administrator of the Web server where your pages will be published to ensure that you write your script in a language the server supports and follow other rules that vary from server to server. Server-side imagemaps require a lot more work than client-side imagemaps and only expand the reach of your page by a tiny proportion.

Given that, I recommend doing what most Web authors do these days:

- Stick to client-side imagemaps.
- Make sure a block of text links on the page repeats all links that are in any imagemap (or other picture link) on the same page (see Figure 20.2).

Your client-side imagemaps will work great for nearly all visitors. And the text links will serve not only visitors whose browsers don't support client-side imagemaps, but also those with text-only browsers, and those who have turned off the display of images in their browsers to speed up surfing.

20

FIGURE **20.2**

*Always repeat any links
in an imagemap (or any
other picture link) in
text links on the same
page, to serve those
whose browsers don't
support imagemaps or
pictures.*

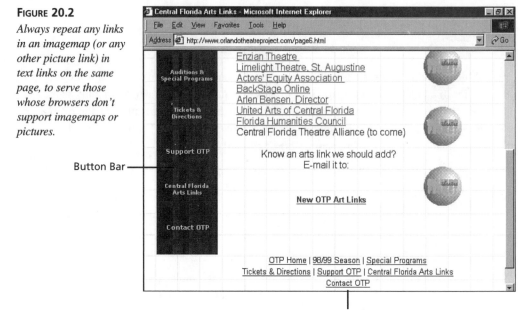

Button Bar—

Text Links

Should you decide to ignore my advice and develop server-side imagemaps,
note that the imagemap creator included on the CD-ROM with this book,
MapEdit, can be used to create either server-side or client-side imagemaps.

Choosing (or Creating) Images Suited for Imagemapping

You can use any GIF or JPEG image for an imagemap, be it one you created or a
copyright-free piece of clip art. But the best image for an imagemap is one that's very
clearly and obviously divided into distinct regions.

It's important that a visitor, upon seeing the image, can instinctively expect different
regions to lead to different places. If the image's regions are not clearly defined, a visitor
might assume that the image is a picture link leading only one place and click it without
carefully choosing a region. Or the visitor might not even realize that the picture contains
any links and fail to exploit the useful tool you have so thoughtfully provided.

For example, consider the image shown in Figure 20.3. This image is a poor choice for an imagemap because it does not appear to have distinct segments or regions. The image shown in Figure 20.4 is a better choice, because it is divided naturally into identifiable shapes that visitors will naturally assume contain different links.

FIGURE 20.3

This image would make a poor imagemap. How would one tell which parts to click?

FIGURE 20.4

This image, very clearly divided into distinct regions, is a better choice.

Creating an Imagemap

The CD-ROM at the back of this book contains MapEdit, a program for adding imagemaps to existing HTML files.

To use MapEdit to create a client-side imagemap, you first create your page (in FrontPage Express or another tool), and insert in the page the image you will use for the imagemap. You then open the page in MapEdit to turn the image into an imagemap, as described in the following To Do.

20

In general, you should finish all other aspects of the page (in FrontPage Express or in another Web authoring program) before using MapEdit to make one or more images in the page into imagemaps.

Why? Well, if you change the size, shape, or other aspects of an image in the page after you create the imagemap, the imagemap may not work properly anymore. In practice, you can probably do some manipulation of the page safely after adding the imagemap, but it's hard to predict which kinds of changes will create problems later and which won't. So it's best to leave MapEdit for the final step.

If after creating an imagemap, you decide you must make major changes to the page (or if you've already made such changes, and discover your imagemap no longer works properly), the best solution is to reopen the page and image in MapEdit (as described in steps 2 through 5 of the To Do) and adjust the regions as needed.

To Do: Create a client-side imagemap in MapEdit

▲ To Do

1. Using FrontPage Express or another tool, create the page and insert in it the image that will become the imagemap.

2. Open MapEdit from the Windows Start menu by choosing Programs, MapEdit, MapEdit.

3. Choose File, Open HTML Document.

4. Navigate to and select the file of the Web page you created in step 1, and then click Open.

5. The list shows all of the image files in the page. Click the one that will serve as the imagemap, and then click OK.

FIGURE 20.5

Step 5: From the images in the page you opened in step 4, choose the one for the imagemap.

Select Inline Image

Select the image to be mapped. You can create a map corresponding to any inline image mentioned in the HTML document.

tomato.gif
tomatoes.gif

OK   Cancel

▼

▼   6. Consider the general shape of the first region to which you want to attach a link: Is it more or less circular or rectangular, or is it a more irregular polygon? Decide what the closest shape is, and then click that shape in the toolbar.

   7. Now click and drag to draw a shape that generally covers the region:

       • For a circle, click in the center of the region, and then drag outward. When the shape generally covers the region, click once.

       • For a rectangle, click in the upper-left corner of the region, and then drag diagonally toward the lower-right corner. When the shape generally covers the region, click once.

       • For a polygon, click one corner of the region and drag to another corner to draw a line. Click the corner you've arrived at to stop that line, and then drag to the next corner. Continue until you have drawn a shape completely around the region, and then right-click.

   > If you don't like the point where you started a shape, press Esc to clear the shape and start over.

FIGURE 20.6

Step 7: Click a shape tool and draw a shape to define the region.

Add Rectangles tool

Add Circles tool

Add Polygons tool

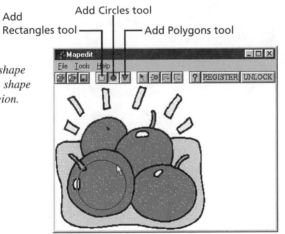

20

▼

In steps 6 and 7, don't fuss too much over trying to perfectly match a shape to a region.

As long as the shape you draw roughly covers the region and does not overlap with other shapes you draw for other regions, it's no big deal if there are some gaps between the shapes covering regions, or if the shape covers a little bit of space outside the region.

Understanding this, you'll find that in most cases you can use the Circle or Rectangle tools to draw your rough shapes, resorting to the more laborious Polygon tool only for special circumstances.

8. Fill in the URL to which a visitor should be taken when clicking this region, and click OK.

FIGURE 20.7

Step 8: Fill in the URL to which this region points.

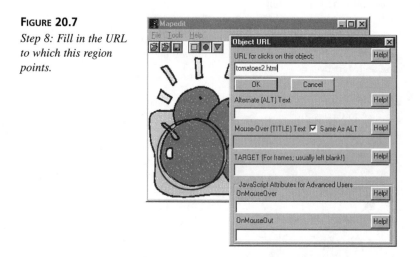

The TARGET field in the dialog box shown in Figure 20.7 is not for entering the name of a bookmark (*target*; see Hour 11, "More Ways to Link") as you might expect, but rather for choosing the *target frame*.

If the HTML file you opened in step 2 will be part of a frames-based Web page, you can enter in TARGET the name of the frame in which you want the file or page opened by this link to appear. See Hour 18, "Dividing a Page into Frames."

▼ 9. Repeat steps 6, 7, and 8 for each region in the image. (You can use different kinds of shapes, and different kinds of URLs, for different regions.)

FIGURE **20.8**

Step 9: Complete the regions.

10. Choose File, Save HTML Document to save the Web page file with its new imagemap added to it.

11. Preview the file in a Web browser to test the links.

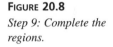

In step 8 of the To Do, you can enter any type of URL: One pointing to a Web site/page (for example, http://www.mcp.com), the filename of another Web page in your Web site, stored in the same folder (page2.html), a link to an email address (mailto:me@server.com), or the name of a file for downloading (resume.doc).

To make the link point to a particular bookmark (*target*), add a hashmark and the bookmark name (#Chapter3) to the URL as described in Hour 11.

▲

Summary

Imagemaps are pretty cool, and not too hard to make. Just be sure you choose an image in which the regions to which you'll attach links are easy for the visitor to recognize.

20

Q&A

Q Can I edit my imagemaps later, after creating them?

A Sure. Repeat steps 2–5 of the To Do, and then use MapEdit's tools to make any changes you like.

Q **Not that I necessarily want to, but assume that I did want to use MapEdit to create a server-side imagemap. How would I do it?**

A Begin by creating a client-side imagemap, just as in the To Do entitled "Create a client-side imagemap in MapEdit" in this hour. Still in MapEdit, choose File, Export Old Server Map. The imagemap script is saved in its own file.

After saving the file, show it to the administrator of your Web server to find out whether any changes must be made to make it work properly on the server, and to learn the rules for publishing scripts on the server, such as in which directory your script must be stored.

Part VI
Getting It Online

Hour

Appendix

HOUR **21**

Publishing Your Page

You didn't become a Web author just to share your accomplishments with your canary. Of course, you want to get your work onto a Web server so it can be visited, loved, and lauded by those burgeoning Web masses.

FrontPage Express is a big help with publishing. By setting up a few defaults and properly organizing your files, you'll wind up with the ability to publish your pages (and then update them later) with a few quick clicks.

At the end of this hour, you'll be able to answer the following questions:

- Where do I publish?
- What should I do before publishing to make sure everything's ready?
- How do I use FrontPage Express to make publishing my page easy?
- Once my page is online, how do I check it out?

About Web Servers

As you've known for about 20 hours, you need space on the hard disk of a Web server to publish your page on the Web.

By now, you probably already know where you intend to publish your page. Nearly all Internet accounts today—whether with a regular Internet service provider or with an online service, like AOL—include a few megabytes of Web server space in the deal (see Figure 21.1). Most folks publish their first Web pages in the space supplied by their Internet providers.

> Note that Web space suppliers usually make a distinction between "personal" home pages and "commercial" pages (those used to promote a business). On the assumption that a commercial page generally gets more traffic than a personal one, suppliers may charge a higher rate for space used by a commercial page.
>
> If your Internet provider gives you free space, the provider may require that the space be used only for a personal page, and may charge an additional monthly fee if you use the space for commercial purposes. (Exceptions may be made for not-for-profits; talk to your provider.)

FIGURE 21.1

For most folks just starting out with Web publishing, it's usually best to use any Web server space that comes free with your Internet or online service account.

Free Web Space Deal

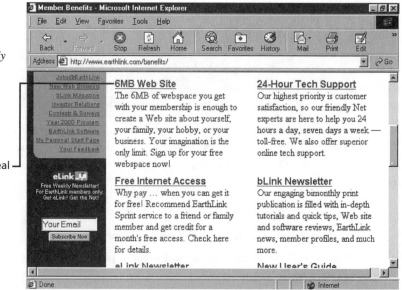

But in case your Internet provider offers no server space to you, here are some other ways to pick up Web server space:

Before choosing a provider for Web space, visit that company's Web page a few times at different hours. If the server sends pages slowly at certain hours or seems to be unavailable from time to time, look for a better-equipped provider.

At work or school—Your employer or school might have a Web server on which you are permitted to store your page. Certainly, if your page is strictly work-related (or school-related), you're most likely to gain permission to publish it on the server for free.

However, note that free access to corporate and university servers is diminishing rapidly as demand grows and as organizations look for ways to earn money from their Internet connections. Also, many university systems, as well as some corporate systems, are overtaxed and might have outdated server hardware or inadequate connection speeds. Using a slow or unreliable system provides poor service to your visitors; forking over a few dollars a month for space on a fast commercial server might be a better choice in the long run than using free space on a poor server.

From a Web-Hosting Service—A growing number of companies online offer Web space "hosting services." Many such services are just Internet providers making a few bucks on the side by leasing server space, often for just a few dollars a month.

You can also find "free" server space offered by a variety of companies sometimes called "online communities." In exchange for your free space, you agree to include required advertising on your pages (see Figure 21.2). Examples are Yahoo!'s GeoCities community (www.geocities.com) and Talk City (www.talkcity.com). The freebies are for personal pages only; these sites also lease space to business pages.

Given the availability of free space from Internet providers, these are usually a poor compromise; the ads annoy your visitors and restrict your design options, and many users complain of poor reliability from the servers. The one advantage of these services is that they provide online, easy-to-use page wizards for quickly creating your pages. Having purchased and read this book, you don't need the wizards.

It's easy to find Web hosting services by surfing. You can enter the search term Web hosting in any search engine, or visit a site called HostSearch (www.hostsearch.com), a search tool specifically for finding server space (see Figure 21.3).

Some hosting services are set up to offer free or low-cost space for pages with particular worthy topics: arts, non-profit organizations, and so on.

21

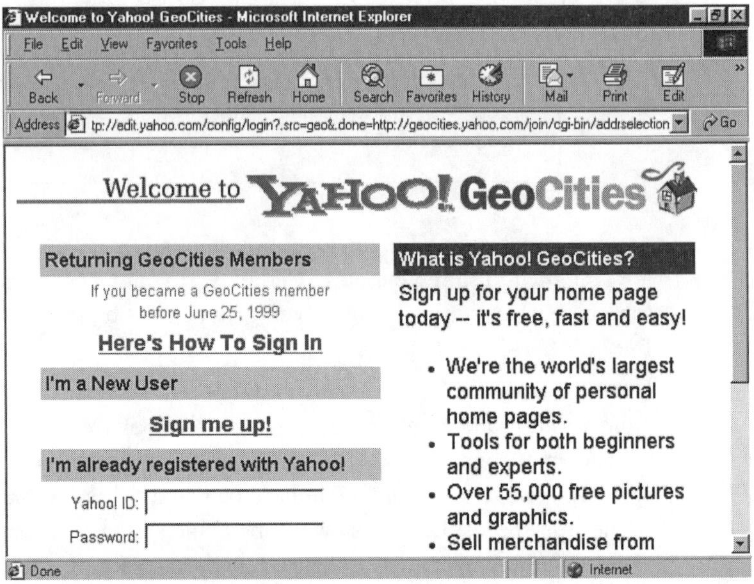

FIGURE 21.2

*You can get "free"
Web hosting services—
just remember that
they reserve the right
to post advertisements
on your Web pages for
your visitors to see.*

FIGURE 21.2

*You can get "free"
Web hosting services—
just remember that
they reserve the right
to post advertisements
on your Web pages for
your visitors to see.*

FIGURE 21.3

*HostSearch is a page
that helps you find
Web server space that
matches your needs.*

Build your own—If your Web page requires extra-tight security (for online sales) or makes extensive use of CGI scripts (especially for forms), an in-house Web server might be your answer. Building your own Web server is a more practical solution (even for relatively small companies) than ever before, thanks to lower-priced server computers (especially Pentium-based PCs), cheaper, simpler server software (primarily from Netscape and Microsoft), and the wide availability of high-speed data lines (such as ISDN or T1).

A Web server is not cheap. The hardware and software for a decent server is coming down rapidly, to a reasonable cost for a small business (under $5000). But the 24-hour, high-speed dedicated Internet connection that a Web server demands might cost more than four times that much—every month. More important, while effectively administering a Web server is getting easier all the time, the job essentially demands one or more full-time experts.

The combined cost of server, connection, and staff now falls within the means of most companies with over 100 employees, or smaller companies whose line of business makes Web service a high priority. For other small companies and for individuals, however, leasing space on someone else's server is a far more sensible option.

Increasingly, commercial hosting services not only provide space, but can also supply (for a higher fee) e-commerce services. The hosting company can take care of processing orders and credit card transactions for you, so you can set up an online store without having to worry about all the e-details.

How Much Space Do I Need?

Good question. Odds are you need very little, starting out.

As I've reminded you over the last 20 hours, the more a page contains, the bigger its file. Pictures (and picture backgrounds) dramatically increase the amount of space a page requires (and the time it takes to appear to a visitor). Sound, video, and large file downloads also may dramatically increase the amount of space you need.

But if you have followed the tips I've offered for keeping the performance of your page sprightly, you'll find that each page occupies very little space. A basic page—a screenful or two of text graced with two or three small picture files and maybe a picture background—typically requires less than 100KB of server space (often a lot less). You can store at least a dozen such basic Web pages in 1MB of server space. (There are 1,024 kilobytes in a megabyte).

21

Most Internet providers and online services supply at least 3MB of free space to each customer; many supply as much as 10MB. That's enough to store 100 basic pages and have a few megs left over for a short video clip or two.

The following To Do shows how to determine the minimum amount of disk space required by your page files.

The following To Do assumes you have stored all of the files for the page—the HTML file or files, picture files, and so on—in the same folder on your hard disk.

To Do: Find out how much space your files need

1. In Windows, open the folder in which your Web page files are stored.

2. Press and hold the Ctrl key, and click all of the files that are a part of the page one-by-one. (There shouldn't be files in the folder that aren't part of the page, but if there are, don't click those.)

3. When all of the files are highlighted, you'll see the amount of space they occupy reported at the bottom of the folder window. The Web page in this example (which includes two screenfuls of text, two pictures and a picture background) requires only 5.16KB of space!

FIGURE 21.4

Step 3: Read the size of the combined files.

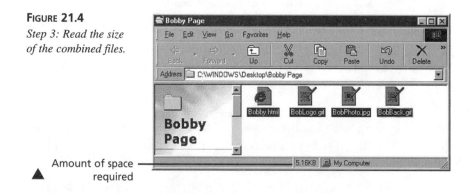

Amount of space required

Preparing to Publish

Before publishing, you'll want to have acquired your server space and given your page a final once-over. (Even if you miss a mistake, you can easily fix it later and publish the correction, as described in Hour 23, "Testing and Updating Your Page.")

The last thing you need to do before publishing is to get some important information from whomever is supplying your Web server space. Specifically, you'll need to know the following:

- *Does the server have the FrontPage Extensions on it?*—As you know from earlier hours, some of the cooler stuff you can do in FrontPage Express—such as interactive forms (Hour 17, "Editing HTML")—will only work properly when the page is published on a server equipped with special Microsoft software called the *FrontPage Extensions*. But even if you do not use any of these features, it's important to know whether the server has the extensions, because the extensions affect the publishing steps.

- *The name of the communications protocol required for uploading your files*—(If the server has the FrontPage Extensions, you can skip this one.) Many servers allow you to use the Web protocol (HTTP) for uploading files, whereas some require that files be uploaded via FTP. (FrontPage Express supports both methods.)

- *The complete address and path where your files will be stored*—You'll need to know the complete URL of the directory in which your files will be stored, including the server name, path to your directory, and the name of your directory. Ideally, you'll have your own separate directory for all your files. Having your own directory prevents conflicts that might arise if any other file on the system (a page, image, or other file) uses the same filename as one of your files.

It's standard practice to name the top page of a multipage Web site `index.htm` (or `index.html`).

But unless you have your own directory on the server, do not name any page `index.htm(1)`. Although this name is often used for the top page in a multipage Web page, if the directory already contains a file called `index.htm`, the server will reject yours—or overwrite the other!

- *The rules or restrictions for filenames on the server*—Different server platforms have different rules for filenames. For example, DOS-based servers and some UNIX servers do not permit filenames longer than eight characters or file extensions of more than three characters. Ideally, you'll find out about such restrictions before you create and name your files. But, if you composed your page without first finding out about the server, you should check for naming restrictions and change any filenames as needed.

21

If you find you must alter any filenames, be sure to check and adjust any links between pages before and after publishing.

- *Your unique username and password for gaining upload access to the server* Your server supplier should give you a username and password for uploading your files.

If you get server space from your Internet provider, the username and password you use to publish will probably be the same ones you always use to connect to the Internet.

Publishing from FrontPage Express

Most server providers prefer that you *upload*—copy your Web files from your PC to the Web server—using an Internet tool called FTP.

If you're familiar with FTP, you can always do it that way. But the publishing facilities built in to FrontPage Express can be a lot easier to use. More important, when you make changes to your pages online (as you learn to do in Hour 23), FrontPage Express can publish those changes in about two clicks.

So even if you do know FTP, I recommend giving FrontPage Express's publishing tools a shot anyway. (And if you don't already know FTP, there's no need to learn now—at least for publishing purposes.)

To Do: Publish a page

1. In FrontPage Express, open the HTML file you want to publish.
2. Choose File, Save As.
3. Under Page Location, type the full URL that a visitor would use to reach this page after it's published, and then click OK.

If your Internet connection does not open automatically after step 3, close whatever dialog boxes or messages that appear, and then connect to the Internet and start over at step 2.

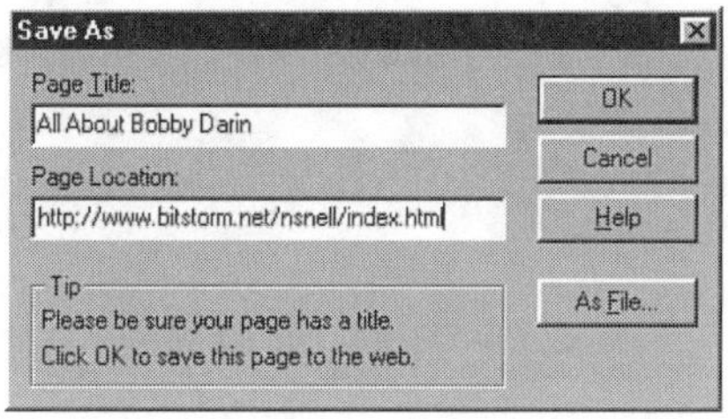

FIGURE 21.5

Step 3: Put the page's URL-to-be in Page Location and click OK.

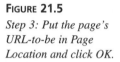

4. Your Internet connection opens, and, after a moment, you are prompted for "authentication information" (your username and password). Type the information in the boxes provided, and click OK.

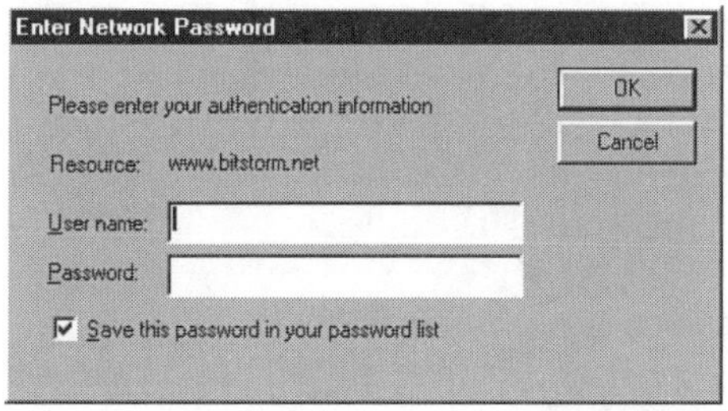

FIGURE 21.6

Step 4: Type your username and password, and then click OK.

5. What happens next depends on whether the server is equipped with the FrontPage extensions:

   • If the server *does* have the FrontPage extensions, you're all done. In a few moments, a message appears to report that the files have been uploaded. They are now on the Web, available to all.

   • If the server *does not* have the FrontPage extensions, the Welcome screen of the Web Publishing Wizard appears. Click Next.

21

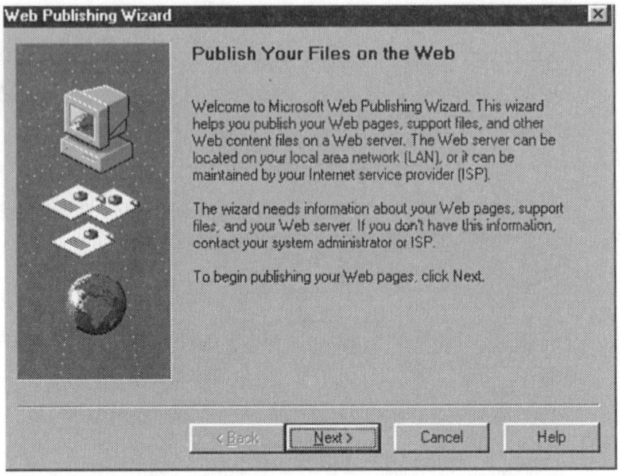

▼

FIGURE **21.7**

*Step 5: If the files
do not publish
automatically, the Web
Publishing Wizard
appears. Click Next.*

6. A box appears, reporting that you must Specify a Connection method. Click Next.

7. Open the Connection Method list, and choose the uploading protocol required for uploading to this server (FTP or HTTP). Then click Next.

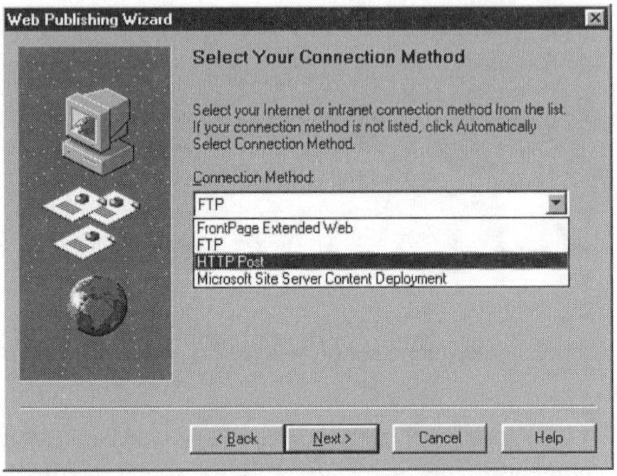

FIGURE **21.8**

*Step 7: Choose the
uploading protocol.*

8. Fill in the address of the server and the name of the directory in which your page files will be stored. Then click Next.

▼

Some servers are set up so that when you log on, anything you upload automatically goes into your private directory (without you having to specify it).

When that's the case, you can leave the Subfolder box blank in step 8. If you *do* specify a directory in the Subfolder box, that subfolder will be created as a new directory *inside* your regular one, and the files you're about to upload will go there.

For example, if all of my files automatically go to the nsnell directory anyway, and I type **nsnell** in the Subfolder box, the files will upload to the folder nsnell/nsnell.

9. Click Finish. In a few moments, a message appears to report that the files have been uploaded. They are now on the Web, available to all.

FIGURE 21.9

Step 8: Fill in the server address and directory name.

Web Publishing Wizard

Specify the FTP Server and Subfolder

Type the FTP server name and subfolder where you publish your files.

FTP server name:

ftp.sample.com

Subfolder containing your Web pages:

nsnell

URL for your Web server and directory:

http://www.mcp.com/

< Back   Next >   Cancel   Help

FIGURE 21.10

Step 9: Click Finish to send the files to the Web.

Web Publishing Wizard

Publish Your Files

The Web Publishing Wizard is ready to publish your files to the Web server named http://www.mcp.com/. To publish your files and close the Wizard, click Finish.

< Back   Finish   Cancel   Help

21

Viewing Your Page Through the Internet

After you publish, you must test your page through the Web, viewing it exactly as your visitors will. Besides, it's fun to see it online.

To view your page online, just open your browser, connect to the Internet, and go to the same address you typed in step 3 of the To Do for publishing. Explore your page, evaluating its appearance and testing all of your links.

- If you find any mistakes or anything else you want to change, see Hour 23.
- If you want to learn how to announce your page to the world (so visitors can discover it), see Hour 22, "Announcing Your Web Presence."

> If you named your top page `index.html` (as suggested in Part 2), that page opens automatically when a visitor surfs to the server directory without specifying a filename. For example, if the user enters the URL `www.server.com/sally/` in his browser, the `index.html` file in the `sally` directory opens automatically.

Summary

Publishing is a simple activity (and relatively foolproof) as long as you've taken care in the preparation of your page. Simple mistakes, like putting files for the same page in different directories, are the kinds of things that most often cause publishing problems.

If you are careful with your filenames and locations, obey your server's rules, and follow the publishing steps, you'll find publishing one of the more satisfying aspects of authoring—the reward for a job well done.

Q&A

Q I want my own "dot com," as in `www.steve.com`. How do I get one o' those guys?

A You need your own Internet domain, which is a little more ambitious than first-time Web authors are ready for. But by now, you're probably ready (if you have the cash), and certainly motivated. You learn how to get a domain in Hour 24, "Developing Your Authoring Skills."

Q What if the HTML standard changes? Will my page suddenly not work in browsers that conform to a new standard or support new extensions?

A Updates to HTML are backward-compatible; in other words, when HTML changes, new tags and attributes are added, as are new ways to do old things. But older approaches and tags still work indefinitely.

In Hour 23, you'll learn about testing your page's HTML online. And in Hour 24, "Developing Your Authoring Skills," you'll learn that not only is HTML still evolving, but also it is morphing into something new: *XHTML*.

Q How do I update my page when it changes?

A That, too, is coming in Hour 23. But first, you need to learn how to announce your newly published page to the world; see Hour 22.

21

HOUR 22

Announcing Your Web Presence

After your page is on the server, it doesn't do you much good if nobody knows it's there. You need to get the word out, so anyone who might have an interest in your page knows it's there and can find it easily.

In this hour, you learn how to announce your page to the world. At the end of the hour, you'll be able to answer the following questions:

- Where are the major Web search pages on which my page should be listed?
- How do I get listed on the search pages?
- In what other ways can I publicize my page?
- How do I broadcast an email announcement to my friends, family, or clients?

Listing Your Page in Web Search Pages

There are two kinds of people whom you may want to know about your Web page—the people you know and the people you don't know.

You will inform the people you know directly, as you learn to do later in this hour. But the most efficient way to inform the people you don't know is to get your page listed on the major Internet search services, including the following:

- *Yahoo!*   www.yahoo.com
- *Excite* (see Figure 22.1)   www.excite.com
- *Lycos*   .lycos.com
- *Alta Vista*   www.altavista.com
- *InfoSeek*   www.infoseek.com
- *WebCrawler*   www.webcrawler.com

Figure 22.1

Excite, one of the Web search pages to which you'll want to add your page.

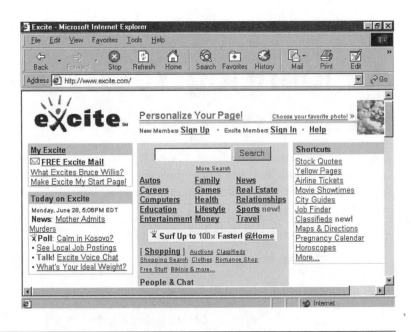

If your page covers a particular subject, it's a good idea to use the search pages to find other pages about the same subject and explore them.

Many such pages offer a list of links to related pages; when you find such a page, you can email its Webmaster to ask that a link to your page be added to the list. (An email link to the Webmaster usually appears on the same page as the links.) You can also add to your Web site your own list of links to related pages, thus returning the favor.

22

When your page is properly listed by these services, folks will find your page whenever they search for something related to your page's subject, title, or *keywords* (see Hour 5, "Choosing a Title, Text Colors, and Other Page Basics").

Actually, some search pages will find your page all by themselves. Services, such as Excite and Alta Vista use programs, sometimes called *spiders* or *crawlers*, to methodically search the Web and add new pages to their search pages.

But by adding your pages to these and other search pages manually, you get them listed more quickly, and you improve the chances that they'll be categorized properly—which improves the chances that your page will be found by people who will actually want to see it.

Each search page has different rules for adding new pages. You always begin by navigating to the search page's top page. From there, by hunting around, you can usually find instructions, a button, or some other indication of how to add a site.

When adding the URL of a business site to search pages, do searches to find out how your competitors are listed. Then, be sure your page is associated with the same categories or keywords.

That way, when anyone does a search that finds your competitors, they find you, too.

To Do: Add your site to Yahoo!

1. Go to Yahoo! at www.yahoo.com.

2. Explore Yahoo!'s categories and choose the precise category in which your page belongs.

3. Scroll to the bottom of the page (see Figure 22.2), and click Suggest a Site.

4. Read the Suggest a Site page (shown in Figure 22.3) for tips on properly listing your page with Yahoo!

If the category you chose in step 2 was too broad, Yahoo! will display a message to that effect and ask you to choose another, more specific category before proceeding.

---

5. Scroll to the bottom of the Suggest a Site page (see Figure 22.4), and click Proceed to Step One.

FIGURE 22.2

Step 3: Click Suggest a Site at the bottom of the Yahoo! category that fits your page.

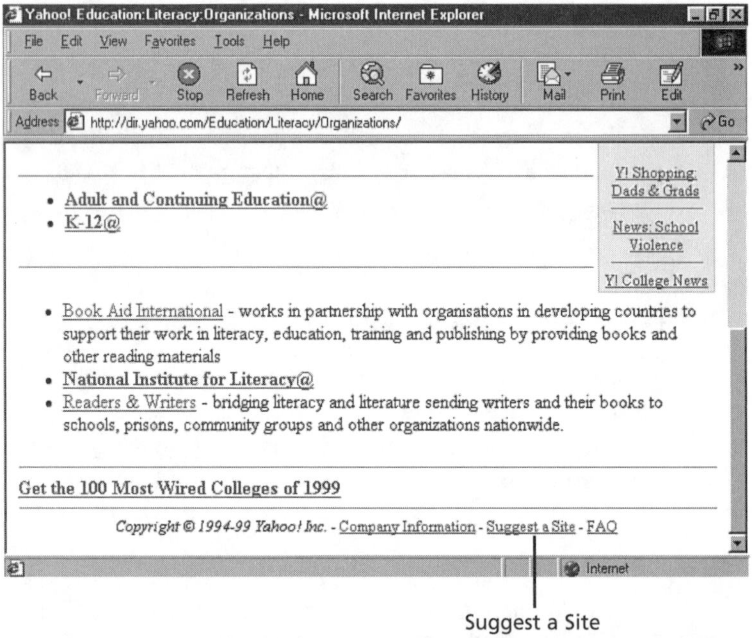

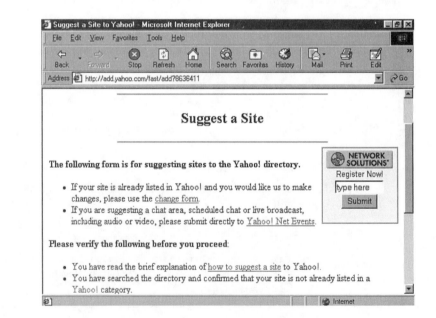

Suggest a Site

FIGURE 22.3

Step 4: Study the Suggest a Site instructions.

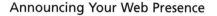

FIGURE 22.4

Step 5: Click Proceed to Step One.

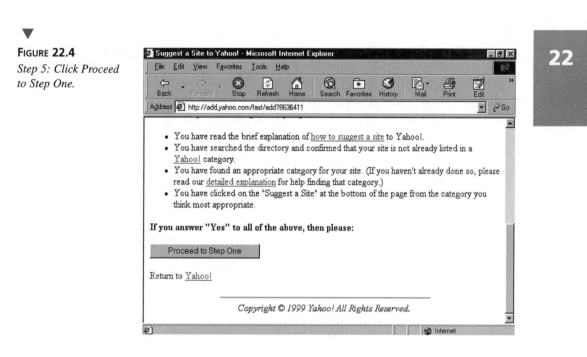

22

6. Scroll down to the Site Information form (see Figure 22.5), and type the title and URL of your page or site, plus a brief Description.

The description you type in step 6 will appear in the search results whenever someone's Yahoo! search finds your page. Word it carefully, to help searchers determine whether your page contains what they want. Be sure also to include in the description keywords related to the page's topic.

7. At the bottom of the Suggest a Site page, click Proceed to Step Two (shown in Figure 22.6).

8. Continue through steps two, three, and four, filling in all information requested and clicking the button at the bottom of the page to proceed to each new step.

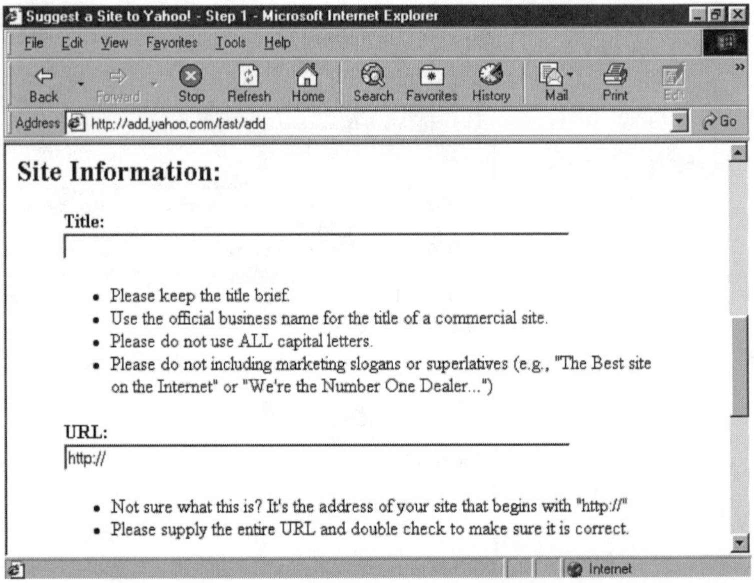

▼

FIGURE **22.5**

Step 6: Fill in your page's title, URL, and a brief description.

FIGURE **22.6**

Step 7: Proceed to Step Two.

▲

When you add a site to many search pages, including Yahoo! and Excite, the URL does not show up in the search page immediately. You may have to wait two weeks or longer before your addition becomes official.

To Do: Add your site to Excite!

Like all spider-based search tools, Excite crawls around the Web cataloging its contents, and it will eventually catalog your site. But by suggesting your site, you'll get it listed more quickly.

1. In your Web browser, go to Excite www.excite.com.

FIGURE 22.7

Step 1: Go to Excite.

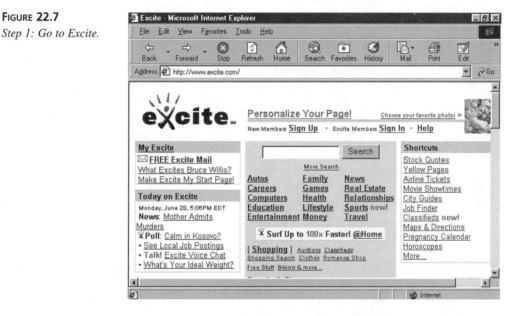

2. Scroll to the bottom of the page (see Figure 22.8), and choose Add URL.

3. Fill in the form (shown in Figure 22.9) with the URL of your page (or top page of your site), your email address (so Excite can contact you if necessary), the language the page uses, your general location in the world, and the general category. Then click Send.

FIGURE **22.8**
Step 2: Choose
Add URL.

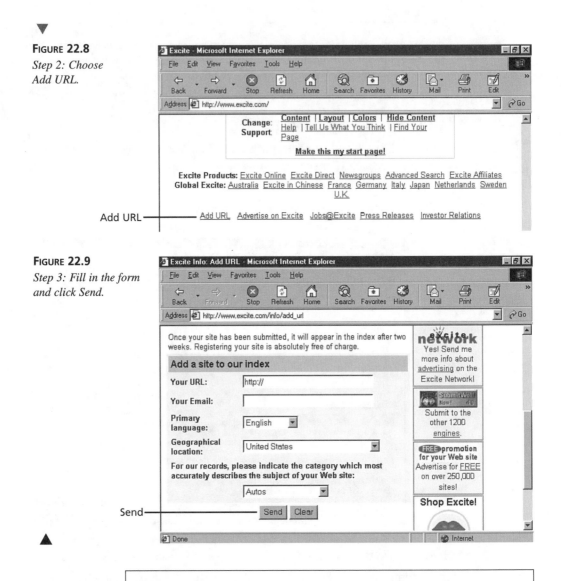

FIGURE **22.9**
Step 3: Fill in the form
and click Send.

To make sure your page is located and properly cataloged by Web spiders, be sure to carefully and thoughtfully phrase the page's title, description, and keywords in the Page Properties dialog box. Refer to Hour 5 for help.

Getting in Multiple Search Pages at Once

Recently, some commercial services have emerged that offer (most for a fee) to list your site with many of the most popular search pages and spiders, all in one quick step.

Such services charge from as little as $10 to more than $100. Note that these services submit not only to the major search engines, but also to hundreds of topic-specific search pages.

> You can find more Web promotion sites by entering the term **site submission** or **web promotion** in any general-purpose search page.

Check out

- *Site See* (see Figure 22.10)   www.site-see.com
- *Submit It!*   www.submit-it.com/

FIGURE 22.10

Site See is one of the many site submission services available online.

Publicizing Your Page off the Web

Don't forget that not all ways to publicize your Web pages are on the Web (or even online). Be sure to list your Web site address

- In your email signature
- On your business cards
- On personal or company stationery
- In company advertising and marketing collateral

Remember: In theory (and in reality, too!), everyone among your acquaintances who will visit your Web page has Internet access, and, therefore, he or she probably has an email address, too. So a great way to make a targeted announcement to people you know is to broadcast an email message announcing your page's URL.

To broadcast an email message, compose the message and include in the To: portion of the message header the email address of everyone you want to receive the message (see Figure 22.11). In most email programs, you separate the addresses with semicolons (;), as shown.

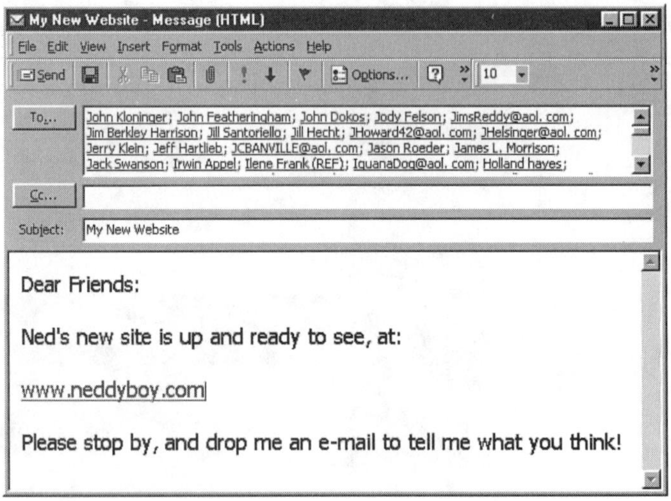

FIGURE 22.11

Broadcast an email message to announce your page.

Summary

If a page falls on the Web, and there's no one around to hear it, does it make a sound? I dunno. I shouldn't ask dumb questions I can't answer. The point is that after you create and publish a Web page, your job isn't done. It pays to advertise.

22

Q&A

Q Do I have to check or update my listings on the search pages?

A Well, after adding your page to the search pages (and after the addition has been made formal on search pages that make you wait a few days), you should always find your listing and test it to make sure it works as advertised.

After that, you can pretty much forget about it, unless you change your Web page's address or filename. Anytime you make such a change, you must change your listings in the search pages to match.

HOUR 23

Testing and Updating Your Page

You haven't simply published a Web page. You've established a Web presence—hopefully one that will expand and evolve with time (most do). After your page is online, it's important to know how to update it—so you can improve and enlarge it over time—and how to test it so you can keep it performing reliably for your visitors.

At the end of this hour, you'll be able to answer the following questions:

- How do I ensure that my Web page looks good, no matter what browser the visitor is using?
- How do I check out how my page looks when viewed by visitors using varying display resolutions?
- How do I keep my links working smoothly?
- How do I evaluate my page's ease-of-use for visitors?
- How do I update my page whenever I need to (or when I just plain feel like it)?

Testing Your Pages

Okay, as you've worked on your page, you've evaluated its appearance by previewing it in Internet Explorer, and by now you've checked out the page online through Internet Explorer. So that means it's perfect, right?

Not necessarily. There are all sorts of little glitches that you may not be aware of until you go looking for them. The next few sections show you how to thoroughly test your page after it's online so you can make sure your visitors have precisely the experience you want them to have.

Testing Browser Variability

You know your page looks and functions fine when viewed through Internet Explorer 5. But what about the rest of the Web population—those using earlier versions of Internet Explorer, or those using various versions of Netscape Navigator or any of a dozen other browsers? How will your page look to them? Figures 23.1 through 23.4 illustrate how the exact same page can appear dramatically different in different browsers.

To make sure your page's appearance is acceptable to all, you'll want to view your page online through a variety of different browsers, just to see if any serious problems arise when using browsers other than Internet Explorer 5. If you discover any problems in a particular browser environment, you must decide whether to adjust your page to eliminate the problem (which may involve compromising some of your formatting or other fancy features), or to sacrifice the performance of your page for one segment of the audience to preserve its performance for another.

Don't worry about whether the page looks identical through all sorts of browsers. It won't, and it doesn't have to. The question is, does the page look OK in every browser? Is all of the text legible? Do the links work? If a picture or other element does not appear, does something else on the page fulfill the same function?

For example, if you have a bunch of links in an imagemap that does not appear (or doesn't work) when displayed through a particular browser, are duplicate text links available? If your company logo doesn't show up, is the company name presented in a heading? If the background doesn't show up, is all of the text legible without it?

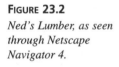

FIGURE 23.1

Ned's Lumber, as seen through Internet Explorer 5.

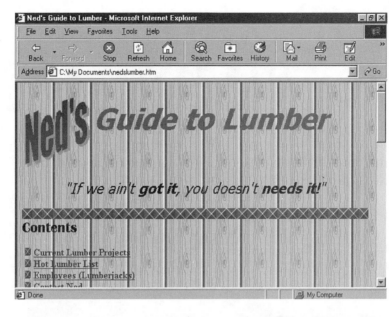

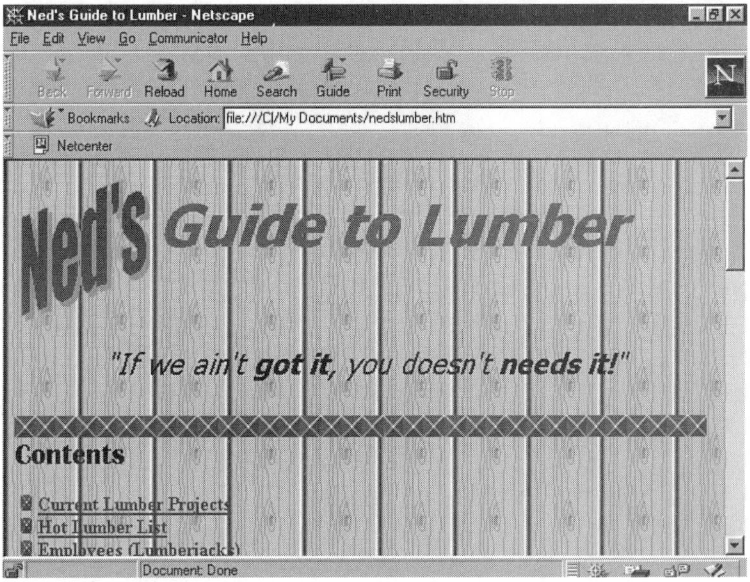

23

FIGURE 23.2

Ned's Lumber, as seen through Netscape Navigator 4.

FIGURE 23.3

Ned's Lumber, as seen through Cello.

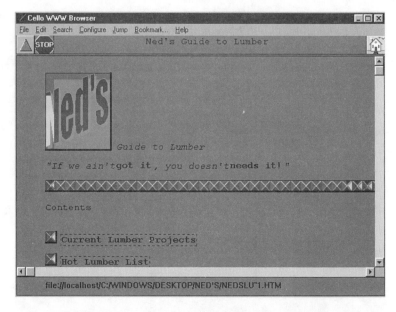

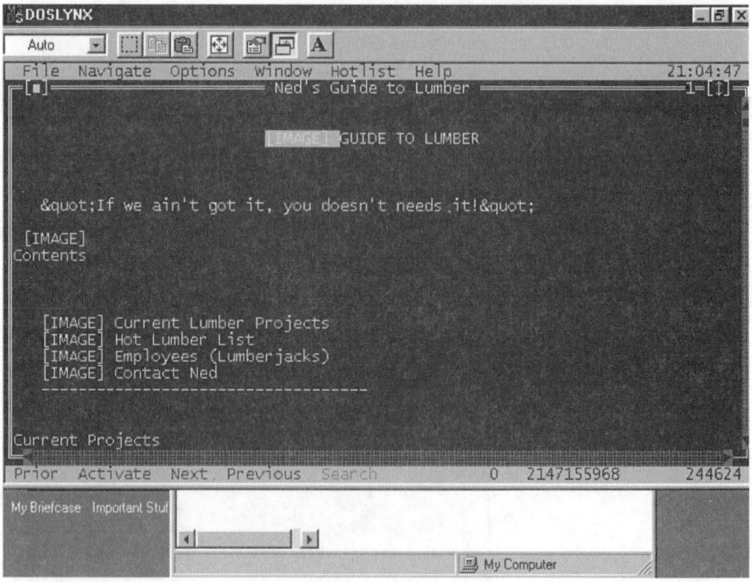

FIGURE 23.4

Ned's Lumber, as seen through DOSLynx.

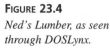

It's a good idea to keep some other browsers around to see how the other half sees you. You can download many different browsers from the Web for free. A good place to start is the Tucows Internet software directory (www.tucows.com), from which you can download many different browsers (see Figure 23.5).

You can also find the download addresses for various shareware and free-ware browsers in Appendix B, "Online Resources for Web Authors."

FIGURE 23.5

The Tucows directory at www.tucows.com is a good place to pick up various browsers for testing.

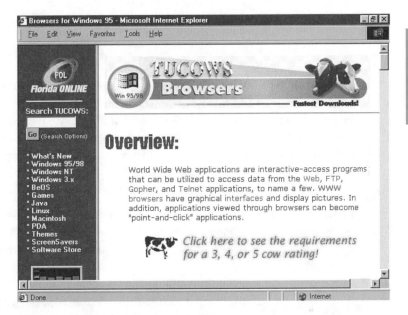

23

Which browsers should you test in? Well, the overwhelming majority of the folks online browse the Web through Internet Explorer or Netscape Navigator, so you need to test in the latest version of each of those "Big Two" browsers, at the very least.

But keep in mind that not everybody keeps up with the latest browser versions, so a page that looks fine in the current version of IE or Navigator may show some trouble when viewed through a browser from just a year or two ago.

If you rummage through the CD-ROMs you have lying around (especially any that were bundled with computer books), you may find some that have older versions of IE or Navigator you can use for testing your pages.

You'll often see outdated computer books for sale in big bins at bookstores, sometimes for as little as $2. (It breaks my heart.)

Often those books include CD-ROMs that have obsolete versions of various Web browsers. For a few bucks, you can pick up some old browser versions for testing, and also pick up a lovely artifact of computer history. For

> example, if you find the first edition of this book in the blow-out bin, you'll
> get a 1998 version of Netscape Communicator (including Netscape's Web
> authoring tool, Composer, which you'll learn more about in Hour 24,
> "Developing Your Authoring Skills").
>
> Check the book's copyright date before buying; a browser from any year
> before 1997 is probably too old to bother with.

Also, each of these browsers is available in different versions for different types of
computers. For PCs alone, you can get IE5 in three different "current" versions: a 16-bit
version (offered primarily for Windows 3.1, but it'll run on Windows 95/98/NT), the
regular 64-bit version (on the CD-ROM with this book), and a 128-bit version for top-
of-the-line PCs, like those with Pentium III processors. Add to these the various IE5
versions for other system types (such as Macintosh), and you must realize that there's
really more than one "IE5" to consider. (There are several different "Navigators" too.)

If your page looks okay in the most recent versions of Navigator and Internet Explorer
(all versions released within, say, the last two years), you can rest assured that it
probably looks okay to most folks on the Web—but not necessarily all.

> Remember that Netscape Navigator is found by itself, as "Navigator," but
> also bundled with Netscape's email program and other tools, such as
> Composer. You can use either one for testing.

Once you've tested for the Netscape/Microsoft world, there remains about 10 to 20 percent of Web users whose view of your page you don't know. Of those, many probably
use one of the many flavors of NCSA Mosaic, the original Web browser, now largely
defunct.

Beyond Mosaic, you may want to test in

- Older, graphical browsers that don't support recent Netscape/Microsoft extensions,
  such as Cello (see Figure 23.3)
- Text-only browsers, such as DOSLynx (see Figure 23.4)

While such browsers are on their way out, you'll need to test in them and adjust your
page as needed if you really want it to behave properly for absolutely all potential visitors. However, you must accept that doing so inevitably forces you to restrict your page
to the most minimal formatting.

If you're really concerned about reaching everyone, supply your page in two versions: a fancy, extension-rich version and a very plain HTML 2-based version—and offer either from a universally visible top page. (This is also a great way to accommodate differing connection speeds and patience levels. The version provided for older browsers usually also includes little or no multimedia, so those with slow Internet connections can enjoy your pages without waiting an eternity for them to appear.) See Figure 23.6.

FIGURE 23.6

To take advantage of advanced formatting while still supporting older browsers, you can create two versions of your pages—one simple, the other fancy—and give your visitors a choice between the two, from the top page.

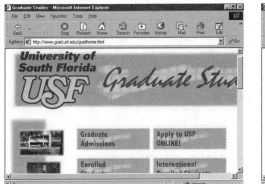
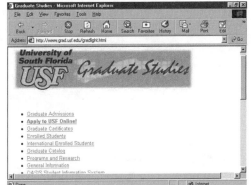

Testing at Different Resolutions

Within the last year or so, it's become standard practice to design Web pages to look their best when displayed on a computer screen running at 800×600 resolution, the most common setting used by most folks on PCs and Macintoshes today.

It's an effective compromise: Users of computers running at the minimum Windows resolution of 640×480 need only do a little scrolling to see all of an 800×600 Web page, while the page will appear acceptably large to those using higher resolutions.

Figures 23.7 through 23.9 show how the same Web page (one designed for 800×600) appears to visitors at three different resolutions.

You may recall that I recommended running your PC at 800×600 when using FrontPage Express. If you do, and design pages to look good on your own screen, you're designing for 800×600 without even having to think about it!

FIGURE 23.7

A page designed for 800×600 resolution on a display running at 640×480. The visitor must scroll to see the whole page.

Display resolution is only a factor when pages contain pictures, tables, forms, or frames. The layout of a page containing only text is automatically fit to the size of the window in which it is displayed.

Tables and horizontal lines will automatically refit themselves to varying resolutions when you have specified their width as a percentage of the window, not as a number of pixels (see Hour 8, "Organizing Text with Tables and Rules"). However, when a table contains pictures, the results of that refit may not be appealing. Always test such pages at varying resolutions.

FIGURE 23.8

A page designed for 800×600 resolution on a display running at 800×600. The page image neatly fills the window.

FIGURE 23.9

A page designed for 800×600 resolution on a display running at 1024×768.

When evaluating your page, it's smart to check out how it looks at varying resolutions. To do that, you must change your display resolution in Windows, and then view the page.

- To change your display resolution, open Windows Control Panel, and double-click the Display icon. Choose the Settings tab, and drag the slider control labeled Screen Area (in Windows 98) or Desktop Area (in Windows 95) to the resolution you desire (see Figure 23.10).

- After changing resolution, when you open your browser, you may find that the browser window is no longer fit perfectly to maximized "full screen" size. To make the browser fill the screen, double-click the title bar at the very top of the browser window.

FIGURE 23.10

Drag the slider control under Screen Area to change display resolution in Windows.

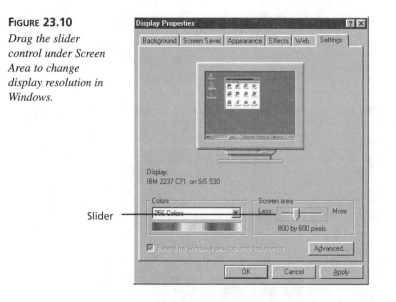

Slider

If you think changing resolutions this way is a pain, you can download a free program called BrowserSizer from ApplyThis Software, at www.vasile.com/racecar/stampware/browsersizer/.

BrowserSizer provides a simple menu from which you can easily change the size of the browser window (either Internet Explorer or Netscape Navigator) to a size that mimics the way the browser would appear at a particular resolution. This gives you a fast and simple way to see how you page looks in varying resolutions.

Testing Link Validity

Finally, it's important to test all of the links in your page.

Once you've verified the links among your own files—between your pages and to images and external media—you needn't recheck them unless you change a file. It's good practice to retest all such links any time you make any changes at all to your Web site. Even seemingly small changes to a single page can sometimes inadvertently scramble links.

When your page contains *external* links—links to other people's Web pages or to any file other than those you control on the server—you'll need to check these links often, because the files they point to might have moved or their names might have changed. I recommend checking all external links at least once a month.

Evaluating Your Page's Ergonomics

The preceding sections in this hour have explained only how to check your page's technical integrity. But what about its fuzzy qualities—its look, its feel, its *mise-en-scéne*? And what about its interaction with visitors? Can they find what they came for? Do they see the parts of your message you want them to see? Do they naturally follow paths through your page to certain items, or are they frustrated by a lot of blind alleys and backtracking?

The best way to answer these questions would be to gather some friends (ideally friends who don't already know too much about your page or its subject) and cooperative strangers and watch them browse your page (no coaching!). Watch what they choose to click and what they skip. Note any time they move down a path and fail to find what they expected or hoped to find. And, of course, listen to their comments.

Finally, remember always to use a signature with your email address. That way, people can send you comments and constructive criticisms.

> Here's one final way to check out your pages: Anytime, anyplace you have an opportunity to visit your pages away from home, do it. In particular, look for opportunities to test your pages through other types of computers (such as Macintoshes) and varying connection speeds. You may find such opportunities
>
> - When visiting friends who use the Internet
> - At a local library that has public Internet terminal
> - At work

Updating Your Page

Okay, you've found some stuff you want to fix, or updates to make. What's the procedure?

Begin by editing the original files on your PC in FrontPage Express. (You cannot edit the copies of the files that are on the Web server; you must work with what's on your PC.)

After making all of your changes and testing the results offline in one or more browsers on your PC, start the publishing steps exactly as you did in Hour 21, "Publishing Your Page." Choose File, Save As to open the Save As dialog box (see Figure 23.11).

Here's the cool part: FrontPage Express remembers the server name and all of the other stuff you entered when you originally published the page. So as long as you change nothing on the Save As dialog box and simply click its OK button, that's all you have to do. The changed files are uploaded to the server, replacing the old pages, using the same settings you entered when you first published this page. (Depending on how your server and Internet account are set up, you may be prompted to sign on to the Internet or to supply your authentication information, but that's the most you'll have to do.)

FIGURE 23.11

Click OK on the Save As dialog box (without changing anything) to publish changes to a Web page.

Save As	☒
Page Title:	OK
Bobby's Page	Cancel
Page Location:	Help
http://www.cathycorp.com/bobby.htm	
Tip	As File...
Please be sure your page has a title.	
Click OK to save this page to the web.	

> Of course, you must retest your page after uploading changes. But you knew that, right?

Summary

Evaluating and updating your Web pages is no big deal, and it's a critical step in making sure your page does the job for which you created it.

Perhaps more importantly, testing and updating your page are important practices in improving as a Web author. Each time you republish your pages, they get better and better, and you gain experience and confidence. So get in the habit of seeing your pages not as "finished" works that you upload and forget, but as works in progress, regularly benefiting from your enhancements and fine-tuning.

Q&A

Q **My page works great in both IE5 and Navigator, but shows some problems in other browsers. The problem is that I don't want to give up the cool stuff in my pages just to make them compatible with everybody's browser. What do I do?**

A Many Web authors in that situation put a disclaimer on the top page, saying "This page best when viewed with Internet Explorer" or words to that effect. Often, the disclaimer is accompanied by a link to Microsoft or Netscape for downloading a compatible browser. The disclaimer in effect says, "If you wanna enjoy everything my page offers, go get an up-to-date browser."

A few years ago, I would have called that practice a cop-out, a callous disregard for those not willing to dance to Microsoft's or Netscape's tune. But like it or not, so much of the Web today works properly only through one of these browsers that anybody using another browser is likely to be encountering problems with more than half of the pages he visits. That person has already decided to accept that many pages won't look quite right to him, which takes you off the hook (a little).

Q **I installed some other browsers for testing, and now when I go online, one of those browsers opens instead of Internet Explorer. And when I do use IE5, it doesn't work right. How do I get IE5 back?**

A Most browsers want to be your only browser, so when you install them, they have a bad habit of making themselves the "default" browser on your PC, the one that opens automatically for most Internet activities.

The easiest way to make IE5 the default browser again is to reinstall it from the CD-ROM, which should also fix any little troubles in IE5 that may have cropped up since you installed the other browsers.

That won't get rid of the other browsers, which will remain ready for your Web page testing. But it will make IE5 the default Web browser again, so that the other browsers don't appear unless you deliberately open them.

23

HOUR 24

Developing Your Authoring Skills

This is it—*la chapitre finale*. And guess what? I tell you nothing here that immediately adds to your authoring skill set. (I know…it's a cheap trick. It's like when they forced you to show up for the last day of high school and then let you goof off all day anyway.)

What you do get in this hour is a graduation speech, or rather, a send-off with a purpose. If you've hit most or all of this tutorial, you've built a pretty solid foundation as an author. But there's always more to learn, always that one new trick that can make a good Web page into a great one. You now possess all the prerequisites needed to understand more advanced authoring information that you may find in other books or on the Web. So in this last hurrah, you'll find tips for developing your new skills.

At the end of this hour, you'll be able to answer the following questions:

- How can I get my own "dot com," my own *domain*, as the address of the pages I publish?

- When I outgrow FrontPage Express, what's next?
- What practices can help me grow as a Web author, no matter what tools I use?
- What can I read now to take me to the next level?

Getting Your Own Domain (Your Own "Dot Com")

If you simply take some space on someone else's server, your page will be accessible through the Web, but it won't have the sort of catchy Web address that gives you a Web identity, such as www.buick.com. Instead, your page's address is expressed as a directory on the server; for example, www.serviceco.com/neddyboy/fredo/.

If you want to have your own Internet name, you must register your own Internet *domain*, and then have that domain set up on the server on which you will publish your pages.

When you check to see whether the domain you want to use is available (as you will in the next To Do), you may receive a message that the name is available for purchase or lease, for a particular sum.

Because a domain costs only $70, a number of companies have snapped up every domain name they can think of that anyone might want to use. But they have no intention of using the names; they intend to sell them, often for much more than $70.

Because the technical details of setting up your domain on the server must be taken care of by whomever controls your server, I recommend having your Internet provider (or whomever else controls the server you use) take care of both registering and setting up your domain for you. Most providers will register a domain for a small fee, or even for free.

Whether you set up your domain yourself or have someone else do it, you still must pay some fees to Network Solutions, the organization that manages domains for the Internet. At this writing, Network Solutions charges $70 to establish the domain, which includes two years of keeping the domain. After that, you must pay $35 per year to maintain it. Typically, if your provider sets up your domain, it can also collect the fees and forward them to Network Solutions for you.

While you might need help setting up the domain, you can choose the name all by your-self. The trick is that the domain must be absolutely unique—it can't be the same as any other domain already in use. You can use Network Solutions' Web site to find out whether the domain you want is available, as described in the following To Do.

> The final part of the domain name can be `.com` (commercial site, the most common), `.org` (organization, like a foundation or other not-for-profit), `.edu` (educational institution), or `.net` (network). If you're not sure what to use, you're probably a `.com`.
>
> There is an advantage to being a `.com`, as opposed to an `.org` or other domain type. The `.com` suffix is so common that many Web users—particu-larly newcomers—have a habit of assuming that all addresses end in `.com`. Tell people your page is at `www.nedco.org`, and a surprising number of them will try to reach you at `www.nedco.com`, and never understand why you're not there.

24

To Do: Choose a domain name

1. Think about what you want your Internet domain to be; for example, `www.cathy-corp.com`. Have a few options ready, in case one or more are already taken.

2. Visit the Network Solutions Web site at `www.networksolutions.com`.

FIGURE 24.1

Step 2: Visit Network Solutions.

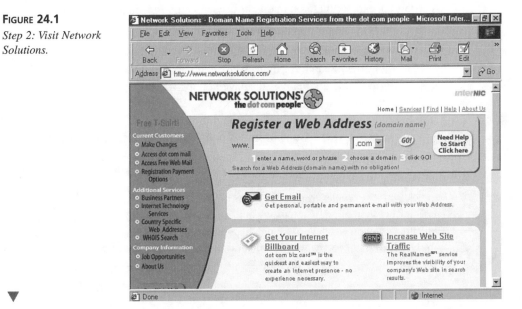

▼ 3. In the box at the top of the page, type the domain you chose in step 1, and click the Go button to the right of the box.

> When typing your proposed domain in step 3, don't precede it with the http:// or the www part. These are part of a typical Web site address, but not really part of the domain. For example, if you want your Web site address to be http://www.wild.com, just type **wild** in step 3, and use the list box provided to choose the .com suffix.

FIGURE **24.2**

Step 3: Type your chosen domain in the Search box.

4. A report appears, telling you that your chosen name is or is not available.

   • If the name *is available*, proceed to step 5.

   • If the name *is not* available, you can try a different name in the box labeled Search for more Web addresses, or choose from among any available alternatives displayed on the report.

> You can click the Continue button on the right side of the report to display buttons for two optional services:
>
> • *Reserve*—You can reserve this domain right away through Network Solutions by agreeing to use Network Solutions as your server provider. You pay $119 for the first two years.
>
> • *Register*—If you know all of the technical information about the server on which you will publish, you can go ahead and register now. (But I still recommend having your server supplier take care of this step.)

▼

FIGURE 24.3

Step 4: The site tells you whether the domain is available or taken.

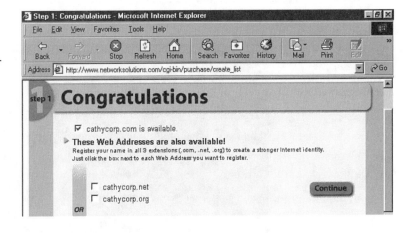

5. Contact your server provider ASAP, and fill out the paperwork to register the domain.

> After you set up your domain, you will have all new settings to use when you publish pages: a new server address, new username and password, and so on. The person who sets up your domain on the server will give you this information; don't forget to use it when you start publishing to your new domain.

Advancing to New Authoring Tools and Techniques

Sculptors start with Play-Doh and work their way up to marble. And like a sculptor, if you continue authoring, your needs will one day advance beyond FrontPage Express's capabilities.

The next few pages describe some of the leading Web authoring environments and related tools. Any of them would make a fitting next step for an experienced FrontPage Express author.

Microsoft FrontPage 2000

If you've cut your authoring teeth in FrontPage Express, the logical (but not exclusive) step up is to FrontPage 2000, the full-fledged (and not free) Microsoft Web authoring environment for Windows 95/98/NT. Figure 24.4 shows FrontPage 2000 in action.

24

You can get FrontPage 2000 in the Premium edition of Office 2000 (bundled with Word 2000, Excel 2000, and so on), or by itself.

FIGURE **24.4**

FrontPage 2000, Microsoft's commercial Web authoring software.

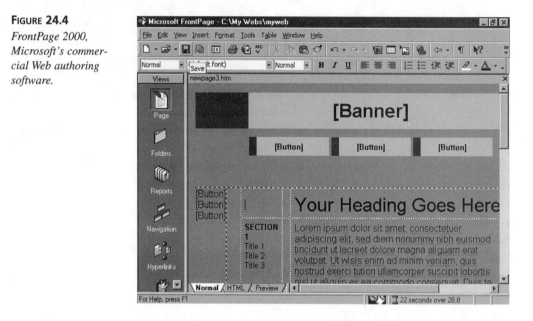

Like most high-end Web authoring tools, FrontPage 2000 includes facilities for creating and editing Web graphics. But what you get depends on how FrontPage is packaged when you buy it:

- Buy FrontPage 2000 as part of the Office 2000 Premium edition, and you also get PhotoDraw, a sophisticated graphics editor.

- Buy FrontPage 2000 by itself, and you get Image Composer, a perfectly competent graphics editor (just not as feature-rich as PhotoDraw). You also get Gif Animator, an add-in to Image Composer that you can use to create GIF Animations (see Hour 16, "Creating Your Own Animations.")

Why FrontPage 2000? Well, performing most of the basic tasks you already know is almost identical in both FrontPage Express and FrontPage 2000. You won't have to relearn how to do most things you already know how to do. That frees you up to move ahead to the things FrontPage 2000 does that FrontPage Express doesn't do.

For example, you insert a picture in FrontPage 2000 exactly as you do in FrontPage Express—same toolbar button, same dialog boxes. But after you insert that picture, you'll discover a Picture toolbar that appears automatically whenever a picture is selected. The toolbar offers buttons for all sorts of advanced stuff, like adjusting the contrast and brightness of the picture, or positioning the picture "absolutely"—locking it into an exact spot on the page, as you would in a desktop publishing program. FrontPage 2000 also supports all of the WebBots and FrontPage Extension-based features you may already have used in your Express pages, and adds a whole range of new ones.

Besides expanding on Express's page-authoring capabilities, FrontPage 2000 adds a site management facility that's especially valuable when you begin to manage Web sites with many interlinked pages. The facility (see Figure 24.5) can show you a diagram of a whole Web site and of the interrelationships among the pages. From this view, you can add and delete pages to and from the site and move pages around. FrontPage 2000 automatically updates the links and navigation bars on other pages in the site so that everything still works together properly.

You can learn more about FrontPage 2000 at www.microsoft.com/frontpage/.

You can download a trial version at www/microsoft.com/frontpage/trial/.

24

FIGURE 24.5

FrontPage 2000 features a site management facility.

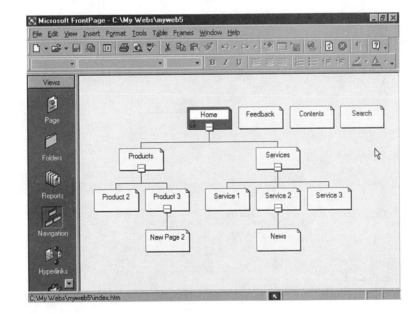

If you have ambitions to become a professional Web author in a company, there's another good reason to learn FrontPage 2000.

Most companies want the Web authors they hire to be able to use a range of Web authoring tools and possess other skills, as well (such as Java or CGI programming). But FrontPage is currently the most widely used Web-authoring application, so knowing how to use it is essential for any job-hunting author.

Macromedia Dreamweaver 2

Dreamweaver 2 (see Figure 24.6) "…is the solution for professional Web site design and production," according to its maker, Macromedia. What that really means is that it's an all-around Web authoring tool that includes advanced graphics creation and editing facilities, site management, and more.

It's similar to FrontPage 2000 in most respects, but a little more powerful, a little more difficult to learn and use, and more expensive. While FrontPage 2000 (and Adobe PageMill, described next) suit both beginners and pros, Dreamweaver is really for ambitious Web authoring professionals who want every bell and whistle at their command.

FIGURE 24.6

Macromedia Dreamweaver 2.

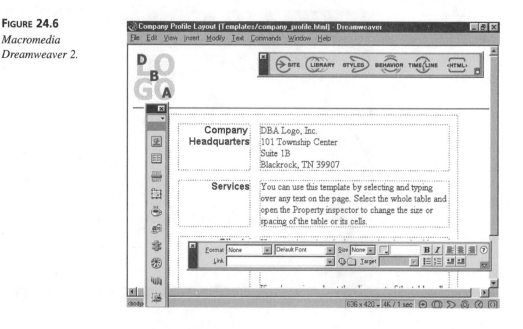

You can learn more about Dreamweaver at
www.macromedia.com/software/dreamweaver/.

You can download a free trial at www.macromedia.com/software/dreamweaver/trial/.

Adobe PageMill

Adobe is known for professional graphics, desktop publishing software, and fonts. So Web authoring is a natural extension.

Adobe's PageMill 3 (see Figure 24.7) is an easy-to-use, all-purpose Web authoring environment that includes site management, publishing, and sophisticated graphics and font tools. One nice feature of PageMill is that you get real WYSIWYG preview of pages (as they would appear in Internet Explorer 5) right from within the PageMill interface (even animations and Java applets play in the preview).

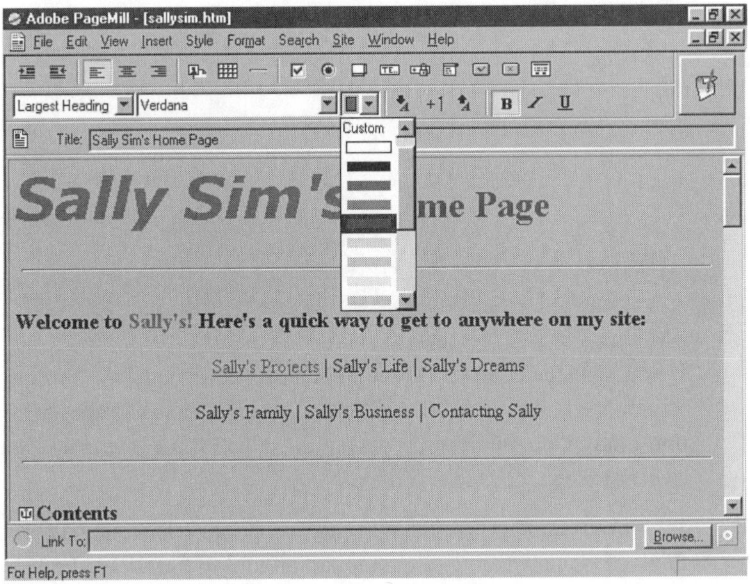

24

FIGURE 24.7

Adobe PageMill 3.

You can learn more about PageMill at www.adobe.com/prodindex/pagemill/.

A free trial is available at www.adobe.com/prodindex/pagemill/demodnld.html.

Netscape Composer

Just as Microsoft bundles its browser suite with a free Web authoring tool (FrontPage Express), Netscape competes by supplying a Web authoring tool in its Communicator suite: Netscape Composer (see Figure 24.8). Actually, Netscape did it first—FrontPage Express was Microsoft's retaliation to Composer!

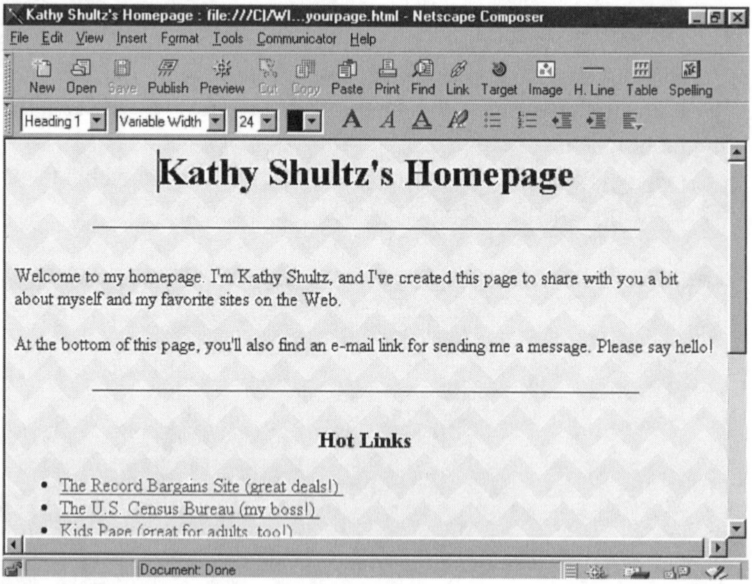

FIGURE 24.8

Netscape's free Web page editor, Composer, part of the Communicator suite.

If you have the complete Communicator suite, you have Composer; you can open it from within Navigator by choosing Communicator, Page Composer from the menu bar. If you don't have Communicator, you can download it for free from Netscape, at www.netscape.com/download/.

Who needs another freebie Web authoring tool when one has FrontPage Express? Well, I think of Composer as a nice companion tool to FrontPage Express.

Composer does a few things that FrontPage Express doesn't do; for example, it has a spell-checker, it offers a greater range of options for controlling the appearance and position of pictures in a page, and it includes a handy toolbar button for instantly previewing a page's appearance in a browser. FrontPage Express, on the other hand, makes publishing a lot easier than Composer does, and offers the Forms Page Wizard, WebBots, and other unique features.

So if you have both Composer and FrontPage Express, you can switch back and forth between the two, as necessary, depending on what you're doing—and you still haven't paid a dime.

The Future of Web Authoring: XHTML

Every time the HTML standard changes, there are new formatting tricks and other capabilities to apply in Web pages, and everybody runs out to get new tools (or learn new tags) to apply those features. So to some extent, your "moving up" as a Web author depends a lot on how and when HTML "moves up."

The current HTML standard is HTML 4, and there won't be an HTML 5. Instead, HTML is merging with another document formatting standard, XML (eXtensible Markup Language) to create a new standard for the Web pages of the future: XHTML (extensible HyperText Markup Language). In fact, you can already see some XHTML-based Web pages online; the page in Figure 24.9 is an example. (Note the filename extension .xhtml in the address bar.)

For general Web authoring, XHTML will be very similar to HTML. But the new language will be applied much more broadly than the old, and will be used to enable browser-like features in such devices as Digital TVs, portable phones, and even "auto PCs"—computers you use in your car. Estimates predict that by 2002, 75 percent of the viewing of Internet documents will take place on such "alternate platforms." To accommodate this change, XHTML is being designed to be highly *portable* (able to work on lots of different kinds of devices), while also being *extensible* (easily upgradeable with new capabilities).

24

FIGURE 24.9

An early XHTML page online.

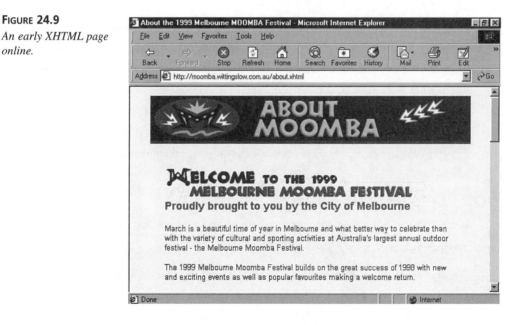

As a Web author, it'll be a few years before you have to think much about XHTML, and by that time, there will also be WYSIWYG tools that crank out XHTML the same way that tools like FrontPage Express crank out HTML today. (Already there are very simple tools for converting existing HTML files to XHTML format.) But if you plan to do Web authoring in the long term, keep your eye on XHTML. It is the future.

How to Grow as a Web Author

What can you do next? How will you advance to the next level? And more important, how can you keep a keen edge on the skills you've already mastered? Here are a few important habits you can adopt to prosper and grow.

Observe

When on the Web, don't just browse. Think about the pages you visit. Study them carefully, not at a technical level, but at an aesthetic one. If a page impresses you, ask yourself why. Is it the images, the layout, the writing, the colors, or some combination of these factors? Bookmark sites that impress you and visit them often. Make a mental catalog of what grabs your interest (or loses it) as a browser. Odds are, many other people respond the same way.

Dissect

When a page really impresses you, save it on your PC (in Internet Explorer, choose File, Save As) and then study it offline. Consider such questions as

- What types of image files were used and what properties are applied to them?
- What is the flow of text elements and properties on the page?
- What special techniques show up in the HTML code if you view the source file?
- In a multipage Web site, how much information is on a page?
- How many pages are there, and in what ways are they interlinked?

For Further Reading

Here are some Sams titles that make excellent advanced reading following this tutorial:

Sams Teach Yourself FrontPage 2000 in 24 Hours (by Rogers Cadenhead)

Sams Teach Yourself FrontPage 2000 in 21 Days (by Denise Tyler)

Laura Lemay's Web Workshop: Graphics and Web Page Design (by Laura Lemay, Jon M. Duff, and James L. Mohler)

Sams Teach Yourself Web Publishing with HTML in 21 Days (by Laura Lemay and Denise Tyler)

The Bridges of Madison County (by Robert James Waller—not a Sams book, but it'll help to get your mind off Web authoring)

Summary

You've picked up a great start, and now you know as much about Web authoring as you may ever need to. But there's always more to learn, always room to grow.

In the meantime, thanks for the 24 hours. And please come back to this book for a refresher anytime. We're always open.

24

APPENDIX **A**

Setting Up the Programs on the Bonus CD-ROM

This appendix describes how to get started with the valuable programs and files included on the bonus CD-ROM you'll find inside the back cover of this book. The appendix is split into two sections:

- "Setting Up the Programs" explains how to copy the programs and files from the CD-ROM to your computer's hard drive, so that you can use them at any time without the CD-ROM.

- "What's on the CD-ROM?" describes each program, tells how to start the program after it has been installed, and tells where in this book you can learn more about using the program.

The programs on the bonus CD-ROM require a computer running Windows 95, Windows 98, or Windows NT.

Setting Up the Programs

To install any of the programs and files on the bonus CD-ROM, begin in Windows, and close any programs that are running (except Windows). Then follow these steps:

1. Insert the *Sams Teach Yourself to Create Web Pages in 24 Hours*, Second Edition CD-ROM into your CD-ROM drive.

2. Wait a few moments. If a screen with this book's title appears, go on to step 3. (If not, open My Computer from your Windows desktop, double-click the icon for your CD-ROM drive, and double-click "Start.exe.")

3. From the welcome screen of the CD-ROM, choose Third-Party Software. Then, click the "View Software List" link in the CD-ROM interface to view descriptions of the software available on this CD-ROM.

   Use the scrolling list of Third-Party Software to read a brief description about the product, visit the official Web site, or install the product on your computer.

4. To install anything you see on the CD-ROM Menu, click the "Install (product name)" link. The Installation Wizard for the program you selected opens, and it leads you step-by-step through the installation of the program you selected. Simply follow the instructions that appear.

   IMPORTANT: To ensure that FrontPage Express is included when you install Internet Explorer 5, begin setting up Internet Explorer 5 as described in Steps 1 through 4. When you see a choice between **Install Now** and **Install Minimal**, choose **Install Minimal** (see Figure A.1) then click Next. On the dialog box that appears, open the list box nearest the top of the dialog and choose **Full** from the list (see Figure A.2). Then click Next to continue the installation.

FIGURE A.1.

To include FrontPage Express, first choose ***Install Minimal***.

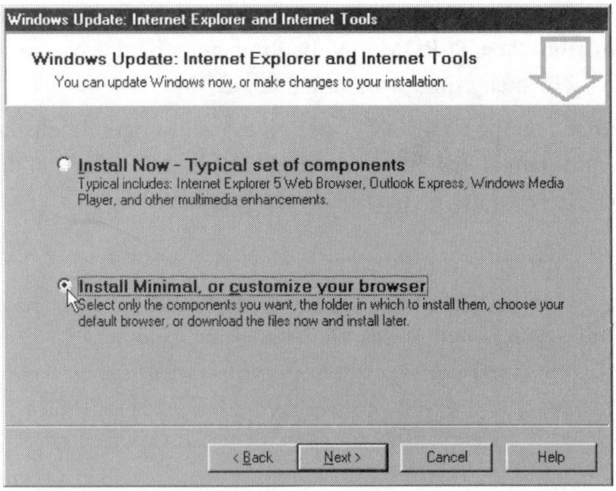

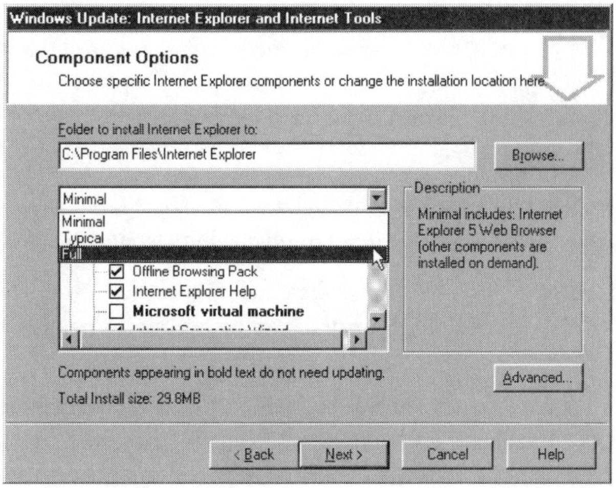

FIGURE A.2.

*On the Component Options dialog box, choose **Full** in the drop-down list box*

5. When you have finished installing a program, the CD-ROM Menu reappears, so you can install another program, if you want.

6. When finished installing programs, click the Exit link at the bottom of the CD-ROM Menu. Then click Yes on the credits screen.

A

> Some programs may prompt you to restart your computer to complete the installation. If you must restart, but still want to install more programs, repeat steps 1-3 to re-display the CD-ROM Menu.

What's on the CD-ROM?

The following sections describe all of the programs and files included on the CD-ROM at the back of this book.

Internet Explorer 5 (with FrontPage Express)

Internet Explorer 5 is Microsoft's all-purpose Internet suite. It includes not only a Web browser, email program, and newsreader, but also FrontPage Express, the principal Web authoring tool used in the examples and exercises in this book. You can use FrontPage Express to create and publish Web pages, and use Internet Explorer to evaluate those pages (and, of course, to surf the Web!)

- To start FrontPage Express from the Windows Start menu, choose Programs, Accessories, Internet Tools, FrontPage Express.

- To learn more about using FrontPage Express to create Web pages, see Hours 2–22.

IMPORTANT: When installing Internet Explorer 5 with FrontPage Express, be sure to follow the installation note shown on page 398.

JPEG Graphics

A great selection of graphics is included on the CD-ROM. You can use these graphics in Web pages you create, or use them to practice the techniques you learn in this book.

- To locate the graphics files when adding them to a Web page, insert the CD-ROM (and close the CD-ROM installation program, if it opens), and look in the following folders:
- D:\Gfx\WebGfx contains three folders: Banners (Web banners), Buttons (various styles of navigation buttons you can attach links to), and Textures (background pictures).
- D:\Gfx\Fun contains a collection of fun images.
- D:\Gfx\Photos contains three folders of photographic images: Animals, Everyday, and People.
- D:\Gfx\Backgrounds contains more great images for picture backgrounds.
- D:\Gfx\Business contains business-related photographs.
- To learn more about using these files in Web pages you create, see Hours 13–16 and Hour 20.

HTML Assistant Pro 97

Supplied here in a trial version, HTML Assistant Pro 97 is a full-featured editor for composing and editing HTML, the underlying code used in Web pages. This program is not used as the principal Web-authoring tool in this book, because FrontPage Express is a better choice for beginners. But as a companion to FrontPage Express, HTML Assistant Pro is valuable for creating Web pages divided up into frames, and also for general HTML editing tasks.

- To start HTML Assistant Pro from the Windows Start menu, choose Programs, HTML Assistant Pro 97, Pro 97.
- To learn more about using HTML Assistant Pro to edit HTML files, see Hour 17.
- To learn more about using HTML Assistant Pro to create Web pages divided into multiple frames, see Hour 18.

MapEdit

Supplied here in a trial version, MapEdit is a tool for creating the type of images you see in Web pages wherein clicking different parts of the image activates different links. It's a handy companion to FrontPage Express for adding button bars and other such sophisticated features to Web pages you create.

- To start MapEdit from the Windows Start menu, choose Programs, MapEdit, MapEdit.
- To learn more about using MapEdit to put multiple links in one picture, see Hour 20.

Paint Shop Pro 5 (with Animation Shop)

Supplied here in a trial version, Paint Shop Pro 5 is a sophisticated image drawing, painting, editing, and conversion tool. You can use it to create new images for inclusion in your Web document or to convert, edit, or prepare images you've acquired from other sources. Paint Shop Pro includes a companion product, Animation Shop, which you can use to create animated graphics for your Web pages.

- To start Paint Shop Pro 5 from the Windows Start menu, choose Programs, Paint Shop Pro 5, Paint Shop Pro 5. To start Animation Shop from the Windows Start menu, choose Programs, Paint Shop Pro 5, Animation Shop.
- To learn more about using Paint Shop Pro to create graphics, see Hours 13 and 16. To learn how to create animations with Animation Shop, see Hour 16.

NetZip

Supplied here in a trial version, NetZip is a Windows compression/decompression utility that allows you to conveniently decompress ZIP files and other compressed formats commonly downloaded from the Internet.

This capability is important for decompressing Web authoring programs and graphics collections you may download from the Internet, and also for compressing large files you offer to others online. When you install NetZip in a Windows environment, it automatically updates the File Types registry so that when you open any ZIP file, NetZip opens automatically to decompress the file and extract any separate files within the ZIP archive.

- To start NetZIP, double-click any ZIP file.

Adobe Acrobat Reader

This program enables a Web browser (Internet Explorer or Netscape Navigator) to display documents stored in Adobe Acrobat (PDF) Format, a format commonly used for documents distributed through the Web.

A

APPENDIX B

Online Resources for Web Authors

Browsers and Other Net-Surfing Programs

- Cello

  www.law.cornell.edu/cello/cellofaq.html

- Client Software Directory

  www.w3.org/hypertext/WWW/Clients.html

- DOSLynx

  ftp2.cc.ukans.edu/pub/DosLynx/readme.htm

- Microsoft Internet Explorer 5

  www.microsoft.com/ie

- NCSA Mosaic

  www.ncsa.uiuc.edu/SDG/Software/Mosaic/

- NeoPlanet

  www.neoplanet.com

- Netscape Communicator (Composer)

  www.netscape.com/download

- Tucows Directory of Internet Clients

  www.tucows.com

General Web Authoring

- Browser Inconsistency Knowledge Base

  www.governor.co.uk/browsers

- Builder.com

  Builder.com

- Developer.com

  www.developer.com

- E-tips

  www.etips.net

- Free Tools for Web Site Construction

  freeware.intrastar.net/htmladd.htm

- Jonny's HTML Headquarters

  www.webhelp.org/main.html

- Netscape Developer's Edge

  developer.netscape.com

- PageResource.com

  www.pageresource.com

- Web Developer's Virtual Library

  Wdvl.com

- Web Toolbox

  www.rtis.com/nat/user/toolbox

Clip Art, Animation, and Templates

- A+B+C Web Graphics & Fonts

  www.abcgiant.com/

- Absolute Designs

  www.absolutedesigns.com/

- Animation City

  www.animationcity.net/

- Animation Factory

  www.animfactory.com/

- BAM Technologies's Web Templates Page

  bamtech.hypermart.net/templates.htm

- Barry's Clip Art Server

  www.barrysclipart.com/

- Clip Art.com

  www.clipart.com/

- Clip Art Universe

  www.nzwwa.com/mirror/clipart/

- Dragon's Free Web Graphics

  www.silet.com/

- Free 3D Graphics

  www.jgpublish.com/free.htm

- GIFart.com

  www.gifart.com/

- Templates from the Spider's Group at Stanford

  www-pcd.stanford.edu/mogens/intro/templates.html

- Web Diner

  www.webdiner.com

B

Java

- FreeWare Java

  www.freewarejava.com/

- Java Applet Directory

  www.gamelan.com/

- Java Boutique

  javaboutique.internet.com/

- Java Repository

  java.wiwi.uni-frankfurt.de/

- Sun Microsystems Java Home Page

  java.sun.com/

- Yahoo Java Directory

  www.yahoo.com/Computers_and_Internet/Programming_Languages/Java/

General-Purpose Software Download Sites

- Download.com

  download.com

- Freeware Files

  www.freewarefiles.com/

- Shareware.com

  shareware.com

- Shareware Junkies

  www.sharewarejunkies.com

- Tucows Directory of Internet Clients

  www.tucows.com

Plug-Ins, Helpers, and Other Browser Accessories

- Adobe Acrobat Reader

  www.adobe.com/

- Macromedia Shockwave & Flash

  www.macromedia.com

- Microsoft Free Downloads

  www.microsoft.com/msdownload

- Plug-In Plaza

  browserwatch.internet.com/plug-in.html

- Plug-In Gallery & Demo Links

  www2.gol.com/users/oyamada/

- RealAudio/RealVideo

  www.real.com

GLOSSARY

alignment   The way text or another object is placed within a page layout. Left-aligned text lines up to the left margin, right-aligned text lines up to the right margin, and centered text is centered between the left and right margins.

animated GIF   A special kind of computer image file that plays as a brief animated clip when viewed through a *browser*. See also GIF.

applet   A small program or application, particularly one written in *Java*.

background   A color or image that covers the entire area behind the text and pictures of a Web page.

bookmark   An invisible marker in a Web page that provides a spot to which a *link* can point, so that a link can take a *visitor* straight to a specific spot within a page. Bookmarks are also known as targets or anchors in some Web authoring programs.

browser   A program that enables you to view Web pages, such as *Internet Explorer* or *Netscape Navigator*.

bulleted list   A list of items in which each item is preceded by a marker, a "bullet" or some other symbol character. See also numbered list.

cell   The individual boxes that make up a *table*. One cell appears at each intersection of one row and one column.

CGI (Common Gateway Interface) One method for creating scripts that make some advanced Web page features work, such as *forms*. See also Java, JavaScript, and Visual Basic.

character formatting Formatting that changes the style of text characters, such as applying *fonts*, bold or italic.

check box A small, square box used to select objects in a program or a Web page *form*. Clicking an empty check box inserts a check mark there, indicating that the object or option next to the check box is selected.

client A software tool for using a particular type of Internet resource. A client interacts with a server on which the resource is located. Browsers are clients.

clip art Graphics, photos, and sometimes other media (such as sound and video clips) published in collections for convenient use in creating Web pages and other publications.

close tag An HTML *tag* required at the end of a block of code beginning with certain tags. Close tags begin with `</`.

Communicator See Navigator.

dialog box A box that pops up in Windows programs to provide the options necessary for completing a particular task. Different tasks display different dialog boxes.

domain The address of a computer on the Internet. A user's Internet address is made up of a username and a domain name. Every Web server has its own, unique domain, and can play host to other domains, as well.

download The act of copying information from a server computer to your computer. See also upload.

Dynamic HTML (DHTML) A set of enhancements to the standard *HTML* Web language that enable a Web page to include a variety of advanced features and formatting. (DHTML features function only when the page is viewed through a DHTML-compatible browser, such as Netscape Navigator versions 4.5–5 and Internet Explorer versions 4 and 5.)

email Short for *electronic mail*. A system that enables a person to compose a message on a computer and transmit that message through a computer network, such as the Internet, to another computer user.

email address The Internet address used in an email program to send email to a particular Internet user. The address is typically made up of a username, an @ sign, and a domain name (`user@domain`).

Explorer See Internet Explorer.

extensions Nonstandard enhancements to HTML that can add features to Web pages. The features can be viewed only through browsers that support the extensions. See also FrontPage Extensions.

FAQ file Short for Frequently Asked Questions file. A computer file, often made available on the Internet, containing the answers to frequently asked questions about a particular topic or Web site.

flame Hostile messages, often sent through email or posted in newsgroups, from Internet users in reaction to breaches of netiquette.

font A particular style of text.

font size The relative size in which text appears onscreen.

form A part of a Web page in which users can type entries or make selections that are then collected and processed. Forms require either the *FrontPage Extensions* or a *script* on the server.

frame definition document An HTML document whose purpose is to define the *frames* in a frame-based document as well as to identify the content files to go in each frame.

frames Multiple panes in a browser window, each of which displays a different Web page file. Web authors design frames pages to enable visitors to use the frames together as a single, multidimensional Web page.

freeware Software available to anyone, free of charge (unlike shareware, which requires payment).

FrontPage 2000 A Web-page authoring program from Microsoft, sold by itself and also included in the Professional Edition of the *Office 2000* suite. See also FrontPage Express.

FrontPage Express Included on the CD-ROM with this book, a free Web-page authoring program from Microsoft, similar to *FrontPage 2000*, but lacking advanced features, such as site management.

FrontPage extensions A set of programs which, when installed on a Web server, enables *forms* and some *components* in Web pages created in *FrontPage 2000* and *FrontPage Express* to perform their tasks without the aid of a *script*.

FTP Short for File Transfer Protocol. The basic method for copying a file from one computer to another through the Internet, often used for publishing Web page files by *uploading* them to a server.

GIF   Short for Graphics Interchange Format. A form of computer image file, using the file extension .GIF, commonly used for *inline images* in Web pages. See also animated GIF.

heading   A short line of text, often set large and bold, that marks the start of a particular section of a document, such as a Web page.

horizontal line   In a Web page, a straight line that divides sections of the page horizontally. Sometimes also known as a horizontal rule.

HTML   (HyperText Markup Language) The document formatting language used to create Web pages. The files produced by Web authoring programs like *FrontPage Express* are HTML files.

HTTP   (HyperText Transfer Protocol) The standard protocol used for communications between servers and clients on the World Wide Web.

hyperlink   See link.

imagemap   A picture in a Web page that contains multiple links; clicking different parts of the picture activates different links.

inline image   An image that appears within the layout of a Web page.

Internet Explorer   A browser for the World Wide Web, created by Microsoft.

internetwork   A set of networks and individual computers connected so that they can communicate and share information. The Internet is a very large internetwork.

intranet   An internal corporate network, usually a local area network, that is based on Internet technologies such as TCP/IP and Web browsers.

Java   A general-purpose programming language sometimes used to add advanced capabilities to Web pages.

JavaScript   A programming language for creating scripts that add functions to Web pages.

JPEG   Short for Joint Photographic Experts Group. A form of image file, using the file extension .JPG, commonly used for inline images (and sometimes for picture backgrounds) in Web pages.

link   Short for *hyperlink*, an object in a Web page that takes the visitor to another page, downloads a file, or starts some other action.

link source   The part of a link that a visitor actually sees in a Web page and clicks to activate the link. (The other part of a link is the *URL*.) A link source can be some text, an *inline image*, or a part of an *imagemap*.

list box   In a *dialog box*, *toolbar*, or Web page *form*, a small box with a downward-pointing arrow at its right end. Clicking the arrow opens a list of options the user can click to select one to appear in the box.

mailto: link   A link in a Web page that, when clicked by a visitor, opens the visitor's email program and creates a new message pre-addressed to a particular person.

marquee   A line of text that repeatedly scrolls across part of a Web page, used as an attention-getting device.

Navigator   Sometimes called *Netscape*, a popular *browser* program from *Netscape Communications*. Navigator is available in a suite, called Netscape Communicator, that also includes programs for Web authoring, email, and other activities.

Netscape   Short for Netscape Communications, a software company that developed and markets a popular Word Wide Web browser called *Navigator*. Some people casually refer to Navigator and Communicator as "Netscape."

network   A set of computers interconnected so that they can communicate and share information. Connected networks together form an *internetwork*.

newsgroup   An Internet resource through which people post and read messages related to a specific topic.

numbered list   A list of items in which each item is preceded by a number, and the numbers go up as the list goes down. See also bulleted list.

Office 2000   A suite of application programs from Microsoft, available in several versions. The "Professional" version for Windows 95/98/NT includes *FrontPage 2000*, Word, Excel, and other popular programs.

paragraph   Any block of text uninterrupted by a paragraph mark (¶).

paragraph break   The space between two paragraphs, in which a hidden paragraph mark appears.

paragraph formatting   Text formatting, such as *paragraph styles* or *alignment*, that can be applied only to a whole paragraph or paragraphs, never to only selected characters within a paragraph, such as *character formatting*.

paragraph style   The principal form of text formatting on a Web page. Paragraph styles include six levels of *Headings*, a style for Normal text, and several different styles for creating lists.

password   A secret code, known only to the user, that allows the user to access a computer that is protected by a security system.

script   An external program opened by a link in a Web page to perform some special function.

search page   A Web page on which a visitor can search the Web or other Internet resource for particular information.

server   A networked computer that serves a particular type of information to users or performs a particular function. On the Internet, servers called Web servers store Web page files and deliver them through the Internet to *browsers* upon demand.

shareware   Software programs that users are permitted to acquire and evaluate for free. Shareware is different from *freeware* in that, if a person likes the shareware program and plans to use it on a regular basis, he or she is expected to send a fee to the programmer.

signature   A block of text on a Web page, usually near the bottom, that identifies the page's author or the *Webmaster*. Signatures often include a *mailto: link* to the author's email address.

style   See paragraph style.

symbol   A character that's not on the keyboard, such as a copyright symbol. In *FrontPage Express*, you add symbols to your pages from a special *dialog box*.

spider   A program that searches methodically through a portion of the Internet to build a database that can be searched by a *search page*.

table   A box or grid used to arrange text or pictures in neat rows and columns.

tag   A code in the *HTML* language.

TCP/IP   (Transmission Control Protocol/Internet Protocol) The fundamental internetworking protocol that makes the Internet work.

template   A preformatted Web page (containing sample text and pictures) that a Web author copies and edits to conveniently create a new page.

title   The name that identifies a particular Web page. A Web page's title appears in the title bar at the very top of the browser window.

toolbar   In a program, a row of icons, buttons, and *list boxes*, usually near the top of the program's window, you can click to perform common tasks.

undo   A feature of *FrontPage Express* and some other programs that enables you to reverse an action you performed by clicking a button on a *toolbar* or choosing a menu item. Undo is useful for undoing mistakes.

UNIX   A computer operating system widely used by Web servers.

upload   The act of copying information *to* a server computer from your computer. See also download.

URL   Short for Uniform (or Universal) Resource Locator. A method of standardizing the addresses of different types of Internet resources so that they can all be accessed easily from within a Web browser.

username   An identification name for a user, used in tandem with a *password* to gain access to a computer or network that's protected by a security system.

visitor   A casual way a Web author may refer to the people who will access his or her creations through the *Internet* or an *intranet*.

Visual Basic   A multipurpose programming language from Microsoft, often used for Web page *scripts* and for automating tasks in *Office 2000* programs.

Webmaster   The person responsible for the management and maintenance of a particular Web page or Web site, sometimes (but not always) also the Web page's author.

Web site   A group of individual Web pages linked together into a single, multipage document. Web site also is sometimes used to describe a whole Web *server* or all pages on a particular *domain*.

wizard   Automated routines, used throughout Windows, for conveniently performing a step-by-step procedure.

Yahoo!   A popular *search page*.

INDEX

C

X - Z

IMPORTANT: To ensure that FrontPage Express is included when you install Internet Explorer 5, begin setting up Internet Explorer 5 as described in Appendix A, under "Setting Up the Programs." When you see a choice between **Install Now** and **Install Minimal**, choose **Install Minimal**. On the dialog box that appears, open the list box nearest the top of the dialog and choose **Full** from the list. Then click Next to continue the installation.